WHEN GIANTS ROAMED THE SKY
KARL ARNSTEIN AND THE RISE OF AIRSHIPS FROM ZEPPELIN TO GOODYEAR

OHIO HISTORY AND CULTURE

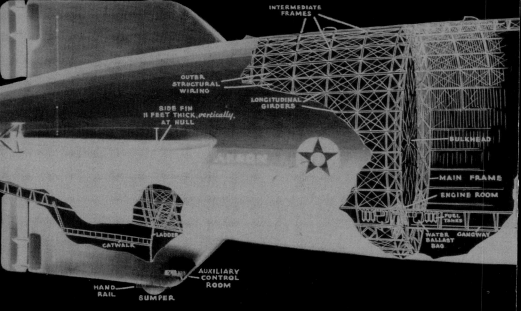

INTERMEDIATE FRAMES

OUTER STRUCTURAL WIRING

SIDE FIN 11 FEET THICK, *vertically,* AT HULL

LONGITUDINAL GIRDERS

BULKHEAD

MAIN FRAME

ENGINE ROOM

FUEL TANKS

GANGWAY

WATER BALLAST BAG

LADDER

CATWALK

AUXILIARY CONTROL ROOM

HAND RAIL

BUMPER

WHEN GIANTS ROAMED THE SKY

KARL ARNSTEIN AND THE RISE OF AIRSHIPS FROM ZEPPELIN TO GOODYEAR

Dale Topping

Edited by Eric Brothers

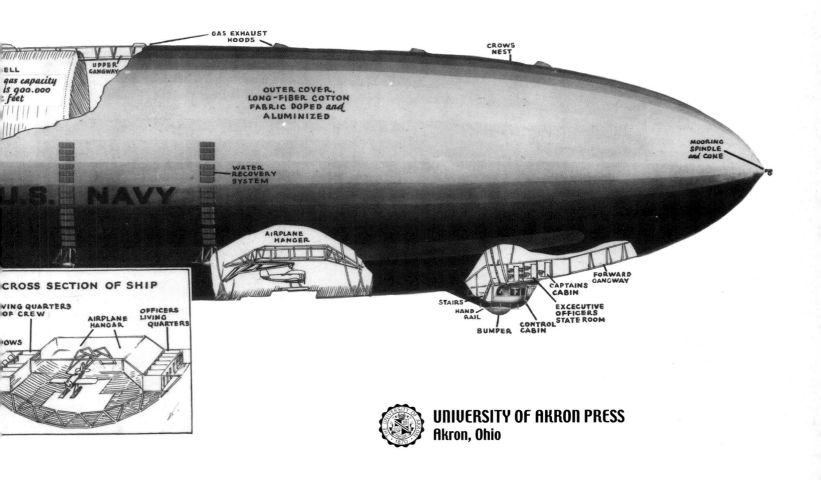

GAS EXHAUST HOODS

CROWS NEST

UPPER GANGWAY

ELL

gas capacity is 900.000 feet

OUTER COVER, LONG-FIBER COTTON FABRIC DOPED *and* ALUMINIZED

MOORING SPINDLE and CONE

WATER RECOVERY SYSTEM

U.S. NAVY

AIRPLANE HANGER

FORWARD GANGWAY

CAPTAINS CABIN

STAIRS

EXECCUTIVE OFFICERS STATE ROOM

HAND RAIL

BUMPER

CONTROL CABIN

CROSS SECTION OF SHIP

IVING QUARTERS OF CREW

AIRPLANE HANGAR

OFFICERS LIVING QUARTERS

OWS

UNIVERSITY OF AKRON PRESS
Akron, Ohio

All inquires and permissions requests should be addressed to the publisher, The University of Akron Press, Akron, OH 44325-1703

Manufactured in the United States of America

First edition 2001

LIBRARY OF CONGRESS CATALOGING-IN-PUBLICATION DATA

Topping, A. Dale (Alanson Dale), 1917–1993.
     When giants roamed the sky : Karl Arnstein and the rise of airships
from Zeppelin to Goodyear / by A. Dale Topping ; edited by Eric
Brothers.— 1st ed.
          p. cm. — (Series on Ohio history and culture)
     Includes bibliographical references and index.
     ISBN 1-884836-69-0 (cloth: alk. paper) — ISBN 1-884836-70-4
(pbk.: alk. paper)
     1. Arnstein, Karl, b. 1887. 2. Aeronautical engineers—United
States—Biography. 3. Airships—United States—History. I. Brothers,
Eric, 1958–   II. Title. III. Series.
TL540.A715 T67   2000
629.133'24'092—dc21   00-011014

CONTENTS

EDITOR'S PREFACE

DALE TOPPING made significant contributions in documenting the history and technology of lighter-than-air flight, which includes balloons and airships of all types, those wonderful vehicles whose lift derives primarily from their buoyancy in air. For more than three decades he served as editor of the bulletin of The Lighter-Than-Air Society, an organization founded in Akron by Goodyear blimp builders. During his tenure as editor, he established the reputation of the bulletin, later called *Buoyant Flight*, as a leading forum for the exchange of knowledge about the branch of aeronautics known as Lighter Than Air. He immersed himself in lighter-than-air history, reading hundreds of volumes on the subject, and became a respected critic of such literature. His equally strong command of the subject's technical and historical aspects won him acclaim the world over. He elevated the level of discourse in this area by his high standards of scholarship, years of dedication, and ceaseless pursuit of the truth.

Dale Topping was born in West Lafayette, Indiana, on March 8, 1917, the day Count Zeppelin passed from this world. The coincidence later caused many to wonder if the old gentleman's once-strong enthusiasm for airships could have been transferred to a new arrival a hemisphere away. Education came naturally to Dale, as son and grandson of professors at Purdue University. He earned a degree in civil engineering in 1940, and, like his mentor, Dr. Arnstein, worked for a bridge construction company. He then went to the Missouri School of Mines and Metallurgy to obtain his master's degree. During World War II, Topping worked in the defense industry, joining Goodyear Aircraft Corporation in Akron, Ohio. He was an airframe structural engineer in the Research Division, when the company was building blimps for the U.S. Navy. In 1949 he earned his Ph.D in theoretical applied mechanics from the University of Illinois. Rather than pursue a career in mining or the oil industry, Topping returned to Goodyear Aircraft Corporation to lead the structural analysis research and development group as a specialist in fabric stress analysis. It was in this capacity that he began to work with people who had played a major role in designing many of America's airships—fabric being a principal airship component. His association with Dr. Arnstein, in charge of engineering at GAC and former Zeppelin designer, grew into a life-long friendship. During social gatherings with the Arnsteins, Topping learned of the triumphs and tribulations in the Zeppelin designer's career. Later, Dale spent many a

Saturday morning with Arnstein discussing the events and personalities who shaped Arnstein's life. Topping committed the conversations to paper in a series of notes. After Arnstein's death Topping realized the notes would make a good beginning for a book about Arnstein's life, but more information would be needed. When Topping retired in 1982, he systematically began his research, even visiting the sites in Czechoslovakia, France, Switzerland, and Germany where Arnstein had lived and worked.

Dr. Topping worked on the biography of his mentor, Dr. Arnstein, as time allowed, for the last ten years of his life. Sadly, in 1993, his 76th year, Topping died unexpectedly. It was his last wish to see this manuscript finished and submitted for publication. Fortunately, Dr. Topping left a wealth of meticulous notes and an outline, as well as correspondence with Arnstein's widow, coworkers, acquaintances, and many other airship historians to serve as a guide. I consider it a great honor to have been asked to prepare Dr. Topping's manuscript for publication, and I hope that it will serve as a fitting tribute to both the author and subject of the biography.

Eric Brothers

AUTHOR'S PREFACE

WHY DID I WRITE THIS BOOK? To tell the story of one of the truly great engineers of the twentieth century—Dr. Karl Arnstein—known for his work on the famous cathedral at Strasbourg, his engineering on the elegant concrete Chur-Arosa Railway bridge, and most of all, for designing more than eighty giant airships. This is the story of his coming to the United States from Germany, bringing with him his famous twelve "disciples"—twelve renowned German engineers and their families—and creating America's largest dirigibles. Later, it tells of his work for the company that became a major defense contractor in World War II, producing more than 150 blimps for the U.S. Navy, more than 4,000 fighter airplanes, and components for countless other military aircraft. His remarkable career continued to the brink of the Space Age. Along the way there was criticism, much of it unfair or uninformed, which he endured stoically, privately, and patiently. There is within this the story of repeated kindness and consideration for others that his modesty and professionalism did not allow him to trumpet.

During my twenty-five years as an engineer at the Goodyear Aircraft Corporation in Akron, Ohio, I came to know Dr. Arnstein, and was keenly aware that "the Doctor" was so called with great respect and affection by my fellow engineers.

It was only after I started writing reviews of airship history books—about the time Dr. Arnstein took mandatory retirement in 1957 at age seventy—that I really came to know him.

After his retirement, Dr. Arnstein remained at Goodyear Aircraft for three or four years as a consultant. One of his concerns was to investigate compartmentation of nonrigid airships (blimps), on which I was assigned to work. It was then that he began to stop at my desk from time to time for discussions.

The first such conversation of which I recorded notes occurred on February 20, 1958. After I became editor of The Lighter-Than-Air Society Bulletin in 1959 (*Buoyant Flight,* as it has been called since 1971), my conversations with Dr. Arnstein, or my record of them, became more frequent and were more often at his home on Saturday mornings. These notes have provided me with a nucleus of information, which since my retirement, I have supplemented with additional research for this book.

Dale Topping

ACKNOWLEDGMENTS

The author and the editor gratefully acknowledge the individuals named below who helped to bring this book into being. They have shared their recollections, knowledge, insights, research, photographs, artwork, advice, expertise, and most of all, their time. Sadly, some of them are no longer with us to see this book in print; we hope it would have pleased them. There are other persons whose names were not recorded and now elude memory who also provided support and valuable assistance during the course of writing this book. If you are among them, your kindness is appreciated, and please forgive us for the omission. Thank you one and all.

William F. Althoff
Bertha M. Arnstein
Dr. W. Gerald Austen
Kurt Bauch
Peter M. Bowers
Isa von Brandenstein
Donald W. Brown
Paul Rendall Brown
Dr. Michael J. Carley
William Cody
Captain Al Cope, USN (Ret.)
Kenneth L. Cordier
Nick Costakos
Roy Cotton
Dr. Tom Crouch
Cary J. Dell
F. Marc de Piolenc
Mark Essex
Maynard L. Flickinger
Cheryl R. Ganz
Nicole Gaffney
Sig Geist
Roger Gilruth

Elton Glaser
Bud Graske
Dr. Vernon Hacker
David Hill
James E. Hill
George Hodowanec
Craig Holbert
Robert E. Hunter
Charles M. Jacobs
Gordon L. Jeppesen
Darlene Kamperman
William F. Kerka
Thomas A. Knowles
John Kovac
Marvin A. Krieger
Kriemhilde I. Livingston
John Lust
Sue Mann
Robert F. Martin
Fritz Mayer
Norman J. Mayer
Robert McLaughlin
Dr. Carolyn Mehl

Dr. Wolfgang Meighörner
Dr. Jeannine Meighörner
John Mellberg
Dr. Henry Cord Meyer
John V. Miller
Gary Morgan
Kent O'Grady
Donald E. Overs
Steve Paschen
Robert Peacock
Carl Pennig
Amy M. F. Petersen
Richard Peuser
Beth Pratt
John Provan
Dr. Douglas H. Robinson
Dr. Robert S. Ross
Vincent J. Rubino
Manfred Sauter
Norbert Schlegel
Lyle Schwilling
James R. Shock
Dr. Richard K. Smith

Lillian Sokol

Brian Steinkirschner

Patrick Tabatcher

Dr. Theodor H. Troller

Bill Turner III

J. Gordon Vaeth

Richard Van Treuren

Else Wagner

Jack L. Waldman

Hepburn Walker Jr.

Captain George F. Watson USN
  (Ret.)

Richard W. Widdicombe

Dr. Delmus Williams

E. Donald Woodward

Rick Zitarosa

WHEN GIANTS ROAMED THE SKY
KARL ARNSTEIN AND THE RISE OF AIRSHIPS FROM ZEPPELIN TO GOODYEAR

Biography is the only true history.

—Thomas Carlyle (1832)

We cannot afford wantonly to lose sight of great men and memorable lives, and

are bound to store up objects for admiration as far as may be; for the effect of

implacable research is constantly to reduce their number.

—Lord Acton (1895)

Karl Arnstein, Zeppelin designer, at the age of 39. (Goodyear Tire and Rubber Co.)

INTRODUCTION

At Goodyear-Zeppelin, and later at Goodyear Aircraft Corporation, he was known as *Doctor* Karl Arnstein, or simply, "the Doctor." The title was uttered with respect, and with appreciation for the engineering knowledge embodied in this man. As a young engineer, I knew little about Arnstein, but I knew of his work in designing the U.S. Navy's huge dirigibles in the 1930s.

How Karl Arnstein came to be involved with designing large, buoyant aircraft is a story of fate and opportunity. He certainly did not dream of becoming an aircraft designer while he was making a name for himself as a structures analyst for a civil engineering firm. But his career, like that of so many others, was diverted by World War I. Arnstein's work with structural analysis had brought him into contact with one of the formidable figures of early aviation history, Count Ferdinand von Zeppelin, and that meeting altered the course of his life.

Count Zeppelin's improbable machine, the cigar-shaped rigid airship, is one of the most marvelous inventions in the history of aeronautics. At the dawn of the twenty-first century, it is difficult to appreciate that the aerial leviathans from the first four decades of the twentieth century represent anything more than a quirky oddity, an evolutionary dead end in the progress of human flight. But when these giants roamed the skies, they were not curious relics of a bygone era, or considered to be living dinosaurs from the antediluvian past of aviation history. In their day, they were at the forefront of technology. They led the way in taking passengers into the airy realm in the serene comfort to be expected of a great ocean liner. They could cover greater distances and carry more people in safety than the contemporary airplanes. They led the way in flying higher, and were the first to demonstrate the techniques for making aircraft from metal, not wood.

1

Despite a shaky beginning, Count Zeppelin and his engineers were able to bring some perfection to the type of airship that is forever linked with its originator's name. Almost from the start, the retired army general's dedication to his invention was contagious, and despite numerous setbacks, a nation rallied to his support. The Zeppelin airships became a symbol of German technological skill and showed the world that Germany would be in the forefront in mastery of the skies. Zeppelins were an ideal vehicle to show off the nation's daring, skill, and courage on a world stage, and in some eyes, to serve as a display of military superiority. Peter Fritzsche in his book, *A Nation of Fliers*, notes that "Just as the Eiffel Tower stood as a monument to French republican virtue and the Brooklyn Bridge attested to the excellent industry of ordinary Americans, the great duralumin dirigibles displayed the technical virtuosity of and material achievement of the German people. . . ." Some saw "zeppelins as the most technically expert means to conquer the air, an achievement 'inscribed in the guest book of eternity.'"

Zeppelins developed as a means of transportation, as a way to cross oceans faster and more reliably than steamships, which were their only rivals in the days when airplanes were limited to a few hundred miles' range. And, unlike noisy, bumpy, cramped airplanes, Zeppelins could carry people through the ocean of air in greater comfort and style, in an age when that mattered. As airship historian John Provan has said, they were the Concordes of their day—sleek, faster by far, elegant, indulgent, slightly out of reach. The promise of the airship as the ultimate in aerial transportation was not truly eclipsed until after the introduction of the commercial passenger jet. Some may argue today that it would still be better to travel for a few days in the relaxed, free-ranging environment of a flying hotel than subject oneself to being immobilized in a flying sardine can for a few hours.

Zeppelins were great things—huge, imposing, formidable—yet vulnerable, too. They were awe-inspiring to anyone who saw one. Nothing larger has ever flown, except in the realm of science fiction movies. Zeppelins stir the imagination even today. Picture stepping outside to look up at an object the size of an ocean liner or an office tower floating overhead, lighter than air. Pretty amazing, even for someone jaded by knowledge of supersonic jets and interplanetary rockets.

This is the story of one man who, more than anyone else, brought knowledge of Zeppelins to America, as the designer—architect if you will—of these great ships of the sky. Certainly, there were those who found fame and celebrity piloting the airships, or merely flying in them, and others who developed the means to produce them, but in an important sense, Karl Arnstein refined the Zeppelin's design to affirm the technological achievement and all that went with it. Arnstein pioneered the way aeronautical design was approached in a time when there were no precedents for determining the strengths and resulting capabilities of flying structures. Aerodynamics was in its infancy. Stress analysis was making the transition from a study of large, ponderous, immobile constructions such as bridges to aerial structures made of new, lightweight metal alloys. The goal of making the least material do the most influenced thinking in design from then on; there was a parallel trend in architecture and in engineering.

That Arnstein could bring his airship design expertise to America is largely the doing of Paul W. Litchfield, visionary chairman and president of the Goodyear Tire and Rubber Company for three decades, and unwavering promoter of the idea of commercial Zeppelins operating from the United States. It was this dream that spurred the development of the Goodyear-Zeppelin Corporation, a concern that today is a predecessor of a division of Lockheed Martin. Litchfield hoped that building a fleet of scouting dirigibles for the U.S. Navy would open the way to constructing at least a dozen passenger Zeppelins of similar design. These airships would then form the basis of an airline that could carry travelers from the continental United States to the heart of continental Europe, or to South America, or Asia—something no airplane of the time could hope to do, or hope to do economically. Litchfield believed in a common sentiment of the Zeppelin age, that in passenger travel, "comfort . . . appeals to more people than does a little greater speed."

At a time when Germany was on the brink of losing all that it had developed in Zeppelin technology, Litchfield brought the seeds of this modern aeronautical technology to the United States hoping to "grow" airships in a land "where the soil was not salted to prevent their fruition." The place for this experiment: Akron, Ohio. And were it not for the Great Depression, maybe this would have all come to pass: an industry devoted to building enormous, silvery, rigid airships, and flying them around the globe year-round. The town known for its tire making, the Rubber Capital of the World, might have become the "Zepp City." It certainly seemed possible on a hot August day in 1931 when the first Goodyear-built Zeppelin was christened as a U.S. Navy ship by no less a person than the First Lady of the United States. The air was full of promise, and the 785-foot-long aerial giant—the biggest yet built—floated gently in its dock, the largest clear-space building in the world. More than two hundred thousand people showed up to witness the event, a throng that not even the vast airship dock could contain. Those who could not get in and others out of earshot could still listen in, because the ceremony was broadcast live across the nation. The airship, the first of its class, carried the name of the city in which it was born and the hopes of its populace. The moment the colossal airship rose gently from her moorings may have been the zenith of Arnstein's career, a moment when the future held so much promise of great things to come, personally and professionally. Already, a sister ship to the USS *Akron* was under construction. Surely, orders to build a fleet of passenger airships would follow. Karl Arnstein would design them. Goodyear-Zeppelin would construct them. The skilled jobs created would be a boon to the local economy. That was the dream.

Chapter 1 EARLY INFLUENCES

Karl Arnstein did not intend to pursue a career in engineering. Nevertheless, he became a pioneer in the field of stress analysis, the means by which an engineer can state with some degree of certainty that materials used in a structure will be strong enough to perform the task desired of them. He applied this knowledge to save a cathedral tower from collapse, to design structurally efficient bridges, to create a building that was both aerodynamic and the largest enclosed space without pillars, and most notably, to perfect the design of giant **airships**—both the **Zeppelin** type and **blimps.** (Words in boldface type are included in the glossary.) He became the head of engineering for a company that at one time employed 30,000 in the construction of a wide range of aircraft and aerospace components for national defense. He said that "in the more important phases of my life you will see that most of the basic changes have not been consequences of my own plans but rather of mere accidental happenings of little apparent significance." Yet in retrospect, the successive developments in his career do show progress, and a thread of connectivity. His interest in art, architecture, mathematics, and philosophy ultimately found expression in engineering. He was not a born tinkerer—his interest in high school was to become a mathematics professor. How did he end up an engineer? To understand that, one must first find out something about the man and the environment in which he was raised.

Karl Arnstein's parents lived in a world of silence. Both Wilhelm and Ida Arnstein lost their hearing in early childhood. Although Wilhelm retained a slight ability to hear, Ida was totally deaf. In an age before the invention of hearing aids, to have both parents hearing-impaired was a challenge to raising a family. Ida was also mute, but Wilhelm was able to speak, and both he and his wife communicated with each other and their children by sign language and by lip reading. Though each was of Jewish descent, they attended a school for the deaf which was run by Catholic nuns.

Karl Arnstein at age 5.

(Lockheed Martin)

Wilhelm Arnstein was born on 14 April 1847 in Wotitz, a country town in Bohemia about thirty miles south of Prague on the rail line to Vienna. Modern maps show it as Votice, in the Czech Republic. Wilhelm's parents had a general store there, and during his early childhood Karl visited his grandmother for vacations, his grandfather having died some years earlier.

As a boarding student, Wilhelm was sent to the Institute for the Deaf in Prague run by the Catholic Church from 1855 to 1861. At the age of fourteen, he began study at the Academy for Lithography where he graduated in 1865. Wilhelm joined the Association of Lithographers and was employed by the firm of A. Thun in Brünn (modern Brno, the second largest city in the Czech Republic), located some 130 miles east of Prague. He worked there from September 1867 until November 1875. Wilhelm then returned to Prague, where he was employed by a book-printing firm until his retirement.

Ida Feigl was the daughter of Dr. Leopold Feigl, a physician for the general staff of the Austrian Army in Bohemia (part of the present-day Czech Republic). Her mother was Amalia Reach of Prague. Dr. Feigl died of cholera on 13 September 1856 at the age of forty-three. He contracted the disease while attending victims of an epidemic, and for his unselfish work he was given a posthumous citation. Still a child, Ida was now fatherless and handicapped by hearing and speech deficiencies. She also attended the Institute for the Deaf and it was there she met her future husband, Wilhelm Arnstein. We do not know much of Ida's young adulthood, but she became reacquainted with Wilhelm after he returned to Prague. They were married on 7 August 1881.

Their marriage produced three children: Poldi, the daughter and the oldest; then Karl, who was born 24 March 1887, and later a younger brother named Otto. All were fine, healthy, normal children except that Karl lost the hearing in his right ear during a childhood illness.

They were a devoted family. Wilhelm was a strict but wise father who wanted to guide his children toward high goals, though the family income was modest. By the 1890s, they were living in a small but immaculate apartment in the Koenigliche Weinberge, the King's Vineyard. Simply known as the Weinberge (its Czech name is Vinohrady), the community was a "solid, middle-class inner suburb" of Prague and home of the future first president of Czechoslovakia, Tomás Masaryk.

The reason for the Germanic names of the neighborhood and members of the Arnstein (ARN-stine) family may need explanation. At the beginning of the twentieth century, the population of Bohemia was approximately two-thirds Czech and one-third German, but

The family of Wilhelm and Ida Arnstein, about 1900. The children, standing, are Karl, Poldi, and Otto.

(Karl Arnstein Collection/University of Akron Archives)

most of the Germans were concentrated along the borders with Germany in what later became a part of the Sudetenland. The presence of so many Germans in the region gave Hitler the pretext to take over Czechoslovakia in 1938–39. After World War II, the Czechs made sure there would be no repeat annexation of their lands by expelling the Germans. In Prague the German share of the population was 13 percent in 1880 but fell to 6 percent in 1900 when the total population had doubled. Bohemia then was part of the Austro-Hungarian Empire ruled by the Hapsburgs, an arrangement which made the Czech nationalists unhappy, but was agreeable to the Germans. The official language of the Austrian-centered empire was, of course, German.

Ida had accepted the Roman Catholic faith, likely influenced by her teachers at the Institute for the Deaf, although she did not officially join a Catholic church. Wilhelm's religious views are not precisely known. We do know that the family was befriended by a Roman Catholic priest who visited them often and gave them helpful advice. Karl was confirmed in the Roman Catholic faith early in his adulthood. His choice of Catholicism, he told a friend many years later, was inspired by the kindness of the priest who had befriended his parents and of the nuns who ran the school where they had been educated. His mother's influence no doubt figured prominently as well: she gave young Karl a rosary to carry in his pocket when he went to take school examinations, especially important or difficult ones. As an adult, Karl would attend Mass every Sunday, go to confession and communion regularly, and see to it that all four of his children were raised as Roman Catholics.

As a boy, Karl proved to be a brilliant student, especially in mathematics. A report card from his school days noted that he not only had perfect grades but perfect deportment. By taking special examinations he was able to win scholarships that would allow him to attend a *realschule* (a type of high school) and later a university. The family circumstances being modest, these scholarships were essential.

In 1897 Karl was accepted at the Nikolander Deutsche Staatsoberrealschule, which emphasized the study of science and modern languages. The Nikolander school required several years of study in two foreign languages and probably was where Arnstein first learned English. He was also fluent in German and Czech since Prague was a bilingual city. The school curriculum was heavily weighted in mathematics and science to prepare graduates for later specialization at the university level.

The student body at the Nikolander school was of high caliber, and Karl was the second youngest in his class. A precocious youngster, he was assigned to a strict but sagacious arithmetic professor, and to a talented physics teacher. Arnstein proved to be doubly exceptional. When all of the other students were stuck trying to solve mathematical problems, Karl would obtain some difficult equations or a complicated analytical problem and solve them every time.

In addition to his studies, Arnstein still found time to concern himself extensively with literature, art, and stamp collecting. At the age of sixteen, Karl, not satisfied by the lectures of mathematics professors and the prescribed textbooks of the institution, started his own technical library. Arnstein graduated summa cum laude as one of the top students in his class, one of the best in the school's existence. Unfortunately, despite Karl's academic excellence, there was no guarantee that he could continue his schooling. His parents did not have the money to send him to university. However, Karl's brilliance as a student at the Nikolander Realschule and even earlier had marked him as one who could earn a scholarship and make good use of it.

At first, it was not Arnstein's talent in mathematics that was to be recognized for further education. Instead, he was offered a scholarship in art. Many years later he remarked, "They surprised me by offering me a scholarship in art at the University of Prague. I surprised them by not accepting it." But he had a great interest in art, which he satisfied later in life by collecting prints and etchings. He also had natural artistic talent, perhaps acquired from his father, who, though not an artist, had to make exact drawings in his profession of lithographer.

Impressed by his talent, Karl's high school art teacher had encouraged him to become an artist. But his father, Wilhelm, who was making no more than a modest living as a lithographer, advised his son to take engineering so that he could use his talent for drawing more profitably. Karl was not eager to seize upon his father's suggestion of engineering as a profession. Instead, he accepted a scholarship with a concentration on mathematics and courses in philosophy at the University of Prague. "When I finished high school in 1904 my ideal was to become a mathematician," Karl later said. That year Arnstein entered the University of Prague, the oldest university in central Europe. It was founded in 1348 by Charles IV, and its original building, the Carolinum, still exists as part of the modern Universitas Carolina, or Charles University.

Even with a scholarship, Arnstein still had to find time to earn money to support his studies. As he had at the Realschule, Karl tutored students in mathematics. He soon gained the reputation of being able to help a student pass the rigorous mathematical portion of the *Matura,* an exam required of the students in many countries to be accepted into a university. His days were often long, first attending his classes, then tutoring, and finally going home and studying to prepare for his own classes the next day. In addition to his academic studies, he completed the requirements for a teaching appointment.

Only two blocks away from the university stood a building with a Baroque facade, the German Technical Institute (Deutsche Technische Hochschule). Once a Jesuit seminary, after 1786 it became the engineering school which today is called the Czech Technical Institute. The proximity of the two schools was to prove fateful. Karl became interested in descriptive geometry and wanted to study it, since mathematics was his major subject. But descriptive geometry, although based on solid geometry, is not a mathematical subject. It is the science of drawing, of the exact representation of subjects composed of geometrical forms. Perhaps Arnstein was drawn to it by his interest in art, or possibly by the idea that he might combine his interests in mathematics and art.

Descriptive geometry was not taught at the university, but a course in the subject was offered at the Technical Institute. When Karl went to register for the course he was asked if he was able to pay for it, which he could not afford to do. Thinking of his options, he quickly said, "No, I want to apply for a scholarship." He was told that scholarships were available only to those students taking a full engineering curriculum.

Confident of his ability, and not intimidated by the idea of carrying two full course loads—one at the university and the other at the institute—he turned to a friend standing behind him in line and asked, "Which is the easiest: civil, mechanical, or chemical engineering?" The friend (doubtless a mechanical or chemical engineering student) answered, "Civil engineering!" That is how Karl Arnstein entered the civil engineering profession.

For the next four years, Karl pursued his studies in mathematics and civil engineering with full course loads at the two institutions. At university, he also indulged his interest in philosophy (perhaps his real first love, although for practical reasons he took those courses only as his minor). Remarkably, he completed all of the studies required for a degree in philosophy except for writing a dissertation. Many years later, he told his wife that the study of philosophy had enabled him to accomplish his work, to deal with people, and to weather adversity.

His curiosity in descriptive geometry presumably was satisfied by the course he took, but Karl's inquisitive young mind found still other interests. "I took a general engineering course because of the mathematics, geometry, and physics offered with it," he said, "and found the studies so fascinating that I became a structural engineer, so to say, against my intention." A course he had in bridge engineering was taught under the direction of Professor Joseph Melan, an internationally known designer and consultant on bridges. He became one of the most important influences on Karl Arnstein's life.

Melan was born in Vienna in November 1853 and graduated from the Imperial Technical Institute as a Diploma Engineer in 1876. He taught there for ten years before becoming professor of structural mechanics at the Royal Technical Institute in Brünn, where he was appointed chancellor in 1895. In April 1902, he was called to the German Technical Institute in Prague as professor of bridge structures, and there he remained. Arnstein remembered him as a man of few words, thin and of delicate health, but a genius when it came to analyzing structures.

During his career, Melan helped to calculate the design of many bridges in Europe and the United States. Among American bridges, he worked on the Williamsburg cable suspension bridge and the Hell's Gate steel-arch bridge in New York City. Melan also was involved with projects other than bridges, such as the restoration of the 164-foot tower of Jacobs Church in Brünn in 1901.

Melan's fame rests on the reinforced-concrete system named for him that he developed in the 1890s. His system was patented in Austria-Hungary as well as in other countries and was awarded the Gold Medal at the World Exposition in Paris in 1900. Using this method, numerous bridges and buildings in Austria, Switzerland, Italy, Germany, and especially in the United States were successfully constructed. Most of the bridges, with the exception of those built in America, were designed by Melan himself.

Although he was not the first to embed iron netting or steel rods in concrete, Melan developed the scientific theory for employing structural steel shapes as reinforcement. Melan's system was put into practice extensively in the construction of reinforced-concrete arch bridges. By 1906 Melan was a pioneer in the theory of pre-stressing, a method extensively used today to tension concrete to withstand shrinkage and deformation.

It is not surprising that Karl, with his talent and love for mathematics, should have found Melan's courses intriguing. Arnstein became one of his best students in bridge engineering. On a personal level, Arnstein later recalled that "Melan showed me the importance of utilizing every minute in the day."

Arnstein also had found a way to combine his love of art with the practical nature of engineering, as several drawings he did for his courses in bridge structures at the German Technical Institute in Prague attest. Done on heavy cardboard, they survive in a volume

Professor Joseph Melan, Arnstein's mentor in structural analysis. (A. D. Topping Collection/University of Akron Archives)

marked *Brückenbau* (bridge structures) in gilt letters on the outside. The drawings are notable for Arnstein's incredible attention to precision. Details such as tiny rivet heads are drawn freehand—even the shanks of the rivets are shown as tiny dotted circles drawn by compass in India ink. Arnstein also made some drawings of structures as they would appear at the site, beautifully done in watercolor wash, looking more like architectural renderings than mechanical illustrations. One drawing shows a bridge with several arches crossing a scenic valley. Another shows the facade of a reservoir pumping station, and in this one young Karl let his artistic imagination have free rein. Over the double door, "1908" is ornately shown inside a carved wreath between two pilasters with urns and balustrade at the top. Above the windows on either side of the doors are two human figures. On the left is a male figure with a long beard holding a trident representing Neptune, on the right is a female figure with a tall vase resting on her hip. All details are well executed, and it is not surprising that Karl was so proud of this work that he took it with him on his later moves.

But aesthetics alone will not ensure a successful structure. Bridge design demands a thorough understanding of the stresses imposed upon the construction materials, and (prior to the development of aircraft at least) received the greatest attention in engineering analysis because the consequences of failure could be so catastrophic. More precisely, stress analysis is a method of predicting what will happen to a structure when it is in service. If one is dealing with a machine part or small piece of a larger structure, it is usually possible to test it by itself to see what happens. But one cannot build a bridge merely to see if it will collapse when a truck drives across it. For new bridge designs, a method of prediction is necessary, and this method had not existed with any degree of sophistication until the seventeenth century. In the design of bridges, the **loads**—the forces compressing, stretching, bending, or twisting a structure—are ordinarily well established, so the problem becomes one of determining the behavior of the structure under those loads. Stress analysis is concerned not only with the internal forces—the stresses or strains within a structure or one of its components—but with deformations and deflections of those parts subjected to an outside force. Arnstein was alert to this concern even as a student. One day when he was studying an equation that determined the deflection of a beam he found that a math constant had been ignored. Curious, he wanted to ask Melan about the omission, but Melan's assistant refused to let Arnstein talk to the professor. Learning of the question, the assistant dismissed Arnstein's observation, saying, "the constant must be zero to make the theory agree with the tests." Arnstein could not believe the theory was valid if arbitrary assumptions were required to make it work. Something must have been overlooked, so Arnstein asked to see the references describing the tests. After studying them, he realized that the constant applied not only to the beam but to its support. This insight enabled Arnstein to predict the reaction of beam and support and thereby calculate the beam stresses. Confident that he had solved the problem with the theory, he wrote a paper on the subject and to avoid the assistant, mailed it directly to his professor. Melan liked it so much he submitted the paper for Arnstein to an Austrian technical journal. It was accepted for publication, a great distinction for the twenty-three-year-old student.

More importantly, Melan was sufficiently impressed that when his assistant left to take another job, he offered the position to Arnstein, who accepted not so much for the honor but because of the financial inducement. "Suddenly I was rich," he recalled. The sum was equivalent to a not insubstantial twenty-five dollars a month. He could not refuse such a princely stipend.

By 1909 Karl was nearing graduation, and the position enabled him to go on to earn a doctorate, while at the same time contributing to the support of the family household where he still lived. His job entailed working with students, grading papers, and assisting Professor Melan with his consulting work. It was a most significant step in young Arnstein's career. In stress analysis he had found a subject in which he excelled, as well as a discipline which promised a rewarding career. And, Arnstein was now the protégé of one of the giants in the field. Their friendship would last the remainder of Melan's long life.

Arnstein later said of his academic occupation: "My happiest years were [spent] there, where my time was divided between teaching structural analysis and working on great bridge projects." During this time Arnstein entered a competition, and won a prize for the Lorraine Bridge in Bern, Switzerland. As a graduate student, Arnstein had more time for his own creative work and had another paper published.

While teaching, Arnstein arranged for a student, a man of modest means, to complete his work over a summer vacation, thereby saving the student the cost of another year's study. When the former student got a job, he felt indebted to Arnstein and so called his employer's attention to his teacher's publications. Soon afterward, and on the recommendation of Melan, Karl received an offer of a position with the engineering firm of Eduard Züblin and Company. Although Melan would have liked Arnstein to stay as his assistant, he counseled him to go into industry for the financial rewards. In 1911, Karl became chief engineer of the division for "bridges and unusual structures in reinforced concrete" at Züblin's office in Strassburg (present-day Strasbourg, France; throughout the text, geographic names are spelled as they were at the time the story takes place).

Like Melan, Arnstein enjoyed academic life, but had not yet completed the work for his doctoral degree. Züblin, however, offered him a larger salary than even his mentor, Melan, was receiving. Also, to his relief, Arnstein found that he would be able to complete his doctorate while working for Züblin. Arnstein completed the work and received his degree from the Deutsche Technische Hochschule zu Prag in January 1912. The large diploma, authorized in grand, ornate script by the Austro-Hungarian emperor, "his Apostolic Majesty Franz Josef," later would be displayed prominently in the Arnstein home. Advanced degrees in engineering were not common in those days, and Arnstein was always proud of his earned doctorate.

Arnstein's new job required him to move away from his native city of Prague and take up residence in Strassburg. Living away from home for the first time, Karl found himself in a city of rivers and canals—and, appropriately, bridges. His employer, Eduard Züblin, was a Swiss mechanical engineer who had become interested in the new field of reinforced-concrete structures. He was influenced by François Hennebique, a French pioneer in reinforced concrete, whose name is often mentioned with that of Melan. After serving as a representative for Hennebique in southern Germany and Strassburg, Züblin founded his own business. It became one of the most reputable engineering firms in Europe, designing structures in Germany, Switzerland, Italy, and Alsace. Züblin did not take safety requirements lightly, and he required exact and painstaking calculations for all of his projects. He valued a man like Arnstein, whose strength was his knowledge of stress theory. Arnstein recalled him as a "self-made man with no college training" who nevertheless succeeded by his judgment, which Karl thought "showed almost supernatural inspiration." Züblin hired Arnstein to head the technical department of his Strassburg office because of a demanding project the company was undertaking. It was not just a construction project, but a rescue mission to save the tower of the Strassburg Cathedral from collapse.

Still the most prominent and famous structure in Strasbourg, the Cathedral of Notre Dame (or Münster-Strassburg, as Arnstein knew it) was begun in the twelfth century. It is one of the great Gothic landmarks of Europe and a UNESCO World Heritage site, notable for the art that decorates it inside and out. The cathedral is located in the heart of the city, and faces a bustling square lined with colorful shops and sidewalk cafes. Built of reddish-gray sandstone, the cathedral's most striking characteristic is its northwest tower—a solitary lacework steeple "pointing like a finger to heaven" (a matching second steeple was never completed). The ornate spire rises to a height of 466 feet (142 m), and was for nearly four centuries the tallest structure in Europe. French author Victor Hugo called the spire "a veritable tiara of stone with its crown and its cross . . . a gigantic and delicate marvel." However, in 1912 the lofty, filigreed stonework tower and the magnificent rose window adjacent were threatened with destruction due to settling of the cathedral's foundation, which was built on an earlier structure from the ninth century. With his lifelong love of art, Arnstein was pleased that this great cathedral would provide the problem for his first important assignment in stress analysis. In later life, he always had a large print of the cathedral in his study and he delighted in its Gothic sculptures.

Arnstein served as stress analyst and scientific consultant to the architectural committee responsible for shoring up the cathedral. He was assigned the task of determining the strength requirements of the new foundation both for the long term and for conditions occurring during construction. The task of a stress analyst was perhaps the single most important one in the design process, both difficult and crucial to the safety and success of the whole operation. After all, one does not casually dig around the foundation of a seven-hundred-year-old masonry tower 466 feet high, nor can one risk performing full-scale tests on such a structure. Stress analysis, based upon empirical knowledge of the behavior of structural materials as well as theoretical reasoning, offered the economic and practical solution.

Arnstein determined that the innermost supporting pillars of the tower were no longer carrying their share of the load, and that the lighter, outer pillars were buckling from the weight. His solution to keep the cathedral tower from toppling over involved putting a reinforced-concrete ring ten feet high and ten feet wide under the west wall of the structure. Additional reinforced-concrete braces fifteen feet wide and two feet thick were put in place at the tower corners. The nearly seventy-thousand-ton tower pillar then was supported by a concrete collar and hydraulic jacks while another reinforced-concrete structure was installed at the base. Let down from the jacks, the entire load of the tower and walls would be supported by a new, deeper foundation.

The actual reconstruction work on the cathedral began in 1912, although the engineering work started the year before Arnstein arrived in Strassburg. Arnstein worked on the calculations and preparations for nearly two years, while also working on his doctorate. The tower reinforcement would continue into the next decade. At his office, Arnstein worked on various bridge projects.

Karl Arnstein was not the only immigrant from Prague in Strassburg. Another who soon arrived was Karl Paul Helma, who, as a student in civil engineering at the German Technical Institute in Prague, had taken laboratory courses in bridge design as a pupil of Arnstein. Helma was actually more than three years older then Arnstein, having been born in 1883 in Saxony. After his graduation from the Institute, Helma obtained a position at Züblin and Company in Strassburg and was assigned to Arnstein's department. With much in common, the two young men became good friends. This friendship would be tested

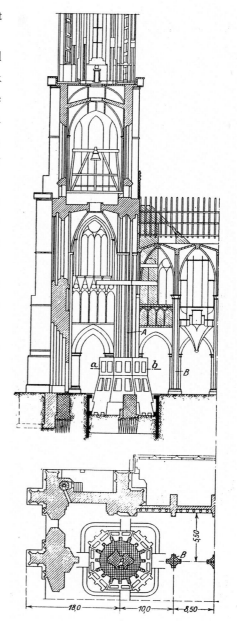

Cut-away side and top views of the Strasbourg Cathedral showing the concrete reinforcement to the tower's foundation for which Arnstein calculated the loads. Measurements are in meters. (Karl Arnstein Collection/University of Akron Archives)

years later, as Helma continued to reappear in the life of Arnstein. Karl also became friends with a couple who, like himself and Helma, moved to Strassburg from Prague. The husband carried the name of an aristocrat, and his wife was a musician from a middle-class family. They wanted children, but were unable to have any. Learning of this, Karl was able to assist as a go-between in the couple's quest to adopt a child born out of wedlock to a married physician and his mistress. Arnstein maintained a friendship with the adoptive parents and their family throughout his life. This gesture is indicative of Arnstein's willingness to assist friends in trouble. It would not be the last time he would generously offer to help both friends and associates in need.

By the latter part of 1912, Arnstein's attention was directed primarily at another project in the easternmost Swiss canton—the one Germans call Graubünden and the French call Grisons,—where the rivers run granite gray. Chur, the capital, lies in the valley of the upper Rhine. In the gray alps above Chur is a remote village called Arosa, situated more than a mile high and about sixteen miles up the Plessur River valley. Nowadays, the destination is sought for winter sports and summer vacations. Formerly, Arosa was noted for its tuberculosis sanitariums which provided patients the benefits of clear mountain air and sunshine. Tuberculosis then was a much feared and often lethal disease, and those afflicted were kept in isolation in villages such as Arosa. The only way to reach it from Chur was by horse-drawn vehicle on a tortuous, unpaved road ascending 3,800 feet (1,160 m).

A more efficient and faster means of travel eventually became necessary, and in July 1911, the Chur-Arosa Road Company was founded. In January 1912, construction of a narrow-gauge electric railway began. From Chur, the route resembles a fish hook as it climbs eastward up the Plessur River valley. At the bend is the village of Langwies, where the line crosses the gorge on a bridge that today is a showpiece of the Swiss National Railway. The contract for the design and construction of that bridge was let to Ed. Züblin and Company, of Strassburg. As head of the company's stress analysis group, Karl Arnstein was entrusted with the planning and calculations. For its time, the bridge design seemed daring. It called for a bold arch span 328 feet (100 m) across supporting a roadbed with improbably thin-looking columns 138 feet (42 m) high. Also unusual for the time, the structure was to be built of reinforced concrete, exceeding in its measurements all designs in reinforced concrete then known. The Langwies viaduct would be the longest and tallest reinforced-concrete bridge in the world, and its slender delicacy excited the admiration of professional engineers all over the world.

Concrete was seldom used in bridge construction because the purchase and transportation costs of sand and cement were too high. However, at Langwies a scarcity of building stone as well as an abundance of gravel and sand immediately suggested reinforced-concrete construction. Arnstein found that although an excellent grade of sand and gravel was available, the temperature extremes in the Plessur Valley were such that the concrete would crack if it was made to conventional specifications.

The strength of concrete depends on the proportions of its ingredients—sand, gravel, cement, and water—as well as the properties of the aggregate (the sand and gravel). More water tends to make wet concrete easier to handle and pour, but the end result is weaker concrete. When two materials as different as concrete and the iron used to reinforce it are combined, other problems arise. The materials do not expand at the same rate, so that when the temperature changes after they are bonded together, internal stresses are set up which can lead to cracking. Also, concrete shrinks as it sets and this shrinkage must be taken into account.

If too much concrete was used, the internal stresses would cause it to crack off the viaduct arches. To prevent cracking, Arnstein proposed to cut the design safety factor for the concrete in half, but at the same time to try to make the concrete twice as strong as the specification called for. "Some people thought I was crazy," Arnstein later recalled with a laugh. But by his calculation, stronger construction would substitute for bulk to support the structure's weight. The Swiss railway engineers agreed and that is how the bridge was built.

Work on the pioneering structure began in August 1912, overseen by Arnstein and a team of seven other engineers. More than 9,680 cubic yards (7,400 cu m) of concrete and 364 tons (330 tonnes) of iron reinforcement were needed for construction. To build the arch, a unique fan scaffold made of wood was first erected. The shape minimized the need for timber, but even so, the support work alone required over 700 cubic meters of wood. Transporting all of the structural materials required over 1,000 four-harness horse carts to travel on the poor road. The slender, cross-braced trestles which would support the road bed on either side of the arch were similarly erected from the valley floor. Although they appear thin, they are still a meter (3.3 ft) thick. At its apex, the arch is 2 meters (6.6 ft) thick, and the legs broaden to only 4 meters (13 ft) width at the base.

During the bridge's construction, Arnstein stayed several months in the isolated village of Langwies. He subsisted on the limited selection of food, which consisted primarily of hard rye bread "black as shoeshine," hard smoked ham, sour red wine, cheese, and a kind of dried beef. He complained of the monotony of this diet although he admitted the beef was very good. Entertainment was nearly nonexistent.

As a diversion, Arnstein and a few of the younger engineers decided to try mountain climbing. They climbed above the snow line before realizing that they would not reach the summit of the mountain and found themselves in danger of falling from the narrow ledges.

Climbing down can be more unnerving than climbing up. Arnstein feared for his life, but they all managed to return safely to the village. Despite this scare, Arnstein later looked back on his months in Langwies as among the most interesting and enjoyable times of his life.

Construction on the bridge continued during the next two years. As the concrete structure was completed and hardened, the magnificent fan-shaped scaffold was dismantled. It had done its job well: the bridge's top layer showed scarcely a centimeter of settlement after the concrete had set. "At this critical moment I was up on the small wooden platform . . . directly under the arch," Arnstein recalled. He watched as the jacks were released. "Everything performed perfectly. We rejoiced. Forgotten was the inconvenience of our diet . . . which we had suffered for so many months."

By July 1914, the pale gray viaduct was finished. Its total length covered 287 meters (942 ft), with the arch alone spanning more than a third that distance. The narrow-gauge roadway perched 62 meters (203 ft) above the Plessur River.

The railway bridge at Langwies was significant because it demonstrated that a structure's design could be optimized by using stress analysis. In other words, the bridge was made strong and durable while using a minimum of materials. Even though the structure was built on an obscure spur line in a little-traveled part of the small country of Switzerland, the engineering community soon recognized the Langwies bridge as the most significant bridge of its type in the world. As one appreciation of the accomplishment noted: "This functional structure, set so lightly and naturally into the landscape . . . owes its elegant appearance in no small part to the basic observance of the laws of stress analysis, especially the exhaustive consideration of the stresses developed by shrinkage and temperature variation in all parts of the structure." The bridge demonstrated the principle "form follows function," a defining theme in the aesthetics of modern architecture. Arnstein's work in stress analysis contributed to this new approach to construction, proving it was possible to build large, engineered concrete structures without fear they would collapse.

Arnstein took great pride in the Langwies bridge, especially in the thin pillars supporting the railway above the main arch which he felt gave the bridge its unusual gracefulness. He always felt that a good engineering work would turn out to be beautiful. The unprecedented slenderness of the pillars is possible only because Arnstein had shown analytically that they could safely carry the design loads without buckling. A less capable engineer would have made them unnecessarily thicker because he would have been unable to prove that slender columns were adequate.

After the bridge was finished, the project's chief engineer, Gustav Bener, wrote: "This

The Langwies Viaduct for the Chur-Arosa railroad in Switzerland. Arnstein's analysis of the bridges's structural requirements directly influenced the design of the reinforced-concrete span. (Karl Arnstein Collection/University of Akron Archives)

bridge is a brilliant proof that structures of building materials taken for the most part from their immediate surroundings and dimensioned according to their stresses, themselves produce to the human eye a match with nature as pleasing and inspiring as that of the high reaching branches of a pine tree." Bener's phrase, "dimensioned according to their stresses," is the key to understanding the bridge's design, and that was Arnstein's responsibility. As proof Arnstein was correct in his calculations, the Langwies viaduct is still in service, still a showplace of the Swiss National Railway system, commemorated in the Transportation Museum in Lucerne by a mural-size photograph.

Langwies today remains a small village, a stop on the rail line, with a beautiful, typically Alpine station. A bench has been strategically placed there where one may sit and admire the view of the bridge and its scenic mountain backdrop. The bridge still has a practical purpose, as well as being pleasing to the eye. Before the bridge was finished, the mail wagon took six hours to go from Chur to Arosa by road. In 1914, the journey by rail took an hour and thirty-five minutes. Now the train makes the run in one hour.

The Langwies bridge was not the only project getting attention at Züblin's Strassburg office. In 1913, Arnstein's department originated a design for a reinforced-concrete bridge at Freiburg, Switzerland. This structure with two broad arches, the Perolles Bridge, would have been larger than the one at Langwies. Despite the Züblin team's design efforts, when the bridge was finally built, it was made to a much different plan. However, Arnstein's knowledge of stresses in concrete was not wasted, but applied to designing a silo to contain iron ore for a Belgian steel company. To protect the silo's thick walls from freezing and thawing stresses, Arnstein's solution was to set them partially underground. By 1914, Arnstein had developed a solid reputation in stress analysis for reinforced-concrete structures. Züblin sent Arnstein to Russia to do preliminary analysis on a project to build that country's first large, reinforced-concrete silo. The Züblin company hoped to construct it, but the outbreak of World War I prevented that.

Archduke Ferdinand of Austria was assassinated in Sarajevo on 28 June, 1914. This event touched off World War I, and on 28 July, Austria declared war on Serbia. Arnstein's assistant, Helma, was called to serve in the Austrian army. Later, Arnstein, also an Austrian national, was required on short notice to return to Prague where he soon would be drafted into the Austrian army. No one expected the war to last long.

Chapter 2 THE ZEPPELIN PHENOMENON

A few years before the war, while Arnstein was working on the restoration of the Strassburg Cathedral foundation, he had the opportunity to climb into every part of the cathedral's tower. From its heights, he could take measurements, admire the stone carvings and spend time "looking down over the quaint old roofs of beautiful Strassburg." One day from this lofty vantage, Arnstein saw "a shining horizontal cylinder on the horizon, growing larger." He soon recognized it as a Zeppelin, which he watched as it flew over and circled the steeple. "I was deeply impressed," he remembered. He thought it a beautiful sight. Little could he imagine that this apparition would one day take him away from the work he liked so well and into a new and different field of engineering. Later, Arnstein came to regard seeing the airship as an omen.

Today, it is hard to imagine the emotional impact caused by a glimpse of that aerial curiosity, a Zeppelin. A contemporary account gives an appreciation of what Arnstein saw and felt:

This balloon, floating in space . . . defies exact reproduction or description. Picture an enormous long polygonal-shaped mass of a startling whiteness sailing two thousand feet above us. The propellers, which murmur like innumerable bees, made the canvas shiver along its rigid structure. . . . It was all so full of life, vibrating with so joyous a sound and so harmoniously lovely in its setting, that one could scarcely believe it a man-made thing. . . .

At last we caught it again, just in time to see it sail over the mountains, a truly lovely sight. Its white color, which had been so alive and gay, had changed to a mist, blue and airy, on which the elegant forms of its framework were delicately shadowed, the color of light blue violets, so simple that it was one with the mountains over which it hung—and then it vanished in the air.

. . . It was so beautiful, not pretty, but beautiful, agreeing with the laws of Greek art and nature . . .

How did these aerial leviathans come into being? The idea of a steerable balloon, or **dirigible**, was almost as old as ballooning itself.

Ferdinand Graf von Zeppelin. (Lockheed Martin Collection/University of Akron Archives)

The balloon, as humanity's oldest means of sustained flight, was invented in France in 1783. While a balloon's vertical movement may be controlled by its pilot, the course it follows across the sky is wherever the wind takes it. As early as 1784, various schemes were tried to make a balloon steerable—what the French called a *ballon dirigeable*—so that it could be navigated from one point to another regardless of the wind's direction. The efforts were unsuccessful, because no method of propulsion existed that was light enough to be carried aloft and powerful enough to overcome even a gentle wind acting on a balloon's large surface. Propulsion technology made great strides in the next hundred years, and by the end of the nineteenth century, a number of experimenters had been able to demonstrate, with varying degrees of success, that a tapered balloon could be motor propelled against the wind. However, these vehicles could barely lift the weight of their one or two man crews, were grossly underpowered, and in design were little more than elongated, gas-filled bags with a wicker basket and motor slung underneath. A retired army officer in southern Germany had an idea that was far more grand. He envisioned no less than an aerial train, a series of balloons held together like sausage links that could be driven through the skies. In its final form, this train became an air ship, capable of navigating the sky as easily as a waterborne ship sails the ocean. The realization of this particular dream of flight largely owes its existence to the determination, will, and courage of that one man: Ferdinand Adolf August Heinrich, Graf von Zeppelin. He is generally acknowledged as the inventor of the **rigid airship,** and the story of the Zeppelin Company is inseparable from its founder.

Graf Zeppelin (Count Zeppelin) was born on 8 July 1838 in the German town of Konstanz, on Lake Constance (the Germans call the lake the Bodensee). This scenic body of water that separates Switzerland from southwestern Germany would later be the scene of the count's earliest aeronautical experiments.

Zeppelin's career was in the army of his native Württemberg, and in 1863, the count, then a young officer, obtained a leave of absence to travel to the United States to be a military observer in the American Civil War. He even secured an audience with President Abraham Lincoln to get a pass permitting him freedom of movement with the Union Army. After a month of military life attached to the Army of the Potomac in Virginia, the twenty-four-year-old Zeppelin grew restless, and decided it might be more interesting to travel. He headed north to Niagara Falls and then west to Wisconsin, where he joined a group of adventurers—two Russians and two Native Americans—on a journey to the source of the Mississippi River. Ill-equipped for such a journey, the expedition got lost and ran out of food. Escaping disaster, the party managed to reach St. Paul, Minnesota, in August.

When Zeppelin arrived in St. Paul, an aeronaut named John Steiner was offering tethered balloon ascensions for a price. Steiner was a former member of the Union Balloon Corps, which had been disbanded before the battle of Gettysburg. Count Zeppelin made his first balloon ascension with Steiner, and in conversation with the balloonist learned that Steiner had an idea for a "long and slender" balloon with a rudder, which would enable it to "reach its destination more smoothly and more surely." This could only have been a dirigible balloon.

Years later Count Zeppelin would say that his first idea for his namesake airships came to him at St. Paul, obviously from John Steiner. However, he did not at that time conceive of the compartmented, rigid metal framework of **Zeppelin** airships and it was not until March 1874 that he wrote in his diary, "Thoughts about an airship." By then, Zeppelin had returned to Württemberg and had already distinguished himself as a cavalry officer.

A decade later the French engineers Captain Charles Renard and Arthur-Constantin Krebs constructed an elongated, pointed-at-the-ends balloon. Below it was suspended a long keel supporting a pilot and an electric motor powered by heavy batteries. It was this *dirigeable*, or steerable balloon, named *La France*, that in August 1884 became the first such vehicle to fly away from its starting point and return against the wind. The speed obtained by *La France* was too low to be practical, but Count Zeppelin perceived in it a threat to Germany, and began to urge development of a German airship. His opinion won him no friends in high places. At that time those who envisioned powered flight were widely considered to be crackpots, and it is true that his rigid airship concept was not achievable with the technology of the time.

Nevertheless, Zeppelin rose through the ranks and became an ambassador to the king of Württemberg, serving in Berlin. But he bristled at the Prussian domination of the unified German states, and he expressed his opposition in an official memorandum at the end of his diplomatic duty. It proved costly. Only months after he was given a division command, he was reviewed unfavorably for reasons that remain obscure. Count Zeppelin's military career ended when he was given the rank of lieutenant general and forced to retire in December 1890. Count Zeppelin did not take to his rocking chair, however—he was a man of both energy and ideas. Zeppelin's diplomatic contacts with the military and scientific elite had allowed him access to the technological innovations of his day, and he was impressed by the military implications afforded by balloons and the earliest dirigibles. Still alarmed by what he thought was French superiority in the development of dirigibles, Zeppelin, in retirement now, had time to work on his airship project in earnest.

The concept of a large, rigid balloon that could be maneuvered at will through the sky was born and could now be nurtured by this brusque, cast-out general. His concept consisted of a rigid framework covered with fabric to give form to the airship and to protect the internal structure from winds. The outer cage of lengthwise girders was braced by transverse **rings** stabilized by wires, generally on the principle of a bicycle wheel. Between the rings were secured a series of cylindrical bags, the **gas cells**, which provided lift according to Archimedes' Principle. This buoyancy was derived because the cells contained a gas (the lightest element, hydrogen) that was lighter than the surrounding air. In Zeppelin's design, the gas cells could expand and contract, or "breathe," as the ambient atmospheric pressure changed during ascent or descent of the airship, while the rigid structure (enveloped with a lightweight, streamlining cotton fabric) maintained its shape. The gas within these cells was not pressurized. This was the main difference between Zeppelin's idea and other airships of the day, which retained their shape by the pressure of the lifting gas pushing outward on their exposed **envelopes** (as do today's blimps). The Zeppelin airship had to be built large because the weight of the enclosing framework for small airships is, in practice, too great.

Although Count Zeppelin had taken some college level technical courses, he was fully aware that he was not a trained engineer. He eventually hired Theodor Kober to do the necessary engineering work. Kober completed a design which was submitted to a government commission headed by the renowned physicist, Hermann von Helmholtz, and which included stress analyst, Dr. Heinrich F. B. Müller-Breslau. He is the same engineer who, with Arnstein, contributed to the structural design of the bridge at Langwies in 1913.

Müller-Breslau found the design had deficiencies in strength. Kober and Zeppelin came up with a crude solution, which Müller-Breslau then corrected, using "a frame made up of multiple stiff longitudinals securely attached to 'stiff cross walls or partitions.'" Müller-Breslau also enlarged the airship to get greater lift and replaced the hemispherical ends of the cylindrical body with tapering ones. This was very much the configuration of the *Luftschiff Zeppelin 1* (LZ 1), the count's first airship.

Other engineering problems had to be resolved. Zeppelin had to find a light, strong metal with which to build his airship, and someone who knew how to produce it. The only man in Germany in a position to help was Carl Berg, a pioneer in the aluminum industry, who became the second largest shareholder (the count being the largest) in Zeppelin's corporation, the Joint Stock Company for the Promotion of Airship Travel

(Aktiengesellschaft zur Förderung der Luftschiffahrt), organized in 1898. Berg fabricated all of the aluminum components of the early Zeppelin airships. The pieces of LZ 1 were made by Berg's company and shipped to Zeppelin's floating construction hangar at Manzell on Lake Constance.

In this huge wooden shed on a raft, the "Crazy Count's" folly took shape. The LZ 1 would have a gas volume of 399,000 cubic feet (11,300 cu m) divided among 17 separate gas cells held under a thin cotton covering. Overall, it was 420 feet (128 m) long and 38.5 feet (11.7 m) in maximum diameter. Below the faceted, cylindrical hull were two metal boat-like control **gondolas**, each containing a 14 horsepower (10 kW) engine; each drove two propellers on outriggers. Although the ambitious craft was completed late in 1899, the count cautiously waited until summer of the next year to demonstrate his vehicle. Suspense grew in Friedrichshafen, the little lakeside town nearest the floating shed. A storm nearly wrecked the fragile craft when its shed was blown from its moorings. When the big day arrived, journalists and local people crowded the shore to witness the event. Prominent persons from business and science also were invited. Finally, Count Zeppelin strode onto the floating platform, doffed his cap and the LZ 1 flew for the first time. The maiden flight on 2 July 1900 covered three and a half miles. It was judged a qualified success. The craft rose to a height of 1,300 feet, but the steering vanes were rudimentary, and the engines labored to keep the ship under control. To make the ship ascend and descend also required sliding a heavy weight between the fore and aft gondolas—not a practical method of control. The cigar-shaped structure also proved less rigid than anticipated. Not without promise, the airship nevertheless demonstrated that the design needed more refinement if it were to achieve its goals of speedy, long-duration flight. But the money for development was gone. The LZ 1 was dismantled in 1901 after only three flights. The Joint Stock Company went bankrupt and, eventually, everyone but the count's new chief engineer, Ludwig Dürr, was laid off.

His fortune seriously depleted, Count Zeppelin was discouraged, but only temporarily. After the king of Württemberg permitted a lottery to raise funds for a new airship, LZ 2 was constructed with Dürr in charge. The new airship had dimensions similar to LZ 1, but was powered by 80 horsepower (60 kW) engines. But, on its second flight in January 1906, both engines failed and the airship had to be free-ballooned to a landing near the village of Kisslegg. It was tied to the ground with ropes, but during the night, high winds came up, and the second Zeppelin was so badly damaged it had to be dismantled.

The failures could easily be explained, and the weather was an unfortunate, freak occurrence. After this setback, the count said he would build no more airships, but his optimism and perseverance prevailed and soon he sought funds to build a third airship.

With the help of another lottery, the count raised enough money to build the LZ 3. First flown on 9 October 1906, it was reasonably successful. Count Zeppelin found some support among officialdom and the scientific community in Berlin. His stature and popularity was also growing with the general public, who were beginning to think the indomitable old soldier was not so crazy after all. He proposed to sell the LZ 3 and the next two Zeppelins to be built to the government, in order to fund development of an airship that could carry five hundred troops without needing a special lifting gas. Count Zeppelin envisioned an airship using hot air as a lifting agent. However, no sufficiently light heat-resistant materials then existed to build such a craft.

Now interested in Zeppelin's ideas, the German Army agreed to buy the LZ 3—if the airship could make a twenty-four-hour endurance flight to a designated point and return. The LZ 3, even with several modifications, was not able to do that. So, a larger, more powerful airship was built, the LZ 4, with the government paying 400,000 marks toward its construction. On 1 July 1908, the LZ 4 created a sensation with a twelve-hour flight over Switzerland and back to Manzell, the longest flight by any aircraft up to that time.

Zeppelin believed he was ready for the endurance flight, and it began on 4 August 1908, with the destination Mainz. On the return trip the next morning, engine troubles developed which made a stop necessary not far from the village of Echterdingen, near Stuttgart. Here the mechanics from Daimler, which had provided the engines, could be called on to repair them. In midafternoon as repairs were under way, and reminiscent of the misfortune that befell LZ 2, a storm came up and tore the LZ 4 from its moorings. It caught fire and burned. Three crewmen aboard escaped with minor injuries. The cause of the fire was a mystery until a later investigation showed that the rubberized fabric of the gas cells, when violently torn, produced an electric discharge that caused sparks. The tear also permitted the hydrogen in the bags to form a combustible mixture with oxygen in the air. Touched off by the spark, a rapid fire consumed the airship. Stunned, the seventy-year-old count rode the train back to Friedrichshafen in silence. He could see no way out; he was finished. But then something happened that would become known as the "miracle of Echterdingen."

The story of Count Zeppelin's airships—full of dramatic setbacks and triumphs—was familiar to the German public. A four-hundred-foot object flying about the sky would excite a lot of interest even today, but in 1907 and 1908, nothing like it had ever been seen. The count had become a national hero, a grandfatherly patriot and forward-looking military man, who was all the more endearing because his strict formality was tempered by his twinkling eyes, a jaunty school cap and voluminous white handlebar mustache. The public began pulling for Count Zeppelin to succeed. Achievements like the Swiss flight only

The Zeppelin LZ 4 is docked in its floating wooden hangar on Lake Constance. Moored at one end, the hangar could swing to align with the wind, making it easier to handle the airship in and out of its dock. The Zeppelin's complex and aerodynamically inefficient array of control surfaces is clearly visible. (Lockheed Martin Collection/University of Akron Archives)

fired its enthusiasm more, and the public tracked the progress of the twenty-four-hour flight in the morning and evening newspapers. News of the latest disaster spread fast, and by the time Count Zeppelin arrived home, telegrams had already arrived offering money to help. The next day letters poured in with more offers of financial help. A manufacturer sent 50,000 marks, collections were taken up in the offices and business plants, and schoolchildren emptied their piggy banks.

This outpouring was a tribute to a most remarkable man and his persistence. The day after the loss of the LZ 4, a onetime critic who had been won over to Zeppelin's cause, Dr. Hugo Eckener, came to see the count. Zeppelin was going through a pile of mail, and in response to Eckener's greeting, he smiled slyly, saying, "Here, you see, you are already over 100,000 marks, and more is promised. If it keeps on like this, I shall end by having as much trouble spending the money wisely as I formerly had in raising it." More than 6,000,000 marks in donations eventually came in.

The money was put into a trust, the Zeppelin Fund, and on 8 September 1908, the Luftschiffbau-Zeppelin GmbH (Company) was founded with a capital of 3,000,000 marks which was later increased to 4,000,000 marks. The city of Friedrichshafen provided land for a factory. The building of Zeppelins was suddenly a promising business, not merely the hobby of an eccentric aristocrat. Henceforth, the Zeppelin name would become synonymous with rigid airships, regardless of manufacturer or country of origin.

The count now needed a business manager. Rather pre-emptively, he received a telegram asking for the position from Alfred Colsman, the son of an aluminum manufacturer and the son-in-law of airship parts fabricator Carl Berg. The count was well aware of Colsman's business acumen, and he also knew him as a man he could trust.

Colsman was thirty-five when he gave up his position as a member of the board of directors at the Carl Berg firm to join Zeppelin. His genius in the company was later overshadowed by the more flamboyant Eckener, but it was Colsman who organized the Zeppelin concern with its many subsidiary companies, building it so well that it still survives today.

Retired general Zeppelin envisioned the War Ministry as the customer for his company's products, but after taking a rebuilt LZ 3 and a new airship, LZ 5, the army placed no more orders. To stay in business, Colsman suggested setting up an airline to fly passengers commercially, capitalizing on the public's enthusiasm for airships. Zeppelin disliked the idea of being reduced to the sordid commercialism of making money, instead of making a patriotic contribution to the safety of the fatherland. But there was no other alternative.

Colsman secured the backing of Albert Ballin, head of the Hamburg-Amerika shipping line, to form a new company called Deutsche Luftschiffahrts-Aktien-Gesellschaft, more

Count Zeppelin, crewman Georg Hacker, and captain Dr. Hugo Eckener in the control gondola of the Zeppelin
Schwaben, *c. 1911. (Lockheed Martin Collection/University of Akron Archives)*

commonly known as **DELAG,** the German Aerial Transportation Company. DELAG set up headquarters in Frankfurt am Main in 1909, and German cities vied to be first to build a hangar for the new passenger airships. But the beginnings of the new company were not promising—the LZ 7 was wrecked in the Teutoburg Forest on an inaugural flight carrying journalists from Düsseldorf on 28 June 1910, and the LZ 6 was accidentally burned in its hangar at Baden-Oos in September of the same year.

Colsman was serving as business manager of DELAG as well as of Luftschiffbau-Zeppelin. After the loss of the LZ 7 *Deutschland,* he needed to replace his luckless airship captain. He shrewdly persuaded Hugo Eckener to take over as flight director of DELAG. In time, Eckener's name recognition with Zeppelins would rank second only to the count's.

Hugo Eckener was born in 1868 in Flensburg, a German seaport on the Baltic. In his youth, sailing was Eckener's sport, and he gained a reputation among his friends for his ability to predict the weather and the wind by studying the sky and water. The young Eckener was an avid scholar with a variety of interests. He studied at the University at Berlin and the University of Leipzig, where he wrote his doctoral thesis on "Variabilities in Human Perception." After receiving his degree, Dr. Eckener did not settle into a profession. After a mandatory year in the German army, he studied economics, then became a freelance journalist and served as a music and drama critic. It seems that his journalistic pursuits brought in little money, but he apparently had income from his father's cigar factory or from his wife's fortune.

In 1900 the couple went to Friedrichshafen so that Hugo would have a quieter place to work than in Munich. The newspaper *Frankfurter Zeitung* asked him to report on the second flight of LZ 1. Eckener wrote a report of it which he, himself, would describe as "cool and critical." In 1905, he witnessed the first ascent of LZ 2 and wrote another critical report, but this time, there was a surprising reaction from Count Zeppelin. He called on Eckener, thanked him for the friendly tone in which he had written about the count personally, and then explained to Eckener, who was not an engineer, that some of the statements in the article were inaccurate. A few days later, he invited Eckener to dinner and Eckener was so impressed with the count's personality and the practicality of his ideas that he offered to publicize his cause.

Following the phoenixlike rebirth of the Zeppelin cause after the disaster at Echterdingen, Colsman persuaded Eckener to become the Zeppelin firm's director of public relations. After the DELAG airship LZ 7 *Deutschland* was stranded in the Teutoburg Forest, largely due to poor judgment by its commander, Colsman gave Eckener the post of flight

Passenger Zeppelin Deutschland II *(LZ 8) was wrecked by gusty winds when it was brought out of its Düsseldorf hangar on 16 May 1911. There were no injuries to any passengers, but the airship's commander, Hugo Eckener, vowed never again to let public expectations overrule his judgment about flying conditions. (Lockheed Martin Collection/University of Akron Archives)*

director for all DELAG airships. On 6 February 1911, Eckener received his airship pilot's license, and was appointed manager of DELAG.

A few months later, impatient to fly with a full load of paying passengers, Eckener wrecked the LZ 8 *Ersatz Deutschland* by bringing it out of the hangar when there was too much crosswind. It was a novice's mistake which he would never make again. DELAG was at a crossroads. The last five Zeppelins had all been ruined, and doubts about Count Zeppelin's rigid airship concept returned. Hesitantly, the board of DELAG, which represented the mayors of the several cities from which DELAG intended to operate, ordered another airship. This became the LZ 10 *Schwaben*, which incorporated many improvements, and proved there was substance to the count's vision after all, with the help of unusually good weather and Eckener's insistence on cautious handling.

There were more setbacks—*Schwaben* burned on the field at Düsseldorf in June 1912 in an accident similar to LZ 4's—but DELAG was well established and eventually had three ships flying in commercial service by 1913. Count Zeppelin stayed active, even piloting DELAG airships to cities from where they were to make their first commercial flights. By the end of the year, Zeppelins had flown more than 30,000 passengers over 90,000 miles without death or injury. In contrast, the first passenger-carrying airline utilizing airplanes did not start operating until January 1914, and then it only carried one passenger at a time over a route of 18 miles.

Meanwhile, as the Zeppelins were enjoying some commercial success, they finally began to win favor as potential military weapons—viewed especially in the role of bomber and long-range scout. While building the DELAG ships, the Zeppelin Company also built for the German army the LZ 9 and LZ 12, each larger, faster and capable of carrying more load than their predecessors. At last, the German navy became interested, and the first navy Zeppelin, LZ 14, was delivered in autumn 1912, to serve as the Navy L 1. But the navy wanted a larger airship with a longer range for its purposes, and it ordered a second airship that incorporated several ideas of its own designer, Felix Pietzker. The Zeppelin factory's LZ 18 would have a brief career as the Imperial German Navy's L 2. (Both the German army and the navy adopted a numbering system independent of the builder's or works number.)

To be able to get his airship into existing hangars while still gaining more lift, Pietzker inverted the keel used along the bottom of previous Zeppelins and put it inside the hull. The engine gondolas (or cars) were also raised and wind screens filled the remaining gap below the hull. This was a fatal mistake, since the flammable hydrogen lifting gas released through the pressure relief valves at the bottom of the gas bags had nowhere to escape (no chimneylike gas shafts were provided at this stage of development), and the wind screens prevented the wind from safely taking it away. As the ship rose, the vented hydrogen mixed with air in an explosive combination. Twenty-eight crewmen perished in the fire which consumed the ship.

Only a month before, in September 1913, the first navy airship was wrecked at sea with the loss of fourteen crew members. These were the first fatalities despite the many other accidents that befell the count's airships. Zeppelin was outspoken in his effort to assess blame on the navy and he quarreled heatedly with the navy minister. In time, Colsman managed to heal the breach, but the embittered Zeppelin was marginalized and remained with the company primarily as a figurehead.

By the time war broke out in August of 1914, twelve airships had been delivered to the army and three to the navy. Pressed into military service, the three DELAG-operated airships went to the army, and Eckener went to the navy, where he was assigned to train airship commanders. The Zeppelin airship, long intended to serve the military needs of the Fatherland, would finally be tested in that role. As the Zeppelin Company went to a wartime footing, production expanded greatly, and there was an influx of government personnel concerned with the product the army and the navy were purchasing. The engineering staff grew rapidly. Within a few months, Karl Arnstein also would be joining the Zeppelin firm.

Chapter 3   THE STRESS ANALYST IN FRIEDRICHSHAFEN

When Arnstein returned to Prague, he was conscripted into the Austrian army engineering corps as a "sapper" with the rank of private. Before bestowing undue credit upon the Austrian military for recognizing Arnstein's engineering talent, consider his duties. In military terminology, a sapper is a soldier who specializes in the construction of trenches and earthen fortifications. Arnstein, at age twenty-seven with a doctorate in technical science and engineering experience, was put to work digging trenches.

As a new recruit, he had to undergo the usual drills, which included marching and calisthenics, which he particularly disliked. Several weeks after his induction, he was on the exercise grounds when his commanding officer, a major, called him into his office.

"What do you know about airships?" the officer demanded to know.

"Nothing," replied Arnstein.

"You son of a bitch!" grumbled the major. "How did you get this soft assignment?" he asked, waving a piece of paper. It was a telegram ordering Arnstein to report to the Luftschiffbau-Zeppelin Company in Friedrichshafen, Germany, for three months.

The answer to the major's question was as mystifying to Arnstein as to the major, but these were the orders, and so Private Arnstein went to Friedrichshafen. He started work at Luftschiffbau-Zeppelin in March 1915.

Arnstein had been in Friedrichshafen once before. While still employed by Züblin in Strassburg he had been sent there as a consultant to advise Zeppelin on the construction of an underground hangar for his airships. This had military advantages, since the giant German army and navy Zeppelin hangars would be prime targets for enemy aircraft bombardment in time of war. Dr. Karl Jaray, a professor of architecture at the University of Prague, was also consulted. Their studies proved that the project was not feasible and the underground hangar was never built.

In one discussion, Count Zeppelin said to Arnstein, "If you can calculate the stresses in this hangar's trussed roof structure, why couldn't you calculate the stresses in my airships? My engineers tell me it is impossible."

Arnstein replied that he was sure the stresses could be calculated, although it would be considerably more difficult than calculating stresses in the hangar roof truss, and there would be some difficulties in determining the aerodynamic loads. Later, Arnstein remembered his conversations with Zeppelin on the hangar proposal and airships and speculated that these may have led to his assignment to Friedrichshafen in 1915.

By 1914, Zeppelin had largely retired from an active role in his airship company. But with the outbreak of World War I in August 1914, the old soldier was again aroused. Now he pushed the development of, surprisingly, not airships, but large all-metal bombing airplanes. He wanted the man in charge of the Zeppelin Company's structural analysis, Claude (Claudius) Dornier, to undertake this project.

Dornier, about three years older than Karl Arnstein, had been engaged in bridge engineering when Count Zeppelin found him and brought him to Luftschiffbau-Zeppelin in 1910. He was first employed as a stress analyst in the research division, assigned the task of investigating other metals to replace aluminum and wood in aircraft structures. One such study examined the feasibility of a steel Zeppelin of 2,825,000 cubic foot (80,000 cu m), which Count Zeppelin hoped to fly to New York by 1916. Dornier also has been credited with the development of **duralumin**—a lightweight aluminum alloy with enhanced strength characteristics—for use in airship structure. Dornier was destined to become famous as a builder of airplanes, with his name among the great ones in aeronautical history.

Dornier was in charge of structural analysis for the Zeppelin Company at the time. When Zeppelin took Dornier away from airships to head up the airplane (actually, the flying boat) subsidiary, a serious personnel gap was left in the research division. Dornier left behind him at Friedrichshafen not only a position that had to be filled, but a problem that was plaguing the current Zeppelin airships as well.

As Luftschiffbau-Zeppelin cast about for a replacement for Dornier, Paul Jaray, an aerodynamicist on the staff, suggested his older brother, Dr. Karl Jaray, who was now a docent at the German Technical Institute in Prague. The elder Jaray was interested, because although he was thirty-eight years old, he was still subject to the draft. The offer had to come through the German government since Jaray was an Austrian citizen, but Zeppelin apparently had no trouble in arranging such appointments. Before Luftschiffbau-Zeppelin's official offer of a position arrived, however, Karl Jaray had accepted a different assignment. Asked if he knew of anyone else who could do the job, Paul Jaray replied that Arnstein was a brilliant stress analyst.

Jaray had met Arnstein while conferring with Count Zeppelin about the underground hangar, and the reputation of Professor Melan's bright assistant would have been known at the German Technical Institute in Prague. Did Zeppelin recognize the name of the engineer from Züblin when it was transmitted to him from Jaray? In either case, the result was the mysterious order that summoned Arnstein to Friedrichshafen. Once Zeppelin wanted Arnstein to replace Dornier, it did not take long to locate the stress analyst–sapper. Upon his arrival at Luftschiffbau-Zeppelin, Arnstein found that Dornier had left nothing except an elementary study, but it was of no practical use to Arnstein in handling his next assignment.

As the war intensified, airships in production or already in service began to exhibit problems requiring urgent remedy. The first such problem Arnstein faced was the tendency of ring girders—the circular crosswise frames—to buckle near the top of a Zeppelin's hull. This became a high priority problem in March 1915 when the navy airship L 5 (LZ 28) experienced a girder failure in the top of a ring amidships. That the minor strain induced when opening a valve to vent gas should have resulted in a girder failure showed the inadequacy of Luftschiffbau's stress analysis. Arnstein soon decided that the trouble was with the ring design. The ring was not a true circle but a many-sided polygon, with wires running from each point or vertex to each of the other vertices except the two bordering on either side. Even so, the wires to the nearest points made shallow angles with the ring girders, making the ring in compression sensitive to any deflections due to external forces. Arnstein recommended removing these shallow-angled wires. His ability to explain the failure, and to show how to prevent it by a design change, attracted favorable attention. At the end of ninety days, Count Zeppelin requested a three month extension of Arnstein's assignment. The Austrian War Ministry wrote back, "Keep him for as long as you need him." The nearly twenty-eight-year-old Arnstein stayed for the duration of the war—in fact, for the next ten years. Recalling this change in the course of his destiny many years later Arnstein said, "That's the way that life is."

The first airship Arnstein was called upon to investigate extensively was LZ 38. Design of the LZ 38 had been started in August of 1914 and it was the first of the largest Zeppelins built up to that time. Airships of this type were 1,126,500 cubic feet (31,900 cu m) in volume, 536 feet (163.5 m) long, 61 feet (18.7 m) in diameter and powered by four 210 horsepower (157 kW) engines. Such a craft could carry 6,391 pounds (2,905 kg) of bombs across the North Sea for a raid on England and return. It was under construction when Arnstein arrived, and made its first flight on 3 April, 1915. The ring buckling problem was especially

Interior of the German Navy airship L 2 (factory number LZ 18) of 1913, before inflation of the gas cells. The hull's simple main rings and length-wise girders are readily seen, and the triangular-shaped keel is visible at the bottom. (Karl Arnstein Collection/University of Akron Archives)

important to avoid in the new class of airships. Although construction on subsequent airships had started, it was not too late to make the type of change Arnstein recommended.

Arnstein's analysis was general and may be said to have applied to all the airships current at the time. Arnstein reported to Ludwig Dürr, who had been Count Zeppelin's chief engineer since the days of LZ 1. But Dürr by this time was also plant engineer with many other responsibilities, and had little time to give to structural problems. He did spend some time with his new employee and was at first concerned by Arnstein's conclusions, but then decided the new stress analyst was right.

Having quickly found an answer to the ring-buckling problem, Arnstein was asked to determine the forces acting on airship fins. To discover what information was already available to help him in this task, Arnstein asked Dürr, "What are the loads?" Dürr replied, "There are none." Dürr, like Zeppelin, erroneously believed that there should be no loads on an airship, since it was essentially a part of its environment, the air. Arnstein was incredulous. He knew that the structure itself had loads imposed by gravity and dictated by the way in which the girders were joined. An airship structure was subject to loads just as surely as a bridge or building would be. Arnstein persisted. "Not even dynamic loads?" he asked, meaning by this the forces exerted by the air in steering the airship. "Oh, yes," said Dürr. "We have some wind tunnel data for that." Arnstein was reassured by this answer, and used the data along with measurements he made of stresses on an airship's tail fins at rest to determine the strength the fins would need in flight. The **factor of safety** for that ship turned out to be four, meaning the structure was reasonably calculated to be four times as strong as any load it was likely to encounter. Four was a very conservative number, and in certain applications a factor of two was accepted. A word about factors of safety from Arnstein himself is appropriate here:

The term "factor of safety" is a much mis-used and misunderstood term, even among engineers. Specific "factors of safety" . . . have no meaning whatever . . . without the complete details of how the calculations are made. It is sometimes *erroneously* supposed that this factor refers to a ratio between the *actual* strength of a structure . . . and the *actual* worst loads to which the structure will be subjected. Such a ratio might be termed a "factor of excess strength." . . . If its value is much more [than one-to-one] the structure will be, generally speaking, a poor engineering job—unnecessarily heavy, cumbersome and expensive. . . . The term "factor of safety" as used in airship design, and in the *best* engineering practice everywhere, can be defined as the ratio between the engineer's *best estimate* of the strength of the structure and his *best estimate* of the worst loads to which it will ever be subjected. As the engineer realizes that he can never hope to consider completely all of the factors involved he makes this factor considerably greater than 1:1, the excess being frankly a "factor of ignorance."

Arnstein's academic training in analysis complemented Dürr's hands-on approach to airship design. Dürr had neither the theoretical basis nor the mathematical background

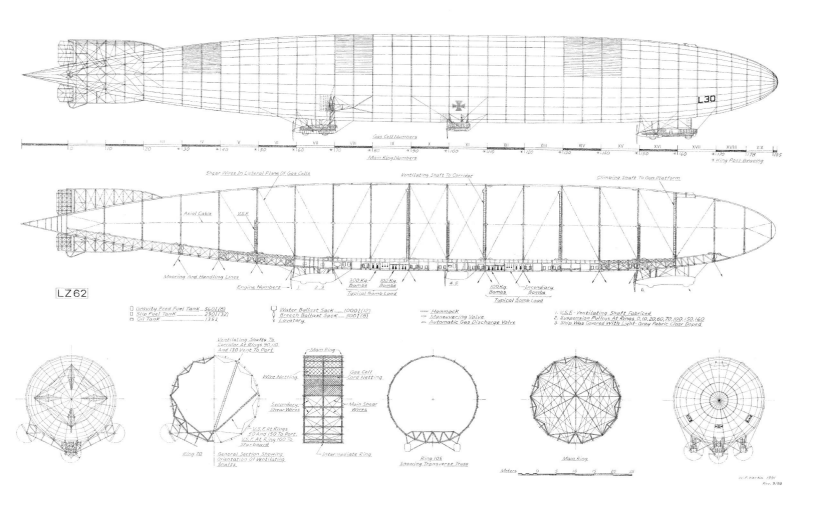

Plans of the LZ 62, which became the German Navy's L 30. This was the first Zeppelin for which Arnstein had full responsibility of structural design. Details of Arnstein's patented hull structure of king-post supported main rings may be seen in the cross-section views. (Drawing by William F. Kerka)

for stress analysis, but he was an intelligent experimenter and his experience with Zeppelin design was unparalleled. A shrewd and practical engineer, he designed more by feel and intuition based on his experience than by analytical considerations. He could read only the simplest drawings, and never looked at the design in the period between its preliminary layout stage and the time the parts began to be fabricated in the shop. This stage is precisely the time when a stress analyst must do his work; previous activity was mere speculation—drawing pretty pictures one might say—and after a part was designed and fashioned, who wanted to change it? Arnstein did respect Dürr, though at first he viewed him with some amazement. Dürr also had good judgment in recognizing talent in people. Once he saw what Arnstein could do, he put him in charge of structural design.

The first Zeppelin for which Arnstein is known to have had complete responsibility for structural design was LZ 62, which became the German navy's L 30. It was the first of the "super Zeppelins" which had been ordered by the German Admiralty in July 1915, and was ready to fly in May 1916. The L 30 was more than half again as large as any of its predecessors, a quantum leap that Dürr could not have dared with his experimental step-by-step approach. This airship, of 1,949,600 cubic foot (55,200 cu m) volume, was 649.4 feet (198 m) long and 78.4 feet (23.9 m) at its maximum diameter. It was powered by six 240 horsepower (180 kW) engines, two of them mounted in cars offset from the ship's keel for the first time. This airship was also the first to incorporate Arnstein's innovation in the design of its structural rings. From his previous work on the LZ 38 ring problem, he saw the advantage of reducing the number of sides or facets forming the ring, but he was told that the many segments of the ring were all needed to support the lengthwise girders that stretched the outer cover over the hull. Arnstein's solution relied on smaller, auxiliary girders set halfway between the main longitudinal girders to maintain the outer cover's shape. The auxiliary girders were supported by perpendicular struts or king posts from triangular trusses formed by the remaining main-ring girders.

To analyze the hull structure of a rigid airship, Arnstein developed a method of analysis which over the years has been much revised and improved. He wrote: "In early rigid airships, methods for calculating stresses in the hull framework were taken from other fields of engineering, mostly civil, and applied with as much judgment as experience permitted, but as the art grew, many new and novel treatments were devised." Analyzing the stresses and strains on an aircraft is more complex than determining the same forces on a simple structure held by its own weight on the ground. An aircraft can be pulled and pushed in many directions. The stress analyst must know what conditions the aircraft is expected to encounter, and to what loads they will subject the structure. To analyze all of the forces acting on an airship structure required solving so many calculations dependent on one another that the actual labor involved made this type of analysis impractical. Arnstein described the way out of this dilemma: "To arrive at a reasonable solution, the airship engineer turned to methods of calculation involving simplifying assumptions and relied on full-scale or model tests to confirm the validity of these assumptions." Put another way, "If you do not use mathematics, and if you do not make assumptions, you are not doing stress analysis." Arnstein believed that aerodynamics theorist Theodor von Kármán expressed the balance of needs when he wrote: "I believe that the engineer needs primarily the fundamentals of mathematical analysis and sound methods of approximation. . . ."

Arnstein focused on two primary areas in determining the stresses to which a rigid airship hull is subjected. The first was figuring out where the strains were inflicted on the lengthwise girders of the ship. Would the girders break and the hull snap in two? The whole hull could be subjected to bending by aerodynamic forces. Also, if concentrations of weight and buoyancy were not evenly matched, gravity and lift could be pulling up and down unequally, distorting the girders. The second area of concern was the stresses across the airship, in the rings that maintain the airship's cross section. If these rings failed, the hull could collapse. Complicating matters further, both the rings and longitudinal girders form a series of facet-like panels, which are braced by diagonal shear wires that keep the pieces aligned and carry the **shearing forces** that try to pull it apart. Although the spindly-looking duralumin girders appear to maintain a Zeppelin's shape, it is the miles of rigging wire that keep all of the elements in proper tension to one another.

Arnstein's early attempts at generalized formulae for determining the stresses for this type of structure assumed that the longitudinal girders carried all the bending, and the shear wires carried all the shear forces. But he found the problem complicated by the inability of wires to carry compression. They may go slack under some conditions and not in others, which makes calculating the structure's overall strength difficult. One can measure the force it takes to pull a wire to its breaking point; but how does one measure the forces that would cause a slack wire to break? That's not so easy! Determining the force it takes to stretch a solitary girder to its breaking point, or compressing it until it breaks is relatively simple. But this is not so for a structure made of many rigid pieces wired together. Arnstein pioneered analysis of Zeppelin structures by using methods learned from Melan and from work he had done on his own doctoral thesis.

The best stress analysis in the world is only as good as the data on which it is based. The determination of loads is usually the province of the aerodynamicist, and Arnstein had become friendly with Paul Jaray, who had come to Friedrichshafen in 1912 to work on airplanes but went to Luftschiffbau to work on Zeppelins in 1914. As an aerodynamicist concerned with preliminary design, Jaray would establish the external lines of the airship, in contrast to what stress analysts would call the real work of design: the structural layout, the mechanisms, the determination of loads and their distribution, and the analytical proof that the proposed vehicle was structurally adequate. However, Jaray's aerodynamic work was entirely on drag and airship performance, and he was never able to give Arnstein any useful data on structural loads. Aerodynamic load data is difficult to obtain and requires relatively costly wind tunnel model tests with numerous measurements to define pressure distributions. Aerodynamics still remains a more empirical discipline than does stress analysis. Determining the structural strain caused by the force of air pressure was a difficulty that was to plague Arnstein throughout most of his career.

Today, the analysis of a rigid airship hull would be programmed for a fairly large computer using **finite element analysis** to measure the forces at many points along the hull's surface. But in 1915, neither the theory nor the modern electronic computer existed. The chief aid in computation was the slide rule. It was a painstaking process to consider all of the forces acting on the structure. Teams of human calculators would check and double-check mathematical equations. There were many unknown quantities. A single arithmetic mistake could jeopardize weeks of labor—and it meant starting over from the beginning. The results could be meaningless (such as a calculation showing a limp wire in compression). With pages of calculations in hand, there was considerable trial and error to fit the numbers to a three-dimensional model of the forces. The equations had to be compared to their diagrammatic representations, which led to new revelations; often, the calculations based on the diagrams might contradict the earlier computations. Initial assumptions might be revealed as wrong, negating all subsequent calculations. Then, all of the component forces had to be equal. One stress calculator described the experience—the ordeal—thus:

When all forces were found to be in balance, and when all deflections proved to be in correspondence with the forces elongating the members, then we knew that we had reached the truth.

It produced a satisfaction almost amounting to a religious experience. After literally months of labor, having filled perhaps fifty foolscap sheets with closely penciled figures, after many disappointments and heartaches, the truth stood revealed, real, and perfect, and unquestionable—the very truth.

Ideally, a designer would do his own analysis, but, especially in wartime, there are schedules to be met and there is never enough time. A division of labor is necessary, and the necessary skills for an analyst and a designer are not the same. A designer must be a good draftsman, while a stress analyst needs a knowledge of mechanics and mathematics. In aircraft, both must understand the need for minimizing weight while meeting the strength requirements. It is not enough that the structure be strong enough, it must also be light enough.

Weight subtracts directly from an aircraft's payload capability and hence from its usefulness. In an airship, if the volume of lifting gas is increased to offset an increase in weight, then the weight of the structure is necessarily also increased, and more power is required to maintain speed. And the additional power extracts its price in engine and fuel weight.

In practice, this often means that the designer must be concerned with geometrical and manufacturing considerations, leaving it for the analyst to show that the design, often derived from intuitive considerations based on experience, is structurally strong enough. This divergence of concerns sometimes leads to arguments, for example:

Designer: But you haven't proved that this design won't work.

Stress analyst: It isn't my job to prove that it won't work. My job is to prove that it will work, and I can't prove that this design will work.

Sometimes the analyst can refine the calculations and be less conservative in estimating the requirements for strength. It then becomes the analyst's duty to suggest a modification that will give a structure adequate strength, and can be proven adequate. More rarely, an analyst may suggest making a design lighter.

Psychologically, a stress analyst should be a skeptic who must try to find something wrong with the design. The designer naturally dislikes this attitude since it seems to disparage his or her work. On the other hand, the stress analyst may feel that the job is incomplete if nothing is found wrong; surely the analyst was not hired merely to echo the designer.

A stress analyst must start with correct—or at least conservative—loads and make assumptions based on a sound knowledge of mechanics and mathematics. An analyst must also know the strength, weight, and stiffness of the materials from which the structure is to be built. In the case of Zeppelins, one of the principal structural materials has been aluminum or its alloys. Duralumin has roughly the same strengths as mild steel, which was the commonly used metal in civil engineering structures. Duralumin was a superior material for aircraft, because it weighed only about one third as much as steel, but its disadvantage was that its stiffness, or resistance to bending, was only a third that of steel. The latter is not so great a disadvantage as might at first be supposed, since the stiffness of a structural part depends not only on the material of which it is made, but on its shape. Thickness (more precisely, the cross-sectional area) is important to strength, as is the form it is given: a thin sheet of metal can resist bending better if it is corrugated than if it is flat.

It is not generally recognized that the Zeppelins pioneered the use of aluminum alloys in aircraft when airplane builders were still relying on wood, wire, and doped fabric. And since the alloy was only six years old in 1915, its production met with occasional difficulties when it was fashioned into bent-up or rolled structural shapes like angles, channels, and "hat sections" (pieces that in cross section resembled a man's brimmed hat).

In November 1915, when Arnstein had been with Luftschiffbau-Zeppelin only a little more than eight months, he was sent to Dürener Metallwerke to discuss manufacturing and quality problems. Such a trip was beyond the duties of an ordinary stress analyst, but by this time Arnstein was already in charge of structural design for LZ 62 and it was a matter of utmost concern. The problem was that the recent shipment of small lattice bars used in bracing a Zeppelin's longitudinal girders had been understrength. The Zeppelin builder clearly was having problems getting enough quality materials to meet the demand for airship orders. Luftschiffbau also wanted Arnstein to get assurance the company would be guaranteed material for four airships. However, problems persisted. A month later, Arnstein was again in Düren, this time to express concern about irregularities in rolled metal sheet delivered to Luftschiffbau. The metal works had to scrap 13,200 pounds (6,000 kg) of finished and rolled sections the previous week, which brought up another subject Arnstein came to discuss, which was policies on saving scrap metal and its disposition. He also ordered materials to build airships at a Zeppelin branch factory in Potsdam.

Although by 1916 Arnstein had charge of structural design as well as analysis, he did not have much contact with German navy personnel except on trips to the airship bases. In those days, aircraft design was not the cooperative venture between manufacturer and military consumer that it would later become. Design calculations were not submitted to the customer but kept as a company secret. The German navy representative made his own calculations, although he would sometimes come and ask Arnstein questions, which under the working agreement he had no right to do. Nevertheless, Arnstein would recall that he did discuss his work with the navy representative occasionally.

Luftschiffbau-Zeppelin furnished the German navy (or army) nothing but an airship that had passed two trial flights—extended to four flights for the first airship of a new class. The four trial flights consisted of a preliminary trial or shakedown flight, a speed flight, an endurance flight, and a height flight. The height flight remained as one of the two test flights required of every new Zeppelin; indeed, the first flight Arnstein had after joining Luftschiffbau-Zeppelin was a height flight. It impressed upon him the importance of altitude to airship survival, and making airships able to reach high altitudes he came to regard as paramount. For the wartime Zeppelins, flying high meant safety from attack, and until the end of the conflict, the tactical advantage Zeppelins strove to maintain was the ability to climb away from their winged adversaries. The defending airplanes struggled to rise into the increasingly thinner air where the new Zeppelins roamed. At those heights, the advantage of buoyancy prevailed over limited horsepower and purely aerodynamic lift.

As the first of a new type, the LZ 62 of course had to undergo all four test flights before acceptance, and the first flight took place on 28 May 1916. This airship was the most advanced of its day, reflected in its enhanced performance: it was larger, faster, sleeker, more powerful, and higher climbing. Luftschiffbau-Zeppelin custom dictated that anyone who worked on the design or construction of an airship must fly in it. Therefore, Arnstein was aboard to witness firsthand the correctness—or errors—in his stress analysis. The flight offered an opportunity for the airship builder to find and correct defects not previously recognized. Evidence of Arnstein's attention to such matters is noted in his report from the flight. Among other things, he found that the framework's stiffness was satisfactory. No **shear deflection** was visible even in the most critical case with almost the entire crew divided between the forward and aft cars (gondolas). This was welcome proof that he had calculated the loads correctly and the ship was built to specification. Another concern was vibration from the motor gondolas. But, as per design, the wire cables suspending the cars remained almost completely taut during flight, thus limiting vibration. Effects of **ballast** bags, fuel tanks, and car suspension on walkway vibration also were carefully observed, and Arnstein noted solutions to any deficiencies.

More evidence of Arnstein's troubleshooting work at Luftschiffbau is found in a business trip report. On 17 February 1917, he went to Ahlhorn, a German navy airship base near the North Sea, to investigate damage that occurred to LZ 79 (the navy L 41). He was accompanied by two engineers from Luftschiffbau and another from the Zeppelin plant at Staaken where the airship was erected (the factory at Staaken, a suburb of Berlin, was built to maintain production in the event the airship construction sheds in Friedrichshafen were destroyed by Allied attack). Arnstein met with the commander of L 41, his executive officer, and two navy engineers to determine the cause of the damage. Arnstein argued, based on the known strength of the ring frame, that the operator must have allowed a high overpressure in one gas cell to damage the frame. But impartially, Arnstein also pointed out manufacturing errors: one in the bracing arrangement used at Staaken and inadvertent omission of some bracing wires. Repairs were made, and Arnstein returned to Friedrichshafen.

On 8 March 1917, Count Zeppelin, the man who had brought the rigid airship to worldwide prominence, died at the age of seventy-nine. He was visiting his airplane factory in Berlin when he fell ill. At word of the news, the houses in Friedrichshafen were hung with black-bordered flags. A special train from Friedrichshafen took several hundred guests, among them "officials and workers from Luftschiffbau with financial manager Colsman," to the funeral in Stuttgart on 12 March.

The funeral procession was conducted with the solemn ringing of the bells of all

Stuttgart churches. Ten thousand mourners paid Zeppelin the last honor. The German kaiser laid a lilac wreath on the coffin. The king and queen of Württemberg said goodbye at the open tomb of the airship pioneer whose work they had energetically supported from the outset. During the burial, two airships cruised over the cemetery and threw out bunches of flowers over the grave, while an airplane squadron uninterruptedly made circles in the sky. The day of mourning, including speeches by the clergy and prayers, ended with a twenty-four-gun salute. At the same moment, in Friedrichshafen all the church bells began to ring. In the evening, the city of Stuttgart held a memorial service at the art museum, at which Colsman gave the only speech, as the family had wished.

During his stay in Friedrichshafen, Arnstein had come to know the old count and admire him as a colleague. "When I first met this small friendly man and looked into his youthful bright eyes I was immediately overwhelmed by his unusual lovable personality," Arnstein recalled. "Zeppelin's success was the success of a personality more than of an engineering nature. Only a man of such clean character and deep faith could go through the catastrophes he had been through and *not* lose the following of the people, who, as a rule, only follow the successful ones," Arnstein related.

"He was a sensible, simple, kindly man who knew that he knew little about engineering, and gave his engineers their way," Arnstein later reminisced. "When there had been a failure—and there were many in those days—he would sit in the conferences listening to everyone expressing views as to what had happened. But, after an hour or two, he would say, 'Make it 50 percent stronger or 100 percent stronger if necessary—it doesn't matter what actually happened.'"

Speaking of Count Zeppelin years later, Arnstein recalled many times having walked with the count out of the factory gates and across the field to an airship, and he particularly recalled the time when the count's first airplane was flown to Friedrichshafen from Staaken. The count was jubilant. Arnstein believed that Zeppelin saw the airplane as the way of the future. The flight showed that the rigid airship was no longer the sole option for long-distance air travel.

Max Freiherr (Baron) von Gemmingen-Guttenberg succeeded as head of Luftschiffbau-Zeppelin upon the death of Count Zeppelin. He is a surprisingly obscure figure in the history of Zeppelins, and since he had a significant influence on the life of Karl Arnstein at one point, we should understand who he was. Zeppelin's older sister, Eugenia, married Baron Wilhelm Friedrich Karl von Gemmingen-Guttenberg in 1860, and son Max Ferdinand Ludwig was born 29 June 1862. Max earned a doctor of philosophy degree, and he was on hand to help his uncle at the first flight of LZ 1. "Captain Gemmingen" was assigned to the motorboat *Württemberg* to follow the airship and take it in tow immediately after it landed on Lake Constance. Although Gemmingen was not a shareholder in Count Zeppelin's original 1898 company, the Aktiengessellschaft zur Förderung der Luftschiffahrt, he was a founder of the firm Luftschiffbau-Zeppelin which came into being after the miracle at Echterdingen, in September 1908. By 1914 he had served on the army general staff with General Erich von Ludendorff, who became a personal friend. He also knew Field Marshal Paul von Hindenburg, chief of the German general staff and, later, the second president of the German republic.

At the beginning of World War I, Gemmingen was fifty-two and over the age for military service. However, he volunteered and asked to be assigned to the *Sachsen*, one of the DELAG airships the German army conscripted for service upon the outbreak of war. The *Sachsen* was under the command of Ernst Lehmann, who would later figure prominently in Zeppelin history. Lehmann was happy to get Gemmingen as his general staff officer, and described him as "an expert and a nobleman in the finest sense of the term; upright, able, fearless, and free. Everyone on board liked him." The two became good friends, and served together aboard a succession of airships until Count Zeppelin's death.

When Gemmingen took control of the company he did not make any drastic moves, and Colsman, who was close to the Zeppelin family, continued to run the company as he had for the count. Gemmingen's experience was more that of a military man and flyer rather than that of a businessman or an engineer. Additionally, he suffered from ill health which may have limited his effectiveness as chairman. After the breakup of the army airship service in late 1917, Lehmann spent the remainder of the war at the Zeppelin company and stayed on after the armistice of November 1918 with the title of assistant manager.

While changes were occurring at the top levels of the company, Arnstein continued to divide his time serving as structural designer and as the company's troubleshooter. Problems arose as the German navy increased demands on their airships and crews and forced them to operate beyond the limits of their intended performance. In the winter and spring of 1917, chief of the German Naval Airship Division, Fregattenkapitän Peter Strasser, ordered modifications to allow the airships to fly higher. There was new urgency to make the changes: British fighter aircraft now had incendiary bullets to shoot at the Zeppelin bombers.

Dr. Max Freiherr von Gemmingen succeeded Count Zeppelin as head of Luftschiffbau-Zeppelin. (Karl Arnstein Collection/University of Akron Archives)

Existing airships and those in production were modified. All unnecessary weight was reduced. On each airship, one engine and the bulky propeller outriggers were removed, and the control and engine cars were replaced with ones that were smaller and lighter. Half of the bomb release mechanisms were eliminated and the gun mounts stripped. In some cases, the side engine cars were moved forward on the hull to make the ships less tail heavy. This condition, caused by too much weight in the airship's stern could, if uncorrected, make the ship difficult to control at great heights.

During this time, Arnstein was called to one of the bases to modify a Zeppelin for a high-altitude raid. The captain took Arnstein aside and asked him if the work couldn't be slowed, hoping that the airship would not be ready to participate in the upcoming raid. Raids could be made only about one night a month when there was no moon, so the deadline was firm. Arnstein replied that his orders were to get the airship ready as soon as possible. Nothing more was said. The airship took part in the raid and was shot down with the loss of all on board. Dismayed by this news, Arnstein's conscience troubled him deeply, and he lost sleep pondering the rightness of his refusal.

The structural changes to lighten the Zeppelins created their own problems, and to correct them Arnstein had to visit the airships at their operational bases. In one such instance, in April 1917, he went to the navy airship bases at Hage and at Ahlhorn. Again, he kept a notebook to record his activities during the eight-day whirlwind trip. At Hage he inspected the old L 11 (LZ 41), relegated to use as a training airship. He noted that it exhibited the usual wear and tear, plus it had several cracked main rings, two of which "had been broken a long time and patched with wooden rails and cord." This indicated to him that airships could still be kept flying after sustaining damage, even with simple repairs, although the ships would not be suitable for frontline service. At Ahlhorn Arnstein had a conference with the commander of L 40 (LZ 88) to diagnose a problem regarding the tendency of the airship to fly out of balance because its stern was too heavy, causing its skipper to make a hard landing. Since the airships were forced to fly ever higher to avoid being shot down, this was a problem that would have to be addressed in future designs. Meanwhile, Arnstein was trying to help fix the ships already in service.

The next day, Arnstein visited the Zeppelin factory at Staaken, where he found girder bracing problems in an airship under construction. He also saw how construction practices differed from those in Friedrichshafen, especially in the assembly of airship nose and tail sections. This was not necessarily detrimental, and some of the local innovations might find broader use, such as experiments with aluminum-coated alloy to reduce corrosion. One day later, he returned to Ahlhorn to investigate the failure of engine cars supports on the navy's L 44 (LZ 93) and damage to L 45 (LZ 85) suffered during a hard landing. These airships, among the first built with the weight-reducing changes Strasser had ordered, were only recently constructed (L 44 was commissioned 1 April; the L 45 on 7 April). Arnstein found a deficiency in the detail work on the L 44, so he sketched an improved design for a bracket. Repairs at Ahlhorn were proceeding with day and night shifts, but Arnstein noted there were difficulties since the workforce included soldiers who "were little suited for such precise construction." On 17 April, he met with navy engineers to agree on a Zeppelin production schedule.

Maintaining his busy pace, on the following day Arnstein conferred with three navy engineers and the commanders of the airships L 40, L 41, L 43, and L 44. The subject of airship tail heaviness was revisited, the same problem Arnstein already had discussed with the L 40's commander. One cause was the gun platform at the airship's stern. It would be easier to keep the ship in trim with no platform, but one commander placed great value on this defensive gun emplacement and argued to retain it.

On 19 April Arnstein noted, "End of work." and complained that only two of the mechanics sent from Friedrichshafen arrived in time to help; therefore, he recommended the permanent stationing of one or two mechanics at Ahlhorn. He also recommended that Zeppelin crews be given a pocket slide rule to use for trim calculations, saying that two commanders had "half humorously" suggested that a slide rule should be a part of the airship's inventory (this may have been the first suggestion for an onboard computer in aircraft).

Although the higher-flying Zeppelins were successful in rendering the British airplane defense obsolete, new difficulties were encountered at high altitudes. There was no way to forecast wind conditions so far aloft and, still worse for the bombers, crews were unable to see intended targets because of the distance and frequent intervening cloud cover at low altitudes. Another difficulty was the engines lost power due to the reduced amount of oxygen at high altitudes, and there was danger to crew members from cold and anoxia. With full bomb load, the Zeppelins could not fly much higher than 16,500 feet (5,033 m). Strasser already decided that the Zeppelins must fly still higher to be safe from British attack. So, by June 1917, Arnstein had a new technical challenge—to develop an entirely new class of airship with the ability to fly above 21,000 feet (6,400 m). The new ships were called "height climbers." Designed as highly efficient thoroughbreds, these airships would sacrifice much to be able to bomb from high altitudes, and be built so lightly that only highly trained crews could fly them safely. Their lightness also gave them another advantage: long range. Later, appreciation of this performance would give birth to the idea of using Zeppelins for transoceanic passenger travel.

Arnstein flew aboard one of the later airships, the navy L 51 (LZ 97), for one harrowing height test flight in July 1917. An incident occurred during the flight that dramatically demonstrated to Arnstein the need to vent air pressure from a Zeppelin's hull. On the earlier Zeppelins, the top portion of the outer cover was left porous to permit valved hydrogen to escape. A hydrogen vent shaft—a fabric chimney leading to a valve—was introduced on L 34 (LZ 78), leading to the belief that the porous cover could now be sealed. Starting with L 49 (LZ 96), the entire outer cover was doped or "Cellonized" with weather-resistant varnish to reduce skin friction. The Zeppelin's commander, Walter Dose, later recalled what happened aboard the L 51:

> We were descending from a high altitude and, with the outer cover completely and tightly Cellonized, there was no way for the [air] pressure to equalize. First thing we knew, there was a shriek of tearing metal amidship then a grinding crash. The pressure outside had caused the longitudinal girders in the lower midships portion to bend inward between the main frames, and they fractured in many places. . . . Despite the severity of the damage, which required nineteen days to repair, the airship landed safely.

Arnstein escaped with his life and was happy to provide a simple remedy: thereafter vent holes forward and aft were provided in the outer cover.

Strasser made further demands to lighten even the height climber Zeppelins. He wanted more weight saving in the framework, even if it meant allowing some structural failure. "A single ring fracture is no calamity," Strasser asserted. This weight saving could be done only at the cost of reducing the factor of safety. To reduce the structure, Arnstein decided to increase the spacing between main rings in the hull from the standard 10 meters (32.8 ft) to 15 meters (49.2 ft), with two of the lighter immediate frames at 5-meter (16.4 ft) intervals. When Eckener learned of this he came to Arnstein much disturbed. Eckener, who tried to volunteer as an airship commander when war broke out, had been put in charge of training airship captains and crews. Although Eckener was not an engineer, he could appreciate the risks of the lighter construction, especially in airships with novice crews. Arnstein told him that increasing ring spacing was the only thing he could do; it was imperative that the airships get above the British incendiaries. The navy's L 53 (LZ 100) was the first Zeppelin with the 15-meter ring spacing. It was delivered to the North Sea airship base at Nordholz, where Eckener was stationed at the time, and commissioned on 21 August 1917.

It was now almost two and a half years since Arnstein had started his "three-month assignment" with Luftschiffbau. A sample of Arnstein's troubleshooting duties during this period have already been shown. A record of his engineering creativity during this time can be seen in his patents. He applied for his first patent on 13 October 1917 for an "Assemblage Point Device." It offered a way to join girders to form a boxlike structure with four sides, which had seldom been used because of the difficulty of making riveted joints

A pre-World War I German postcard showing the double-wide hangar at Leipzig with two DELAG passenger airships inside. Its grand opening on 22 June 1913 was attended by the King of Saxony and Count Zeppelin. *(Courtesy Eric Brothers)*

This British postcard portrays "The Great Double Event" of 24 September 1916 when the German Navy Zeppelin L 32 was shot down in flames by aircraft (at left) and the L 33 was forced to land by an artillery barrage (right). Such victories were quick to be used in propaganda; this colorful card was produced less than a week after the event. *(Courtesy Charles Jacobs)*

A patriotic German postcard from World War I showing an early Army Zeppelin accompanied by two biplanes. Note the Zeppelin's external keel from which the engine gondolas are suspended and the top-mounted gun platform. A series of these cards, illustrated by artist Hans Rudolf Schulze, were sold to raise money for soldiers' charities. (Courtesy Eric Brothers)

SCIENTIFIC AMERICAN

JANUARY 1925

The January 1925 issue of Scientific American *featured this dramatic illustration of the USS* Shenandoah *moored to its sea-going tender, the USS* Patoka. *The accompanying article asks, "Can Huge Dirigibles Supplant Our Ocean Liners?" (Courtesy Eric Brothers)*

Curiously, the only airship ever depicted on a United States postage stamp was Germany's Graf Zeppelin. To compensate for the absence of U.S. stamps depicting American dirigibles, stamp collectors created these air mail labels in several colors featuring the USS Akron. *(Courtesy Charles Jacobs)*

These images (above, below, right) are an example, like the Goodyear blimp, of the creative ways in which Goodyear used airships to promote tires. *(Goodyear Tire and Rubber Company Collection/University of Akron Archives)*

Workers perched on ladders and scaffolds cover the exterior of the USS Macon *with cotton fabric, November 1932. The* Macon *was covered stern to bow; while the USS* Akron *was covered nose to tail. (Lockheed Martin Collection/University of Akron Archives)*

The souvenir edition of the Akron Beacon Journal *for 8 August 1931 included this ad sponsored by First City Trust and Savings Bank. The illustration is misleading: the USS* Akron *may have been "another (air)'ship,'" but it was the first rigid airship produced by Goodyear-Zeppelin. From the appearance of the tail fins, this Zeppelin more closely resembles the USS* Los Angeles *than the* Akron. *(Private Collection)*

"Rosie the Riveter" was an important icon in the United States during the Second World War; she was the representative of all women working in the war effort, taking the place of men gone to fight in the armed forces. Good-year employed many women in its plants in Akron producing war materiel, though this particular Rosie worked in a ship-building yard in Los Angeles. (B-26 Marauder Archive/University of Akron Archives)

This is perhaps the most famous photo of a World War II U.S. Navy patrol blimp, which Goodyear Aircraft used in a color-tinted advertisement lauding their K-ships' record in safely shepherding a convoy of merchant ships. (The Lighter-Than-Air Society Collection/University of Akron Archives)

in the inaccessible corners. However, such box girders were inherently more efficient (stronger for the same weight, or lighter for the same strength). Arnstein overcame the problem by inserting U-shaped pieces and cutting away part of the box walls. A second patent on the general subject of joining box girders was applied for on 5 November 1917, and before the war was over, Arnstein applied for two more patents relating to box girders and ways to join them, to make trusses, for example.

Most or all of these ideas were incorporated first in the Zeppelin Company's LZ 62 (navy L 30), not coincidentally, the first airship for which Arnstein was fully responsible for the structure. Since LZ 62 was commissioned in May 1916, the patents seem to have been something of an afterthought during the exigencies of war. The technological advances embodied by the patents were not overlooked, however. In the summer of 1917, Wilhelm, the king of Württemberg, honored six Zeppelin company engineers, including Arnstein and Paul Jaray, with the Wilhelm's Cross for their technical contributions.

Arnstein's life had been transformed by the war. His days as a stress analyst of bridges seemed remote. But late in the war, a reminder of those times turned up in Friedrichshafen. It was Paul Helma, Arnstein's former Züblin associate. Helma, who had been serving as an engineering officer in the Austrian army, requested and received with Karl's help a position in Arnstein's Theory of Airship Structures Division. It was not the first nor would it be the last time that Helma would follow Arnstein in his career. Neither knew it at the time, but their professional association would continue for decades.

The war had created a huge demand for Zeppelins for military purposes. Ever-growing military requirements pushed the development of ever-larger Zeppelins that could fly faster, farther, and higher than their predecessors. In a few short years, the knowledge of building and operating airships had advanced on a scale unprecedented in peacetime. With Germany building dozens of airships, the state of the art progressed most rapidly there. Most of Germany's rigid airships were built by the Zeppelin Company because it had the skilled workforce and ability to mass-produce these aircraft. With greater numbers built, Zeppelin designs became more refined and efficiently engineered. But the advances were not all the result of a quantitative advantage—there was a qualitative improvement as well. Trial-and-error methods of construction gave way to scientific calculation of the mechanical forces involved. Structural as well as aerodynamic considerations increasingly entered into dirigible design, spurred by the need to make airships as strong and as light as possible to achieve maximum performance. This knowledge helped to make the Zeppelin Company the pre-eminent supplier of rigid airships. Arnstein played a pioneering role at each step of this technological evolution. He quickly learned to apply his civil engineering knowledge of massive, immobile structures weighing thousands of tons to enormous mobile constructions that floated in air. Within a little more than three years Arnstein had become one of the world's few experts in rigid airship design and had developed a reputation as an innovator of airship structures. Such knowledge literally would open up a new world for Arnstein. However, all of the circumstances that would bring this to pass were not yet in place. In the meanwhile, the world was still at war, and even global conflict is no deterrent to romance. Arnstein's life was about to change course yet again.

Chapter 4 LOVE AND WAR

When he first arrived in Friedrichshafen in 1915, Arnstein rented a room at a house on Olgastrasse just off the main street through the western part of the town. Next door, on the corner, was a home occupied by the five granddaughters of Arnstein's new landlady. The parents of the five Jehle (YEH-lee) girls had died several years earlier, and they were watched over by their maternal grandparents, aunt, and housekeeper. The girls' father, physician Dr. Bernard Jehle, had died from tuberculosis at the age of forty—not long after the youngest child, Bertha Maria, or "Bertl," was born in 1898. After the death of the girls' mother, Ida Miller Jehle, ten years later—also from tuberculosis at age forty—the grandparents moved in with the girls and they continued to live in their large and comfortable house with its beautiful garden.

Even before Arnstein arrived, there was a Zeppelin connection with the Jehle home. In the years up to World War I, there were no good hotels, apartments, or other similar places to stay in the small town of Friedrichshafen. When Alfred Colsman arrived to become Zeppelin's business manager in 1908, a company official arranged for him to stay with the Jehle family, and later, he moved his family into rooms upstairs.

Bertl was impressed by Colsman, who stood over six feet tall, and she became fast friends with his three daughters. One of the Colsman daughters was Bertl's age, and the two girls watched the early Zeppelin trial flights from the roof. In the mornings, Bertl could watch Count Zeppelin turning out in a carriage with two horses from his nearby residence on his way to the hangar where the Zeppelins were built.

The war years also brought a change in Arnstein's social life. When he first arrived in Friedrichshafen, Arnstein knew no one, but he soon became acquainted with Paul Jaray, the brother of Dr. Karl Jaray, the man who had recommended Arnstein to Count Zeppelin. Although both the Jarays and Arnstein came from Prague, and Paul had attended the German Technical Institute, Arnstein and Paul Jaray had not met before. Still, they did have much in common, and they were soon associated professionally.

Paul Jaray came to Luftschiffbau as an aerodynamicist, and is credited with **streamlining** the Zeppelins. He reduced their aerodynamic drag resistance by half to meet a German navy requirement, and as a reward, was named head of Luftschiffbau-Zeppelin's preliminary design group.

Paul Jaray would have a more personal and lasting influence on Karl's Arnstein's life well beyond their professional association. It began soon after Arnstein's arrival in Friedrichshafen, on a Sunday afternoon in late March 1915, when Jaray and his wife invited Arnstein to tea at their home. Paul Jaray had married Olga Jehle, the third of the five Jehle sisters from Friedrichshafen. On this particular weekend, Olga's youngest sister, Bertl, was visiting from her Roman Catholic boarding school in the nearby town of Lindau. Bertl, age seventeen, was in her last year at the school, run by nuns, called "The Englische Fräulein." Since it was Bertl's last year of high school, she was permitted a few visits with her sister in Friedrichshafen, so it happened that Bertl was present when Arnstein came to tea. It was Bertl's first meeting with Karl.

Arnstein was then just twenty-eight, having celebrated his birthday on 24 March, a slender young man of medium height (five feet, eight inches) with hazel eyes and dark brown, wavy hair, through which an early bald spot at the top of his head was already visible. He was wearing a suit that consisted of black-striped pants and a cutaway coat, which was the fashion in those days for anyone in a leading position and was what he wore at the Zeppelin company. At this first meeting, Bertl was impressed with his reserved and modest but friendly demeanor, and his lack of conceit. He was a complete gentleman, she thought.

A half century later, Arnstein would remember how well Bertl played the piano. He especially enjoyed her playing of Schumann's "Träumerei." She was wearing a green corduroy dress, and her hair was in two long braids, each tied with a bow—a detail he would always remember. It can hardly have escaped his notice that this was a pretty and vivacious young woman. Still, romance did not bloom quickly, because of their age difference. He thought she was too young. This impression may have been heightened that summer when Bertl and her sister Mimi played a prank on Karl. The mischievous girls slipped over to their grandmother Rosa Miller's house, where Arnstein still roomed, and while he was at work, went upstairs and filled the pockets of his coat with stones as it hung in his closet.

Later in 1915, Arnstein moved to a house on Riedleparkstrasse to be nearer his job at the Zeppelin factory. Arnstein would live there for the next four years, but his move did not terminate his contacts with the Jehle family. Meanwhile, in the fall of 1915, Bertl went away to a German teacher's college near Stuttgart, for training in home economics. She graduated two years later, but found that because of the war, the German government would not go ahead with plans to add home economics teachers in the grammar schools. With her teaching career on hold, Bertl, who also had studied horticulture, found work as a gardener for a private estate in Friedrichshafen. Next she worked as a gardener for a resident home the Zeppelin Company operated for its employees, and later served as the housemother. During this time, the friendship between Karl and Bertl continued to grow.

The inescapable backdrop to this romance was the war itself, which had reached stalemate until the United States entered on the side of the Allies in the spring of 1917. On the ground, the armies of both sides battled with great losses to capture and hold small parcels of land. On the home front, Germany suffered shortages because of an effective Allied naval blockade and an inability to manage economic policy. In 1916, military leaders had assumed control of the economy to improve the allocation of limited supplies of raw materials to the war effort. The military leaders—among them chief of staff of the army, Hindenburg, and Quartermaster General Ludendorff—gave authority for war production to the army and large industrial firms. Priorities were set in order of importance to the war effort, primarily skewed toward munitions production. The imbalance resulted in a free-for-all, with a few industries monopolizing scarce commodities and fueling inflation as costs were passed along to the army and then to the consumer. This helped to create a black market that further disrupted and corrupted the mechanisms of supply. A poor harvest in 1916 and chronic labor shortages only worsened matters.

The privations of an effective naval blockade caused Germany to engage in unrestricted submarine warfare on shipping, especially the lifeline of transport ships from the United States and Canada bringing food and war materiel to the Allies. The German submarine policy and a diplomatic blunder—the Zimmerman letter, in which it was revealed that Germany had promised American territory to Mexico in exchange for its assistance—led the U.S. Senate to declare war on Germany on 6 April 1917. The United States, with seemingly limitless manpower and natural resources, would tip the balance in favor of the Allied cause. However, the abdication of the Russian tsar, the collapse of the succeeding provisional government, and the Bolshevik Revolution that same year gave hope to Germany: the revolutionary government under Vladimir Lenin signed a separate peace in March 1918 removing Russia from the Allied coalition. Later that month, Germany launched a last major offensive in France and Belgium. After initial victories, and an advance within thirty-seven miles of Paris, the German army, exhausted and lacking reserves, faltered. The Allies, invigorated with fresh U.S. troops, counterattacked in July and August and began to push back the German army. The realization that victory was no longer possible demoralized

Germany's fighting forces. As one historian put it: "the deprivation and anxiety of the previous three years were eclipsed by a last surge of social solidarity and patriotism. But after the initial 'victory' had turned into a massive and unmistakable retreat, the moods of the Front and home front changed abruptly." Tired, disillusioned soldiers went on strike. In September, the Central Powers lost their eastern flank when the Bulgarian government signed an armistice. Ludendorff saw that "the only alternatives to a military collapse in the west and an Allied invasion of Bohemia and southern Germany were an armistice and a negotiated peace." Internal opposition to the war intensified, and by October a cessation of hostilities seemed to be the only means to prevent chaos and the spread of revolution. The German command viewed an armistice as a chance to regroup, not a surrender, but it was too late. Other Central Powers—Austria-Hungary and Turkey—capitulated. In early November, German navy sailors mutinied, Ludendorff resigned, the kaiser abdicated, and an armistice came into effect on November 11.

What was the wartime record of Count Zeppelin's airships? Ever since the miracle of Echterdingen in 1908, the German people had embraced Zeppelin's invention as their own. They had watched the passenger airships of DELAG fly overhead in the years before the war. Those who could afford it had flown aboard them. When the war came, they looked to the Zeppelin as a weapon that would win the war for Germany, and later on, one that would avenge them upon the British, whose blockade was creating shortages and hardship. But the Zeppelins did not win the war, nor did they break the blockade. By the time the old count died in 1917, the Zeppelins had been supplanted as bombers by the Gotha and other large airplanes. Toward the end of the war, the numbers of airships had dwindled.

The Zeppelin in combat had difficulty proving itself as a major weapon. During the first year of the war some naval Zeppelins had been used as sea scouts, aiding reconnaissance of the German High Seas Fleet. The German army had employed the airships primarily as bombers in the east. Beginning in 1915, the German navy also used the Zeppelins as bombers, hoping to take the war directly to England. At first prohibited from bombing London, because the kaiser feared the repercussions of bombing his cousin, King George V, the Zeppelins attempted some nighttime raids on dockyards, factories, railroads, and the like. Soon, though, the war was taken to the heart of London, in a vain attempt to disrupt the government, military command, and war-related activities. In reality, the Zeppelin raiders usually succeeded only in arousing the populace against the Zeppelin menace, and their bombs rained down haphazardly on civilians and largely nonstrategic targets because of poor aiming. The airships' limited success as bombers was surpassed by the psychological effect they had early in the war as silent, untouchable, indiscriminate killers, and the public felt outrage at its own vulnerability. The Zeppelins posed a serious threat, if not in causing vast amounts of physical damage, at least in tying up precious resources for home defense that could have been used at the front. (The strategic implications of these early air attacks would be realized more devastatingly a generation later, when German airplanes blitzed English cities, bombing civilians as well as military targets.) The risks the Zeppelin crews took to make their raids were far greater than the risks to those on the ground, especially once the British defenders were able to shoot down the Zeppelins with incendiary bullets—almost guaranteeing a flaming, meteoric end to the flammable ships and their crews. The situation was no better on the eastern front, and in 1917, the German army deemed it had suffered enough losses and suspended its airship operations, giving its remaining dirigibles to the navy. Under the zealous leadership of Peter Strasser, naval Zeppelin raids continued and intensified, despite growing losses. Only Strasser's death in August 1918 halted the operations. The Zeppelin had not been very successful as an offensive weapon in World War I. Its true value was reconnaissance, as the eyes of the navy.

Statistically, the Zeppelins had grown in number and sheer size during the war. Their volume had grown from 777,000 cubic feet (22,000 cu m) in 1914, to 1,130,000 (32,000) in 1915, to 1,942,300 (55,000) in 1916, to 2,401,000 (68,000) in 1918. As can be seen, they more than doubled in size once Arnstein came to Friedrichshafen; this growth was possible technologically in no small part because of the innovations he pioneered. The Zeppelins' power increased from 600 to 1,600 horsepower (450–1,200 kW), and their speed increased from 47 to 75 miles per hour (75–120 km/h). Bomb loads reached nearly four tons by war's end. Not counting the 18 airships of rival **Schütte-Lanz,** a total of 88 wartime Zeppelins were constructed. Production increased to the point where the Zeppelin factory took only six weeks to build an airship. The numbers belied a tragic reality: the German army lost half of its 52 airships; the German navy lost 53 of its 73 airships. Flight crew casualties surpassed 450—the death rate of airship crews exceeded that of airplane crews and the submarine service.

Beyond the tally of airships built and lost, there was a human dimension to the Zeppelin town in wartime that should not be forgotten. Toward the end of the war, the employees of the aircraft and armament industries in the Friedrichshafen area, who came from all parts of Germany, numbered about 8,000. The original population of Friedrichshafen was only about 8,000, so it can be understood that the price of food and shelter rose rapidly. The pay was good, but the work week was six days of ten to twelve hours, and the rising prices resulted in a decline of real wages. Rumors of huge profits made by the companies added to discontent, which was further aggravated by the appearance of wealthy invalid guests, for the Bodensee (Lake Constance) was, and remains, a resort area

The L71, the last Zeppelin delivered to the Imperial German Navy, rises from the factory field at Friedrichshafen. One of the later "height climber" class of airships, it featured small, streamlined control and engine gondolas. It was lengthened from 694 feet to 743 feet (211 m to 0226 m) in October 1918. It survived the war to be surrendered to England. (Karl Arnstein Collection/University of Akron Archives)

with a mild climate. These visitors made the difference between rich and poor all too apparent. Even the Württemberger military men stationed there were incensed at poor food and price gouging. All over Germany, hopelessness and anger grew. "Sailors' councils joined workers' councils in taking over Kiel and other port cities," notes historian Jay M. Winter. "The revolt in the navy quickly spread to the home army and to the industrial working class, putting an end to both the monarchy and the war."

Signs of opposition to the war had appeared as early as 1916, and as the fortunes of war turned against Germany and the Central Powers, the political turmoil increased. Socialist and communist voices in Germany grew louder, emboldened by the success of the 1917 Bolshevik Revolution in Russia, whose leaders would end that country's participation in the Great War early in 1918. Many among Germany's working class also sought an end to the fighting, and with it, a new political order. Friedrichshafen may have been a sleepy backwater in this revolutionary uproar, but even it did not escape the growing discord. A peace demonstration occurred on 22 October 1918, when about one hundred workers marched from the Maybach engine plant to the town hall shouting, "Down with the war. Up with the German Republic!" It had become obvious to everyone but a few that the war was lost. Two days later, two hundred to three hundred men took part in another protest. A strike was called for Saturday, 26 October, but all the big plants closed to forestall it. Still, some four thousand men, including about sixty soldiers in uniform, marched to the town hall for speeches. On this day some threats of violence occurred—"a young radical man from Motorenbau" yelled at Colsman from atop a gravel pile, "For you, too, Herr Colsman, we have a bullet."

In Friedrichshafen as elsewhere, civil unrest grew, and on 5 November a general strike was called. A soldiers' and workers' council elected by acclamation demanded immediate peace, abdication of the kaiser, socialist revolution, and a seven-hour workday. Arrests followed, and the workers' and soldiers' group met at the town assembly hall to determine how to free its jailed strike leaders. Colsman, not intimidated, strode into the volatile situation. After listening to one speech, Colsman was allowed to speak. He sounded an eloquent plea for a peaceful settlement, and, in this event, negotiations were successful. By 9 November red flags flew in the city of Friedrichshafen. Church bells rang out calling the people to a meeting at the assembly hall at 9:30 in the morning, where speeches celebrated the revolution. A crowd of eight to ten thousand people paraded through the streets, all marching to fill the town square to overflowing. More speeches were made, and after about half an hour, the crowd broke up to go home or to the local rathskeller for a stein of beer. By the following day, 10 November "most large municipalities in Germany were in the hands of Workers' and Soldiers' Councils."

The battlefield hostilities ceased with the armistice on 11 November 1918, but an uneasy truce remained at home as centuries-old monarchies gave way to volatile republics. The terms of the peace treaty would demilitarize Germany and threaten the continued existence of any firm that had supplied war material, especially aircraft. The future of Luftschiffbau-Zeppelin looked bleak. With no way of foretelling the political upheaval and economic chaos that would engulf Germany in the next few years, the Zeppelin Company diligently set out to resume its prewar passenger airship business.

Chapter 5 POSTWAR TRANSITIONS— AND THE AMERICANS

Gemmingen's illness had left the Zeppelin Company without strong leadership, which contributed to the ultimate showdown between Eckener and Colsman on the company's future. As an airman rather than a businessman, Gemmingen's sympathies doubtless lay with Eckener's urge to continue building Count Zeppelin's airships rather than with Colsman's adherence to sound business principles.

Shortly after the armistice Gemmingen embraced his friend Lehmann's scheme to fly the last Zeppelin built for the navy, L 72 (factory number LZ 114), which was still in Friedrichshafen, to the United States. The plan was accepted by the company, although it was strongly opposed by Eckener, whom Gemmingen had appointed to the board of directors. It was eventually vetoed by the German government because of the opposition anticipated from the Allied powers.

In objecting to Lehmann's grandiose—or simply audacious—idea of flying L 72 to the United States, Eckener offered a different idea: a small airship to fly the 370 miles (600 km) from Berlin to Friedrichshafen. The phenomenal time savings that only Zeppelin travel could offer were revolutionary compared to land-based transportation. Postwar rail connections in Germany were poor, and it was estimated that up to twenty hours' travel time could be saved via a passenger airship service. Even against the best prewar rail schedules, the time savings still could be nine to twelve hours. The need for a connection to the nation's capital, Berlin, was obvious. Friedrichshafen, the southern destination, would serve as the country's gateway. One could take a ferry across Lake Constance to Switzerland, and from there, travel by rail to France or southern Europe. More important to the future of the Zeppelin Company, Gemmingen thought this modest demonstration could advertise the speed, safety, and convenience of airship travel. The board of directors approved the idea, and work commenced on the first commercial Zeppelin to be built in more than five years. Arnstein, of course, handled structural design and analysis.

The airship, works number LZ 120, was unlike any that had preceded it. Fully streamlined, the graceful curve of the hull was unbroken by the straight lines of any cylindrical "can" section amidships. It resembled an elongated teardrop, with four tail fins at the rear and three engine gondolas along the sides and the bottom. Where all earlier Zeppelins had control cars suspended from struts and wires, the LZ 120 design had its combined control car and plush passenger cabin mounted flush with the bottom of the hull. The passenger seats were arranged facing each other across a small table, in the style of a compartmented railway carriage, with a grandly arched window at either side. Each of the five compartments would seat four; sometimes additional wicker seats could be accommodated. Additionally, there was a private cabin forward (available at twice the fare), two washrooms and a small buffet aft. A radio room occupied space behind the front cabin—the "control car"—equivalent to the bridge on a seagoing vessel. Here were the rudder and elevator wheels, engine telegraphs, ballast and gas valve control panels, and navigation table. At 396 feet (120.8 m) long, the new airship was shorter than all of its Zeppelin predecessors, and its maximum diameter of 61.3 feet (18.7 m) was comparable with the LZ 40 of 1915. The latest Zeppelin had a lifting gas volume of a mere 706,300 cubic feet (20,000 cu m)— less than a third of the height climbers and more on par with the DELAG passenger airship *Sachsen* of 1913. However, the efficient LZ 120 would have a useful lift of eleven tons— a weight one third larger than *Sachsen* could lift. What is more, its aerodynamically clean shape gave the LZ 120 the highest trial speed yet achieved for an airship, 82.4 miles per hour (132.6 km/h) while not even at full throttle. The new airship was christened *Bodensee* and flew for the first time on 20 August 1919. Four days later, the ship went into passenger service.

The concept of a regularly scheduled airline, although it dated to the prewar DELAG days, was still a novelty. However, the vast experience in building and operating Zeppelins in wartime held a promise that peacetime schedules would prove regular. Indeed, for the next three and a half months, the *Bodensee* made daily flights, alternating northbound trips to Staaken outside Berlin on odd-numbered days of the month with southbound trips on the following day. Often, there was time for local Berlin excursions, and for a while, intermediate landings at Munich. It proved so popular that a second similar but larger airship was planned for a service to Stockholm. The new airship, LZ 121 *Nordstern*, was similar in design to the *Bodensee*, but an extra ten-meter-long gas cell amidships allowed it to carry thirty passengers. With the coming of winter, DELAG closed its flight operations on 5

After World War I, the Zeppelin Company resumed passenger airship service with the LZ 120 Bodensee. Originally less than 400 feet (120 m)
in length, it had only one-third the volume of the last wartime Zeppelins. (Lockheed Martin Collection/ University of Akron Archives)

The cabin of the Zeppelin Bodensee *was designed to carry twenty passengers, but up to six more persons could be accommodated in wicker chairs in the aisle. With the control car at its front, the 80-foot (24 m) long hull-mounted gondola also had washrooms and a buffet. (Karl Arnstein Collection/University of Akron Archives)*

December 1919 and proceeded to modify the *Bodensee* to make it the size of the *Nordstern*.

Then the blow fell. In January 1920 DELAG was forced to suspend operations when the Interallied Control Commission enforced the Versailles treaty clause that mandated: "No dirigible shall be kept." No distinction was made between military and civilian airships, and both of DELAG's new Zeppelins were ordered to be surrendered to the Allies. Because some naval Zeppelins that were to have gone as war spoils to France and Italy had been wrecked by their crews immediately after the war, the commission decided that the two commercial airships would substitute as partial compensation. Accordingly, the *Nordstern* was delivered to France where she was flown as the *Méditerranée* and the *Bodensee* went to Italy and was renamed the *Esperia*. The Zeppelin Company was now in a real bind. Forbidden to make military aircraft and hemmed in by a size restriction on any commercial Zeppelins it could produce, the company resorted to a job-saving tactic it had once tried in the lean times before the miracle at Echterdingen—it produced aluminum kitchen utensils. Using the company's initials as a trademark, the "Ellzett" logo appeared on cake pans and cooking pots, as well as some elegantly shaped vases and pitchers that were often given a gold, blue, rose, or green-colored finish.

Karl and Bertl Arnstein at the time of their wedding in September 1919. (Karl Arnstein Collection/University of Akron Archives)

During the previous two years, the friendship between Karl and Bertl Jehle deepened. By 1919 Arnstein was steadily employed working on the LZ 120, and the couple decided to marry. The Arnstein relatives were Austrian. "What?!" they said, "Marry a small-town German girl? German cooking is unfit for a man to have to eat over a lifetime. She must come to Vienna and learn to cook." So, in the summer of 1919 Bertl went to Vienna and took culinary lessons from Karl Arnstein's sister, who had become Mrs. Fred Korn. It was in Vienna at the St. Margareten Catholic Church, not far from the Schönbrunn Palace, that Karl Arnstein and Bertha Marie Jehle entered into the bonds of holy matrimony on 18 September 1919.

Something of Arnstein's stature within the company can be inferred from a compliment his new wife received. Not long after Bertl had married Karl, Mrs. Colsman said to her over tea, "Here you have caught the biggest fish in the pond," and remarked about her own unmarried children, "none of my five daughters have caught anything."

After the war it was difficult to find a good place to live, and the newlywed Dr. and Mrs. Arnstein stayed for a few months in a loft apartment on Friedrichshafen's main street. Eventually, they were lucky enough to get an apartment at 4 Klosterstrasse, only a block or two from the Jehle house where Bertl had been raised. The Arnsteins occupied the second of the three floors, and were also allotted a garden space behind the big house. The house also was not far from the summer castle of the former king of Württemberg—former because Germany was now a republic—and that garden would become a valuable asset in the tough times to come.

While the Zeppelin Company was fighting to survive in the strict postwar environment imposed by the Interallied Control Commission, others pursued the advantages of airship flight—most notably, the British. Some factions within the British Royal Navy had long perceived the military potential of rigid airships, but they had been largely unsuccessful in fostering a homegrown Zeppelin industry prior to 1914. Once the war was on, officials within the Royal Navy continued to push for a fleet of British rigid airships, despite the objections of First Lord of the Admiralty, Winston S. Churchill. A few indigenous rigid airships were constructed in England before and during the war, but their technology trailed that of their German counterparts. To close the technology gap, many elaborate efforts were undertaken to obtain the latest Zeppelin intelligence.

In contrast to Britain's half dozen obsolete prototypes, Arnstein's successful "super Zeppelin" design, first embodied in the LZ 62, was repeated during the war in more than fifty airships. The British were in luck when one of the class, the German navy Zeppelin L 33 (LZ 76), was forced to land in Essex, England, on 24 September 1916. The British captured the crew and secured the wreckage. They soon set to work to build copies of this airship. The result, after slight modifications, produced the British navy airships R 33 and R 34, but these were not finished until after the war was over. With the German competition effectively neutralized by the Versailles treaty, Great Britain took the lead in postwar development of the long-range rigid airship.

On 2 July 1919, the R 34 set out from East Fortune, Scotland, to fly to the United States. It arrived safely at Mineola, Long Island, New York, on 6 July after a flight lasting four and a half days. Thus, the first airship to fly the Atlantic was British, not German, a stinging blow to the pride of those in Friedrichshafen who hoped to be first. A few days later on 9 July the R 34 took off and made the return flight, landing at Pulham, England, on 12 July. Nevertheless, it was an airship of Arnstein's basic design which made the first east-to-west crossing of the Atlantic Ocean by any aircraft and the first transatlantic round-trip flight by any aircraft. (It should be noted that in May 1919 the U.S. Navy's four-engine flying boat NC-4 had made the first transatlantic flight, in stages, from New York to Lisbon via Newfoundland and the Azores. In June, British aviators John Alcock and Arthur Whitten Brown flew a twin-engine Vickers biplane from Newfoundland to Ireland, but crash-landed in a bog.)

Aboard as observer on the R 34's westbound flight was Lt. Commander Zachary Lansdowne, U.S. Navy. Lansdowne would play a major role in the history of America's airship program a few years later, and his presence on the R 34 was indicative of the United States Navy's keen interest in rigid airships. Taking Lansdowne's place on the eastbound flight was Colonel William N. Hensley of the U.S. Army Air Service. Hensley's mission in Europe was to acquire information on European airships and airship stations. He was also to investigate the availability of a Zeppelin airship for possible purchase by the army, despite the fact that the U.S. Navy had been made solely responsible for developing America's military rigid airships. There is some evidence to suggest that outspoken airpower advocate Brigadier General William "Billy" Mitchell, then chief training and operations officer of the Army Air Service, was behind Hensley's mission. The purchase of a Zeppelin also would have been in violation of the Versailles treaty, which the United States had not signed, and prohibited by the fact that the U.S. and Germany were technically still at war.

However, the United States felt that it was entitled to some compensation for the two airships it was to have received according to the treaty, but which had been wrecked along with others at the German Naval Airship bases at Nordholz and Wittmundhaven following the armistice. The airships were destroyed by flight crewmen who did not wish to see their Zeppelins fall into enemy hands. At the time of the German revolution, the flight personnel of the Naval Airship Division remained loyal to the kaiser, but seamen and ground personnel took control of the airship bases and, on 9 November 1918 the airships were hung up, their gas cells were deflated, and their hulls shored in place. Some airship men remained at the bases after the war, and on 23 June 1919, after the scuttling of the German warships at Scapa Flow, they pulled away the supports and freed the suspensions, allowing the empty airship hulls to crash to the floor, destroying them.

The L 72 (builder's number LZ 114) was never delivered to the German navy and was still in possession of the Zeppelin Company, so, on a technicality, it might be available for purchase. Hensley went to Friedrichshafen to meet with the Zeppelin officials on 5 September 1919, but on that same day, the Allies refused to consider L 72 private property. Instead, the Interallied Aeronautical Commission of Control awarded what would have become the German Navy's L 72 to France, where it served a four-year career renamed the *Dixmude*.

While in Friedrichshafen, Hensley discovered that Luftschiffbau-Zeppelin had plans for an airship on the drawing board, the LZ 124, that was larger than any previous airship with a volume of 3,500,000 cubic feet (98,000 cu m). Gemmingen supported the plan to build a Zeppelin for the United States Army. The Zeppelin Company, faced with the probability of having its aeronautical activities halted and its hangars razed, was pleased to see an opportunity to develop an American tie. In a state of euphoria, Hensley asked for and received from Washington a sum of money with which to negotiate a contract, which was signed by himself and Colsman on 26 November 1919. Less than a week later, on 1 December, he was told in no uncertain terms that the secretary of war, Newton D. Baker, who had never authorized the contract, had ordered the project abandoned. Hensley protested, but was overruled. He reluctantly informed the Zeppelin Company of the cancellation in mid-December; then, on 6 January 1920, he asked Luftschiffbau-Zeppelin to replace the contract with an option good for six months, to which the company agreed. All was to no avail. Hensley returned to the United States a frustrated man with no Zeppelin purchase order to show for his efforts.

Before Hensley left, another American turned up in Friedrichshafen and took a trip in the airship *Bodensee*. He was Harry Vissering, a wealthy Chicago manufacturer of railroad equipment. His interest aroused, he spent considerable time in Friedrichshafen and became friends with Eckener, who was still director of DELAG, the operating company, and with Lehmann, who spoke English better than any other officer of the Zeppelin Company. Vissering returned to the United States in 1920 with the idea of starting a New York–Chicago airship line. This failed to materialize, but Vissering was on such good terms with the Zeppelin Company that he became its official representative in the spring of 1920. This relationship would bear fruit four years later.

The U.S. Navy was not idle during Hensley's semiofficial maneuverings. The navy had become interested in the large rigid airships during World War I, and the joint Army-Navy Airship Board had in 1917 funded a design team headed by Starr Truscott, a University of Michigan graduate who had previously been employed on the Panama Canal. Truscott's team of designers produced drawings for an airship of 889,000 cubic foot volume, with wooden girders like those used by the Schütte-Lanz Company, rather than of metal as used by the Zeppelin Company. It was not built.

On 11 July 1919, Congress passed a bill appropriating money for two rigid airships, one to be constructed in the United States and one to be procured abroad. The first of these was the navy's ZR-1, the USS *Shenandoah*. Truscott and his crew based their initial design on the German navy's L 49, one of Arnstein's "super Zeppelins" which had been forced to land in France in October 1917. For its second airship, on 5 December 1919 the navy agreed to buy from the British His Majesty's Airship R 38, then under construction. Unnamed, it would be given the U.S. Navy designation ZR-2.

Meanwhile, the procession of Americans who traveled to the "Zeppelin Mecca" of Friedrichshafen continued. U.S. Navy Commander Ralph Downs Weyerbacher, a thirty-one-year-old Naval Academy graduate who had also done postgraduate work at the Massachusetts Institute of Technology, was soon to be in charge of building the USS *Shenandoah*. He decided that one thing he needed to learn more about was the calculation of the structure (that is, the stress analysis of a rigid airship), and he persuaded the navy to send him to Germany to learn what he could. Since the United States and Germany were technically still at war, he encountered some difficulty, but eventually was able to visit the Zeppelin manufacturing sites at Friedrichshafen; Staaken; and Düren, where duralumin was made. At Friedrichshafen he talked with Colsman and Dürr, but with his special interest in analysis, Arnstein was the man he wanted to see, and he was not allowed to do so. Weyerbacher felt that Dürr was not really a designer but a supervisor of construction and erection, which at that time he was.

While Luftschiffbau-Zeppelin struggled to survive after the termination of the *Bodensee* and *Nordstern* operations, its future appeared moribund following the collapse of the negotiations with Hensley for LZ 124. Karl Arnstein had doubts as to whether he should continue his career in airships. Indeed, he doubted if any more Zeppelins would be built. During this period he received a call from his former employer, Züblin and Company, to come for an interview. Upon his return from the interview, Arnstein told his wife, Bertl, that he thought Züblin was no longer a place for him to further his career.

Arnstein was not the only one uncertain about the future and his place in it. Across Germany the threat of revolution and counterrevolution shadowed the Republic. The Weimar government had difficulties maintaining social order, relying on volunteer paramilitary forces which it could not always control. The fear of social upheaval was only heightened by a sense of uneasiness brought about by the deteriorating economic situation following the war. During 1919 Germany's industrial production reached an all-time low, agricultural production had not recovered to prewar levels, and millions of demobilized soldiers appeared on the labor market. The German people were unsure if their government could withstand the pressures brought about by the Versailles treaty sanctions. The victorious Allies continued to finalize the terms of peace, taking from Germany 13 percent of its territory and 10 percent of its population. Germany was stripped of colonies and export markets. The Allies also imposed reparations payments. Their motivation initially was revenge, but practically it was to make Germany pay for war damages and debts.

Eager to dismantle or destroy any remaining technologically advanced German weaponry, the Allies demanded examples of these as war spoils. When Germany denied them, as had been the case with some airships, suitable compensation was expected. Therefore, during the summer of 1920, negotiations were carried on to determine the value of the seven Zeppelins destroyed at war's end at Nordholz and Wittmundhaven. In October 1920, the Conference of Ambassadors meeting in Paris decided that the *Bodensee* and *Nordstern* should be confiscated to replace two of the destroyed naval airships. The conference also decided that the German government should pay for the other five destroyed Zeppelins in gold marks, or by constructing a civil type airship in lieu of cash payment for those powers desiring this option. However, this protocol was not signed by the Conference of Ambassadors and the German minister until 30 June 1921.

This clause concerning the building of a new airship opened the way for the United States to procure an airship from Germany. David Lloyd George, the British prime minister, is said at this meeting to have turned to the American ambassador and suggested that the United States might like to acquire one, but nothing was done until Vissering heard about it. Vissering had been talking to many people and, among others, U.S. Navy Admiral William A. Moffett, the recently appointed head of the new Bureau of Aeronautics, and to U.S. President Warren G. Harding. Because of President Wilson's illness, the executive branch had been run on more or less a caretaker basis during the last months of his term, but Harding displayed a relatively energetic approach in grasping the opportunity to acquire a new airship at no cost to the United States.

By this time the Zeppelin people in Friedrichshafen were becoming fearful that the Allies would demolish their big construction hangar, and saw the Americans as the only hope for the survival of the Zeppelin airship business. The United States wanted a 3,500,000 cubic foot volume airship such as Hensley had sought. The Allies, via the Conference of Ambassadors, refused to allow that on 17 August 1921. For one thing, Britain and France feared the military uses of an airship that size. Besides, Britain already had the U.S. Navy as a customer for its smaller R 38, and was not eager to have its recent enemy Germany compete with British industry. But a week later, the tragic crash of R 38 during a trial flight caused a change of attitude. The British had to take the blame for the loss of the R 38 and the lives of forty-four crew, including sixteen of the most experienced personnel of the U.S. airship program. Significantly, the R 38, about to enter U.S. Navy service as ZR-2, was a postwar copy of a German height-climber Zeppelin. Arnstein had designed the height-climbers with a low factor of safety in order to maximize their performance in the thin air of high altitudes. The British copy was faithful to the original, but when R 38 was subjected to abrupt turning maneuvers in the dense air at low altitude, its lightly built frame broke in two. In the subsequent accident investigations, the airship's British builder was faulted for failing to calculate the structure for aerodynamic loads. Unfortunately, he had been killed in the crash.

The tragedy gave an increased sense of urgency on the American side, and by December 1921, a compromise had been worked out. The airship for America could be of the size of the German Navy L 72 (LZ 114), about 2,470,000 cubic feet in volume—slightly smaller than the R 38 had been, and ironically, what the Americans had first sought. Since this airship was to be provided as compensation for two wartime Zeppelins, the German government was to pay the cost, not the United States. The Zeppelin Company could not afford to build the airship gratis, and made known their cost estimate. While the German government wanted to pay as little as possible for the airship's construction, the United States government expected the amount to cover its entire cost. The Zeppelin Company was stuck in the middle. If its cost estimate exceeded the likely compensation award, the deal might fall through, and the construction hangar would be demolished along with any hopes of continuing the airship business. On the other hand, what would be gained if the contract was approved but the cost of building the new airship bankrupted the company? The Interallied Aeronautical Commission of Control set the all-important price at 3,000,000 marks, based on a favorable estimate of the value of L 65 and L 14, the two destroyed airships the United States was to have received. In the German view, the generous figure was more than the two wartime airships deserved, but the British general who assessed their worth was likely considering as well the value of Anglo-American relations, strained by the loss of the ZR-2.

Eckener did not want to build another L 70–type airship like the late wartime Zeppelins that were lightly built "height climbers," nor one like the comparatively small airships *Bodensee* and *Nordstern*. He had a vision of a stronger, more perfect airship that would demonstrate the Zeppelin Company's ideas for a transoceanic passenger carrier. An airship of wholly new design would cost more, but Eckener was able to negotiate this with the U.S. officials. Already, Zeppelin's rival Schütte-Lanz in Germany and some investors in the United States—including former Assistant Secretary of the Navy Franklin D. Roosevelt—were pursuing the idea of building an Atlantic passenger airship. An airship could halve the time it took to cross the sea by ocean liner. There was no other viable aerial competition: no airplane of the day could match the endurance or load-carrying ability of an airship, and no airplane could perform the ocean-crossing flight except as a death-defying stunt.

The contract between the U.S. Navy and Luftschiffbau-Zeppelin for the compensation airship was finally signed on 24 June 1922. The agreed-upon price was 3,031,665 gold marks, which was a loss for the Zeppelin Company, but one that would be made up by separate contracts for delivery of the airship to the U.S. and subsequent training of American crews. It had been nearly three years since Hensley had appeared on the scene, but the protracted negotiations had delayed demolition of the Friedrichshafen hangars to accommodate the Americans. The hangars of rival builder Schütte-Lanz at Mannheim and at Zeesen had already been destroyed.

Four of the provisions of the contract are especially noteworthy. At the insistence of the Allies, the compensation Zeppelin was to be a nonmilitary airship used strictly for civilian purposes. Thus, this airship, the ZR-3 *Los Angeles*, was provided with Pullman-like accommodations for twenty passengers. As a historical fact, it was never operated as anything but a navy aircraft, used primarily as a training airship and for publicity purposes. Not until 1930 was permission sought and obtained from France and England for the airship to participate in military maneuvers. The comfortable accommodations were never used by paying passengers, although they were appreciated by frequent prominent guests on board.

Another requirement, at the insistence of the Zeppelin Company, was that payment from the German government must be in gold marks. Arnstein had a role in this crucial decision. By 1921, Colsman had made Arnstein, at age thirty-four, an officer of Luftschiffbau-Zeppelin with responsibility as a *prokurist*, which meant that he could, with the signature of any other *prokurist*, commit the company to anything—for example, payment on orders for material. Obviously, only management of the highest rank was accorded this responsibility.

Arnstein was present when Colsman was discussing with Eckener whether to ask for payment for the new airship in gold marks or in standard German marks. Colsman preferred gold marks, but Eckener argued that the inflation evident in Germany at the time would pass and values would return to normal, so that it would be sufficient to take payment in regular currency. Colsman asked Arnstein for his opinion, and he answered that it would be best to take payment in gold marks. This became the company decision. If payment in unsecured German currency had been accepted, the subsequent runaway inflation would have been disastrous for Luftschiffbau. Considering this possibility years later, Arnstein would comment that although Eckener had written an economic treatise, he was not a very good practical economist.

A third provision of the contract was that the airship should be delivered to Lakehurst, New Jersey, by a German crew. Colsman was opposed to this because it meant that if for any reason it did not succeed in flying across the Atlantic, the company that he had built for Count Zeppelin would be ruined, for there would be no payment. There were no facilities en route, so it would have to be a nonstop flight, and while R 34 had flown the Atlantic east to west in 1919, it had started from Scotland, not Germany. The new Zeppelin would have to make the longest over-ocean flight ever attempted.

But would not the Zeppelin Company come to an end anyway? The entire enterprise was at a crossroads, with the future beyond building one more airship much in doubt. Even now, the company was more than just an airship factory. The company survived after 1919 while no airships were being built, largely to the credit of Colsman who had developed the company's nonairship subsidiaries. The commercial alternatives began with unglamorous pots and pans and slowly became more sophisticated—subcontracts for automobile and truck transmissions, drive-trains, motors of various kinds, wood products, industrial gases and chemicals, participation in various aviation ventures, partnerships with metal works, housing construction, and even a motion picture subsidiary in the empty hangar at Staaken. All this was occurring during Germany's horrendous inflation that saw the great wartime profits of the company almost vanish. To gamble all this on the success of a transoceanic airship flight was to Colsman unwise, if not to say foolish. The board of directors, however, was stacked with airship men who saw this as the last chance to realize the dream of commercial airships flying over the globe. They saw the Zeppelin Company as an airship company. All those by-products of Colsman's were a means of survival, but the airship for America was the real thing.

Alfred Colsman, the Zeppelin Company's business manager. (Karl Arnstein Collection/University of Akron Archives)

Colsman carried the onus for the Hensley fiasco, and also for failing in 1920 to secure a partnership with American industrial interests seen as vital to the company's future. Therefore, Colsman was outvoted. The company would stake its reputation—and survival—on the delivery of a Zeppelin to the United States.

The controversy split the Zeppelin organization into two factions: those who backed Colsman, and those who backed Eckener. One would expect Arnstein, whose work dealt solely with design of the Zeppelins, to favor Eckener's view, because if there were no airships Arnstein would have no job. But this was not so. Looking back many years later, Arnstein was decidedly pro-Colsman, a view that may have been colored by later events. In any case, with the decision to sign the contract and deliver airship LZ 126, the Zeppelin the Americans would christen the USS *Los Angeles* (ZR-3), the balance of power shifted to Eckener. When Gemmingen died a couple of years later, Eckener became chairman of the board of directors. The decision would be a fateful one for Karl Arnstein.

A fourth condition of the contract stated that the airship was to be "constructed in accordance with plans and specifications approved by American inspectors stationed at the builder's works." The Germans were not prepared for the U.S. Navy's interpretation of this, which was that the Americans were to have access to "the German design methods, theoretical calculations, stressing procedures, and the basis for the use of particular structural items throughout the airship." Even during the war, the Zeppelin Company had not provided this sort of information to the German navy and army, because much of it was considered a company secret. It was a condition that clearly showed the difference between the American and the German systems of procurement, in their dissimilar attitudes regarding the division of design responsibility between the customer and the supplier. This arrangement would create problems later that would be a cause of great aggravation to Arnstein.

What prompted the Americans to be so meddlesome? It stemmed from the loss of the ZR-2, the British airship R 38. The ship's customer, the U.S. Navy's Bureau of Aeronautics, lacked experience, so had been hesitant to contradict the British concerning what it felt were weaknesses in the R 38 design. But the loss of the R 38 convinced the bureau that its own calculations were as good as anyone's and it was not about to accept a design without understanding it—not even one from Luftschiffbau-Zeppelin. The bureau had some very competent people, foremost among whom was Charles P. Burgess, Starr Truscott's stress analyst and the man who wrote what is still considered to be the definitive text on airship design in the United States, and Jerome C. Hunsaker, who had design responsibility for all U.S. Navy airships in World War I and in 1921 became head of the Design Division of the navy's Bureau of Aeronautics.

It is clear that Luftschiffbau-Zeppelin valued its own strength calculations, and Arnstein, as stress analyst, was a closely held and vital company secret. According to Ralph Weyerbacher, who had been in charge of erecting the *Shenandoah*, and had been in Friedrichshafen, "There was no two ways about it. Arnstein was the brains of the outfit, though the Zep people took pains to hide this. In fact, when I was there in 1919 and 1920, they even hid Arnstein's person." When the American position became clear to the Germans, some opposed accepting it, the most prominent of whom was Dürr, who had labored in secret for four years to develop the design of LZ 2, and whose inclination toward secrecy had not diminished with the years. But Eckener was wise enough to see that the alternative was the death of his vision of Zeppelin transport, for which he would ruthlessly brush aside any obstacle or individual. He had the power and prestige to have his way, and the contract was signed. Two Americans came to oversee the Zeppelin's construction, Lieutenant Commander Garland Fulton and Lieutenant Ralph G. Pennoyer, who opened the U.S. Navy inspector's office in Friedrichshafen in July 1922.

It took some time before Fulton discovered Arnstein, who was kept away from conferences with him while Dürr and Lehmann stonewalled or evaded questions about airship design. Finally, after threats of canceling the *Los Angeles* contract, and upon Eckener's orders, Arnstein was finally called into a conference on the design of the passenger gondola and hull strength in November 1922. Fulton found, however, that he was still not being given the information he wanted. In his "Notes on Personalities" of 15 December 1922, he wrote of Arnstein, "Personally he is very pleasant and cordial but, evidently acting on instructions, shows some reluctance about giving detailed information. Appears to be broad minded and would like to leave Friedrichshafen, which he considers has a very narrowing influence."

This was Arnstein's first professional contact with the U.S. Navy Bureau of Aeronautics in what was to become a long and usually friendly relationship. What the Americans expected in the way of technical information, he found, was far more than the German army and navy representatives had asked for in the past. The Americans wanted to be a full partner in the design. Luftschiffbau people were not used to that. As Arnstein would say years later, "In Germany and Britain, the contractor has more responsibility and more freedom to design as he believes best—then if his product passes all the tests, that's that."

Even with continued prodding, Luftschiffbau resisted sharing company knowledge. As late as January 1923, while the new airship was well under construction, Lehmann wrote on behalf of the company: "The method of strength calculations is one of the most *vital business secrets* of the Luftschiffbau-Zeppelin.... In the opinion of the Luftschiffbau-Zeppelin, it is not at all necessary for the Navy department to have these calculations for any reason in connection with this ship." Furthermore, he added, "It is not an obligation for the Luftschiffbau-Zeppelin to submit a stress analysis, but it is up to the Inspector to make one of his own." This proprietary zeal was hardly the American view, and after a threat to cancel the contract, the American position prevailed. Fulton expressed his view of the situation in March 1923: "It should be realized that German psychology, methods, habits and language are all different from our own. The Zeppelin company . . . always enjoyed very special privileges from the government, their only previous customer, and have, therefore, had a free hand in regard to building airships. This independence coupled with secrecy carried to an extraordinary length, even for Germany, and a somewhat narrow viewpoint about certain matters, coming mainly I think from the isolated position in Friedrichshafen, has created a state of mind which requires a process of education and time to dispel."

By the time Fulton wrote these lines, the conflict of viewpoints had been decided in favor of the customer, and Fulton was sending information obtained from Arnstein and others back to Washington. There, C. P. Burgess evaluated the data and was able to apply some of it to the ZR-1, then being erected. Jerome Hunsaker congratulated Fulton on the material he derived from interviews with Arnstein and commented, "I have not tried to puzzle out the calculations, but the general method is ingenious. I suspect it will give about the same results as ours, but it will take a long time to find this out" (the bureau's methods were largely developed by C. P. Burgess).

Meanwhile, Arnstein had been given the title of chief constructor. This title corresponds in American usage to chief engineer or chief designer. The difference from his former status was that now he was responsible for all aspects of design and not merely structure, so that the individuals responsible for power plants, electrical systems, aerodynamics, and so forth, who had formerly reported to Dürr, now reported to Arnstein, who reported to Dürr.

While Arnstein was being hidden from the Americans, he was busy perfecting the techniques that would allow building a Zeppelin regularly capable of transoceanic flights. The technology for producing a flying structure strong enough and light enough for the task was nearly at hand, but no airship existed to prove it could be done commercially. One of the last wartime Zeppelins, L 59, had proven it had the range in an abortive resupply mission to German troops in East Africa. Before the airship's commander was tricked by a false radio message into believing the mission was futile, the Zeppelin flew nonstop 4,200 miles before returning to its base in Bulgaria. However, such a ship was unsuitable as a commercial carrier. The postwar *Bodensee* and *Nordstern* were more advanced in design, but far too small for crossing oceans. The British military rigid R 34 had proved the flight was possible, but it barely made it across the Atlantic before running out of fuel. Clearly, something bigger and bolder was needed, and Arnstein began to develop his ideas on how to accomplish the feat. A record of his inventiveness can be found in his patents from the years 1920–25.

All but one of these more than twenty patents were intended for rigid airships, although two (for a wire and rope clamp and clamping device) had other applications. His patent, "Rigid Frame for Airships," had its roots in the problem Luftschiffbau-Zeppelin asked Arnstein to solve in 1915, the weakness in Zeppelin frames. His solution was to refine the early inefficient Zeppelin hull rings by adding stronger triangular and then diamond-shaped trusses. This system was less susceptible to buckling and supported the lengthwise auxiliary girders that helped to maintain hull shape. His new patent extended the support across not just one but several longitudinal girders, while retaining a strong diagonal truss structure. The goal was to build bigger, but lighter framing, without sacrificing strength as had been necessary in the "height climbers." This new design was a milestone in the progress toward larger airships. Three more American patents were applied for in April 1922 relating to airship ring structures. Other patents from this creative time in Arn-

Hugo Eckener and Ludwig Dürr pose by the chart table in the control car of the ZR-3 Los Angeles. *One of Arnstein's patented box girders with flanged lightening holes is visible in the control car support at left. (Lockheed Martin Collection/University of Akron Archives)*

stein's structural design career include improvements to airship mooring devices, tail surfaces, hull bracing, and gas cells.

The patent "Hollow Girders in Light Structures" shows how to make boxlike girders simply from bent-up metal sheet, where excess weight in the girder walls is reduced by punching out holes. Lightening holes were not new, but what was novel was strengthening them by giving them flanged edges. Girders made this way are easier to produce than the truss girders used in previous airships. Those had to be formed from many short, stamped struts, each hand-riveted across the longitudinal segments. Hollow box girders with lightening holes were used successfully in the *Los Angeles*, and they became a hallmark of the Arnstein aircraft structure. Flanged lightening holes found uses in structures other than Zeppelins, such as in making airplane wing ribs and control surfaces. It may be his most influential and successful invention.

Other patents, "Stabilizing Apparatus for Rigid Airships" and "Stern Construction of Rigid Airships," develop the idea of extending girders entirely through an airship's hull in several places to securely anchor the fins. The resulting **cruciform** tail structure was first used in the airship *Los Angeles* and on all subsequent German-built Zeppelins. A patent submitted in October 1923 for a "Rigid Airship" is the beginning of the "deep ring," a new idea in airship structure, which Arnstein would famously develop as a replacement for wire-braced-only rings. This and a subsequent patent showed ways to make ring frames strong enough to omit miles of crisscrossing stabilizing wires and still keep gas cells in place.

Since analytical methods are not patentable, Arnstein's patents provide us with some record of his creative life during the early 1920s. Three of them influenced later development of airship construction in both Germany and the United States. The patent for easy-to-manufacture girders made of metal sheet with flanged lightening holes found wider application, not only in heavier-than-air craft, but for other structures for which weight must be closely controlled.

All of these developments had been considered the proprietary innovations of the Zeppelin Company, even though they were largely the product of Arnstein's imagination. Since he was a principal source of new ideas in Zeppelin design, he was considered to be a valuable company asset worth guarding—or at least not publicizing. However, the Americans, especially those in the U.S. Navy's airship design bureau, had discovered the Zeppelin company's talented engineer. Arnstein soon would be a company secret no longer. But before he would become known as the designer of the *Amerika-Zeppelin*, Arnstein faced some personal choices that would unfold amidst a colossal economic crisis in Germany.

Chapter 6 A ZEPPELIN FOR AMERICA

Zeppelin LZ 126—popularly called the ZR-3 and destined to be christened the USS *Los Angeles*—when completed in 1924 was the largest airship ever built by the Zeppelin Company and the largest airship in the world. It was 658 feet (200 m) long and 90.7 feet (27.7 m) in diameter at its largest section. The Conference of Ambassadors had authorized it to be no larger than the L 70–class Zeppelin of the war (about 70,000 cubic meters, or 2,470,000 cubic feet in volume). Since both the Germans and the Americans wanted to build a larger airship, it is perhaps not altogether surprising that when this airship was complete, space was found for 2,600,000 cubic feet (72,800 cu m) of inflation gas—the increase officially attributed to cumulative inaccuracies of design and construction. The enlargement was not admitted by either the Zeppelin Company or the United States until after the airship was delivered.

As chief designer as well as head of stress analysis, Arnstein was able to incorporate some of the ideas he had patented, or would patent. Not all of the innovations in the ZR-3 were patented, such as the diamond-truss ring elements. The keel design, described as five-sided where earlier keels were all triangular, was unique, as was the gas bag netting. The car was similar to, but larger than, the car of the *Bodensee*, placed against the hull rather than suspended below as in the wartime Zeppelins.

ZR-3 was the first Zeppelin to have accommodations where up to twenty overnight commercial passengers could sleep. The seats were rather like sofas with three cushions, providing ample space for three people to sit, and adequate length for one person to lie down. The fold-out berth above was positioned directly over the seat. There were five such compartments, two on one side of the aisle and three on the other, each with two seats and two upper berths. Curtains could be drawn for privacy at the center aisle. The radio cabin took the remaining space immediately behind the pilot's compartment. As in the European hotels of the time, the bathroom was down the hall, at the rear of the 75-foot (23 m) gondola. The crew slept in hammocks in the hull, above the keel.

Erection of the structure proceeded under Dürr's direction but hit a snag when the new Maybach engines were not ready, resulting in a delay of several months. Meanwhile, Eckener had been teaching his captains how to fly the Atlantic. Of course, he had never flown it himself, but he understood that it was a matter of weather. Based on weather maps of the North Atlantic available from previous years, he showed them how to fly the most advantageous and safest route around the storm centers. As Hugh Allen put it, "The airship captain flies by the weather map rather than the compass."

Gemmingen died on 4 March 1924, and from that time Eckener took complete control of the company. Colsman, because of his disagreements with Eckener, found himself in an increasingly difficult position. (A few years later Colsman would resign, his departure induced by Eckener's "tactically clever conduct.") Bitterness between the two men grew to the point that "Colsman would not set foot in Friedrichshafen if Eckener was in the city—and vice versa." The Arnstein family, being friends of both Colsman and Eckener families, were dismayed and saddened by the Colsman-Eckener feud, and Arnstein thought Colsman had been badly treated.

While the Colsman-Eckener affair simmered on the back burner, the engines from Maybach arrived and erection of the LZ 126 proceeded rapidly to completion. The airship began to be called the ZR-3, which was the American navy's designation for their newest airship.

In Germany, the public was becoming aware that a new sky leviathan was coming into existence in a hangar in remote Friedrichshafen. Eckener had not forgotten his journalism and public relations experience. The first big publicity splash came on 28 June when the German magazines *Die Woche* and the *Stettiner Illustrierte Zeitung* featured stories about the new "giant" airship, both featuring a photograph of Arnstein. In *Die Woche*, no other individual is mentioned besides Arnstein, who is recognized as Luftschiffbau's chief engineer.

In July, a new book, *Fünfundzwanzig Jahre Zeppelin-Luftschiffbau*, (Twenty-five Years of Zeppelin Airship Construction) was published, describing the engineering development of all the Zeppelins, including the latest. The author is listed as "Dr.-Ing. L. Dürr," but the idea was most probably Eckener's, for he knew the value of publicity. Dürr was unlikely to write a book to commemorate his own career or to give away his cherished secrets, and he gave Arnstein most of the work of writing it. The publicity would help raise money for the next airship the company hoped to build, but if the ZR-3 was to be the last Zeppelin, it should be celebrated in a burst of glory.

By September, the time was approaching for the first of five test flights that the airship would make before starting on its long flight to Lakehurst, New Jersey, where it would be turned over to the U.S. Navy. Arnstein was aboard on all of these flights, but he was asked by Luftschiffbau not to make the American flight. The thought may well have been that if the ZR-3 did not make it, Arnstein, and their apparent last hope, might be lost.

Eckener planned to use the test flights and the transatlantic flight to conquer the adverse effect of the British R 38 disaster in 1921 and the more recent loss of the German-built *Dixmude* (LZ 114) in December 1923. Press representatives were invited from all over the world. The crew was besieged by questions and by cameras taking both still and moving pictures. "We were filled with pride and joy," wrote airship pilot Anton Wittemann, "when we saw how our ship shone to some degree as a symbol, and that we had been called to present to the world this marvel."

Eckener intentionally chose a day of threatening weather. After some difficulty getting safely out of the hangar door, the airship took off and flew through gusts of rain over the Bodensee. During a full-speed run, a crankshaft counterweight broke loose in one of the engines and went through the crankcase. The incident was minor and the airship returned to the hangar after a flight of two hours and forty-seven minutes, but wild rumors had spread about the engine shutdown, and one foreign newsman reported that it had broken down completely.

After repairs and replacement of all crankshaft and counterweight bolts with stronger ones, the ZR-3 was ready for its second test flight. Besides the flight crew, there were on board others who had contributed to the structure, including, of course, Arnstein and an American contingent headed by Commander Garland Fulton.

6 September was a beautiful day, and Eckener had planned a flight to show off Luftschiffbau's latest Zeppelin. This time eighty-six persons including the German crew and U.S. Navy observers were aboard, plus two movie cameramen and many German and foreign newspaper correspondents, all generating, as Eckener expected, favorable publicity for the airship.

One other American aboard, although little noticed, was J. M. (Jack) Yolton, foreman of Goodyear's aero workshop. He had been sent to Friedrichshafen during the final stages of the erection of ZR-3, and now was riding in the egg-shaped aft engine gondola. His log of the flight is in rather amusing contrast to the flowery and fervently nationalist account of Wittemann, one of Eckener's captains. Where Wittemann wrote concerning the

The newly-completed German-built ZR-3 is walked out of its hangar late in the summer of 1924. It would be delivered to its customer, the U.S. Navy, via a transatlantic flight that October. (Goodyear Tire and Rubber Co. Collection/University of Akron Archives)

takeoff, "Soldiers brought the ship out of the hangar in glorious weather and, among the sounds of the Army band playing the national anthem, in which the spectators as a body joined with enthusiasm, we took off. This moment of the takeoff is to us a most exalted memory. With hats and kerchiefs waving, in many eyes the tears of emotion could hardly be held back. With a roar the motors set in on command, and in a few minutes we ascended to a height of 300 meters."

Yolton writes more laconically: "8:30 A.M. . . . crew on board ready for the weigh-off. For this flight Captain Flemming was in charge, 250 men on lines, 50 men on two cars, about 350 soldiers standing by. Hands off at 8:33." Later, he resumes, "Ship walked to the east field pointing towards Maybach motor plant. Large crowd to witness takeoff. Kept back by soldiers. Weigh-off. O.K. 9:00 A.M. In flight."

Yolton was impressed by the reception the airship received over Munich two hours later: "Thousands of people greet us from below. Have never seen such a reception. Street cars stop. Whistles blow." The ZR-3 turned toward the west and headed for Stuttgart, and flew over the grave of Count Zeppelin.

Several Swiss cities sent requests for a visit from the *Amerika-Zeppelin*. Eckener was pleased to oblige. On the morning of 11 September, Eckener waited for the wind to change, so the airship would not have to be pulled from the hangar tail first into the wind and then be turned almost completely around for takeoff—a dangerous maneuver. After some delay, ZR-3 took off with eighty people aboard, including Garland Fulton and a contingent of newsmen. After one and a half hours of flight tests over the Bodensee, the ZR-3 headed west toward Basel, where Eckener had to take care not to cross the French border. The airship then headed for Lucerne and Zurich, where the streets were crowded with people waiting to see the airship, before returning to Friedrichshafen after a "short" flight of eight hours and twenty-five minutes. During this and other test flights, motor troubles persisted. Would the airship be able to make the transatlantic flight?

As publicity ballyhoo about the airship grew, letters requesting Zeppelin visits poured in from cities all over Germany and as far away as Copenhagen and Stockholm. Eckener determined "to show the last Zeppelin to the German Fatherland to say farewell" to as many German cities as possible. The last flight was to start early in the morning, but during the night of 24 September a wind storm arrived. At 6 A.M. the crew gathered in the hangar, and listened to the wind howling outside, knowing that taking the airship out of the hangar was out of the question. But the wind abated, and by 9 o'clock, ZR-3 with seventy-one persons including Arnstein aboard, was already up in the air.

After about an hour of experiments over the Bodensee, the long trip was begun. The route would carry the airship over towns in the northernmost corners of Germany by day's end.

During the night the crew practiced navigation with radio or compass bearings and lighthouses. Rain and heavy weather to the east forced them to spend the night cruising along the coast of Sweden before heading to Berlin at daylight. The airship cruised over streets and housetops crowded with cheering people, dropped a large mail pouch by parachute, and radioed greetings from the mayor and Reich president. After about three-quarters of an hour of showing off the "Swabian masterwork," it was time to head for home. The flight ended after thirty-three hours and thirty-two minutes. All had gone well, and the airship was deemed fit for the long journey across the Atlantic.

As the flight test program progressed, publicity about the *Amerika-Zeppelin* and its designer spread. The Prague German-language papers soon recognized that the much-talked-of Dr. Arnstein was a native of their own city. Articles in the *Prager Tagblatt*, the *Prager Presse*, and other Prague newspapers began to refer to him as the "builder [*erbauer*] of the *Amerika-Zeppelin*," although he was, in fact, the chief designer. The Friedrichshafen paper *Seeblatt* credits Arnstein only as head of stress analysis. At the other extreme, an article by Bruno Frei in the Vienna paper *Der Abend*, dateline Berlin, claimed that all of the latest Zeppelins including ZR-3 "were entirely his [Arnstein's] work." Of course, that is not accurate either.

Rumors apparently began to fly that Luftschiffbau would become defunct, which was not implausible in view of the Versailles treaty, according to which ZR-3 would have to be the last German-built Zeppelin and the hangars would have to be torn down. Eckener had other ideas, and a dispatch from Friedrichshafen appeared in the *Prager Tagblatt* stating the official company position: "The Luftschiffbau-Zeppelin has, with the Goodyear Tire and Rubber Company, created in the United States a joint new company in Akron in the state of Ohio which . . . will take up the construction of airships in America. For this purpose it is planned to send a small staff of engineers there. The continuation of the work at the Zeppelin works in Friedrichshafen will not be hampered by this." The company further explained that Dürr would remain as technical director in Friedrichshafen, while Arnstein would be provided as technical director of the new company. Among the engineers publicly credited for their part in the success of the ZR-3, seven of ten were to accompany Arnstein to the United States. As the time for the great flight to America approached, there was a crescendo of public excitement about the great new Zeppelin. For better or worse, Arnstein was now becoming a celebrity, praised as an example of the best of German genius and industry. But, of course, he was neither German nor a naturalized

German citizen—he was a citizen of Czechoslovakia. In the glare of publicity, the ZR-3 and its designer, Arnstein, became a subject for nationalistic rhetoric, which was often inaccurate or inappropriate.

Aviation historian Peter Fritzsche notes, "Both Social Democrats and German nationalists recognized the zeppelin as one of Germany's technical 'masterpieces' which instilled a measure of national pride." Groups representing opposing political views each saw their own virtues in the success of the *Amerika-Zeppelin*, and Karl Arnstein and his achievement were invoked in competing claims of German superiority. None of these claims originated with Arnstein, it should be noted, nor did he endorse any of the viewpoints expressed in the often strident press of that era. He wasn't even interviewed directly. These editorial pieces were published to the distress of Arnstein himself, who "was a modest person" and "always reluctant about publicity." Perhaps he was right to be wary of publicity, since the inaccurate information presented in some of these articles was later held against him, especially by critics who wanted to believe that Arnstein concocted the extravagant claims, not the journalists. For the rest of his life, Arnstein "hated to meet with the press, because he said they always took what he said and twisted it around to mean something he didn't intend. He preferred not to be 'quoted.'"

It should be remembered that emotions were running high in Germany, and not just because of the Zeppelin. The economic, social, and political upheaval agitated many factions, and generated an atmosphere that made it "much easier to search for scapegoats than try to comprehend the complex processes which lay behind the decline of specific social groups." Disillusioned supporters of the monarchy and former military men blamed their woes on foreigners (especially the Allies), minorities, socialist revolutionaries, and Jews. These scapegoats were accused of starting the war, losing the war, toppling the monarchy, and accepting the blame and indemnities of the Versailles treaty. Spurred by the pronouncement by General Ludendorff that Germany had been "stabbed in the back" by such traitors, the middle classes—among them academics, professionals, and clergy—began to join in the sentiment against those who were actually least responsible for the calamities of postwar Germany. It should be made clear, as historian Lindley Fraser put it, that "the stab-in-the-back theory is a legend and a myth, put forward by evil men for the concealment of their own mistakes and the furtherance of their aggressive and warlike ends."

Against this backdrop, "all Germany's pride," the ZR-3, was seen by some people as being expropriated by non-Germans. That the ship was going to the Americans gave more ammunition to opponents of the American Dawes Plan, approved in August 1924, which provided a mutually agreed schedule of reparations payments as a precondition of United States economic aid. Some saw this plan as an end to the economic chaos, but the German right wing saw it as legitimizing the "nefarious" Versailles settlement. They viewed this airship, being provided as war compensation, as another valuable German asset being given up by the hated Weimar Republic. And there was some undercurrent of resentfulness among the extremists that the designer of this gem of German technology, the state-of-the-art Zeppelin, was not a German at all, but a foreigner from Prague. The suspicions and distrust from the ultranationalists would reach a climax before the elections in November of 1924, but by then, the new Zeppelin—and soon its designer—would be gone from Germany.

Chapter 7 A WINTER OF DISCONTENT

While the *Los Angeles* was being built, Arnstein had to face important career decisions. Germany was in turmoil in 1923. In January, French and Belgian troops occupied the Ruhr industrial region to force compliance with reparations payments mandated by the Versailles treaty. The German government resisted and began printing money to pay off its debt. Nearly 1,800 printing presses were turning out notes day and night. As a result, the paper mark became nearly worthless, and inflation reached unheard-of peaks. In 1914, a dollar was worth four marks; in 1919, fourteen marks. In January 1923 a dollar would buy nearly eighteen thousand marks, but by November of that year, four trillion marks would not equal one dollar. "For millions of Germans, these figures created a lunatic world . . . in which all value was illusion and monetary fortune fleeting." Bertl found when she became eligible to claim her inheritance at age 21 that its real value had dwindled to a very small amount since it was paid in the depreciated currency. Bertl's share of her parents' considerable estate had, by law, been invested in German government bonds, which had become almost worthless. Tradesmen did not like to part with their goods in exchange for the paper money and, consequently, shopping became difficult. "Grocers would tell you they were all out of things, when you could see those very items on the shelves," Mrs. Arnstein later recalled. "It was my husband's task to take a knapsack and go out in the country to see what food he could get from the farmers. He would be very polite to them and pretend to be interested in all kinds of subjects, and then, if they happened to take a liking to him, they might give him a dozen fresh eggs or some cabbage," Mrs. Arnstein smiled impishly.

"One time," she continues, "my husband went to a farmer's house and the farmer was very gruff. He didn't want to sell him a thing. But there was a man there whom my husband knew and, as this man was leaving, he said to my husband, 'Goodbye, Dr. Arnstein.' Immediately a change came over the farmer. He was all smiles. He went out and got everything he could find—fresh fruits and eggs and vegetables—and loaded down my husband with them. And then, just as my husband was leaving, the farmer said, 'By the way, Doctor, I have a daughter here who is having trouble with her ear. I wish you would look at it.' My husband, you know, is not a doctor of medicine; he is a doctor of mechanical engineering. But he didn't want to lose all those fresh fruits and vegetables by explaining all of this to the farmer, so he said he would see the girl. As soon as he saw the girl he realized he recognized a common ear trouble he had once suffered. So he gave the farmer excellent advice and referred him to a specialist."

The shortages of consumer goods which had started during the war grew even worse afterward. Shoes, clothing (leather, wool, linen, etc.) and furniture were scarce. Important foodstuffs were rationed beginning in 1916. Meat, eggs, milk, butter, and fats became less plentiful, replaced by ersatz (substitutes) or done without. The rations were not enough, and the military always got priority over civilians. Small vegetable gardens were started, and the "much-hated turnip meals" became more prevalent as misguided agricultural policies added to food shortages caused by bad harvests. By the end of 1918, food prices had risen almost 200 percent from 1914 levels. By the last year of the war, it was estimated that one-half of families tracked in a government survey "consumed food purchased on the black market at prices and quantities higher than was officially authorized." Even General Ludendorff admitted that prices in the open food market were "scandalous," but a remedy eluded him. The price of coal—a staple of home heating—had risen, as had clothing prices. Workers in war industries have been alleged to have benefited from the war, but historians agree "there is no evidence that the rise in wages compensated for the rise of prices." The food shortages persisted after the war until July 1919, when the Allied blockade was lifted.

During the postwar period of scarcity, in order to forestall black-marketing, farmers were not allowed to sell to the public except for private consumption. It was a time of rationing, and produce had to be sold to the government to distribute. This contributed to the inflation which peaked in 1923. During these years of hardship and scarcity, Luftschiff-bau-Zeppelin would allow employees to buy small quantities (five yards or less) of the fine Egyptian cotton cloth that was used for the outer covers of Zeppelins. It was excellent material and buyers used it to make clothing. Arnstein was also able to get for Bertl some of the aluminum cookware made by the Luftschiffbau-Zeppelin company when there were no airships to build.

As elsewhere during times of severe inflation, merchants did not want to sell their goods for money that would be worth less each day, while the consumers were anxious to spend it as soon as possible. Luftschiffbau paid its employees twice a week: on Wednesday evenings and at the end of the work week on Saturday noon. After immediate current needs for food, clothing, and such were met, with his lifelong interest in art, Arnstein used any money left over to buy paintings of the nineteenth century Munich school as an investment. He kept those small but fine oil paintings all his life. All was not austerity and distress, however; there were at least two bright spots. Arnstein became a family man with the birth of his first child, Marianne Renate (also called Renée) on 5 July 1920, and a second daughter, Ruth Suzanne, on 16 April 1923.

By 1923 Arnstein had reason to worry about his career in airship building. There seemed to be no future for Zeppelins after the contract for the ZR-3 was fulfilled. Arnstein began to think he would like to obtain a post as a professor at a technical university, for which he thought his talents and nature were better suited, rather than have a career in industry as a member of an engineering firm. One day he received an invitation to submit a paper for a commemorative book honoring Joseph Melan, his former mentor at the German Technical Institute in Prague. Melan, nearing his seventieth birthday, was about to retire. Arnstein drew on his experience in bridge design at Züblin and wrote a paper on long-span reinforced concrete arch bridges designed according to Melan's system.

With Melan retiring, Arnstein thought he might be considered for the position left vacant by his teacher. European universities of the time were small, and a professorship with tenure was a most prestigious appointment. Arnstein thought it would be ideal. In fact, he was asked to submit his credentials to the institute's faculty, an honor in itself. A senate of faculty members had to approve such an appointment. However, it was not to be. Melan was an engineer of great reputation and the position went to one of his two sons, both of whom were structural engineers. Although it was a great disappointment to Arnstein, it was understandable that one of Melan's sons might be given preference.

The Arnsteins' brother-in-law, Paul Jaray, who had been the project director for the Zeppelins *Bodensee* and the *Nordstern*, was also becoming restless. He was working privately on some ideas for streamlining automobiles when he fell ill with tuberculosis. In 1923 he took a leave of absence while he spent several months recuperating in a sanitarium not far from Arosa in eastern Switzerland. Then, with the encouragement of a Swiss financier, he decided to resign from Luftschiffbau-Zeppelin and move with his family to Brennen, Switzerland, to pursue the development and marketing of a streamlined auto, which proved not to be successful. Financially, Paul Jaray would have been better off had he stayed with Luftschiffbau-Zeppelin.

Other people were thinking about what would happen after the American ship, the *Los Angeles* (LZ 126), was completed. It was assumed that the Zeppelin hangars would be torn down and that no more airships would be built in Friedrichshafen. What then would happen to all of the German know-how built up over a quarter of a century? This question was being considered not only in Germany, but also in Washington, D.C.

Harry Vissering, the Zeppelin Company's American representative, tried to interest the U.S. government in a partnership with the airship builder. However, in the United States, it was considered awkward for the government to negotiate for rights to Zeppelin industrial secrets. So Vissering went to the private sector. He succeeded in getting Paul W. Litchfield, then a vice president of the Goodyear Tire and Rubber Company in Akron, Ohio, interested in the possibilities of commercial airship travel. Vissering's role is poorly documented, but his influence is clear; he later became a director of the Goodyear-Zeppelin Corporation, a subsidiary of the rubber company.

The Goodyear Tire and Rubber Company of Akron, Ohio, had been supplying rubberized fabric for balloons and airships since 1911. The company's interest in aeronautics was largely due to Litchfield's initiative, since rubberized fabric was a natural extension of the company's business. Using that material, Goodyear built both military observation balloons and nonrigid airship envelopes in considerable numbers during World War I. In 1917, Goodyear shared in a navy contract to assemble complete airships (blimps) using parts (gondolas, motors) furnished by the Curtiss Aeroplane Company. Goodyear also undertook to run an airship training school and flying field for the U.S. Navy at Wingfoot Lake, east of Akron. After the war, Goodyear's aeronautic department continued to design and build airships, not only for the army and navy, but for commercial purposes. That business was temporarily sidetracked when the depression of 1920–21 forced the Goodyear Company into receivership. After the company was reorganized, Litchfield stayed on, becoming its president and chief executive officer in 1926 and chairman of the board of directors in 1930. His name became almost synonymous with Goodyear's for the next thirty years. A talented executive who built his company into the largest rubber company in the world, he also believed strongly in the future of airships, especially the commercial rigid airship.

As Litchfield recalled in his autobiography, *Industrial Voyage:* "Secretary of War, [John W.] Weeks, and Secretary of the Navy, [Edwin] Denby, called me down to Washington in 1922, and asked if Goodyear would try to procure these [Zeppelin] rights." Goodyear was willing. In October 1922, William C. Young of Goodyear's Aeronautic Sales Department was sent to Friedrichshafen to talk to the Zeppelin people. Goodyear's position was that it would not spend any money to obtain the rights, but would be willing to enter into a joint venture in which Goodyear would build a construction hangar while Luftschiffbau-Zeppelin would supply the technical information. Young reported back that Eckener was willing to deal on that basis.

In the summer of 1923, Litchfield and E. G. Wilmer, who had been made president of Goodyear as a result of the receivership, with their attorneys, went to Friedrichshafen to conclude negotiations and to sign a contract. Litchfield took along his wife and daughter. They stayed at the Kurgarten Hotel, owned by the Zeppelin Company, which was less than a block from the Arnsteins' apartment.

None of the Americans spoke German. During the negotiation, Ernst Lehmann, who spoke excellent English, served as interpreter. On some occasions, and particularly with the feminine contingent, Bertl Arnstein was often called upon to interpret, although her English was not fluent at that time. Litchfield remembered the discussions with the Germans started "at ten o'clock in the morning and lasted until nearly four o'clock the next morning, the hotel sending up coffee and sandwiches from time to time."

The agreement, signed in September 1923, called for the establishment of the Goodyear-Zeppelin Corporation, to be two-thirds owned by Goodyear Tire and Rubber Company and one-third by Luftschiffbau-Zeppelin. All patents owned by the Zeppelin Company and its subsidiaries were to be transferred to Goodyear-Zeppelin. Further, the Zeppelin Company was to make available to the new corporation "suitable and experienced expert personnel." For its part, Goodyear agreed to give the German Zeppelin Company access to its airship patents and to turn over its Wingfoot Lake airship hangar and related facilities to the new corporation should it receive a contract to build a Zeppelin.

As for the "'suitable and experienced expert personnel,'" wrote Litchfield, "one man I particularly wanted was Dr. Karl Arnstein, the chief engineer, whose career interested me from an engineering standpoint." Litchfield, whose own engineering training included a degree from the Massachusetts Institute of Technology, had learned of Arnstein from the navy. During his visit to Friedrichshafen, Litchfield offered Arnstein the position of chief engineer with the newly formed Goodyear-Zeppelin Corporation.

Arnstein did not immediately accept. It would be a giant step. He would have to uproot his family and move four thousand miles across an ocean to a country whose language he had studied in school but had used little since. On the other hand, future prospects for Luftschiffbau-Zeppelin did not look bright, and it was obvious that the American venture was Eckener's and Colsman's hope for the future. And times were bad in Germany. The Weimar Republic was shaky, threatened by revolution from the political left, and even more so from the militarists on the right. That November, not far away in Bavaria, paramilitary demonstrators openly called for a march on Berlin to install a military dictatorship under Ludendorff. Although the revolt was quashed, this so-called Beer Hall Putsch in Munich would give new legitimacy to one of its leaders, an ex–army corporal, Adolf

Hitler. Still, Arnstein considered Litchfield's offer a long time. Finally, one day he and Bertl went to see Gemmingen, whose health was failing fast. He received them graciously and his advice was to accept the American offer.

So on February 14, 1924, Karl Arnstein departed for Akron, Ohio, to negotiate details, inspect facilities, and plan the design offices. At Bertl's request, he was also going to evaluate Akron as a place to live. Arnstein was overwhelmed. After years on a starvation diet in Germany, he had "the fantastic opportunity to eat three huge meals every day" and took advantage of every one of them. During this visit Arnstein attended a celebration marking the completion of the **semi-rigid** airship RS-1, built by Goodyear's Aeronautics Department for the U.S. Army. "It was an impressive evening for me," he recalled thirty years later, "coming from starving Europe to see the tables sagging under the load of a fish and chicken dinner where the motto was 'as much as you can eat.'" He was further amazed that in a corner of the room "two happy people were finishing a friendly argument by throwing pieces of apple pie at each other." It was a heady introduction to a land of plenty and the "life of a happy group of capable and fine engineers" with whom he would soon be working. Six weeks later he returned to Friedrichshafen bearing gifts of things not available in Germany; among them, several pairs of silk stockings and a pair of fur-trimmed boots, which made Bertl feel like a queen. But when she asked him about the sooty, often smelly "rubber capital" Akron, all he said was, "It's a nice town."

It was on this visit to Akron that Arnstein, having tentatively agreed to accept the Goodyear position, discussed the additional Zeppelin personnel he would need. Litchfield expected Arnstein to bring two or three experts with him, but Arnstein thought over the various engineering disciplines in which experts were needed—at least two stress analysts; designer-draftsmen; experts for electrical equipment, outer cover and gas bags, engines, car layout, and furnishings, aerodynamics—and came up with a total of twelve.

"Twelve?!" roared Litchfield. "Who do you think you are? Jesus Christ?" But Arnstein had his way and the story prompted Goodyear publicist Hugh Allen to dub them "the twelve disciples."

Litchfield had insisted on Arnstein, but Karl hesitated. He was still not sure that he wanted to leave Friedrichshafen with its lake, mountains, and scenic beauty for an industrial city in the American Midwest. Still, the Goodyear-Zeppelin job looked like a good opportunity. But was it for someone else? The only other person with comparable design knowledge was Ludwig Dürr. He had been a pivotal figure in the development of the Zeppelin enterprise, and was responsible for construction of all but the first Zeppelin airship. He had graduated from the Royal Mechanical Engineering School of Stuttgart as a Diploma Engineer, and was a shrewd practical engineer, although he lacked the formal analytical training that Arnstein had received. As a candidate for the Goodyear-Zeppelin post, he had other shortcomings. Dürr could be abrasive and distrustful; he usually wore a perpetual scowl framed by his bushy, arched eyebrows, mustache, and goatee. And Dürr could not speak English.

Meanwhile, Litchfield had been much impressed by Lehmann, with his facility in English and his knowledge of airships from the operator's point of view. Possibly on Eckener's recommendation, possibly impatient with Arnstein's vacillation, he promised Lehmann the vice presidency of the new corporation. Litchfield's lieutenants—head of aeronautical sales William C. Young and Herman T. Kraft, Goodyear's chief aeronautical engineer—were dismayed. Litchfield did not need yes-men, and Kraft and Young told him what they thought by letter, because Litchfield was already on his way to Friedrichshafen to close the deal.

Kraft wrote: "Mr. Lehmann has had no experience in the design of airships and knows little about physics and mechanics insofar as design is concerned. While he has been considered a good pilot, the consensus is that this is about the full extent of his capabilities. It appears that it would be advisable to put Arnstein in charge of engineering." Kraft continued, "Through contact with the various members of the Zeppelin organization, I find that Dr. Arnstein is considered first in engineering and design, and seems to have the general support of most of the men in the organization . . ." There was also a warning: "I talked with Dr. Arnstein about his general views of this new organization. He would not consider coming to America to act in any other capacity other than that of being in full charge of engineering."

Bill Young wrote a backup letter to Litchfield the following day in which he reiterated, "I feel that Dr. Arnstein is much more highly regarded by the Zeppelin organization than Lehmann." Eckener was "one big exception" to this consensus, but Young believed Lehmann's ability to speak English better than Arnstein had some bearing on Eckener's preference.

Litchfield's solution to this personnel problem was to make both Lehmann and Arnstein vice presidents, but Arnstein's title specified "in charge of engineering." Lehmann, who had considered himself Eckener's right-hand man and thus the logical head of the new company, was unhappy when he learned about this only after he had come to Akron. However, Kraft's letter to Litchfield urging him to give Arnstein rather than Lehmann the vice presidency for engineering was pivotal in Arnstein's decision to come to Goodyear-Zeppelin. Both Lehmann and Arnstein were made directors in the new company. The course of events and this opportunity in Arnstein's life were always a source of amazement. "How I came over to the United States is still somehow unbelievable and mysterious to me," Arnstein admitted many years later. "If someone had told me that some day I would be an executive of a large firm in the United States, I would have laughed in disbelief. But I think there must be a destiny—whether that of God or simply a working of the laws of the universe." With a smile, he added, "Our church doesn't believe in destiny; isn't it the Presbyterians who do?"

A behind-the-scenes observer at the time was Hugh Allen, whom Litchfield had hired as airship public relations man, and who was to write several corporate histories. His observations on this situation are revealing: "I never felt that Eckener or Lehmann ever gave Arnstein credit for his brilliant mind and his vast experience in design and construction. Eckener, of course, was not an engineer, took his doctorate in economics, moved to Friedrichshafen as a secluded place where he could sail his boat and work on a book on the causes of business depressions and the cycle of boom or bust."

Eckener apparently did not think highly of engineers. As an example, when Litchfield was negotiating for the acquisition of the Zeppelin rights for the United States, he believed that men were far more important than patents, and wanted Eckener's key engineers to go with the package. Eckener had no objection. Arnstein and the engineers arrived in the United States in late 1924, preceded by Lehmann, who had flown from Germany on the Zeppelin ZR-3. That airship is perhaps Arnstein's greatest triumph.

Chapter 8   FAREWELL TO FRIEDRICHSHAFEN

In late 1924, both the ZR-3 and its designer Arnstein were to leave Germany to find new homes in the United States. The ZR-3 was none too large for the 5,000-mile flight from Germany to Lakehurst, New Jersey. Its 43 tons of useful lift, allowing for about 33 tons of fuel, 2.2 tons of oil, and 1.7 tons of water ballast, left just 6.1 tons for the crew of twenty-seven and four American military observers, plus luggage and other supplies. Eckener estimated that would be sufficient to travel 5,350 miles against moderate head winds (about 15 mph) in 96 hours. Two U.S. Navy cruisers, the *Detroit* and the *Milwaukee*, were stationed strategically in the Atlantic to provide weather information and emergency aid should that need arise. It would be the longest manned flight ever attempted by air.

The ZR-3's departure from Friedrichshafen for America was scheduled for 11 October 1924. Excitement over the impending flight rose in Germany. The Zeppelin was seized upon as a symbol of German engineering, of German industry, of German genius, of German greatness, and German loss. Must the German people give up this greatest—and possibly last—of all the Zeppelins? Some in Germany felt it was a part of a wider effort to strip away anything of value created or held by Germans. This sentiment was expressed by Hjalmar Schacht, the respected president of the German Reichsbank and author of the plan that had ended the wild inflation of 1923, ". . . this airship which represents up to this time the pinnacle of human efficiency and engineering, this ship which is the best answer to the slander and libel to which the German people have been subjected for the last ten years. This is to be the last airship of German manufacture, because it is German; hate, revenge, envy, and stupidity still live."

To Eckener, the flight was propaganda for airships, a positive step to overcome some of the hatred focused on Germany since the war. But with blind fervor, nationalist extremists vowed that no foreign country should ever have the ZR-3. There was talk of sabotage. Eckener's life was threatened and a student with a rifle was arrested near the Zeppelin field. He'd boasted he would kill Eckener to prevent the airship's departure.

Reporters again flocked to Friedrichshafen. So did many other people drawn by the chance of a last look at the latest realization of Count Zeppelin's dream. On the morning of 11 October, unexpectedly warm air moved across Friedrichshafen. In those conditions, the heavily laden airship would not lift. Rather than sacrifice fuel or ballast, Eckener postponed the flight until the next day. Some of the disappointed onlookers said Eckener had "lost his nerve." But on the morning of 12 October, the ZR-3 rose through an early morning fog and was gone. For Arnstein, Dürr, Fulton, and the entire city of Friedrichshafen began three anxious days of waiting. On Monday, 13 October, the local newspaper, the *Seeblatt*, printed the first radio messages from the airship and other reports. Meanwhile, in mid-ocean, Eckener was receiving weather reports indicating strong head winds in his path—strong enough that the ZR-3 would probably run out of fuel if it maintained its course. Eckener, with his practiced meteorological sense, deduced that a low pressure area was creating a counterclockwise air flow, and altered course northward to pick up the flow as a tail wind. He rode it around the storm center and down the American eastern seaboard. Confident now of success, Eckener sent a radiogram to Dürr and Arnstein, giving his "Heartfelt compliments on the magnificent achievement of the LZ 126, which tonight easily mastered heavy weather." A similar radiogram congratulated Maybach on the performance of the engines "which already have run over sixty hours without any interruption."

After about an hour of being shown over New York City, the airship landed at Lakehurst, New Jersey at 9:37 A.M. 15 October 1924 after a flight of eighty-one hours. This was the fifth transatlantic flight ever made, the first since 1919, and the first ever from the heart of continental Europe to the United States—and it was flown nonstop. The North Atlantic would not be flown nonstop again until Charles Lindbergh's flight from New York to Paris in 1927.

The news of the safe arrival was quickly flashed to Friedrichshafen, where the time was six hours later. The *Seeblatt* newspaper rushed out an "extra" with giant headlines and a map showing the route of ZR-3. The paper's exultant prose was typical: "With the speed of the wind the joyous news of the successful landing at Lakehurst had spread through the city. On the grounds of Luftschiffbau [over a hundred] cannon shots were fired; joyous bell chimes sounded from the towers of both churches, and flag upon flag was unfurled in the lively streets." That evening, officials and workers of Luftschiffbau held a torchlight parade. After laying a wreath at a statue of Count Zeppelin, the procession made its way led by the town band to the homes of both Dürr and Arnstein ". . . and gave them tumul-

U.S. Navy sailors prepare to help land the ZR-3 Los Angeles *at Lakehurst, New Jersey after the airship's non-stop delivery flight from Germany. Hangar 1 is visible in the background, beneath the Zeppelin's control car. (Goodyear Tire and Rubber Co. Collection/University of Akron Archives)*

tuous ovations." Dürr expressed thanks "with heartfelt words." Chief constructor, Arnstein, accepted congratulations for the management and said, "All of us from the Zeppelin dock, we who saw the work rise from its beginnings, never even for a moment doubted that our Zeppelin would succeed in crossing the ocean. It was a piece of ourselves that we set free into the air Sunday with our most ardent wishes; and from the lowest rigger up to the chief engineer, we were all filled with that happy confidence without which a gigantic accomplishment, be it in a scientific or a technical field, is not conceivable. Now we have the proof. We did not expect it to be otherwise, and we must acknowledge in this joyful hour that all our expectations for this work have been fulfilled." The torchlight procession then proceeded to the lake, where the torches were extinguished in a spectacular manner by being thrown together into the Bodensee.

The airship was commemorated in prose and special medallions; even decorative blown glass Christmas ornaments featured the name "ZR-III." Arnstein's name was included in some of the over-the-top tributes to the airship and its designer after the flight that showed the enthusiasm the LZ 126 generated in Germany.

A poet, Max Heintze, was inspired to create an ode "To ZR-III," which was published in the *Ortelsburger Zeitung*. The seven rather long verses are full of national fervor, invoking the name of Count Zeppelin, the ZR-3 and its flight across the Atlantic. The fifth verse mentions Arnstein, and here it is quoted in full (in a prose translation) to give an idea of the sentiments:

> Our thanks to you, Dr. Eckener
> From all the German people.
> Because you so marvelously
> Guided the airship—so we love you.
> Also we give thanks to the constructor,
> To Dr. Arnstein.
> What you created the world has seen
> On this we all agree.
> Deutschland Hoch!
> Above all the world
> That's what they sang,
> As it rose to the vault of heaven.
> A threefold Hoch!
> Also the crew, man for man.
> That safely went so far.

With the success of the flight, Arnstein was now an even greater celebrity than he had been in the months preceding.

In the United States, the crew of ZR-3 was received with wild enthusiasm. Eckener was feted in several American cities: New York, Cleveland, Akron, Detroit, Chicago, and Milwaukee. At the invitation of President Coolidge, Eckener and flight captains Lehmann, von Schiller, and Flemming were received at the White House in Washington. President Coolidge expressed the wish that the ZR-3's safe arrival might mark the beginning of a new era of peace and friendship between Germany and the United States, erasing the feelings of hostility remaining from the war. And so it did, for a while. Secretary of the Navy Curtis D. Wilbur announced that the new airship would be christened *Los Angeles* "because it came to us like an angel of peace." Of course, it was actually named for the California city.

At Lakehurst, Arnstein's "masterpiece of German genius" was taken into the large hangar that had been built there in 1921 for the navy's rigid airships, which in 1924 numbered two: the *Shenandoah* and the new *Los Angeles*. The *Shenandoah* was not at home; it was off on a journey to the west coast with the U.S. Navy's entire supply of helium keeping it airborne and would not return until late on 25 October. The *Los Angeles* was to become the first and only German-built Zeppelin to be inflated with helium, but it had to wait for the *Shenandoah* to return to Lakehurst. Humorist Will Rogers remarked that the navy now had two rigid airships but only one set of helium.

Helium was a rare and costly substance in 1924, and could only be found as a small percentage of some natural gas deposits in the United States. The U.S. government maintained a virtual monopoly on its extraction and stockpiling (in vast underground wells) for most of the first half of the twentieth century. The most important property of helium for use in airships is that it is an inert gas and will not burn, whereas hydrogen combines readily with oxygen in the atmosphere, which is another way of saying hydrogen will burn explosively.

Helium's other main advantage is that it is the second lightest element after hydrogen. However, helium weighs nearly twice as much as hydrogen under the same conditions of pressure and temperature. The difference is only 8.8 percent, but when the usage is in airships employing millions of cubic feet, the differential amounts to tons of lift gained or lost. With the ZR-3, for example, the loss in useful lift when using helium was 18,500 pounds—almost 23 percent less lift. Despite this loss of lift, and helium's high cost and scarcity, its noninflammability compelled both the U.S. Army and U.S. Navy to adopt helium as the only lifting gas for their airships. For any new airships designed to fly with helium, the importance of decreasing structural weight by designing a more efficient structure would be much greater than before.

The *Los Angeles* had a long and honorable career. Launched in 1924, it was finally decommissioned in 1932, but even after that was used for mooring-out experiments, and its dismantling was not completed until January 1940. The airship's operational history has been well told elsewhere. In Germany it was largely forgotten—no longer a symbol of the greatness of the fatherland.

The importance of the *Los Angeles* has been overlooked, although it is arguably the most important Zeppelin ever built. Its achievements are worth summarizing here. It should be remembered that the *Los Angeles* became the first aircraft of any kind to fly across the Atlantic Ocean from mainland to mainland. And the later Zeppelins would never have been built had not the *Los Angeles* been successfully completed and flown across the Atlantic. Due to Arnstein, the *Los Angeles* introduced structural design innovations which were incorporated into the later Zeppelins. Foremost among these was the full cruciform tail—not until the *Los Angeles* were the spars of an airship's stabilizing fins extended through the hull to the opposite side. If one is to understand the later chapters of the Karl Arnstein story, it is important to remember that this cruciform was Arnstein's own design. The *Los Angeles* was the first Zeppelin for which the distinct aerodynamic loads on the tail structure were determined from wind tunnel tests. This was a modern innovation in its day, but a method that would become standard procedure. The wind tunnel work was done at the Technical University of Aachen by Wolfgang B. Klemperer for his doctoral thesis under the legendary aerodynamicist Dr. Theodor von Kármán. In its fins and control car, the *Los Angeles* introduced Arnstein's patented box girders with flanged lightening holes. Although of lesser importance, the *Los Angeles* was the first Zeppelin to have an aluminized, doped outer cover that gave it the legendary silvery appearance. It was also the first airship to have a windmill electrical generator to power the radio.

In Friedrichshafen, Arnstein prepared for his move to Akron. While Eckener and the German crew of the ZR-3 had their share of the spotlight of publicity, Arnstein had not escaped notice. Eckener and the crew would not be back from America for several weeks, so Arnstein received the attention of the local press.

The journalistic tug of war between the far right of Germany and the liberal newspapers of Prague and Vienna continued. On the one hand, Arnstein was classed with Einstein. As physics professor, Albert Einstein had been on the faculty at the German University of Prague from 1910 to 1913, so his tenure overlapped Arnstein's time at the German Technical Institute (and Arnstein had met Einstein a few times). On the other hand, the nationalists said that Arnstein was merely one among many draftsmen who knew how to use a slide rule—an obvious insult. This flurry of publicity was happily soon over. Always a modest man, Arnstein was embarrassed to be compared with Einstein, and felt as if the Arnstein portrayed in the newspapers had been someone else. Karl thought it was all completely irrelevant to his personal life and professional career.

Long-range planning for Arnstein's transfer to Goodyear-Zeppelin had been under way for months before the great transatlantic flight of the ZR-3. Arnstein realized that as vice-president in charge of engineering of the new company, he would hardly be able to devote his full time to stress analysis. He had decided to take along his two best stress analysts, Paul Helma and Kurt Bauch. Eckener had not given up hope that more Zeppelins would be built in Friedrichshafen, and would maintain at least a skeleton work force supported by the Zeppelin Fund. With Arnstein, Helma, and Bauch all gone, the chief position of chief stress analyst would be vacant.

Arnstein contacted Kármán, then the director of the Aeronautical Institute at the Technical University of Aachen, asking him to recommend a capable young engineer to fill the vacancy. After rejecting Kármán's own assistant because he did not get along with the engineers, Arnstein was sent a candidate from the math and mechanical department, Arthur Foerster. Arnstein liked Foerster, whom he found to be "intelligent and smart." Foerster had only about six months to learn his new job, which, with the help of Helma and Bauch, he quickly mastered. After their departure, he was put in charge of stress analysis, while Arnstein's other principal responsibility of structural design was taken over by another senior designer.

Arnstein wanted Paul Jaray to go to America with him, but Jaray had already left Luftschiffbau-Zeppelin and did not want to come. So Arnstein chose Wolfgang Klemperer, the young Austrian Ph.D. who had recently joined Luftschiffbau. The others to accompany Arnstein to America to build airships were: Herman Richard Liebert, of project engineering, and his assistant, Wilhelm Fischer. Benjamin Schnitzer and his assistant, Walter G. E. Mosebach, would be needed for their expertise in framework design. Eugen Brunner was chosen for work on the car and cabin structures. Leonz Rieger would specialize in engines and gasoline tank installation, while Hans Keck would supervise installation of the control system and engine room equipment. Erich Hilligardt was to oversee the electrical equipment, ballast, and signal installation, and Eugen Schoettel was selected to do the work involving the gas cells and hull outer cover.

On Saturday evening, 8 November, Colsman and Dürr gave a farewell party for the departing group in the casino (cafeteria) of the Zeppelin assembly building. Dürr gave a speech in which he regretted the engineers' departure, wished them well, and hoped that in later years it might be possible to call them back to Luftschiffbau-Zeppelin. Members of the band played, and at the end there was a dance for the young people.

Since the trip to America was to be by ocean liner, first class, it was decided that the engineers must be good representatives of their new employer, and since not one of them owned a tuxedo, each had to get one—paid for by the company.

It was time to go. Bertl and the two Arnstein children were to stay behind and to come to Akron the following spring. Arnstein and the other twelve engineers took the train to Bremen, and on 15 November stepped on board the liner *George Washington*. Also on board was Fulton, who, as U.S. Navy representative, had seen the ZR-3 project through to its successful end. They would see much more of him. Ten days later, SS *George Washington* docked in New York.

Chapter 9 TWELVE DISCIPLES IN THE NEW WORLD

Before the group disembarked at New York, Dr. Arnstein and his twelve engineers posed for photographs with a life preserver from the SS *George Washington* placed prominently in the foreground. A representative from Litchfield sent to meet the men hurried them aboard a train bound for Akron, Ohio. They did not even pause for a day's sightseeing in New York City. A contract for a rigid airship was expected soon, and there was much planning to be done. When the Germans arrived in Akron, however, they did nothing except planning for two years. The contract that Litchfield had so optimistically anticipated was slow in arriving.

Why had they come? I asked Kurt Bauch this question in 1982. Bauch was the last surviving member of the twelve disciples. He replied that the alternative was to be laid off if they had stayed in Germany. At that time it was thought that there would be no more German Zeppelins—the next big airship was to be made by Goodyear. But that expectation changed late in 1925 when Germany was granted a relaxation of limits on civil aviation. This opened the way for the Zeppelin Company to continue building airships. Soon thereafter, Eckener was able to raise enough money to start building a new Zeppelin. It would be the LZ 127, the famous *Graf Zeppelin*, which would fly in 1928. Still, for most of the group of engineers who accompanied Arnstein, the offer to work for the Goodyear-Zeppelin Company meant steady employment, a promotion, and a raise.

Any group of immigrants set down in an unfamiliar country has to make adjustments, some of them quite challenging. "Some conclude that the new locale is just a good place to visit and others are sufficiently impressed to make it their home. Fortunately, most of the engineers were of the latter type," according to Maynard L. Flickinger, who, with Harry H. Haines, was assigned to help the disciples adjust to America. The young engineer's job was to get them settled and assist in their efforts to learn local customs and ways.

Arnstein and the "twelve disciples" pose in a lifeboat of the SS George Washington *after arriving at New York in November 1924. Left-to-right, back row: Erich Hilligardt, Walter Mosebach, Wolfgang Klemperer, Paul Helma, and Wilhelm Fischer. Front row: Hans Keck, Eugen Brunner, Eugen Schoettel, Leonz Rieger, Karl Arnstein, H. R. Liebert, Ben Schnitzer, and Kurt Bauch wearing the life preserver.* (Lockheed Martin)

The disciples came from various backgrounds. Kurt Bauch was born in 1894 in Rudol-stadt, in eastern Germany. He had his first balloon flight as a young schoolboy, and was enchanted by his first glimpse of a giant Zeppelin floating high in the air above a sailboat-ing meet at Kiel in 1912. His unbounded enthusiasm for Zeppelins influenced him later to apply for work at Luftschiffbau-Zeppelin Company in Friedrichshafen.

Besides his native German, Bauch could speak Russian—at that time better than English—and after 1914 he was pressed into service by the German army as an interpreter on the Russian front. He was captured and spent a year in a Russian prison camp before being released at the end of the war. He then applied to Luftschiffbau, and was inter-viewed by Arnstein, who evidently was well impressed, for he hired Bauch for a position in Paul Helma's stress analysis department. This was the group closest to Arnstein's heart and, as Kurt Bauch would soon learn, it was the first place everyone comes when anything breaks, asking, "What happened?" He proved himself a solid, dependable engineer and a good counterbalance to the temperamental brilliance of Helma.

Although the twelve engineers were billed as "veteran designers" of Zeppelins, Kurt Bauch had only two years of experience with airships, but some of the disciples were indeed highly experienced veterans. Benjamin J. Schnitzer graduated from the Höhere Maschinenbau Schule at Esslingen, Germany, and worked for several years in the area of machine design before joining Luftschiffbau-Zeppelin in 1914. There he worked on the design of hull structures and became an assistant department manager. At the end of World War I, he joined the Naatz Airship Company in Berlin, where he was engaged in the planning and design of large **pressure airships** (blimps) using a combination of wire net-ting and envelope fabric. None of the Naatz projects were ever built, and in 1923 he returned to Luftschiffbau-Zeppelin in charge of hull structural design on LZ 126 (ZR-3) under Arnstein.

Herman R. Liebert was another veteran. If Bauch could be described as taciturn and Schnitzer as dour, the word for Liebert was jovial. A native of Dresden, Germany, he joined Luftschiffbau-Zeppelin in 1912 as a weight engineer, one of the most difficult jobs in any aircraft company. Later he moved into the new products department under Paul Jaray, where he gained some experience in applied aerodynamics, and had a part in design of Zeppelins in World War I and postwar through the LZ 126. Although in the United States his technical explanations were sometimes lost in his thick German accent, his engineering competence was soundly based on long experience, and he was both liked and respected. As head of the projection department at Goodyear-Zeppelin, he would draw up the initial plans of virtually every type of airship the company would produce.

Eugen Brunner was born in Germany to Swiss parents in 1880, and this was not his first visit to America. Brunner had come to the United States in 1905 to work in St. Louis as an engineer on the design of railroad cars and in Pittsburgh on a compressed-air locomotive. He returned to Germany and joined Luftschiffbau-Zeppelin in 1910 where he became an expert designer of airship control cars and engine gondolas. A rather small and quiet man, one of Brunner's relatives once remarked that in group photos he was always the one standing next to Arnstein. A newspaper account described him as "a short, rotund bachelor, whose life runs apparently with the regularity of a Swiss watch."

Walter Gustav Mosebach was the youngest of the group, and one of the three who was unmarried. He was born in 1901 in the village of Golbitz, Germany, and spent his childhood in another village, Schkaudiz, where his father was the school teacher and also president of the local horticultural society (it was said that people came from miles around to see his gardens and orchards). "Mosey," as Walter would become affectionately known in later years, absorbed his father's love of gardening and devoted much of his retirement to the intricately arranged flower beds and shrubbery surrounding his home.

World War I brought hard times for the young Mosebach. His father died of war wounds, and, after finishing preparatory school in 1917, Mosebach went to work in a machine shop to earn money to continue his education. He entered the Frankenhausen Polytechnic Institute in 1919, a classmate of Kurt Bauch, and by taking extra courses at night, earned degrees in both mechanical and aeronautical engineering in three years. He was hired immediately by Luftschiffbau-Zeppelin, which was seeking engineers to work on LZ 126 after the contract was signed in June 1922. A one-word characterization of him would be "genial."

Of all the disciples, Arnstein came to regard Dr. Wolfgang Benjamin Klemperer—substitute for Jaray though he may have been—as the most talented. Born in Dresden, Klemperer attended the Dresden Institute of Technology, from which he received a degree in mechanical engineering in 1920, after his education had been interrupted by World War I. He first soloed in an airplane in 1912, and served in the Austrian Air Corps from 1915 to 1918 as an observer, pilot, instructor, and designer. He was twice awarded the Medal of Valor. When the Interallied Commission placed strict limits on powered aircraft in Germany after the war, Klemperer was a leader in the movement to use gliders to keep aeronautical skills alive. He earned Soaring License No. 1 in a small glider dubbed the *Blue Mouse*.

In 1920 Klemperer went to the Technical University of Aachen and became assistant to Kármán in the aerodynamic institute there, while he studied for his doctor of engineering degree. He developed an aerodynamic theory for streamlined bodies such as airships, and in 1922 joined Luftschiffbau-Zeppelin. He worked on and completed his doctoral thesis in the period between 1922 and 1924 under Kármán, and his thesis topic concerned experimental determination of loads on the tail fins of an airship (specifically for application to LZ 126, we may be sure), a subject which had concerned Arnstein since 1915.

Leonz Rieger was the oldest, born in 1879, and a widower. He designed the engine installations, including the propellers, fuel tanks, fuel lines, and water recovery apparatus. A native of Bavaria, he had designed "gears and auxiliaries" for Luftschiffbau since 1909. He was described as "tall, scholarly, and an excellent chess player." Erich Hilligardt was to be in charge of electrical equipment for the Goodyear Zeppelins, but he would return to Germany in 1927 before the design and construction of the first Goodyear Zeppelin began. All were graduate engineers and four of the original group were Diploma Engineers. Of the remaining disciples, Eugen Schoettel was an Alsace native educated in Stuttgart who was in charge of designing the airship's outer cover, ballast bags, gas cells, and valves. Schoettel was liked by everyone. In contrast, Wilhelm Fischer was not. Kurt Bauch once remarked that Fischer would come around and try to show him how stress analysis should be done, but if anyone tried to tell Fischer anything about his own work (he was in charge of engines), he would get angry. A power plant engineer originally from Mannheim, Fischer left Goodyear-Zeppelin in the mid-1930s and worked for another American firm for a time before returning to Germany. The twelfth engineer, Hans F. Keck, adapted well to American life but transferred to the Goodyear Tire Company in the 1930s, as did Fischer, where they worked in machine design.

With the exception of Helma, all of the German engineers rented rooms near the Goodyear Company when they arrived, and later when their families arrived those who were married initially rented houses in the same area of East Akron. Arnstein rented quarters on Dopler Avenue, on the city's west side. After office hours, the Germans went to Akron University to study English. Dr. Charles Bulger, a dean and also professor of German (he had studied at Heidelberg) was a tremendous help to the Germans.

Preceding Arnstein and his disciples to Akron was Ernst Lehmann, who took up residence not too far from the Goodyear-Zeppelin company's chief, Paul W. Litchfield. Lehmann did not have very much to do; after all, he was primarily an airship pilot, and there were no Goodyear Zeppelins to be flown. He spent much of his time writing articles for the *Saturday Evening Post* and working on a book with professional writer Howard Mingos, *The Zeppelins*, which was published in 1927. Lehmann resigned from Goodyear in December 1926. He had become frustrated by the U.S. government's lack of financial support for Zeppelins in commerce. Lehmann had unrealized ambitions, and he decided to return to Luftschiffbau when it looked like Germany might once again build a Zeppelin. He became one of Eckener's captains, and after the Nazis came to power in 1933, he became de facto successor to Eckener.

The twelve disciples were not the only Germans to come to Goodyear during this early period. Another was Wilhelm Siegle, who had been in charge of erecting the LZ 126 under Dürr. But he did not adapt well to American life, and returned to Germany within six months. Arnstein always spoke highly of Siegle's vigilance in spotting and correcting problems on the ZR-3 and his speed in effecting repairs. Then there was Karl Huerttle, a specialist in fabrics and gas cells in particular, who stayed through the construction of the two rigid airships Goodyear-Zeppelin built for the U.S. Navy.

"Most of those who stayed bought automobiles and spent the weekends, Saturday noon through Sunday, sightseeing in northern Ohio and Pennsylvania," wrote Goodyear publicist Hugh Allen. And Akron had "the Liedertafel—a club originally founded in 1855 by German immigrants—where they were warmly welcomed. This association enabled them to rapidly find dentists, physicians, bakers, insurance salesmen, and so forth." Arnstein expressed his appreciation for the reception he and his engineers received: "We found that Akron, in contrast to many other cities, was exceedingly kind and helpful to newcomers." In some cases, the kindness grew into something more. Eventually, three bachelors of the group married Americans.

One of the most popular diversions for the group was card games, especially the nearly forgotten game of skat, and later, bridge. The games were often held at the engineers' homes, wives invited, and provided a much needed opportunity to socialize with friends and discuss life in their new country. When the Germans conversed among themselves they usually spoke in German. Occasionally, as time went on, they might forget when Americans were present. One of Flickinger's assignments was to check the English used by the Germans in papers and reports. Dr. Klemperer, who was very capable in handling the language, was the only one to object to this.

Arnstein also had adjustments to make. Thanks to Goodyear publicity director Hugh Allen, he was an instant celebrity when he stepped off the ship at New York. Once again, Arnstein became the subject of stories exhibiting more imagination than knowledge of their real-life subject. A story distributed by the Associated Press referred to him as "the little German Professor" (he was neither little, nor German, nor a professor) whose "favorite pastime" was "juggling figures." The press concocted an imaginary dialogue in which the Zeppelin company called him in because it had no one who "could divine the heights to which a ship could climb." Arnstein purportedly "drew forth a worn pencil and an old scratch pad, and after figuring a few moments," gave his answer.

"But how do you know you are correct?" Zeppelin officials are supposed to have asked.

"The figures say so and the figures never lie," it is said Arnstein "meekly" replied. All of

this was imaginary, but it generated interest, and nowhere was there more interest in Dr. Karl Arnstein than in Ohio, most of all in the Akron-Cleveland area.

The day after Arnstein arrived in Akron he was called upon to make a speech at a meeting of the Akron Builders' Exchange. The meeting program offered an odd mix of speakers. Ernst Lehmann talked about the airship ZR-3, and Mr. Ralph Stoddard of Cleveland spoke about business predictions for the future. Stoddard predicted great and lasting prosperity; Arnstein predicted a bright future for Zeppelins. "It will be but a very short time before regular air traffic is passing between the old world and the new," he said. "Europe and America will be linked together first; then the other continents will be joined. Already a Zeppelin has made a transatlantic trip in eighty hours that takes a ship much longer to duplicate. England and Holland are planning airship routes to India and the East Indies. Before long, great airlines will gird the earth."

He had been interviewed in New York the day before, and had said in a similar vein, "I say that I am not a dreamer, but I say also that we probably will begin at once to design at Akron an airship of 5,000,000 cubic feet capacity. . . . We do not venture to say how large

The dining room of the proposed Goodyear-Zeppelin passenger airship resembled that of an ocean liner. This artist's rendering shows it decorated in the latest style of the era.

(Goodyear Tire and Rubber Co. Collection/University of Akron Archives)

dirigibles may eventually be built. We believe they will be used primarily for fast mail and passengers with whom speed is of great importance. We believe that from the standpoint of economical operation the smallest airships will accommodate about thirty passengers. Three days for transatlantic passage will be the normal flying time."

The possibility of designing military rigid airships had not crossed his mind. Asked about them, his reported reply was, "Dirigibles for war? Really, we are trying to forget that we made Zeppelins for war purposes. Don't you think that use for them ought to be forgotten? We are thinking now only of the dirigible as a vehicle of peace—a means of commercial transit."

Litchfield was interested primarily in building a commercial airship, but he was uncertain if money to build it would be offered by the government or the private sector. Meanwhile, Litchfield had a good idea of where he would find enthusiastic support for a large airship—not for commerce but for its military potential. It was, after all, the U.S. Navy which had persuaded him to make the deal with Luftschiffbau-Zeppelin in the first place. Goodyear had recently emerged from receivership, and while the company could support a group of engineers for a reasonable time, large amounts of risk capital were not available. Goodyear had no equivalent to the Zeppelin Fund, the money-raising scheme Eckener would use to finance building airship LZ 127, the *Graf Zeppelin*. However, Litchfield believed that adapting a proven military design into a commercial airship presumably would be less expensive. Arnstein would soon become aware of Litchfield's views.

The weekly Goodyear employee paper, the *Wingfoot Clan*, was quick to note the arrival of the *Los Angeles* and to welcome Arnstein and the disciples into the company. After the initial fanfare had subsided, the reality of being strangers in a new home began to sink in. The differences in culture where apparent in December 1924, when a Christmas party was held for all of the engineers from Germany, since their families had not yet arrived. Arnstein was asked to reflect upon how Christmas was observed in his native land of Czechoslovakia. He described a scene much different from the typical holiday festivities in the American Midwest: "For Christmas dinner there is fish soup and boiled and fried carp and after dinner sweets are served. At Christmas time there are big fairs along the streets with fancy cakes for sale in their canvas booths. They sell a wonderful Christmas cake with raisins called 'Vanocka' in Czechoslovakia and 'Weinachts-Strietzel' in Austria." The mood of the party was somber: the disciples, especially those with families, missed their loved ones back in Friedrichshafen. But their mood brightened early in the new year when the paperwork was processed to allow the disciples' wives, children, and—in the case of Fischer, his fiancée—to come to the United States.

As a new vice president of a U.S. company, Arnstein indulged himself and bought an automobile: a grand 1925 Packard sedan. He had only owned bicycles before. Arnstein had a photo taken of him behind the wheel and sent it to his wife as an inducement to get her to come to Akron. Bertl was impressed, and she and the children arrived in April. Now it was Bertl's turn to adjust to life in America. The reunited Arnstein family moved into a yellow brick house at 90 North Portage Path in west Akron. The house was only about a block from a small shopping center. "To show you how European I was," recalled Bertl, "when I went to the grocery store, I put my children in a little red wagon and pulled it behind me." The family also got to ride in the Packard, in one instance taking a

"Ask the man who owns one." Arnstein, who had never owned an automobile before, sent this photograph showing him behind the wheel of his new Packard to his wife Bertl in Germany. He hoped it would be an incentive for her to bring the family to Akron. (Lockheed Martin)

trip to Buffalo, New York, to see Niagara Falls and to search for Native Americans. Arnstein had read about them in the literature of James Fenimore Cooper and Henry Wadsworth Longfellow and had seen "Indians" portrayed in Wild West movies. When he visited their reservation he was surprised—and a little disappointed—to learn that they had adopted modern ways.

Arnstein and his disciples gradually settled into their routines in Akron, and expected there soon would be an order for a new Zeppelin. Arnstein started to deliver numerous luncheon talks to the National Exchange Club, the Rotary Club, the Institute of Aeronautical Sciences, and many other local civic groups promoting the coming age of commercial airships. Meanwhile, the engineers began to work on refining designs for a new training Zeppelin in which the U.S. Navy had shown some interest. These designs were limited by the size of the Goodyear blimp hangar at Wingfoot Lake—at the time, 400 feet (122 m) in length—but that would still be enough to build an airship larger than the *Los Angeles*. In addition to a training version, Huerttle rendered elaborate pen-and-ink drawings depicting Pullman-like accommodations for a passenger version of the airship. One variation of the new Zeppelin might have compartments like those found in European railway carriages, with fold-down beds. A dining room with oval tables seating a dozen each, as in a fine hotel or ocean liner, would be featured in the center of the large cabin. Another drawing proposed a cargo-only Zeppelin, to carry the lucrative airmail over the ocean. A model of the proposed *Goodyear-Zeppelin-1*, a 5,000,000-cubic-foot (140,000 cu m) commercial airship, appeared on a parade float in Akron that summer. There were predictions that Ohio would become the "'hub' of aviation" and that airships would get the "cream of passenger and mail business." Such claims did not seem extraordinary. At the time, the airship's future as a long-range transport seemed inevitable. No winged airplane could compete. But there was a problem: Goodyear's Wingfoot Lake hangar was much too small for a 5,000,000-cubic-foot airship, which was the size Litchfield wanted to build for the U.S. Navy. There was also an advantage: the basic design of this large rigid airship could be built as a commercial variant with relatively minor modifications. In promoting his ideas, Litchfield never lost sight of his goal, which was to produce commercial rigid airships.

Why the emphasis on a 5,000,000-cubic-foot airship, other than the fact it was a nice round number and nearly double the volume of the *Los Angeles?* It had to do with the U.S. Navy's desires for future airships. Before construction of the *Shenandoah* was completed, engineers at the navy's Bureau of Aeronautics (Hunsaker, Burgess, Weyerbacher) were considering what improvements should be made on "the next airship." It was already decided that the *Shenandoah* would be inflated with helium instead of hydrogen. After the hydrogen-inflated U.S. Army semirigid airship *Roma* was destroyed by fire in 1922 with the loss of thirty-four lives it was clear the new airship must be filled with noncombustible helium. It was also recognized that the airship would have a scouting mission with the fleet. Its true value was in long-range reconnaissance as the "eyes" of the navy, not as an offensive weapon—a bomber—as the Germans had tried in World War I.

In March 1924, the navy's Bureau of Aeronautics issued a memorandum setting forth its ideas of what the new airship should be. It proposed that the bureau immediately undertake preliminary studies for a scouting airship of highly advanced design. The dimensions of the navy's Lakehurst hangar dictated that the length of the airship be less than 800 feet (244 m); this would still allow construction of an airship of 5 or 6 million cubic feet (the smaller volume was preferred), but there was no commitment to any dimensions. The memorandum was emphatic in its conviction that if a rigid airship was to have any success as a fleet scout, it would have to carry airplanes, both as a means of defense and as an extension of the airship's ability to gain information.

According to the bureau specification, the airship was to have a cruising speed of 60 to 80 knots (111 to 148 km/h) in order to launch and retrieve airplanes. The specification

called for no less than four airplanes, even though at the time, no method had been worked out for operating planes to and from an airship. Starr Truscott, head of the bureau's design team, believed it feasible, although he doubted that airplanes could be stowed inside. He was certain the means of carrying them—perhaps in an external pod—should be located at the bottom of the airship. Minimum endurance at full speed (80 knots) was to be fifty hours.

Preliminary calculations for the proposed airship had begun in the summer of 1924. To obtain a helium-inflated airship of the desired performance, the bureau's engineers were forced to move away from Truscott's 5,000,000-cubic-foot proposal and settle upon an airship of 6,000,000 cubic feet (168,000 cu m). Its dimensions were about 780 feet (238 m) long with a maximum diameter of 122 feet (37.2 m). By April 1925 the various calculations were compiled and the nameless airship was given the Bureau of Aeronautics designation Design No. 60. It was essentially little more than an enlargement of the fundamentals embodied in Arnstein's design for the *Los Angeles*.

The ZR-1 Shenandoah *was built in the United States and made its debut in 1923, the first rigid airship to be flown with inert helium as its lifting gas. Its design was derived from the German Navy Zeppelin L 49 which was forced down in France in October 1917. (The Lighter-Than-Air Society Collection/University of Akron Archives)*

It did not take Arnstein long to adjust to the realities of the situation, and trips to Washington became a necessity. Garland Fulton, upon his return from Germany, had been put in charge of the **lighter-than-air** (LTA) design section at the Bureau of Aeronautics and influenced all decisions on airship matters made by its chief, the airship-friendly Admiral Moffett. Arnstein was well acquainted with Fulton from Friedrichshafen days, and considered him a friend. However, navy developments depended then as now on appropriations from Congress, and there not much progress was being made. The United States Navy already had two big airships, and had not convincingly demonstrated a need for any more.

The 2,115,000-cubic-foot (59,220 cu m) volume *Shenandoah* had made its first flight on 4 September 1923, and was having an adventurous career that included being torn from its mooring mast in a gale (it survived and was flown back to Lakehurst) and a highly publicized round trip to the United States west coast in October 1924. Following the transcontinental flight its helium was transferred to the recently arrived ZR-3. Then the *Shenandoah* became the vehicle of choice for a planned flight to the North Pole, but it did not take place.

During a flight to the Midwest on 3 September 1925, the *Shenandoah* was caught in a violent storm over eastern Ohio, about ninety miles south of Akron. It broke up in midair and fourteen of the forty-three men aboard lost their lives. Most of the fatalities occurred when the control car broke free from the airship's hull and plummeted into a farmer's field. The middle and aft portion of the hull drifted into the valley beyond, and crumpled in a heap. But the nose section, torn from the hull, still had some of its gas cells intact. It shot upward, taking seven crewmen for a wild ride until they could valve off the helium and land safely—in a tree—twelve miles away. It was before dawn when Arnstein received a telephone call at his home in Akron, and he left the house immediately for the crash site. The other disciples gathered at Goodyear-Zeppelin's offices and once they heard the news, they also hurried to the scene of the accident. The wreckage of the 680-foot-long (207 m) craft was strewn over Noble County in a spectacular fashion that attracted reporters and photographers, sightseers and souvenir hunters, as well as the little-noticed group of engineers from the Goodyear-Zeppelin Corporation.

A Naval Court of Inquiry was convened to try to determine the cause of the disaster. Arnstein, as the structural designer of L 49 on which *Shenandoah* was modeled, was among those called to testify as an expert witness. There were two schools of thought on what caused the accident. One, led by Anton Heinen, a former Zeppelin pilot who had served as a consultant during construction and flight testing of the *Shenandoah*, attributed

The ZR-1 Shenandoah *broke up in the air during a violent thunderstorm over southeastern Ohio on the morning of 3 September 1925. The aft section with 18 men aboard floated down into a valley near the town of Ava. Within hours, crowds of people arrived at the scene, some stripping the ship's carcass for souvenirs.* (The Lighter-Than-Air Society Collection/University of Akron Archives)

the failure to an insufficient number of automatic gas valves. The commander of the airship, Zachary Lansdowne, had earlier in 1925 ordered the removal of ten of the airship's eighteen automatic valves which might allow too much costly helium to escape. When the gas expands due to heating or an increase in altitude, it fills the gas cell completely and then creates a pressure, which is relieved by the opening of the valve before the pressure can become too great. If the gas expands too rapidly, the automatic gas valves will be unable to release enough gas fast enough to prevent possible damage to the gas cell and surrounding structure. Reducing the number of automatic valves to eight limited the safe rate at which the *Shenandoah* could ascend, warned Burgess of the Bureau of Aeronautics. Lansdowne did not think the airship would encounter conditions that would cause such a rate of ascent; he argued that if it did, the sixteen manually operated maneuvering valves operated by orders from the control car could be opened.

In the violent storm over Ohio, the *Shenandoah* was driven upward at rates which finally reached 1,000 feet (305 m) per minute. Heinen argued that the resulting pressure increase in the gas cells had caused the girder structure to break up. Arnstein was called to the stand, and agreed that this might have been a contributing cause of the disaster. The judge advocate asked him to put his opinions in writing. After he returned to Akron and was doing so, he found that his calculations showed that not enough pressure increase could have occurred to damage the structure. Then he thought of something Burgess had told him. Years later, Arnstein gave this capsule description of the whole story:

Lansdowne was a bright young commander who wanted to be an admiral. He flew the *Shenandoah* all over the country and finally flew it full speed into a severe gust. The *Shenandoah* was a German design and was not built for that. But we learned a lot from the *Shenandoah*. Up until then no airship was designed for gusts—there weren't supposed to be any. It was Burgess who first realized what we were up against. 'My God,' he said, 'we haven't even considered such a thing,' and he made up the first design gust conditions, which was to consider the airship as running into a moving wall of air traveling at 30 feet per second [20 mph, or 32 km/h]. We now know we can get gusts as high as 50 feet per second [34 mph, or 54 km/h], but we don't design for them, which is why you can't just fly an airship anywhere.

As he sat at his desk, he thought of Burgess's idea of a vertical wall of air, and wrote to the judge advocate that he could no longer testify that he thought the reduction in number of valves was a cause of the accident. Arnstein now "believed it was entirely a structural failure due to the gust," and offered this as an alternative to Heinen's explanation.

From still another perspective, years later, Arnstein would say, "Eckener . . . had a fine intuition for airship flying. He met storms as a free balloon, . . . and cut power in rough weather, whereas inexperienced American pilots fought storms with full power and all the control they could muster. The loss of the *Shenandoah* illustrates this. Internal pressure could not have caused failure of the airship. The force that sheared it in half could have only come from overloaded tail surfaces fighting the gust."

Arnstein explained, "We didn't lose Zeppelins to gusts during World War I because we didn't fly them any time, anywhere. Maybe once a month, when weather conditions were just right, there would be a dash across the North Sea to drop some bombs on England." One does not encounter the thermal conditions in a maritime environment that can occur over a large land mass, with violent up and down air currents, as had the *Shenandoah*. Ironically, since that airship was derived from the wartime Zeppelin L 49, Arnstein noted: "Sometimes the weather turned bad before they got back. L 49 had been forced to land in France for that reason." If Arnstein was critical of American pilots for disregarding gusty weather, he did not spare designers.

"These airships were not designed for severe loads, and toward the end of the war, when altitude was everything, we built them even lighter." On another occasion, he remarked, "No European designer could possibly imagine the violence of weather conditions in the American Midwest." In short, the phenomenon of air turbulence and its effect on aircraft were little known or understood in 1925. Lansdowne, although he was brought up in Ohio and familiar with the summer thunderstorms of the Midwest, "could not have envisaged the severe, unpredicted disturbances that destroyed his ship and cost him his life."

Burgess and William Hovgaard, a professor of naval architecture at MIT who had become interested in airship design and analysis, testified that the type of failure apparent from examination of the wreckage and available evidence showed that it was due to external gust loadings, though they both had misgivings about the reduction in the number of gas valves. Arnstein believed Hovgaard to be one of the few individuals who made important contributions to airship analysis. However, he thought that Hovgaard's testimony admitted the possibility that the reduced number of automatic valves might have played a role in causing the failure. Arnstein believed they did not.

The *Shenandoah* had been flying over the continent to generate support for the naval airship program by showing the big dirigible to the voters who elect the Congress whose appropriations finance such programs. Of course, the dramatic disaster that overtook Lansdowne and the *Shenandoah* did nothing to improve chances for a naval appropriation for airships. Nevertheless, Moffett, in the midst of the furor, proposed a program of two 6,000,000 cubic foot airships for the fleet (essentially the Bureau of Aeronautics' Design No. 60) and a 1,250,000 cubic foot training airship. Aware of Goodyear's Wingfoot Lake hangar size limit, Arnstein realized the training airship was something they could do immediately, but the airship was never built.

In December 1925 Hovgaard offered a "technical argument" summarizing reasons for the loss of the *Shenandoah*. He made ten recommendations, many of which were followed in improving Design No. 60 for any future airships the navy would ask to have built. The main points were: (1) reduce the **fineness ratio**, the ratio of hull length to diameter, to make the airship fatter to increase resistance to bending loads (like those that broke the slender *Shenandoah*'s hull); (2) build the control car integral with the keel (the *Shenandoah*'s control had been torn loose from the hull and fell free, killing its occupants, including Lansdowne); and (3) locate the engines inside the hull (for similar reasons). Among the other requirements was one for future airships to be of 5,000,000 cubic feet "for war service and commercial operations, with one smaller airship of 1,000,000 cu. ft. for training." Maybe now Arnstein and Goodyear-Zeppelin could get some work, especially if the final recommendation was implemented: "a systematic policy to be followed in the development of rigid airships."

In the meantime, the British had initiated a new rigid airship program centered upon two 5,000,000 cubic foot airships inflated with hydrogen. Two nearly identical airships, built by competing teams, were to provide passenger and mail links to outposts of the British Empire and her commonwealths. One ship was to be built by private enterprise, namely, the Vickers Corporation, through its Airship Guarantee Trust subsidiary, and the other would be built by a government concern, the Royal Airship Works. Inevitably, they were seen as the capitalist ship and the socialist ship. If successful, they could also prove competition to Goodyear-Zeppelin's plans to build a fleet of transoceanic passenger airships. In Germany, Eckener was revitalizing the old Luftschiffbau-Zeppelin with the plan to build an even larger airship than the *Los Angeles* to demonstrate German superiority in producing and operating passenger airships.

In Akron, it seemed that the momentum of the year before was slipping away. If it did not act soon, Goodyear would lose the competitive advantage it gained in assembling its team of German engineers. This situation was frustrating to Litchfield and the disciples. But not all of the developments of past year had been negative. By December 1925, all of the German families had arrived and were settled in their new homes in Akron. In contrast to the previous year's event, that year's Christmas party in America was indeed a happy occasion.

Chapter 10 INVESTIGATIONS AND INVENTIONS

In January 1926, four months after the wreck of the *Shenandoah*, Arnstein and Litchfield were in Washington to testify before the House Naval Affairs Committee on the subject of airship patents. Litchfield was not really prepared. One of the questions directed at him was, "Are there any outstanding patents on the Zeppelin method of construction of ships, of which your company is the owner?" Litchfield replied, "I do not know how much there is to the patents. A great many of the basic patents are pretty old. We do not consider the patent situation as one of the most important features. We wanted to have all these patents made available in America, but how strong they are or how vital they are to the aircraft I am not in a position to state." Litchfield was not even sure of the number of Zeppelin patents for which Goodyear held the American rights. When questioned, he replied, "Dr. Arnstein says from 80 to 100. I thought it was from 8 to 10."

It is easy to imagine a dismayed expression coming over Arnstein's face as Litchfield dismissed the importance of the Zeppelin patents, a number of which were Arnstein's own. Patents were crucial to using the technology of the Zeppelin Company. The general principles of airship construction—such as compartmentation of gas cells or use of ring frames—were not patentable. It was only the details that were, such as *how* these structures were designed and employed. This appreciation was not taken lightly in Germany. After the war, the Zeppelin company's rival, Schütte-Lanz, sued Luftschiffbau-Zeppelin for infringement of its patents. Certain features which had appeared in Schütte-Lanz airships before they had appeared in any Zeppelin were incorporated during wartime into the Zeppelins at the insistence of the German navy in the interest of the greater good of the country, it was claimed. But after the war the matter became important to Schütte-Lanz when the Zeppelin Company began commercial operations with the *Bodensee*. The intervention of the Interallied Commission, appropriating all German rigid airships and stopping their construction, made this academic, but it was considered that the ban on airships would eventually be lifted, as in fact it was. Further, there was LZ 126, built for the United States as a commercial airship, though in the end its entire career would be with the navy. The court battle in Germany was bitter, but in August 1924 an accommodation was reached between the companies and the German government.

At the House Naval Affairs Committee on Airship Patents more surprises were to come. Another questioner asked Litchfield from whom his company had secured the American rights to German airship patents. "From the German Zeppelin Company," Litchfield replied. He was not expecting the congressman to refute this fact by claiming, "As a matter of fact, the German Zeppelin Co. does not at this time own those patents." This was news to Litchfield who answered, "I have never heard that stated, and do not believe this is so." The congressman stated it was a "matter of record" and explained that "all patents of that character were taken over by the Government during the war and transferred by the Alien Property Custodian to the Chemical Foundation Co. of this country."

Arnstein, more familiar with the patent situation—after all, many of the patents were his—replied, "About 15 of the patents are American patents which have been filed in this country, not German Zeppelin patents . . ." Litchfield no doubt tried to minimize the situation by saying, "I would say in this connection that we have never put very much weight upon these patents." If Arnstein grimaced, he could take comfort in Litchfield's rejoinder, "What we are interested in is in getting the practical experience of the Zeppelin company and the long experience which they have had in the construction of these ships . . . and have the organization to go ahead with this work."

The importance of licensing airship technology was not altogether ignored in the United States. In 1921 a company with the nondescript name of American Investigation Corporation (AIC) studied the possible use of airships for a New York to Chicago airline. AIC sought association with the patents of Schütte-Lanz. That company no longer had construction facilities, but it appeared to have the edge over Zeppelin for legal reasons and because its designs, heavily promoted by Johann Schütte, seemed more advanced. In contrast, the Zeppelin Company at that time had failed to find an American corporate backer. The AIC attracted the attention of powerful people. Among the prominent investors were William E. Boeing, president of the Boeing Airplane Company, and Marshall Field, of Chicago department store fame. Other backers included the president of Westinghouse Electrical and Manufacturing Company and the chairman of the Radio Corporation of America, as well as a former assistant secretary of the navy and unsuccessful candidate for vice president of the United States named Franklin D. Roosevelt. In fact, Roosevelt was a vice president of the company.

The lesson over patents was not lost on Goodyear-Zeppelin's vice president in charge of engineering. As Arnstein and his colleagues proceeded to develop ideas and designs for components of their planned big airship, they assiduously applied for patents where they could.

The patent "Hull Structure for Rigid Airships" was assigned to partner company Luftschiffbau-Zeppelin and provided a way to keep large-diameter Zeppelin hull rings from buckling inward, a problem as the number of small, straight segments in a ring increased. In this patent, longitudinal keel girders provided the necessary hull strength, and deep ring construction was unnecessary. The first patent Arnstein applied for after coming to the United States and his first to be assigned to Goodyear-Zeppelin was a refinement on his idea to use a "deep ring" with triangular cross section for rigid airship hulls. Connecting the rings together and running the length of the hull would be keels, built up like the deep rings, to make them much stronger than individual girders. The keels could be run the length of the hull along the top, bottom, or sides of an airship, and they would be large enough to serve as corridors for crew access (to gas cells and valves, for example) not possible with conventional rigid airship construction. Such access was a great advantage, especially in an experimental airship. Arnstein believed the "deep ring with keels" type of construction offered advantages for the construction of airships of 5,000,000 cubic feet in volume or larger.

The second patent filed after Arnstein came to the United States revisited the problem of restraining an airship's gas bags against forward or aft motion. This time he proposed a combination of slack wires and taut cord netting to overcome difficulties that appeared with previous solutions. Paul Helma was co-inventor on this patent, as he was of all of Arnstein's subsequent airship patents except one. Arnstein's solo effort concerned a way to minimize the twisting of prefabricated main rings as they were lifted and placed into an airship hull. Arnstein proposed hoisting two main rings side by side, connected by short girders to resist lateral loads. Two more Arnstein-Helma patents improved the design and fabrication of flexible bulkheads that kept gas cells in place in deep rings. Another patent granted to Arnstein, Helma, and Kurt Bauch solved the problem of fluttering of the hull's fabric cover.

It is worth noting that other members of the Goodyear-Zeppelin team were busy with patentable ideas. Schoettel, Liebert, Huerttle, Klemperer all applied for and received patents. During this period, Bauch and Helma patented the design for a non-rigid airship that would govern the design of the famous Goodyear blimps for the next half century. Most previous non-rigid or pressure airships had control cars suspended some distance below the rubberized cotton "bag" or envelope. The long cables holding the car extended upward to fan-shaped patches of fabric cemented along the outside of the envelope. All of these cables created extra drag, but were needed to keep the airship cars and their engines away from the hydrogen-filled envelopes. Inert helium was now available to inflate airships instead of flammable hydrogen, and to take advantage of this, Bauch and Helma introduced an internal cable suspension system that carried the car's weight to the top of the envelope and brought the car up snugly under the bag. This not only reduced drag, but eliminated the lengthy external cables and patches. In the patent, the internal suspension cables are not attached directly to the envelope, but transmit their load to a fabric **catenary curtain** both cemented and sewed along the upper part of the envelope. In this way, the pull of the cables can be spread over a large area rather than tug at a small patch on the envelope. In 1925, this arrangement was tried in a small Goodyear blimp, the *Pilgrim*. It would become the standard configuration for pressure airships from then on.

The *Pilgrim*, originally fitted with a bag having a capacity of 47,700 cubic feet (1336 cu m), was flown briefly inflated with hydrogen. When it was refilled with the safer alternative, it became the first helium-filled commercial nonrigid airship in the world. However, it was deflated 17 February 1926 as an austerity measure when the Goodyear Company faced a financial crisis. Once Litchfield became president of Goodyear Tire and Rubber Company in 1926, he insisted the *Pilgrim* be returned to service, and it was in 1927. Construction then began on a whole fleet of Goodyear blimps built to a new design. The prototype for these airships was the *Puritan*, which first flew in 1928. During the 1930s Goodyear operated as many as six blimps at one time.

The primary purpose of the Goodyear blimp fleet, which Litchfield dubbed "aerial yachts," was "to interest the public in the big passenger-carrying airships, the company's real objective." They also were to serve as training airships for pilots who would be needed for the big Zeppelins, and would prove to be effective as flying billboards for Goodyear's tires. They, rather than the big rigid airships, were harbingers of the airship's future, not only with Goodyear but with the navy, although Arnstein could not have suspected that at the time. In the mid- to late 1920s, Goodyear-Zeppelin focused most of its attentions to designing a large rigid airship that could be built in civilian or military versions. All they needed was a customer.

The interior of a blimp envelope undergoing an air inflation test. Catenary curtains, the scalloped strips of fabric attached lengthwise near the top of the bag, carry cables which will support the control car at the bottom of the envelope. The areas on the bag outlined by undulating light-colored lines denote reinforcing patches. These strengthened areas will hold bracing cables on the outside of the envelope to keep the tail fins in position. (Goodyear Tire and Rubber Co. Collection/University of Akron Archives)

Chapter 11 THE COMPETITION

As Karl Arnstein struggled in Akron to develop his ideas and analyze concepts for an airship acceptable to the U.S. Navy, events were taking place in Europe that would have a profound impact on his life.

When Eckener returned from the United States after the triumphant flight of ZR-3 across the Atlantic, he found the hangar in which it had been built intact. No one had begun to dismantle it, as called for by the Treaty of Versailles. Though this might be ascribed to inertia, voices were being raised among the Allies saying that destruction of the Zeppelin plant would be self-defeating and "would set the prospects of passenger aviation back by fifty years." The president of the Royal Swedish Academy of Sciences, Dr. Sven Hedin, wanted to use a Zeppelin to retrace the route of Marco Polo's journey to Peking, an idea conceived without much consideration of the operational limitations of airships. Another Swedish scientist, Dr. Svante Arrhenius, argued that demolition of the hangar at Friedrichshafen would deprive scientists of an important technological asset.

Among the Allied governments, the United States favored permitting the Germans to resume aircraft construction, France opposed it, and Britain and Italy wavered. In these circumstances, Eckener grasped at Hedin's idea, saying it was feasible, and that he would meet him in Stockholm to discuss the matter. Another organization, Aeroarctic, headed by the famous explorer Fridtjof Nansen, appeared on the scene with a plan to fly an airship across the Arctic. This project was pushed by Captain Walter Bruns, a former German army airship commander and chairman of the German section of Aeroarctic. Bruns, however, was committed to Luftschiffbau-Zeppelin's rival company Schütte-Lanz, which had in 1922 offered a design for an airship of 5,000,000 cubic feet for polar exploration. Since Schütte's hangars had already been demolished, Bruns proposed to build the airship outside of Germany. Nothing could have made Hugo Eckener more angry, for that would destroy the premise for preserving the hangar at Friedrichshafen.

Eckener had already agreed with Hedin that Luftschiffbau-Zeppelin would build an airship which "would be available to Aeroarctic for two polar flights. . . . For the rest, our company can make use of the airship as it sees fit." Nansen, at Bruns's suggestion, proposed that Aeroarctic petition the Allies for authorization to build the airship. Eckener wrote to Hedin in July 1925 that he would have nothing to do with seeking permission from the Allies, or with Aeroarctic, and would raise the funds to build the airship himself with an appeal to the German people. Eckener's irritation here was not merely with Aeroarctic, but with the Treaty of Versailles, which he felt unfairly and unreasonably put the Luftschiffbau hangars—indeed, the whole enterprise—in jeopardy.

The fund-raising campaign started slowly. A celebration of the twenty-fifth anniversary of Count Zeppelin's first flight in the LZ 1 opened the campaign at Friedrichshafen. The Zeppelin cause received a boost when the signing of the Locarno treaties in October 1925 "restored Germany to her place among the Great Powers" and allowed it entry into the League of Nations. German authorities asked for and were granted a relaxation of prohibitions on German civil aeronautics, including the size, building, and flying of airships.

In May 1926, the relationship between Eckener and Aeroarctic had been patched up by Dr. Hedin, but in this same month another airship, the Italian-built semi-rigid *Norge*, designed by General Umberto Nobile, flew from Spitsbergen across the North Pole to Alaska. This expedition was under the direction of famed Arctic and Antarctic explorer Roald Amundsen, sponsored by the Aero Club of Norway (which had built a hangar at Spitsbergen), and funded largely by the American explorer Lincoln Ellsworth, who was aboard for the flight. Interest in a polar flight by Zeppelin dwindled. Furthermore, it turned out that Aeroarctic was unable to finance the expedition it had proposed, but that did not deter Eckener in his quest to build a new dirigible.

After two years of exhausting effort, the Zeppelin-Eckener Fund had raised only 2.5 million marks of the 7 million estimated as the cost of the new airship. Eckener added 3 million marks of company money, which was enough to start construction. The German government was involved in the negotiations between Aeroarctic and Eckener from the beginning, and eventually provided an additional 1.1 million marks. With this sum, work could begin on the LZ 127, the famous *Graf Zeppelin*, a rigid airship with a gas volume of 3,900,000 cubic feet (109,000 cu m). However, the existing hangar limited the maximum diameter of the airship, so building a ship of that volume resulted in a relatively slender hull with an elongated cylindrical midsection. This configuration and Dürr's adherence to

Arnstein's structural innovations made the *Graf Zeppelin* resemble a stretched version of the *Los Angeles*.

With the airship renaissance in Germany, Goodyear-Zeppelin was no longer the last best hope for the survival of the Zeppelin. The engineers at Friedrichshafen had their hands full with the *Graf Zeppelin* and, later, with subsequent airship projects, so they would have little time to offer well-considered advice and comments to the American sister company. Quite the contrary, Arnstein was asked to come to Friedrichshafen as early as 1926 to serve as a consultant on the design of the new airship, partly to advise the capable yet still inexperienced stress analyst, Arthur Foerster.

As a civil rather than a military airship, the *Graf Zeppelin* had to meet the safety standards of the German Air Ministry. There was no great expertise in rigid airship design at the recently formed Air Ministry, so its representative, Dr. Hans Ebner, later came to Akron and asked Arnstein to look over the stress calculations for that airship. Arnstein spent a day or two going over them and told Ebner that they seemed all right and reassured him that they were done the same way as on earlier Zeppelin airships.

In the United States in 1926, there was still no contract to build a rigid airship. Arnstein knew that Goodyear would be unable to retain its staff of Zeppelin engineers if business prospects did not improve. So, during a visit to Friedrichshafen Arnstein took it upon himself to discuss with Alfred Colsman the possibility of Goodyear-Zeppelin constructing the Dornier Wal flying boat under a licensing agreement. Colsman was business manager for Luftschiffbau-Zeppelin, and general director of the entire conglomerate. He had supported Count Zeppelin's desire to set up a separate airplane construction subsidiary in his earlier days as the count's business manager. The Dornier subsidiary had found some success with its durable metal flying boat, and it became the preferred airplane for a few intrepid aviation adventurers and was purchased by several governments.

Just before Christmas, Arnstein wrote to Colsman summing up his experiences in the past year, "Since my return from Friedrichshafen, I have spent the largest part of my time outside of Akron. We were busy in Washington for weeks. It seems that President Coolidge wanted to defer the airship program, but the Congress, in particular the Committee for Naval Affairs insisted on having it at once." Arnstein remained optimistic that the airship program would survive this tug-of-war, but still thought it wise to proceed with licensing construction of the Dornier airplane by saying, "I have found in Litchfield a profound appreciation for the issue, and think of getting next time the Navy statement of requirements. . . ." Clearly, he was thinking the United States government might be a potential customer.

Claudius Dornier, whose place at Luftschiffbau Arnstein had originally been called to fill, headed the airplane branch of the Zeppelin conglomerate, and he had misgivings about the proposal. Colsman wrote Arnstein in early 1927 to tell him that Dornier was unhappy about the matter, because he feared "that if airship travel were one day to come to naught, you would arise as a competitor."

Arnstein reassured Colsman, first, regarding his own intentions. "I think that the fears of Dornier relative to my personal later competition for him are absolutely unfounded. If I should leave the field of airship structures so dear to me . . . it is highly improbable that I would go into only one related field such as airplane structures. I think that I would go back to bridge structures. And this, according to my strong conviction, will not happen, since I am more than ever convinced of the future of airship construction, though it is not at present a profitable field for action." Arnstein further tried to allay Dornier's suspicions by adding, ". . . I also cannot believe Goodyear-Zeppelin could become a competitor for Dornier. The reasons are as follows. Airplane construction is for Goodyear-Zeppelin only a means to survive, to get over hard times in airship construction. The principal business must and does remain dedicated to airship construction."

Dornier countered by coolly stating that a license agreement would only be profitable if there was a definite annual market. "In America, however, the conditions appear to be unfavorable" due to the pause in air transport undertakings. Dornier could not even begin to calculate a licensing fee without knowing how many units would be produced, but mentioned that negotiations were already underway with various American firms. However, if Arnstein could obtain in Washington promises from the army and navy, and then "communicate to us something positive, then we would, after considering the facts of the case, perhaps decide to break off other negotiations in order to concentrate on your case."

"The Navy would very much desire to place orders for prototype aircraft, especially your Wal type," Arnstein replied, but he doubted they would order more than one example. Meanwhile, Dornier transferred its sales rights to an experienced airplane designer, A. V. Verville in Detroit. Verville had business connections to Ralph Upson, Goodyear's former chief aeronautical engineer who left the rubber company in 1920 to lead the design and development of an all-metal airship. In 1927 his company, the Aircraft Development Corporation, was in direct competition with Goodyear-Zeppelin for a contract to build a navy rigid airship. It would have been awkward to have Luftschiffbau's airplane subsidiary in competition with Goodyear-Zeppelin, but as it turned out, no Dornier flying boats were built in Detroit. However, had Goodyear-Zeppelin started building flying boats, it might have had considerable impact on American aviation as well as on the city of Akron. Dornier later built an enormous flying boat in Germany, the Do-X, to demonstrate transoceanic passenger air travel. Had it been successful, it would have represented serious competition to the fleet of commercial passenger airships that Goodyear-Zeppelin had in mind.

Despite the corporate frustrations of this period, Arnstein could find some satisfaction on a personal level. In April 1926, he was honored by a doctor's degree from the Technical University of Aachen for "rationalizing airship design," as one historian has put it. In lay terms, this meant that he had led the way from empirical trial and error methods (as used by Dürr, for example) to analytical ones by developing and applying the mathematical theory of structures.

To put this honorary degree in perspective, consider that the rigid airship in the 1920s was thought to be the best, if not the only, hope for long distance travel by air. Honorary degrees are seldom given for accomplishments in minor fields, and they are generally reserved for those whose hair is gray and whose accomplishments have been authenticated by time. Arnstein was just thirty-nine. He was unable to leave his work at Goodyear-Zeppelin to go to Aachen for the ceremony. Regularly scheduled transatlantic flying was a decade away, and the *Spirit of St. Louis* was scarcely an idea in the mind of a little-known flier called Charles Lindbergh. To go would have meant taking at least two weeks for the round trip. Instead, he and Bertl celebrated by inviting the disciples, with their wives, to an evening party at the Arnstein home.

Meanwhile in Washington, D.C., numerous hearings on Capitol Hill growing out of the *Shenandoah* inquiry resulted in a five-year program that authorized the construction of two rigid airships, as well as the small Metalclad airship that Upson had been developing. However, Congress omitted to appropriate any funds for the authorized airships. Goodyear's Bill Young went to Ohio Republican Representative James Begg, who succeeded in getting a $200,000 appropriation for airships added to the fiscal 1928 navy funding bill. The amount was far short of enough to build an airship, but it was a start. It was enough that the navy could seek a contractor to help spend it. It did this by announcing a competition in early 1927.

Here at last was something that Arnstein and his engineers could sink their teeth into. Arnstein wrote to Colsman, "Our work here goes well at the start. The date for submission of our bid is May 15 of this year, and we may well know in July what outlook we have for a contract grant." Arnstein had meanwhile interested the navy in improvements to the Maybach engines used on the *Los Angeles*, resulting in "a contract of about $15,000" for engine manufacturer Maybach Motorenbau, a Zeppelin subsidiary.

Goodyear-Zeppelin not only submitted the three best of the thirty-seven designs entered in the competition, but was the only one to bid on the construction, easily winning the competition. But Congressman Begg's amendment called for one rigid airship, not two, to be built for not more than $4,500,000. The navy still wanted two airships.

Arnstein had estimated that Goodyear-Zeppelin could build two airships for $10,000,000. There would have to be some negotiations, and the estimates were carefully reviewed with the other Goodyear-Zeppelin engineers. Estimating costs for an airship of unprecedented size was itself a large and complex undertaking. The new airship was to contain 6,500,000 cubic feet of lifting gas, making it half again as large as the still unfinished *Graf Zeppelin*, more than twice as large as any previous airship, and of innovative design. Much had to be left to engineering judgment, and allowances would have to be made for unforeseeable contingencies. On the other hand, how badly did Goodyear-Zeppelin need the contract? In this case, the competition was of no concern. What was important was how much would the navy be able and willing to pay?

Arnstein was well aware that he had been in the United States more than two years without anything tangible to show to justify his presence. This contract seemed to be the only real prospect for a rigid airship. The fleet of commercial airship transports envisioned by Litchfield could not be built without a large hangar, and the hangar would not be built until there was a contract to justify its existence. As it turned out, the hangar would be built with Goodyear money as an investment in the future of airships.

It would be cheaper to build the navy a second airship to the same design as the first— there would be no need to repeat the design engineering, and lessons learned in building the first airship would reduce the probability of costly errors and waste during construction of the second. Perhaps his first cost estimate had been a little more than what could actually be expected.

Litchfield was going to Washington to negotiate with navy representatives, and he wanted Arnstein to go along to be available if needed to answer technical questions. As they sat together on the train, Arnstein told Litchfield that he could come down to $9,000,000 if it came to hard bargaining. The next morning Litchfield entered negotiations while Arnstein remained at the hotel. Arnstein was eating lunch when Litchfield came into the dining room, clapped him on the shoulder and said, "We have just agreed to a contract for $8,000,000." Telling of this in later years, Arnstein said, "I almost fainted! But Litchfield wanted that contract and he would have signed for any price."

Unfortunately, Congress had yet to provide the navy with the $8,000,000. Bill Young, who knew his way around Washington, now took the initiative. During his career, he talked to every president from Harding to Roosevelt about airships, and at one time had a speaking acquaintance with every senator and half the House of Representatives. From his sources, he learned that Coolidge, who had supposedly been anti-airship, actually had no opinion on the subject. Young obtained an appointment to see the president, and apparently convinced him of the desirability of the two airship program. On 19 March 1928, the House Committee on Naval Affairs received a communication from the president urging that funds be provided for two airships, not just one.

There was other cause for rejoicing. The Arnstein's third child and first son, Karl Frank, was born on 23 March 1928. Goodyear-Zeppelin had won the competition and funding appeared to be in hand, but no contract was immediately forthcoming. Goodyear-Zeppelin could not agree to deliver a single airship for a fixed price of $4,500,000, and the Navy Department refused to go along with a cost-plus contract. More months had gone by, and a new competitor had appeared in the form of the American Brown-Boveri Electric Corporation. It had a nominal connection to the Swiss company, Brown-Boveri Limited and was controlled by the American Shipbuilding Corporation of Camden, New Jersey. Its president was Lawrence Wilder, who has been described as an "economic buccaneer who roved the financial seas of the 1920s." Arguing airships were ships, not balloons, American Brown-Boveri claimed it could build airships cheaper than could Goodyear-Zeppelin. Structurally, a rigid airship has much more in common with an airplane than with a seagoing ship, but being essentially laymen in such matters, congressmen took Wilder's comments seriously, with the result that a new competition was ordered, to close in July 1928.

Arnstein and the other engineers at Goodyear-Zeppelin had not been idle during the interim, and entered the new competition with increased determination. They knew what the navy wanted. Prior to the 1927 competition, the Bureau of Aeronautics had modified Design No. 60, increasing the volume to about 6,500,000 cubic feet by increasing the diameter, which helped give the hull added bending resistance. The bureau further specified a deep ring design with elastic bulkheads to restrain movement of the gas cells. Clearly, the bureau was impressed by Arnstein's work on deep-ring hull design, which had been favorably described by their analyst, Burgess, in his book on airship design.

Design No. 60 was not actually a design. It was not even a preliminary design, but rather a design concept, a picture of what the Bureau of Aeronautics thought the navy should have. Design No. 60 had been conceived from the beginning as an airship that would carry airplanes aboard, primarily for advance scouting, but also to provide defense against enemy airplanes attacking the airship. The designs submitted in 1927 showed various constructions that their proponents thought would be good ways of realizing the concept.

By the due date for the 1928 competition, Goodyear-Zeppelin was able to develop and modify its 1927 proposals, providing more detail and fourteen volumes of data for three different versions of Design No. 60, labeled respectively Project I, Project II, and Project III. The first two differed in the proposed construction of the deep rings, number of engines, and hull interior details. And they incorporated three keels, with four engines aligned on each side along the lower side keels. This arrangement had been suggested by Schnitzer because of the advantages of simple design and structural efficiency if the lower side keels could contain the engines. The disadvantage was that the airflow from the forward propellers would render the aft propellers less efficient. Arnstein thought this problem could be alleviated by refining the design of the propellers, and that the structural advantages outweighed the aerodynamic disadvantages.

Inflation with helium instead of hydrogen allowed the engines to be brought inside the hull with a considerable reduction of drag, hence more speed and lower fuel consumption. Support for the engines along with overall structural requirements led to the three-keel design. The engines might still have been staggered from the keels, but there was considerable economy in design simplicity and weight, interchangeability of parts, and system testing as well as in personnel, in having the engines on one level where a single mechanic could more easily maintain them.

There would be criticism of this design feature from some quarters because it differed from German practice. These critics would have been happier with Project III, which offered an airship more nearly of the traditional Zeppelin type. It resembled an enlarged version of Arnstein's *Los Angeles*, but because of its great size, four keels ninety degrees apart, on top, sides, and bottom, were added. The bottom keel was wider to allow attachment of the control car. The eight engines were mounted in conventional power cars which were staggered around the circumference of the hull and hung from main frames. The bid price for Project III was the lowest of the three. All of the Goodyear-Zeppelin plans provided for the launching and in-hull storage of from three to five airplanes. This was a feature no previous airship had ever had, and it was essential to the bureau's conception of the airship's scouting mission.

The competition proved to be weak. Wilder and Brown-Boveri found that airship designers were not plentiful, and tried to make a deal with Schütte-Lanz. Failing that, they pirated what Schütte-Lanz data was available, and scaled it with a few modifications of their own. Schütte also offered an entry, expressly to expose Brown-Boveri. Schütte had no place to build its airship, but then neither did Goodyear or Brown-Boveri, but both were willing to build a hangar. However, Brown-Boveri was unable to provide stress analysis and other back-up data for its proposal, and neither Schütte nor Brown-Boveri offered what the navy wanted, which was spelled out in Design No. 60. The remaining short list of competitors were too inadequate to be taken seriously.

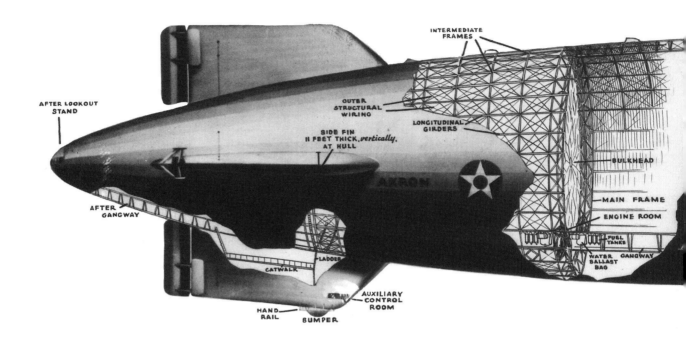

This 1931 cutaway view shows interior details of the scout-type airship Goodyear-Zeppelin was building for the U.S. Navy. A unique fea-ture is the internal hangar bay for airplanes located aft of the control car. The drawing shows a lone float plane in this hangar, not the Curtiss biplane fighters eventually chosen. (The Lighter-Than-Air Society Collection/University of Akron Archives)

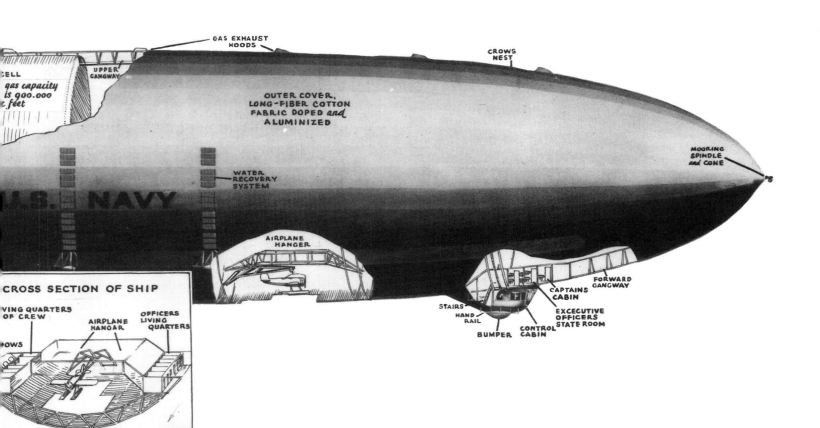

GAS EXHAUST
HOODS

CROWS
NEST

CELL

gas capacity
is 900.000
. feet

UPPER
GANGWAY

OUTER COVER,
LONG-FIBER COTTON
FABRIC DOPED and
ALUMINIZED

MOORING
SPINDLE
and CONE

U.S. NAVY

WATER
RECOVERY
SYSTEM

AIRPLANE
HANGER

FORWARD
GANGWAY

CAPTAINS
CABIN

STAIRS

HAND
RAIL

EXECUTIVE
OFFICERS
STATE ROOM

BUMPER

CONTROL
CABIN

CROSS SECTION OF SHIP

LIVING QUARTERS
OF CREW

AIRPLANE
HANGAR

OFFICERS
LIVING
QUARTERS

OWS

So Goodyear-Zeppelin's three designs won first, second, and third places, and it is hardly surprising that Project III, while rated an excellent design, was passed over in favor of the deep ring design of Project I. Project II had an undesirably complex gas cell system. The bid price of Project I was $5,450,000 for one airship and $7,995,000 for two (just under Litchfield's figure of $8,000,000), but the price bargaining was not over. Finally, on 6 October 1928 a contract was signed—$5,375,000 for one, $7,825,000 for two, with the first to be delivered within thirty months and the second airship fifteen months after that.

The contract signing was a goal Arnstein and his colleagues had worked toward for four years. It was a victory to be savored, but only briefly; too much valuable time already had been wasted. The *Graf Zeppelin* was finished and would begin its first Atlantic crossing five days later, arriving at Lakehurst exactly four years to the day since the ZR-3 landed. Construction on the British airships R 100 and R 101 was also well underway. Goodyear-Zeppelin's lead in creating a commercial airship market was now seriously threatened. Except for drawings, there was no prototype airship—and not a place to start erecting one. In building the navy's new fleet airship, Arnstein was to face the greatest challenge of his life. But first there was a hangar to build.

The contract for Goodyear-Zeppelin to build two rigid airships is signed in Washington, D.C. Goodyear's Paul W. Litchfield is seated at left, next to Secretary of the Navy Curtis D. Wilbur. Witnessing the event are, left-to-right: William C. Young, Karl Arnstein, Jerome Hunsaker (all from Goodyear), Assistant Secretary of the Navy for Aeronautics Edward P. Warner, Fred Wahl, L. H. Baker (both from Goodyear), and from the U.S. Navy's Bureau of Aeronautics, Captain Garland Fulton and M. A. Kraus. (Goodyear Tire and Rubber Co. Collection/University of Akron Archives)

Chapter 12   THE PATENTED HANGAR

Winning the first navy airship competition gave the Goodyear-Zeppelin team confidence that it soon would get a contract for a large rigid airship. It was time to decide where to build it. No one had ever created an aircraft the size of the proposed navy scouting Zeppelins. A suitable location was needed, not just for a building where the airship could be assembled, but a place free of obstructions and large enough to allow the behemoth to be maneuvered in and out of its dock for takeoffs and landings. Goodyear's existing Wingfoot Lake facility was much too small. Also, the property would not easily allow the hangar to be enlarged to the immense proportions required. Another site would have to be selected, but Litchfield was not going to erect the huge structure required until a contract to build the large navy airship was in hand. Even though the second airship competition in 1928 postponed an agreement with the government, Goodyear still expected it would be awarded a navy contract eventually. It was clear, though, that Goodyear would pay for the hangar because it would be needed for the commercial airships that would surely follow the military prototype. When the time came, it would be only prudent to have a hangar design ready to build. Arnstein began to give the subject some thought.

While a hangar was being built, the company would still need a place to fabricate the girders and interior fittings for the navy airship if there was any hope of meeting the delivery date. Goodyear's Akron factory had grown from its original site, Plant 1, with the addition of two more large buildings nearby, Plant 2 and Plant 3. Goodyear-Zeppelin used Plant 3 for its office space and its workshops for making component parts.

A mile or so south of Plant 3, an enterprising and lifelong flying enthusiast, B. E. "Shorty" Fulton, had in 1924 turned the family farm, which lay in a shallow valley, into a flying field. In the national burst of enthusiasm that followed Lindbergh's solo flight nonstop from New York to Paris by airplane in 1927, the city of Akron bought it, turned it into the Akron Municipal Airport with Fulton as manager, and soon built an art deco style terminal building. The city limits were extended to include the entire airport. But securing the Zeppelin business in Akron did not come easily. At first, a $900,000 bond issue to pay for Akron's airport failed to pass. With no airport, there would be no place to build and operate Zeppelins in Akron. At that point, other cities saw an opportunity, and invited Goodyear to move its budding Zeppelin works to their vicinity. One of these was nearby Cleveland and among others were two California cities, Los Angeles and San Diego. To see what the latter had to offer, Litchfield and Arnstein departed 5 January 1928 for California.

They inspected sites in several cities and created quite a stir. The *Los Angeles Times* headlined one story, "Los Angeles May Become World's Zeppelin Center," with the subhead, "Greatest Industrial Offer Ever Made City Comes With Unfolding of $3,000,000 Plant Plans." A second story in the same issue quoted Arnstein on the size and description of the airfield needed. "It should be one and a half miles long by one mile wide," he said, "with the length in the direction of the prevailing wind; . . . The field should lie where the flow of air above it would not be ruffled by mountains, canyons, streams, or other air current creators. And it should be located in a region were the variation between night and day temperatures is as little as possible. Especially should high tension electric wires around such a field be removed."

While in California, Arnstein would have an opportunity to be associated with one of America's most enigmatic Hollywood producers, later to be known for his exploits in aviation. In 1928, a twenty-two-year-old millionaire named Howard Hughes was producing, at unprecedented cost, a movie about the First World War in the air. The film was *Hell's Angels*, and it would have a Zeppelin sequence. For the filming, four models were built, one complete and three cruder ones. Hughes asked Arnstein to "supervise the studio drawings" from which the wartime Zeppelin models were built. After he returned to Akron, Arnstein sent photos, sketches, and blueprints of military Zeppelins. Hughes cabled Arnstein, "Received pictures and sketches cannot tell you how much we appreciate your help," and asked for information on Zeppelin markings and interior details to be airmailed to Metropolitan Studio, Hollywood. "We are building bomb room of Zeppelin at present," wrote Hughes, "and feel we could go ahead more intelligently" with some pictures or a rough sketch of the particulars. With some urgency he added, "We are holding up construction of this set waiting for these pictures or sketches from you," and sent five dollars for the cost of airmail postage. Arnstein sent the sketches and was duly noted as a "technical advisor" in the film's publicity.

When Litchfield and Arnstein went on their scouting mission to California, the *Akron Beacon Journal* began an editorial campaign to persuade Goodyear-Zeppelin to stay in Akron. The Akron Chamber of Commerce was in favor of both getting a municipal airport for the city and keeping Goodyear-Zeppelin nearby. The chamber established an Airport Committee of distinguished citizens, and on 21 February 1928, the chamber had a meeting at which the mayor, members of the city council, and other city officials were present. The Airport Committee said an airport must be secured if Goodyear-Zeppelin was to be saved for the city. It was decided that the city council should authorize a $900,000 bond issue, although it had not been specifically authorized by the voters. That afternoon the council met officially and passed the necessary legislation. With this assurance, the Airport Committee quietly acquired options on the land that would be needed.

Then nothing happened until 6 October when Goodyear-Zeppelin had a signed contract to build the two big airships. Three days later, members of the chamber and the council met with Litchfield to give assurances that the city would meet Goodyear-Zeppelin's requirements for an airport if the hangar were built at Akron. There followed much hard negotiation, and on 22 October a letter was addressed to Litchfield spelling out the combined offer of the city, the chamber of commerce, and Summit County. The city would buy 600 acres and construct and maintain an airport of that size. An additional 70 acres would be furnished for a Zeppelin mooring mast. Roads would be relocated and paved. Sewers, utilities, and airport lighting would be provided. The site would be Fulton Field, at the southeast edge of Akron, but much enlarged beyond what the small airplanes of the day required. Railroad tracks of the Baltimore and Ohio would be moved and made flush to the ground. The chamber would deed 60 acres for the hangar. Summit County agreed to cooperate with changes in roads and to Akron's city limits. On 27 October Litchfield replied that upon completion of the city's plans, Goodyear-Zeppelin would build its hangar at the site indicated, and expressed appreciation for their enthusiasm and cooperation in "the development of Akron as one of the greatest centers of the world in air transportation." Around Akron, people were beginning to call their town the "Friedrichshafen of America."

Now that a location for the hangar was determined, what was needed next was a building. It must be large enough to house the proposed airship during its construction, as well as afterward, and shelter it from the weather—in aeronautical terms, a hangar.

The size of airship which the navy wanted was by this time fixed at around 7,000,000 cubic feet (the completed airships had 6,850,000 cubic feet of gas volume and air displacement of 7,400,000 cubic feet). The forward-looking Litchfield came to Arnstein and said, "Let's not limit ourselves for all time to this size of airship. Make the hangar big enough for a 10,000,000 cubic foot airship." So Arnstein made it big enough for a 15,000,000 cubic foot airship. He later qualified that by saying, "Fifteen million might be a tight fit, but I'm sure you could build a twelve million cubic footer."

Wind can be the greatest enemy of a balloon, and an airship is simply a steerable (dirigible) balloon. On a calm day, taking an airship out of its hangar is a straightforward task. In a crosswind, or a gusty one, an airship halfway out the door could easily be blown against the side of the doorway with possibly severe damage despite all the ground handlers' efforts. With square-ended hangars like those in Friedrichshafen, the problem was aggravated by the swirling of the wind around sharp corners of the building and doors. Wind velocity close in could be twice as great as in the open. The difficulties were alleviated when the wind flowed along the length of the hangar, and Count Zeppelin's original floating hangar had been designed to permit its being rotated into the wind. However, a water-based hangar is vulnerable to stormy weather, and there was considerable inconvenience in building an airship over water. At any rate, that approach was not entertained. Stationary land-based hangars could be situated so that most of the time their doors faced into the prevailing winds (though winds are notoriously fickle).

For the least troublesome hangar shape, Arnstein conceived a long, cylindrical shell of parabolic cross section, arching over the airship inside and supported at intervals by girder arches of the same contour. To minimize the eddying of the wind around the doors, they would be shaped like segments of a parabolic orange peel, with two doors at either end opening like the half shells of a clam. At ground level, the doors would travel on a semicircular track to leave an opening the full width of the hangar, while causing only minor disturbance to the flow of the wind.

A scale model was made, and Dr. Klemperer was given the task of testing it in the wind tunnel. The test served not only to verify the concept, but to determine the distribution of the pressure over the unconventionally shaped structure. To a stress analyst like Arnstein, this was most important since it determined the distribution of the stresses in the structure, and therefore the design of the members of which it consisted. Laymen may be surprised to learn that suction pressures on the lee side of ground structures may be more critical than the direct pressures on the windward side, and furthermore, that a lifting force occurs which if great enough, may remove roofs. In the 1920s, it was still a common practice to ignore these other considerations and design simply for the direct impact pressure on the windward face. Not so with Arnstein, and especially not with this building. The wind tunnel results showed that, for this hangar, a broadside wind created positive pres-

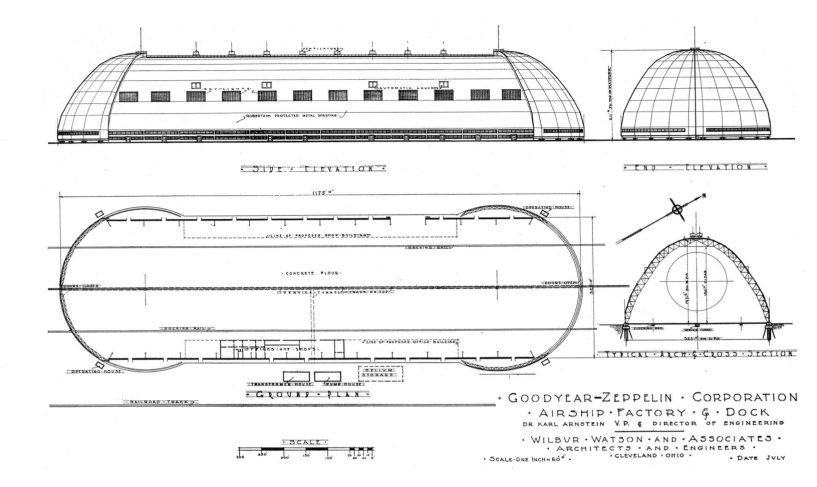

Plan views of the Goodyear-Zeppelin Air Dock. The aerodynamic shape of the structure was patentable. (Goodyear Tire and Rubber Co. Collection/University of Akron Archives)

sure only over about half of the lower windward side, and suction over the remainder and the entire leeward side. If there was any concern, it was not that the hangar would be blown down, but that wind action would pull up its roof. Hundreds of wind deflection calculations attest to the thoroughness of the analysis. Arnstein and his team designed the structure to resist these forces, and he was proud that this huge building had been designed for aerodynamic loads and not according to the conventional wind load criteria of the time. The result was a structure that would be not only the world's largest airship hangar, it would be the world's largest building without interior supports. It would maintain that distinction for nearly four decades.

William C. State, an exceptionally capable engineer who had been with Goodyear since 1901, was by the mid-1920s head of Goodyear plant engineering. There was hardly a more important plant to be built than what Litchfield called the Air Dock, so State transferred to Goodyear-Zeppelin with the title of consulting engineer. For the construction, he brought in Wilbur Watson and Associates of Cleveland. Arnstein had provided the conceptual design of the Air Dock. He now gave Paul Helma, head of his stress analysis department, the task of investigating the structural design. Helma found that the design was not only aerodynamically advantageous, but also economical in weight of steel. Structural efficiency is measured by comparing relative weights of the alternate designs; and although weight in a building is not as important as in an aircraft, structural steel was bought by the pound. Helma also contributed a system of bracing between the arches that relieved the bending and shear forces in the arch girders themselves, and provided lateral stiffening.

Goodyear-Zeppelin's small force of engineers was needed for design and analysis of the airship itself, so a contract was let to the structural engineering firm of Wilbur Watson and Associates for the detail design and erection of the structure. As developed by Watson and his designers, eleven main arches eighty feet apart provided the primary structure, with the arches interconnected by a bracing system proposed by Helma. Only the middle three arches are fixed into the ground. The remaining four on either side sit on rollers to accommodate expansion and contraction of the structure along its length due to temperature variation. At the ends, each of the two door leaves are attached at the top by a floating pin six feet long and seventeen inches in diameter. The four six-hundred-ton doors roll on a standard-gauge railroad track with forty wheels, propelled by a gear five feet in diameter engaging a toothed rack girdling the lower part of each door. One 125-horsepower electric motor and "machinery such as might be required for a long bascule bridge" provided the power to move the doors at speeds up to forty feet per minute and to stop them.

The Air Dock, except for its size, was not entirely unique in its general configuration. One day, State discovered some drawings in the journal of the Society of German Engineers (Verein der Deutsche Ingenieure) that looked familiar. They showed, that, unknown to Arnstein, there were hangars built for DELAG in 1913 at Dresden, Liegnitz, and Posen similar in external appearance to the Air Dock, but much smaller.

On 29 October 1928, with the navy contract for two large rigid airships safely in his pocket, Arnstein optimistically announced to the press: "We expect the hangar for the new navy dirigibles to be completed and ready for starting the assembling of the first dirigible at Fulton Field by next April or May." Construction of the Air Dock began in November, with an earthmoving operation to level the marshy area, clear tree stumps, and to install a large pipe to carry the stream underground and across the airport field. The valley floor consisted of about two feet of muck and twenty-eight feet of sand, gravel, and clay underlaid by solid sandstone. It was deemed best to remove more than a million cubic yards of earth and replace it with six feet of gravel and clay from the adjacent hillside. Reinforced concrete pilings twenty-five feet long, both vertical and inclined, were driven to rock to provide the arch footings—1,300 piles in all. A concrete floor was poured six inches thick onto a six-inch base, using 7,000 cubic yards of mix.

In March 1929, Arnstein, Helma, and Watson applied for a patent for their "Aircraft Hangar and Method of Building It." Neither the parabolic arches nor the orange peel doors were patentable, but the method of accommodating thermal expansion and contraction of the structure was considered unique.

Erection of steel did not start until 20 April 1929, and the first set of arches went up on 22 May, using locomotive cranes with gooseneck booms. Ingeniously, the pre-assembled top of each arch was lifted above the two partially completed sides by a series of counterweights. Temporarily pried open, the sides were allowed to settle back to connect with the arch top once it was brought up through the gap. By using an around-the-clock effort employing eight gangs of riveters, the last arch went into place on 19 September. The south door was put in place and closed by 1 September, and the north doors by 25 November. At first, only the bare skeleton of structural steel was erected; even the doors were put up this way. Incombustible corrugated metal sheathing was added as the work progressed. The roofing was not completed until February 1930. Construction of the first Goodyear rigid airship's ring frames had begun at the enclosed end in early November 1929, before the dock was fully clad at its other end.

Built in eleven months for a cost of $2,250,000, the Air Dock was an engineering marvel featuring gas-tight electrical fixtures, underground helium storage tanks and a pair of clever, swiveling "inclined railway" elevators. During its construction it attracted a stream of dignitaries, and received accolades from Eckener and other aviation notables.

The hangar as finally built had slightly larger dimensions than the one originally proposed by Arnstein in early 1928. According to builder Wilbur Watson, the length was 1,175 feet (358 m), its width 325 feet (99 m) and its height 197.5 feet (60 m). The height from the floor to the platform at the top measured 211 feet (64 m).

Statistics about its interior floor area (364,000 sq ft or 33,852 sq m), roof area (693,000 sq ft or 64,450 sq m), and cubic content (55,000,000 cu ft or 1,540,000 cu m) begged more real-world comparisons. The Air Dock's height is equal to a twenty-two-story building, and the eight and one-half acres (3.4 hectares) of floor would accommodate seven football

Looking toward the north end of the Air Dock on 3 October 1929. Much of the exterior cladding is in place, but the arching doors attached to 6-foot pins 200 feet high have yet to be covered. Construction of the first Goodyear Zeppelin would begin in the Air Dock before the giant hangar was finished. (Goodyear Tire and Rubber Co. Collection/University of Akron Archives)

fields. It was said to be large enough to hold the Washington Monument and the Woolworth Building tipped on their sides, plus the 1920s U.S. Navy aircraft carriers *Lexington* and *Saratoga* with room to spare. Public relations people created photo illustrations that placed the Air Dock alongside the U.S. Capitol or perched the Air Dock spanning the cataract on the American side of Niagara Falls.

Painted black all over, since in physics a black body is the most effective radiator of heat, the Air Dock for years sported the words "Goodyear-Zeppelin" in letters twenty feet high along its sides. On a clear day, its distinctive loaf shape is visible to approaching aircraft from at least twenty miles away. It became the model for a similar steel hangar the navy started building in 1931 at Sunnyvale, California (1,117 by 308 by 198 feet overall), and smaller versions erected in Weeksville, North Carolina, and South Weymouth, Massachusetts, during World War II.

The Air Dock may not be as well known as the Golden Gate Bridge or Eiffel Tower, but it is not unappreciated. It is designated a National Historic Civil Engineering Landmark, is on the National Register of Historic Places, and is listed as a National Historic Site by the U.S. Department of the Interior. Although rarely used as an airship shelter nowadays, it still fascinates as a monument to the Zeppelin era. During a rare open house for a United Way campaign event in 1986, the giant hangar attracted 300,000 curious sightseers. One of Goodyear's 202,000-cubic-foot-volume blimps seemed lost in its vastness. It fit comfortably within the semicircle of just one of the orange peel doors.

One of the most persistent stories about the Air Dock became a subject for the newspaper feature, Ripley's "Believe It Or Not," in 1930. The Air Dock was said to be so large that it had its own weather, specifically, that "sudden changes of temperature cause clouds to form inside the hangar—and rain falls." Arnstein claimed this story was "somewhat exaggerated" and offered a less sensational explanation of the phenomenon, which results mainly from the fact that, except for offices along the walls, the interior space is not temperature controlled. He explained, "The actual facts are as follows: On a particularly foggy morning the relative humidity inside the dock was very high. A sudden temperature drop caused condensation of some of this moisture which fell to the floor in a mist. Whether the amount of water which fell merits the title 'rain' is somewhat questionable."

Early on, there were plans to build an identical hangar side by side with the patented Air Dock, one for construction or maintenance, one to serve as a dock for the fleet of a dozen or so ocean-hopping commercial Zeppelins that Litchfield hoped to build. Unfortunately, Akron would never achieve Litchfield's vision as a center of world air transportation. The promise of the commercial rigid airship was never fulfilled. Still, the city's investment was well repaid during World War II, when the Air Dock became the nucleus of a complex of five huge plants employing, at its peak, 30,000 people.

One oddity surfaced a couple of decades later, in the 1960s, when Akron initiated a city income tax. The city and county, in redrawing the city limits, had offered one more gift to the infant company. The boundary was drawn around three sides of the site, leaving the Air Dock in the county, thus permitting Goodyear-Zeppelin to avoid city taxes. During the wartime expansion, such niceties were ignored; when the city income tax was passed, it was found that of two employees at desks side by side in one of the new buildings, one might have to pay the tax while his neighbor did not.

Chapter 13 A GOODYEAR ZEPPELIN TO BUILD

"Out of sight, out of mind" would never make a good motto for a rigid airship captain, especially where it concerned his ability to see the airship's lower fin from the control car. The lower fin was most vulnerable from an operational perspective, since it carried the rudder surface closest to the ground, and was inconveniently located far away from the cabin where the airship was steered through the sky. The distances involved were equivalent to a few city blocks in the case of an airship like the *Graf Zeppelin* or the one proposed in Design No. 60. If your tail were that far away, you would worry about what harm might befall it if it could not be seen. An invisible tail fin was something to be avoided.

In 1928, Arnstein was preoccupied with project detail and analysis of the structure for the navy's Design No. 60, soon to be designated the ZRS-class airship ("Z" for lighter-than-air, "R" for rigid, "S" for scout)—still the largest aircraft ever built in the western hemisphere. To a professional stress analyst like Karl Arnstein, what had gone before was little more than drawing pretty pictures. True, much thought had been given to the preliminary design and some preliminary calculations had been carried out, but now it was time for action.

The immensity of the design and analysis task may be illuminated by some figures. The airship's structure was 785 feet (239 m) long and contained twelve gas cells separated by eleven main rings, typically 74 feet (22.6 m) apart. There were three triangular keels running the length of the ship: one at the top served as a spine and two more forty-five degrees up from the bottom centerline provided strength against bending, and facilitated access to the structure. Together, these rings and keels served as the primary structure. Neither the rings nor keel were simply single girders connected end to end, however. Rather, the rings were deep rings, actually a ring with in a ring, with the inner ring connected to two closely joined outer rings. A cross-sectional slice through a ring would reveal a triangular girder structure about eight feet on a side. Between the main rings were typically three simpler auxiliary rings for secondary support. The keels formed triangular corridors along the airship's length, connecting the rings. If a ring were a clock, the keels were attached at roughly the 12, 4, and 8 o'clock positions. Parallel to the keels, intermediate girders filled out the spaces to give the hull thirty-six sides. Along its length, the airship's curved, streamlined contour actually was composed of many short, straight girders linking the rings. The girders were Arnstein's patented box girders with flanged lightening holes. This practical solution to obtaining a smooth shape produced a multitude of girder joints, and a three-view drawing had to be made for each unique joint. In all, more than 20,000 detail drawings were made to guide the men who would assemble the airship's parts. The size and complexity of the construction project necessitated the hiring of additional engineers and draftsmen.

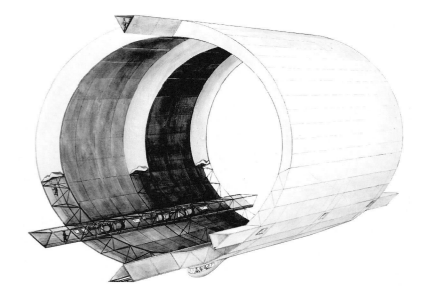

Besides the main hull, there were many other structures to be considered: the tail fins and control surfaces, each as tall as a house; the engine and propeller support structures; the control car with its command and control systems; the nose and mooring cone; and the airplane hangar, which was designed to house five airplanes. The airplane hangars within the airships ZRS-4 and ZRS-5 were unique—no other hangar was ever airborne, before or since.

The gas cells had to be designed to fit into their assigned spaces, shaped around the deep rings and held in place by ramie cord netting. The airship's engines and propellers, control mechanisms, fuel tanks and a water ballast system, a galley and crew accommodations, an electrical system and radio equipment, gas valves and catwalks, and sundry other details primarily of a nonstructural nature also had to be provided.

The main features of the two navy airships to be built had already been outlined by Arnstein in a paper published in early 1928 entitled, "The Development of Large Commercial Rigid Airships." That title may seem to be a misnomer, but all along it had been the idea of both Litchfield and Arnstein (not to mention Eckener in Germany and the builders of the British rigid airships R 100 and R 101 in England) to develop airships for long distances, especially transoceanic travel. Developing an airship for the navy was only a step toward that goal—an essential and important step, the one that gave them confidence that it was all going to happen as the visions of the 1920s foretold.

The principal elements of the "deep-ring design" rigid airship hull are seen in this illustration. The main rings are built up to a triangular cross-section. Similarly-shaped keels run lengthwise at the top and bottom of the hull and part way up the hull sides at the four and eight o'clock positions. The keels provide strength and support loads such as fuel and ballast tanks, engines, and cargo. The rings and keels also provide corridors to allow the airship's crew access throughout the hull interior. (Goodyear Tire and Rubber Co. Collection/University of Akron Archives)

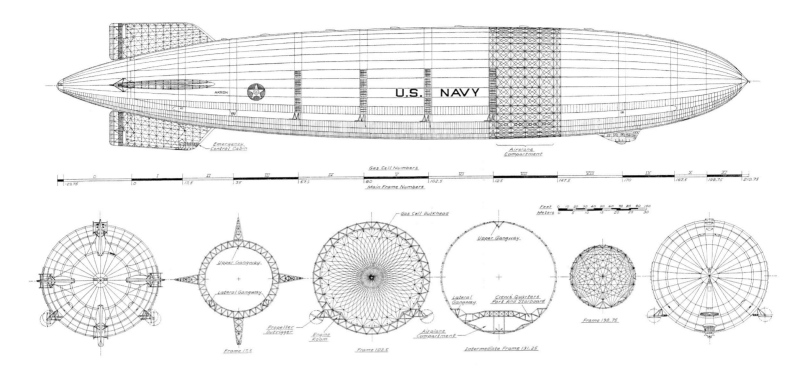

Plan view of the ZRS-4 USS Akron. *The linear scale shows location and number of the gas cells (in Roman numerals) and main frame numbers as measured along the hull in meters. Note that the tail fins are supported by only two main rings, at station 0 and 17.5. Cross-sectional views show features of the main and intermediate rings, and the intricate pattern of the gas cell bulkheads. (Drawing by William F. Kerka)*

Arnstein considered the two navy ships to be experimental airships, test beds for the ultimate commercial vehicle. Even the *Los Angeles* was supposed to be merely a training airship for pilots—commercial as well as navy—and had passenger accommodations unlike the spare furnishings typical of most navy craft. The navy wanted to develop an airship building firm that would supply its future needs, and encouraging a firm to sustain itself by building commercial Zeppelins was very much in the navy's interest.

The optimism at Goodyear-Zeppelin mirrored a national sense of euphoria as 1929 began. The new president, Herbert Hoover, was inaugurated in March. It was a time of prosperity and a rising stock market. Business prospects in general seemed promising, and that was favorable to promoting air commerce, especially the need for transoceanic airships to carry passengers and mail. More than just engineering expertise was needed, and Litchfield hired two additional vice presidents for Goodyear-Zeppelin. One was Dr. Jerome C. Hunsaker, who had served twenty-one years in the navy before resigning his commission in 1926 to take a position in research and development at Bell Telephone Laboratories in New Jersey. During his navy career, Hunsaker had led the navy's design effort on the wartime non-rigid airships, and later on the first American rigid airship, the *Shenandoah*. He also conducted aerodynamic research, developed an aeronautical engineering curriculum at MIT, built the first wind tunnel there, and traveled abroad in connection with his research and as a naval attaché. In his later years he would head the aeronautical engineering department at MIT and serve as the last head of the National Advisory Committee for Aeronautics (NACA) before it was transformed into the National Aeronautics and Space Administration (NASA). In short, he was a distinguished engineer and a fine addition to the staff. Litchfield wanted him to develop a commercial airship operating company. Actually, three different transport companies were organized on paper: International Zeppelin Transport and Pacific Zeppelin Transport, and several years later, the American Zeppelin Transport Company. Considerable planning went into collecting weather data, selecting routes, and determining costs. Efforts were made to track legislation that could benefit airship transportation and lobby on their behalf. The missing ingredient remained someone to purchase the airships.

The other new vice president was Fred M. Harpham, "an Akron businessman, distinguished for his common sense." He was put in charge of the business administration of Goodyear-Zeppelin, which included coordinating relations between Goodyear-Zeppelin and Goodyear Tire and Rubber, the parent company. Surprisingly, it was not Goodyear-Zeppelin with its airship expertise that operated the small pressure airships, the blimps, but the tire company. The blimps were part of its advertising and public relations, and Airship Operations maintained personnel, equipment, and facilities separate from Goodyear-Zeppelin (although there was some interchange between the departments and, of course, Goodyear-Zeppelin did manufacture the aircraft). Business matters concerned with blimp operations became a major part of Harpham's responsibility, especially when the fleet grew to six airships in 1929. These "aerial ambassadors" toured the country promoting Goodyear tires. The blimp fleet today is still regarded as Goodyear's most effective advertising medium.

Besides those two appointments, Harry Vissering, who had started it all back in the Harding administration, was made a director of Goodyear-Zeppelin. Arnstein, too, added some new young engineers to his staff, made up of the engineers who came from Germany with him and members of the old Goodyear aeronautical department. The new engineers included among others Thomas A. Knowles, who would later become president of Goodyear Aircraft, the successor company to Goodyear-Zeppelin; Oscar W. Loudenslager, who would later become head of research and development; and Donald W. "D. W." Brown, then a young draftsman who would later become manager of engineering administration. Long afterward, Brown remarked how lucky he was to have been hired

On 24 May 1929 Mrs. Karl Arnstein christened the Goodyear blimp Mayflower *by breaking a flask of liquified air over the control car railing. Dr. Arnstein is standing directly behind his wife, while Goodyear executives, including Fred Harpham, watch at right.*
(Goodyear Tire and Rubber Co.)

two weeks before the great stock market crash of 29 October 1929. Arnstein personally interviewed every engineer hired at Goodyear-Zeppelin, and later at Goodyear Aircraft, until the influx of new employees became too great for that to be practicable.

Meanwhile, things were also happening in Germany. Theodor Kármán at the Technical University of Aachen noticed a tide of nationalism and anti-Semitism rising. As a Hungarian Jew, he decided to investigate discreetly opportunities in the United States, and in 1929 he was offered a position as director of the Guggenheim Aeronautical Laboratory at the California Institute of Technology. As an added inducement, he was told that a branch of the laboratory for airship studies (ultimately known as Daniel Guggenheim Airship Institute) was expected to be set up in Akron, Ohio. In December 1929, Kármán moved to the United States on leave from the University of Aachen. He had made aerodynamic studies for airships, and in fact, had been Klemperer's mentor, and had found Arthur Foerster for Arnstein and Luftschiffbau. Karl regarded him as a friend, Kármán having visited Friedrichshafen and the Zeppelin works in 1924 at Arnstein's invitation.

The aeronautical event of 1929, however, was the flight around the world by the *Graf Zeppelin* in August. Dreaming about such a trip and making it happen are entirely different matters, and although they had their differences, Arnstein still considered Eckener to be "the world's greatest diplomat" and respected his ability as a Zeppelin promoter. Eckener had given the possibility of a globe-circling flight serious thought during the previous winter. From Friedrichshafen, the *Graf* would fly to Tokyo, where the Japanese had erected a hangar acquired as reparations from Germany after World War I. Tokyo to San Francisco (later changed to Los Angeles) would be the next leg of the journey. The third leg would be from there to Lakehurst, and the final one back to Friedrichshafen.

But how would it be financed? The German government gave Eckener no encouragement. A surprise offer came from the American newspaper tycoon, William Randolph Hearst, who saw that the story of this adventurous flight would sell newspapers. He would pay nearly half the expense of the flight in return for the rights to the story—but with the stipulation that the flight would start and end in the United States. Some German newspapers agreed to pay a much smaller amount, and the rest was made up by mail carried for stamp collectors and the passengers who wanted to be aboard.

So on 1 August 1929, the *Graf Zeppelin* departed from Friedrichshafen for Lakehurst, where it began the official around-the-world flight, and on 8 August left Lakehurst for Friedrichshafen, circled the globe, and after a remarkable voyage, arrived safely back at Lakehurst on 29 August. The lap around the earth was completed in 21 days, counting layovers, or in 11 days, 20 hours, and 34 minutes of flying time. The *Graf* was the first passenger aircraft to make such a flight. The airship then continued once more to Friedrichs-hafen, where its arrival was acclaimed by the nationalistic German press as the true completion of the world flight. Eckener was acclaimed a hero, and there was serious talk about making him president of the republic. However, the commander of the airship was not aboard for the final Lakehurst-Friedrichshafen flight, nor was the passenger list the same. Among those who left the airship at Lakehurst was Commander Charles E. Rosendahl, the U.S. Navy's observer and experienced airshipman, who had survived the *Shenandoah* disaster by free-ballooning the broken nose section to a safe landing.

The *Graf*'s voyage had been marred by one mishap. The Los Angeles airport at Mines Field (site of present-day Los Angeles International Airport) proved to be a less than ideal site for a one-day layover. As the *Graf* circled in the early morning hours before landing, Eckener discovered that there was a temperature inversion—not unusual in the Los Angeles area. The temperature on the ground was colder, while at altitude it was ten degrees warmer and therefore less dense. The airship was more buoyant on the denser, cooler air. To descend through it to land, Eckener had to valve a large amount of hydrogen.

Moored on the field during the day, the heat of the sun caused more gas to be vented from the airship. This was replenished, as was fuel, but the airship was still too heavy to lift off, even though Eckener already had ordered some of the crew to go to Lakehurst by other means. The airship floated in the cool, dense air near the ground but would not rise into the warmer, thinner air above, so Eckener tried to use engine thrust and the aerodynamic lift generated by the shape of the airship's hull. To do that, he had to gain as much speed as possible to get the airship's nose pointing slightly up.

That maneuver seemed to be going all right, but the high tension power lines running across one end of the field at a height of sixty-five feet suddenly loomed in front of Eckener. He could only apply more elevator to tilt the nose up, but this also brings the tail down, and the lower fin hit the ground and scraped. The airship rose, and as it cleared the obstacle, Eckener leveled the airship to ensure that that lower fin would not snag the wires. The fin was damaged, but not seriously, by its impact with the ground. Boxes, cans, vegetables, and cases of ginger ale left behind on the field testified to the struggle to lighten the airship and to get airborne. The *Graf* had escaped disaster by a narrow margin.

Rosendahl, who would become the first commander of the ZRS-4, stood in the control car and watched Eckener's maneuvers with alarm as the airship took off. He later described the episode as "just about the closest call and the most hair-raising experience of my life." Eckener himself admitted to "being numb afterward." At the most heart-pounding part of the maneuver to clear the electric wires, Eckener had to rely on his feel for the airship to avoid disaster. From his position, he could not see if the lower fin would

The Graf Zeppelin *(LZ 127) moors at Mines Field, Los Angeles during its world flight in 1929. The Goodyear blimp* Volunteer *flies in the distance. (Lockheed Martin Collection/University of Akron Archives)*

clear the obstruction. It would be much better if future airships were designed so that the lower fin could be seen from the control car. The desire for this feature would have far-reaching consequences that no one could possibly understand at that moment.

When Eckener got off the *Graf Zeppelin* in Lakehurst, he had business in Akron, and among those greeting him was Arnstein. Eckener also wanted to talk to Hunsaker about plans for an international Zeppelin airship line. It was a few days after the *Graf*'s circumnavigation of the earth according to the rules set by Mr. Hearst, that Maynard "Flick" Flickinger recalled looking up from his drafting table to see a conference going on in Arnstein's office. Dr. Eckener was visiting. Since 1926, when he was assigned to preliminary design, Flick shared an office with Liebert and Fischer, two of the German contingent, and by 1929 he was a well-trusted designer.

Shortly thereafter, Arnstein and Eckener came out to Flick's table. The contract for the ZRS-4 and 5 airships had been signed nearly a year before, and the design was well along, but they were discussing a change in the tail fin. Eckener had not flown an airship since at least 1919 in which he could see the lower fin without leaving his control position, so Eckener's experience at Mines Field must have made an indelible impression. "I like to be able to see the bottom of the lower fin from the control car," Eckener said. Flick was asked to make a drawing showing the control car floor lowered by eleven inches. A second part of the job was to increase the span of the lower fin without increasing its area. That task was assigned to Liebert. There were two reasons the lower fin could not be seen from the control car: the control car itself was reduced to a small bump on the hull for aerodynamic reasons, and the ZRS-4 and 5 hulls were more plump in the middle than previous rigid airships. While this blocked the view fore and aft, a broadly curving hull was preferred because it was less susceptible to bending, just as a short, thick twig is more difficult to snap in two than a long, thin one (this was a concern following the destruction of the long, narrow-hulled *Shenandoah* by excessive wind forces). It had not been possible to see the lower fin of the *Graf Zeppelin* from its control car because the car was placed far forward on the hull in order to construct the airship with the largest diameter possible within the height limitations of the hangar at Friedrichshafen. In retrospect, the importance Eckener placed on seeing the lower fin from the control car is questionable. None of the later German-built Zeppelins would allow this view, and had Eckener insisted on this feature, it is likely that Dürr would have obliged.

However, in the autumn of 1929, no one questioned the need for a visible fin. The gist of the discussion in Akron was apparently not long in being transmitted to the U.S. Navy's Bureau of Aeronautics in Washington. In December 1929, the navy expressed its concern that the control car and fins as they existed on Goodyear's winning Project I proposal made it impossible to see the lower fin from the control car. Burgess addressed this issue in a design memorandum that began, "Operating experience has shown the importance of giving the commanding officer and the elevator man of a rigid airship a clear view of the lower edges of the bottom fin and rudder, in order to avoid striking them against the ground when taking off." Rosendahl also thought it necessary to "have visual communication between the control car and the auxiliary control station in the fin's leading edge." The memorandum discussed five solutions to the problem of seeing the lower fin. None included increasing the breadth of the fins. Burgess considered moving the control car aft, lowering the steering positions by means of a double-deck control car, and using a retractable rearview mirror in which the altitude control pilot could see the fin. Two additional solutions were rejected as impractical. Moving the car aft was considered the best means of making the fin visible, but it would then interfere with the airplane hangar, which was already as far aft as it could be without interfering with the engines.

After further discussions the following spring, an official Change Order No. 2 was issued in July 1930 directing that the airship's control car be moved back about eight feet and its floor lowered about twenty inches. Additionally, the original long, slender fins were shortened in the fore-and-aft direction and lengthened outward to achieve the desired results. All four fins were altered instead of just the lower one because deeper fins were more efficient aerodynamically and gave better control at low speeds, and they were treated the same in the interest of symmetry.

But there were consequences at the joints where the fins attached to the hull. Goodyear's accepted Project I design called for the fins to attach to the hull at three strong points each, at main deep rings 0, 17.5, and 35 (measured in meters forward from the rudder post). With the change, only two main spars of each fin were to be attached to the hull, to main rings at stations 0 and 17.5. Those rings would have to be strengthened. The leading edges on the wider but shorter fins extended beyond ring 17.5 only far enough to be attached at an intermediate ring (at station 28.75) which was not built to carry the load of a main ring. However, since the forward part of fins were now to be attached here, the fins' anchorage was reinforced by four diagonal cables.

Dr. Hugo Eckener and Commander Charles E. Rosendahl. Their near-disastrous experience in the Graf Zeppelin *at Mines Field in Los Angeles inspired the change in the fin design of the U.S. Navy's ZRS airships. (Goodyear Tire and Rubber Co. Collection/University of Akron Archives)*

These changes would not have been made without discussion with the Goodyear-Zeppelin people. Bauch and Helma, the stress men, were strongly opposed to the changes. Arnstein, a stress analyst, could sympathize with their point of view. But Rosendahl was adamant, and Fulton, head of the navy's lighter-than-air design section, took Rosendahl's view. Arnstein maintained a "can-do" attitude: if any problem came up, he could solve it. Besides, he was aware of Litchfield's "The customer is always right" philosophy. He agreed to the change.

Reducing the attachment points from three to two did not create any difficulty from an analytical point of view; it was easier to calculate the loads to the hull with two supports than with three. The real problem was, how had the aerodynamic loads on the fins changed as a result of the changed fin configuration? No wind tunnel data existed showing the pressure distribution over these fins. The National Advisory Committee for Aeronautics was asked to obtain the necessary information, but it would take months.

Meanwhile, the stress analysts could not proceed. But neither was it acceptable to wait for the data. Helma, Liebert, and Klemperer put their heads together and came up with a reasonable estimate, based on their collective experience, and Arnstein approved. When the wind tunnel results arrived, some corrections would no doubt be needed in the stress analysis. Effect on the fin design would probably be minimal and could be handled with minor changes, if it turned out any were needed.

An auxiliary control station in the lower tail fin was included in the Project I design. By necessity, this control room was narrow and spartan, but, from this position, a pilot had better visibility, both of the airship, which was in front of him rather than behind him, and of everything below. There certainly should be no difficulty in seeing the proximity of the lower fin to the ground during takeoff or landing from this vantage, so there was no need for larger fins on that account. Visual contact between the auxiliary and the forward control cars was not an unreasonable feature to have in an experimental airship, as the ZRS-4 was conceived by its designers. However, the aft car was rarely used, and line-of-sight communication between the two control stations was used not at all. It appears that despite the navy's insistence on the change, the fin redesign was unnecessary.

Chapter 14   USS "AKRON," THE NEW QUEEN OF THE AIR

Arnstein and his team were anxious to get started building the navy's airship. They were an enthusiastic group consisting of a few former members of the Goodyear aeronautical department, the remaining disciples and several former Zeppelin men, plus a few young, newly hired engineers. "The Engineering Department grew rapidly to about one hundred people," Arnstein said, "while the fabrication, subassembly and erection people gradually grew to about seven hundred men." Girders and subassemblies were manufactured at Plant 3 and then trucked the mile or so to the Air Dock. Even before the big hangar was finished, assembly of the main rings of the airship began on the Air Dock floor. The first ring was completed with much fanfare before an invited crowd of 30,000 people at a ceremony on 7 November 1929, which included Admiral Moffett driving a golden rivet to complete the main ring. The navy airship *Los Angeles* came from Lakehurst especially for the occasion and circled overhead, escorted by several smaller Goodyear blimps. Moffett, Litchfield, and Arnstein gave speeches broadcast to a nationwide radio audience.

On the home front that winter, the Arnsteins would have a second son, William Gerald, born 20 January 1930. At Plant 3 and in the Air Dock, work continued on the daunting airship project. The first task was to create Arnstein's patented girders from flat duralumin stock. Long strips of the metal, six to nine inches wide, were fed into a press which contoured their edges then punched out lightening holes and flanged their rims. The resulting channel sections were then anodized and varnished to inhibit corrosion. The next step was to rivet the miles of channel sections together to form four-sided box girder sections. When completed, the ZRS-4 would contain 6,500,000 rivets—a number equal to the airship's nominal gas volume in cubic feet—each one squeezed into place by hand.

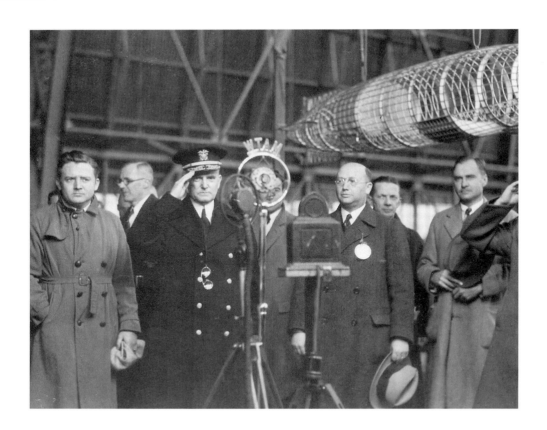

Rear Admiral William A. Moffett (saluting) and Karl Arnstein at the ring-laying ceremony marking the beginning of construction on the USS Akron *in November 1929. The event was broadcast live on the radio networks. A shop model of the Goodyear-Zeppelin with the original long fins is seen in the background.*
(The Lighter-Than-Air Society Collection/University of Akron Archives)

Set on the vast concrete floor at one end of the Air Dock were several sizes of circular wooden jigs that workers used to assemble girders into rings. In March 1930, the first main ring of the ZRS-4 was lifted into place. An incident occurred during that operation that suggests the difficulties encountered during the erection. Kurt Bauch had worked out a system for lifting the huge ring (133 feet in diameter) into place without damaging it. During the erection of large structures, stresses can exist that are greater than any expected to occur in the completed structure. Inside the hangar, cranes were slowly lifting the big ring from a horizontal to a vertical position when there was a loud pop. A rivet had failed. With much profanity, V. W. "Red" Coffelt, who was in charge of erection and had learned his trade in steel construction, lowered the ring back to the floor. He quickly devised his own web of cables, and finally succeeded in hoisting the repaired ring into the desired vertical position. The men in the shop felt that the know-it-all Germans had been shown that Americans knew a thing or two. Bauch seems to have accepted this gracefully, if perhaps with a red face.

The second main ring of the U.S. Navy's ZRS-4 airship is hoisted into position inside the cavernous Air Dock in April 1930. In the background, the first main ring with United States flag is already suspended from the ceiling. The triangular cross-section of the deep rings may be seen clearly. (Lockheed Martin Collection/University of Akron Archives)

Thereafter, more rings were hoisted into place atop a cradle of scaffolding, the intermediate rings placed between, and the longitudinal girders riveted to tie them together.

Meanwhile, the ZRS-4 was given a name. There was no shortage of suggestions for what to call the two airships planned. Moffett preferred naming them after the fallen commanders of the ZR-1 and ZR-2, *Lansdowne* and *Maxfield*, while the assistant secretary of the navy Ernst Lee Jahncke argued for *Alaska* and *Honolulu*. At the suggestion of John S. Knight, publisher of the *Akron Beacon Journal*, Akron's Congressman Francis Seiberling and Ohio's U.S. Senator Simeon D. Fess tried to get the first ship named *Akron* "as a deserved tribute to the world's new lighter-than-air capital." The local citizenry lobbied hard. "We all had developed such a strong personal feeling for the ship in which we all—even our children—believed to have some sort of sponsor rights," Arnstein said. "No airship before or since had more imaginary godfathers and godmothers . . . the whole community followed suit." By May 1930 it was official: the new airship would be named USS *Akron*. The choice was also consistent with the navy's policy of naming its fast oceangoing cruisers for U.S. cities.

It was the first time that an airship had carried the name "Akron" since the ill-fated Vaniman *Akron*, built by engineer Melvin Vaniman for a transatlantic flight attempt in 1911. This earlier airship was the largest non-rigid airship of its time, and had its envelope built by Goodyear's fledgling aeronautical department, largely with the backing of the company's president Frank A. Seiberling. Vaniman's airship was filled with hydrogen, which caught fire during a trial flight in July 1912, and the ship crashed into the sea off Atlantic City, New Jersey, killing all on board.

By 1930, the first effects of the stock market crash the previous October—coming little more than a week before the long-awaited ring-laying ceremony—were starting to be felt in *Akron*. The workers who were crafting the giant airship were happy to have jobs, even if it meant being in the unheated Air Dock. In the cold winters of northern Ohio, the inside of the unheated hangar was not a comfortable place. To make the workmen a bit more comfortable, small heaters were installed to warm canvas tents placed over the jigs and work tables. Summers were hot, but no one missed air conditioning—it was still a novelty in just a few movie theaters.

A problem soon arose—humorous but no less serious—concerning the duralumin airship taking shape. In June 1930, Arnstein wrote to plant superintendent, W. H. Collins, "It is absolutely necessary for us to eliminate the practice of spitting tobacco juice on the structure at the Dock. The Research Department has made some complaints that this will tend to cause corrosion, as well as additional weight." Arnstein realized what he was up against trying to enforce the rules on the workers atop the 150-foot-tall framework. "Inas-

On a platform high up inside the Air Dock, a worker squeezes into place one of the 6.5 million rivets that went into the framework of the U.S. Navy's rigid airship Akron. *The worker on right is preparing to install a bracing wire. Arnstein's box-girder design is clearly in evidence.*
(Lockheed Martin Collection/University of Akron Archives)

much as these men cannot be prohibited from chewing tobacco while working from such a great height, we should try to find some method whereby it will not be necessary for them to cover the duralumin structure with tobacco juice." Arnstein's solution may have prompted the workmen to refrain from their habit altogether—he suggested "some kind of individual paper sack" to collect the juice!

On 26 June 1930, Karl Arnstein, the Czechoslovakian immigrant, became a naturalized U.S. citizen, as did his wife, Bertl. Arnstein obtained his citizenship papers in the minimum time required. "I was enthusiastically determined to become an American citizen in spirit and reality," he later remarked. It was his goal and the company's to have the immigrant engineers of 1924 become part of the local community.

That same month, the novel elastic bulkhead of cord netting designed to keep *Akron*'s gas cells in place was tested in a section of the completed hull. It seemed things were finally coming together in a positive way. On the engineering side, the myriad details of the inside power plant installation, hull-conforming ballast water recovery system, gas cell construction, electrical and mechanical apparatus were being worked out. "There was no clock watching and no thought of overtime pay in the offices while we worked a normal seventy-two-hour week," Arnstein proudly recalled. Morale among the workmen was high despite the dangers of working from 80-foot-tall fire ladders and clambering over an aluminum alloy skeleton as much as 150 feet above a concrete floor. The Great Depression was beginning, but spirits were high because the workmen had a feeling that they were part of something important, something historic. This enormous structure on which they were working was actually going to fly through the air, improbable as that might seem. They were proud to be part of an elite group—and they had jobs.

There were exceptions. In 1931, a Hungarian-born riveter named Paul Kassay, an admitted communist, claimed to have sabotaged the airship. Kassay was a man who liked to tell tall stories about himself to anyone who would listen. He was arrested when he told

Interior of the hull of the USS Akron *under construction, looking forward. Two workers stand in front of a main ring near the center bottom of the photo, nearly lost from view in the array of girders and tail section bracing wires. The outer cover has already been installed on the nose of the airship. The polygon-shaped boxes along the side of the hull are the ship's internally-mounted engine rooms. (Lockheed Martin Collection/University of Akron Archives)*

The USS Macon, *sister ship to the USS* Akron, *nears completion in the Akron Air Dock in February 1933. Most of the hull has been given its outer cover of cotton fabric doped with aluminum powder, but the moving control surfaces (stacked upright on the floor in the left background) have not yet been installed on the fins. The pyramid-shaped protrusions on the back face of the fins are the control-surface hinge points. For a sense of scale, note the worker on the extension ladder in front of the lower fin. Three more men are barely visible at the base of the 80-foot ladder nearest the front of the right fin. (Lockheed Martin Collection/University of Akron Archives)*

two FBI undercover agents that the reason he spit on the rivets he was driving was so the saliva would freeze in the cold, then leave a gap when it melted in the spring. The idea was nonsense, but it created a national furor. Arnstein and Chief Inspector of Naval Aircraft T. G. W. "Tex" Settle issued a statement that sabotage was impossible under the overlapping inspection systems of Goodyear-Zeppelin and the navy. Kassay's work was carefully re-examined. There was nothing wrong with it.

Soon after the Kassay flap, there was another round of accusations in the press. Two workmen named MacDonald and Underwood went to the navy with a tale of "inferior materials and shoddy workmanship" on the dirigible. It was unlikely that if true the matter would have escaped the notice of Settle and his crew of inspectors, but the navy assigned R. D. Weyerbacher, who had been in charge of the *Shenandoah*'s construction, and Lieutenant Karl Schmidt, who had been on Garland Fulton's staff in Friedrichshafen during construction of the ZR-3, to make a confidential investigation. When MacDonald claimed to have been a supervisor on the *Shenandoah*, Weyerbacher knew the claim was false. Two weeks of investigation, including five days' climbing over the airship's hull, showed that there was no basis for the claims of MacDonald and Underwood.

Still later, the press howled a rancorous chorus when the navy announced that the *Akron* was 20,000 pounds overweight. If there was more substance here, there was still no cause for concern. Actually, it was 22,282 pounds over estimate, but that was less than 8 percent over the specification weight and reduced the airship's gross lift by only 4 percent. "Specification weight" is someone's best guess, made at a time when there were little more than preliminary drawings and calculations to go on. The actual final weight is essentially a correction of the preliminary estimate. A few percent for a first-of-a-kind aircraft is neither critical nor unusual.

Preliminary weight estimates tend to be optimistic. All of the major airships had been somewhat overweight from their paper specifications. Of course, with a fixed gross lift, adding structural weight reduces the permissible payload. Some of the extra weight was attributable to changes made by the navy; the rest was Goodyear-Zeppelin's responsibility, and may have been at least partially a result of Arnstein's policy of insisting on conservative stress analysis assumptions and margins of safety.

As the Depression deepened, there was some resentment, especially among out-of-work machinists, that more jobs should be made available to Americans, not the foreign-born immigrants who had been hired to fill the ranks of airship laborers. Arnstein responded to such criticism by pointing out that there were "times when the character of the work of the non-citizen makes his retention advisable" and explained that most were securing U.S. citizenship. Given time, the company would be able to train more American laborers. Meanwhile, work on the airship continued—a bright spot in an otherwise bleak economy. And despite Akron's steadily climbing unemployment rate, the silvery vessel taking shape in its big, black cocoon was something to celebrate, perhaps symbolic of better times ahead.

The navy's new airship was christened 8 August 1931—another big day for the city of Akron. Mayor Lloyd G. Weil declared it a legal holiday, and there were brass bands and much hoopla. The *Akron Beacon Journal* and *Akron Times-Press* put out special editions on pale green and pink newsprint heralding the event. An editorial cartoon showed "the rest of the world" personified as a globe "looking on" benevolently from the clouds at the christening ceremony. For the moment, it did seem as if a spotlight was focused on Akron. Aviation celebrities Amelia Earhart, Frank Hawks, and Jimmy Haizlip attended, and formations of army and navy airplanes by the dozens flew overhead, as did three blimps of the Goodyear fleet. By automobile, bus, and train an estimated 250,000 people poured in from all over Ohio, western Pennsylvania, and as far away as Illinois. One of the throng said the crowd was so large because many in it were unemployed, and having nothing else to do, they went to the airport. There, the Air Dock's north doors were opened to reveal the speakers' platform under the bow of the huge airship draped in red, white, and blue bunting. The cavernous building gave no comfort from the ninety-degree heat, but the crowds still pressed forward to get a better view as the airship's crew "in snow white uniforms" marched into the hangar. More than a dozen dignitaries, including Arnstein, walked onto the platform to the sound of "Anchors Aweigh" in front of "a battery of still and motion picture cameras." Litchfield gave a tribute to the fallen heroes of lighter than air and Admiral Moffett told a national radio audience how the ZRS-4 "represented the vanguard of a vast fleet of airships bringing to the United States boundless opportunities for global commerce." Then Mrs. Herbert Hoover, wife of the president of the United States, did the honors by pulling a red, white, and blue silken cord that released forty-eight racing pigeons from the bow of the airship as she uttered the words, "I christen thee *Akron*! " The band struck up the new national anthem, "The Star Spangled Banner," and the airship was allowed to float up a few feet and the bow was dipped in salute. It was a proud moment for Karl Arnstein.

There was still work to be done. "Before the airship was flown, it had to be put through a series of tests which could yield accurate information only when she was completed, inflated, and in a condition of flight readiness. These tests included general and particular overloadings . . . a strength test of the 'bridge' across the airplane compartment; final ground testing of rudder and elevator controls, engines, and transmissions, fire extinguishing systems, electrical bonding, and the airship's two 8-kilowatt, 110-volt, D.C. generators

Goodyear-Zeppelin President Paul Litchfield (center) and Chief of the U.S. Navy's Bureau of Aeronautics, Admiral William Moffett (at far right), watch as the First Lady, Mrs. Herbert Hoover, pulls a cord to release 48 racing pigeons to christen the naval airship USS Akron. *The event on 8 August 1931 was broadcast to a national radio audience and documented by newsreel cameramen. (Goodyear Tire and Rubber Co. Collection/University of Akron Archives)*

A large crowd dressed in its summer finest filled the Air Dock on the warm afternoon of 8 August 1931 to watch the First Lady, Mrs. Herbert Hoover, christen the USS Akron. *A portion of the airship was left uncovered to allow visitors a glimpse of the interior. Fuel and ballast tanks, ductwork and other details were identified by large signs. (Goodyear Tire and Rubber Co. Collection/University of Akron Archives)*

and their transmission system." There would be tests of all control lines to the moving tail surfaces, ballast bags, and gas cells.

Since this was still a new type of airship, Arnstein was concerned how closely their predictions about loads matched what they would actually find. Arnstein told a reporter, "In the dock, our chief purpose will be to determine the agreement of our stress calculations with actual stresses on the ship." They would do this by concentrating weights at both ends and then center of the hull to bend the ship up and down. Some strengthening was required after the overload tests resulted in some permanent strains, but nothing unexpected. The press and public grew impatient. "Sentiments were running high and expectations great when finally the day of the maiden flight approached," according to Arnstein. It was late September before the *Akron* was ready to try and lift its bulk into the air. "This was not an ordinary event," explained Arnstein, in case there was any doubt. A crowd of 200,000 people gathered on the field of the Akron Airport and the surrounding hills to see "Arnstein's 'baby' "—the biggest flying contraption in the world—actually fly. And see it they did. The ship was brought out of the hangar on a mobile mast by a small army of ground crewmen. It was mid-afternoon, however, before the *Akron* was released from its mooring. Arnstein smiled. Later he said of his team's feelings, "I know all of us were moved when we saw that wonderful structure coming to dynamic life on the 23rd of September about 3:30 in the afternoon."

In the Zeppelin tradition, Arnstein the chief designer was aboard, as were 28 other persons from Goodyear-Zeppelin, including Litchfield, Hunsaker, Flickinger, Coffelt, and eight of the disciples. Arnstein referred to a list of the 112 persons on this first flight. Among other officials aboard were Secretary of the Navy Charles F. Adams; his assistant, David S. Ingalls; Moffett; Fulton; Burgess, Weyerbacher, and nineteen navy inspectors. The nine flight officers and fifty ratings were navy men who had undergone special training, especially in the period since the christening. The airship's first commander was Lieutenant Commander Charles E. Rosendahl, ranking survivor of the *Shendandoah* disaster, observer aboard the *Graf Zeppelin*, past commander of the *Los Angeles*, and author of a then new book *Up Ship!* This book and other publications made Rosendahl, at least in the eyes of the reading public, the leading American spokesman for navy airships and for the rigid airship in general.

As the ground crew let the airship vane into the light breeze, water ballast was released to lighten the craft. When the airship tugged at the crewman with about 600 pounds of net lift, Rosendahl gave the order, "Up ship!" The ground crewmen released the handling lines and the *Akron* rose noiselessly into the air. "At 200 feet, the engines were started, the

"Up ship!" The USS Akron *rises into the sky on its first flight, 23 September 1931. The pyramid-shaped girder structure is the airship's mobile mooring mast. (Goodyear Tire and Rubber Co. Collection/University of Akron Archives)*

hull gleamed as the sun broke through the overcast, cheers broke out, and the pride of the city of Akron was off on its first flight."

"The ship cruised over Akron for one hour and then headed to Cleveland at higher speed," Arnstein recalled: "Wherever we passed we could see the scenery full of humanity attempting to get a glimpse of the new queen of the air. Hundreds of thousands of people stood on the ground, the hills, streets, roofs of buildings . . . Children ran out of school buildings, cars stopped and ships on Lake Erie sounded their horns."

After flying over the east side of Cleveland and then downtown, the *Akron* headed back home for a landing about 7:30 P.M. The National Guard honored the airship's return by firing a salute. "The most impressive recollection I have was the return to the Air Dock, where our friends awaited us," said Arnstein. "Among the many well-wishers were most of the company executives with their families."

The purpose of this test flight, as with others, was to check for possible flaws. The only problem found was a minor one involving the steering, but that was corrected before the airship was delivered to Lakehurst. There were ten trial flights in all. The ninth of these was a forty-eight-hour endurance flight, and Arnstein was again aboard. The course was down the Ohio River valley to St. Louis, and back via Chicago and Milwaukee. Rosendahl was piloting. At one point along this route, it was reported to Arnstein that a control cable was going bad on the starboard elevator. He went to inspect it, and found that it was fraying at a cable sheave. Arnstein knew that trouble might be expected with the other control surfaces as well. A check showed, however, no other cables in immediate danger.

He returned to the control car and reported the situation to Rosendahl who reacted violently by yelling at him. Arnstein got the impression that Rosendahl was near panic, but finally was able to tell him not to use the starboard elevator until Arnstein told him he could. Meanwhile, a new section of cable was spliced in, and the temporary repair was completed in midair within a half hour or so.

The design error was immediately rectified after the *Akron* returned to the Air Dock in its namesake city. Going over the drawings back in his office, he found that one of his designers had made a serious error. He had selected pulley diameters that were too small. Larger diameter pulleys would have to be installed throughout the control system, which had two thousand pulleys in all. The designer responsible for the potentially disastrous blunder was one of the disciples. Arnstein transferred him from Goodyear-Zeppelin to

Pleased with the success of the USS Akron's first trial flight, Karl Arnstein, Goodyear-Zeppelin's chief engineer, and Paul W. Litchfield, the company's president, pose in front of the airship's gangway. (Lockheed Martin Collection/University of Akron Archives)

Goodyear Tire, where he was given work in machine design. It was a move that Arnstein felt he had to make. The consequences of such an error could have been fatal, and it revealed a lack of technical understanding on the part of the designer. As chief engineer, Arnstein dared not keep the man in a position where such a mistake could risk men's lives. He could not let his friendship override his responsibility, though his decision pained him personally. Years later he met the wife of the erring designer in a supermarket. She told him that her husband had never been the same since he left Goodyear-Zeppelin. He had loved his work on airships. Yet he had not been fired outright. Arnstein had done the best he could for his colleague from Friedrichshafen.

The next flight of the *Akron* was its delivery flight to Lakehurst. At five o'clock in the evening on 21 October 1931, Litchfield and Arnstein met with Settle and Rosendahl to sign the papers transferring the airship to the navy. At 5:40 P.M. Rosendahl gave the command "Up ship!" and the *Akron* left its hometown for the last time. "It was a stirring moment," said one emotional witness. "Lumps filled the throats of those hundreds gathered nearby. They applauded. Many eyes were dimmed with tears. A few wept openly. All of them waved a final farewell." Rosendahl circled the city twice and then headed east. "Every Akronite was given a final view of the world's largest and best airship, a triumph of the city's industry," trumpeted the *Akron Beacon Journal*. Arnstein was on board for the overnight flight, as were Hunsaker and a few Goodyear-Zeppelin technicians. Arnstein and Hunsaker would meet Eckener at Lakehurst to discuss the Parker-McNary Merchant Airship Bill introduced in the 71st U.S. Congress. It was just the sort of legislation Litchfield and Hunsaker wanted. If passed, it would make large airships eligible for foreign airmail contracts "to promote income during the period devoted to winning public confidence in regular LTA service." It would also give commercial airships status on par with cargo ships in the American merchant marine.

The *Akron* moored at her new home at 6:34 A.M. on 22 October. Five days after her arrival, on Navy Day, she was commissioned USS *Akron*. Apparently everyone was satisfied with the airship although the top speed was a little short of specification and there were minor mechanical bugs to be worked out—but that was to be expected. She was, after all, only an experimental prototype with a variety of innovative features. Perhaps the most notable feature was the airplane hangar, located in the hull aft of the control car between stations 125 and 147.5. The navy had experimented by furnishing the *Los Angeles*, Arnstein's old LZ 126, with a device allowing an airplane with a special tripod in front of the pilot and with a hook on top to catch a trapeze hung below the airship. On the *Akron* and its new sister ship the ZRS-5, however, the airplane could then be hoisted up inside the airship through a T-shaped opening, to be transferred by an overhead trolley to a storage area measuring 75 feet by 50 feet by 24 feet (23 by 15 by 7 m). Although the compartment was designed to hold five airplanes, no more than four were ever carried. The navy tested several types before selecting Curtiss F9C-2 biplanes as the principal scout aircraft, although different utility airplanes were also used at times. However, it would be May 1932 before the first airplane occupied the hangar bay. Only then could it be said that a hangar had flown.

Another unusual feature of the *Akron* were swiveling propellers, which could be selected independently and used for vertical thrust at takeoff, then rotated into the horizontal position to give forward thrust. When Eckener saw the *Akron* take off in this manner, he was so impressed that he turned to Arnstein and exclaimed, "But this is not a Zeppelin!" Eckener was sufficiently impressed by the airship to call it "a masterpiece of American engineering and workmanship." Admiral Moffett quoted him to the Naval Affairs Committee when one of its members dredged up the unfounded MacDonald accusations in 1932.

This is not the place to recount the adventurous career of the USS *Akron*, but it would impact Arnstein's life twice more. The first time was not long in coming. Moffett had invited congressional members of the Naval Affairs Committee to come to Lakehurst for a flight in February 1932. A stiff crosswind rose as the airship was being taken out of the Lakehurst hangar, the tail broke away from its heavy stern mooring beam, and soared upward. It then came down and smashed the lower fin against the ground repeatedly, as the airship swung parallel to the wind, held to the mast at its nose. There was heavy damage to the lower fin, but only minor damage elsewhere, thanks to the deep ring design. Had traditional Zeppelin construction been used, damage probably would have been more severe. This accident seems to be an example in the classic tradition of aeronauts pressured into flying against their better judgment. One wonders whether Eckener, who himself learned from his mistake with the *Deutschland II* (LZ 8) in 1911, would not have left the airship in the hangar, congressmen or no, and waited for more favorable wind conditions.

Goodyear-Zeppelin sent a team to Lakehurst for the repair job, which would take several weeks. The Goodyear-Zeppelin representative at Lakehurst, dour Ben Schnitzer, was put in charge of the group, which consisted of two designers, a stress man, a materials engineer, and a number of shop personnel. The repairs were made and the last two men, Donald W. Brown, one of the designers, and the materials engineer, Rudy Redman, were ready to return to Akron when Schnitzer inexplicably fired them. After a glum trip back to Akron, the pair went to see Arnstein, who told them to forget it. This episode throws some light on the Arnstein character; the incident would not be the last time Arnstein would defend his engineers against the judgments of others.

Chapter 15 CAUSE FOR CONCERN

With the *Akron* safely delivered to Lakehurst and accepted by the navy, Arnstein could turn his attention to the second airship, the ZRS-5, on which work had already started. The name *Macon* was chosen over other cities' names because Macon, Georgia, was in the home district of Carl Vinson, the powerful chairman of the House Committee on Naval Affairs. The *Macon* would incorporate nearly sixty improvements upon the *Akron*, and these were made primarily to reduce weight or to enhance performance. One such innovation improved the airship's huge gas cells. To replace the **gold beater's skin** gas bags used on earlier Zeppelins, Goodyear had developed a rubberized cotton fabric, and the Bureau of Standards had developed a gelatin-latex compound and impregnated a cotton cloth with it. Both appeared promising, and half the gas cells in the *Akron* were made of one fabric and half of the other, as a service test. The gelatin-latex cells proved to have the best characteristics of lightness and durability so they were installed in the *Macon*. To reduce wind resistance, the engine-cooling radiators which had been attached to the propeller outriggers on *Akron* were put in streamlined housings on the *Macon*'s hull. Three-bladed metal propellers replaced the two-bladed wooden propellers originally specified. The streamlined radiators and outriggers, coupled with the more efficient propellers, gave the *Macon* a top speed of 75.6 knots compared with only 69 knots for the *Akron*. Another visible difference between the two dirigibles was the absence of vent cowl "bumps" along the top of the *Macon*'s hull. Instead, flush-mounted louvers were substituted. Some modification was made to permit the full complement of five airplanes to be carried in the airplane compartment, instead of the three which were all that fit into the *Akron*. The crew's quarters were configured differently on the *Macon* to make them more comfortable. More important, though, were the improvements in performance. Due to refinements in structure and fittings, the new airship's structure weighed four tons less than the *Akron*, giving the *Macon* a corresponding increase in useful load.

By 1932, the Great Depression had deepened. Akron's industrial unemployment rate reached a staggering 60 percent that year. The workers lucky enough to have jobs constructing the ZRS-5 must have wondered what was in store when that airship was completed.

At their convention in the summer of 1932, the Democrats nominated for president Franklin Delano Roosevelt, who had been their vice presidential candidate in 1920 and who was now governor of New York. He also had served as assistant secretary of the navy in the Wilson administration, and had a further, if unhappy, association with airships as a director of the American Investigation Corporation, which proposed to build Schütte-Lanz airships in the United States. Democrats hoped Roosevelt could pull the country out of the Depression. The Republicans renominated Herbert Hoover.

A big event in the airship world that summer was the dedication of the Guggenheim Airship Institute building at the northwest corner of the Akron Airport, across the field from the Goodyear-Zeppelin Air Dock. The idea for the institute originated with Dr. C. F. Zook, president of the University of Akron. In October 1929 he approached the Guggenheim Foundation for the Promotion of Aeronautics, which had funded aeronautical research at several universities. One of these was the California Institute of Technology, where the Guggenheim Aeronautical laboratories were headed by Dr. Theodor von Kármán. The Guggenheims approved funding for what became Daniel Guggenheim Airship Institute (DGAI), to be operated by the University of Akron. Kármán was appointed director of research for the DGAI in September 1930, but since he could not be in two places at once, he asked a former student and assistant of his at Aachen, Dr. Theodor Troller, to become assistant director in Akron.

The City of Akron, with help from the Airport and Aeronautics Committee of the Akron Chamber of Commerce, contributed "an essential sum" for erection of the building. Troller arrived in February 1931, in time to assist with the planning. Bertl and the children had gone to Arizona for the winter, and Arnstein invited Dr. Troller to stay at his home while his family was away. Troller considered this a great honor, having grown up not far from Prague, and knowing of Arnstein as a famous engineer.

One of the most important features of the institute was a large vertical wind tunnel, in contrast with conventional wind tunnels, in which the air moves horizontally. The advantage of the vertical tunnel is that a model can be hung nose downward from the tail; this permits a minimum of interference with the air flow from the model mounts, which can introduce appreciable error into the measurements. The size of the wind tunnel was important because it permitted the use of larger models, and especially in the case of airships, the use of small models can introduce errors in scaling up results to the full-size prototype.

The wind tunnel was dedicated in June 1932. The ceremonies included a speech by Dr. Robert A. Millikan, chairman of the Executive Council of the California Institute of Technology and Nobel Prize winner in physics in 1923. From a contemporary vantage point, one of Millikan's observations is striking. Of the prospect of a four-day journey from Los Angeles to Tokyo, he said, "such a rapid Pacific passage is not now possible by any other than lighter-than-air craft, and there is little likelihood that it will soon, if ever, be done commercially by any other means." This view of the future was, of course, shared by many, and the optimism of Arnstein and Litchfield for the future of commercial airships must be understood in this light.

The two-day program included "technical addresses" on airship topics by a succession of noteworthy speakers, including Troller, Garland Fulton, Hunsaker, and Kármán. Arnstein spoke on "Research and Development Problems Arising in Airship Design." Arnstein concluded the conference with the remark, "Knowing Dr. von Kármán well from past experience, I am sure he will select the most important and far-reaching of the problems for future study, and that he and his able assistants will have a very interesting set of results to present at the next session of this group." As it happened, the test results of greatest interest came from the National Advisory Committee for Aeronautics in November 1932. Its report shed new light on the aerodynamic loads acting on the tail fins of the *Akron*, which had been flying for more than a year, and on the *Macon*, then nearing completion in the Air Dock. Goodyear-Zeppelin engineers concerned with fin loads had followed the testing at NACA, and had obtained the critical data much earlier. Given the new distribution of the air loads, they were able to make revised stress calculations from those estimated in 1930, and from these determine whether the fin design was still adequate. Test results showed that while the total load on each fin was close to the preliminary design estimate, it was distributed differently. The highest pressures occurred farther forward, toward the leading edge of the fin, and the resultant load consequently also moved forward. This finding did not agree with earlier tests made by Luftschiffbau-Zeppelin and the California Institute of Technology. If the latest information was valid, it was important because it indicated that the load carried by the forward spar supporting each tail fin was much greater than originally calculated. The spar's factor of safety, and that of the ring to which it was attached (frame 17.5), were therefore reduced, apparently to less than the specified minimum. In presenting the results to Fulton, Arnstein proposed to reinforce the area. Fulton, however, refused to believe NACA's wind tunnel data. He asked NACA to repeat the tests, and these yielded the same results. Fulton still wouldn't believe them, which dismayed Arnstein.

Politically, Fulton's attitude is understandable. A costly delay in completing the *Macon* would be bad enough, but also the *Akron* would have to be grounded to have its tail reinforced, generating criticism not only within the navy but from the press and possibly the Congress. Fulton would surely catch hell from Moffett. It would be more expedient to discount the NACA data, to avoid the time and expense of reinforcing ring 17.5.

Seeing Fulton's position, Arnstein suggested that brace cables be installed between the fins. This would have distributed a high load on one fin to the other three. Fulton rejected this solution: for one reason, the external cables could pose a danger by getting in the way of ground crew members. For another, the added aerodynamic drag of the cables would make the airship slower. Although Arnstein dismissed these objections, Fulton remained unconvinced.

Arnstein also had learned about a potentially serious problem relating to loads caused by an airship's **dynamic lift**, that is, lift generated by angling the airship's bow upward and driving it forward by its motors to catch the wind below. The problem was not with the hull, but the effect of that angled airflow on the tail surfaces. The fins were not designed to be driven sideways through the air; the more perpendicular they were, the greater the force of air, and the greater the likelihood of failure. There was already wind tunnel data to show that a steeper pitch angle caused higher than expected loading at the fin leading edge and an increased risk of failure. In the design of the *Akron*, *Macon*, and *Los Angeles*, and probably for the *Graf Zeppelin* as well, an angle of twelve degrees nose up had been assumed for design purposes to be the maximum upward angle that an airship operator would attempt to fly. Then Arnstein learned that the *Graf* had been flown with its nose pitched up at fifteen-degree angle. That was alarming. If the factor of safety had been reduced before at a twelve-degree angle, it was now still further reduced at fifteen degrees and the assumed built-in margin of safety would be correspondingly less. What would happen if there was a sudden gust? In the worst case, the wind force could exceed the safety factor and the fin would break, most likely at a place not previously anticipated. Arnstein did not want to take that risk so he continued to urge Fulton to at least add the fin cables to the *Macon*. Finally, before the airship left the Air Dock, Arnstein on his own unilateral initiative, had attachment fittings for brace cables installed in the fins. The navy, however, chose not to install the cables, for the reason that their necessity could not be proven.

In defense of Fulton, the airships were designed to have their structure twice as strong as needed, expressed as a safety factor of about two. The NACA test data did not of itself indicate a reduction of the factor of safety to 1.0, which would have indicated failure if a critical condition were ever encountered, but it did diminish the margin of safety. Likewise, there remained some margin of safety flying an airship with a twelve-degree angle of

Captain Garland Fulton, head of the U.S. Navy's Bureau of Aeronautics LTA Design Branch (The Lighter-Than-Air Society Collection/University of Akron Archives)

nose-up pitch, and apparently even with fifteen degrees. However, for the navy to accept a reduced factor of safety was unwise. Factors of safety are needed to account for uncertainties about forces, materials, and the accuracy of the stress analysis.

Arnstein discussed the situation, including Fulton's intransigence, with Litchfield more than once. Litchfield did not want to add the reinforcements or the brace cables without Fulton's approval, since that could offend Goodyear-Zeppelin's only current customer; commercial airship ventures were on hold as a result of the Depression. Arnstein was not happy with his position in the middle. It had been different at Luftschiffbau. If Arnstein wanted a structural part reinforced, the men in the shop did it without question. At most, someone might go to Dürr who would ask Arnstein about it. Generally there would be no question, and even the shop people would suggest maybe a little more reinforcement here or there. Factory personnel were also flight crew, so they had a reason to take an interest. Arnstein once asked Wilhelm Siegle why he wanted more reinforcement and got the terse reply, "Because [it is] *my* ass in the ship!"

The year 1933 was an unhappy one, and not only for Karl Arnstein. In January, President Hindenburg of Germany had made Adolf Hitler chancellor. In the United States, the Great Depression was at its worst. The *Los Angeles* had been decommissioned in June 1932, to save operating expense to the government. The *Akron*, the navy's only operating airship, had received bad press, not only because of the tail-smashing incident at Lakehurst, but for an incident at San Diego in which two inexperienced sailors failed to let go of ground handling ropes and fell to their deaths. A third hung on long enough to be pulled to safety aboard the airship.

The airplanes aboard the *Akron* had failed to protect the airship from attack in war games; the airship was ruled "shot down," or dive-bombed, more than once. The small hook-on planes, however, had shown great potential as scouts that extended the range and coverage of the carrier system, while allowing the airship to keep its distance from enemy aircraft. Moffett noted this potential in his speech at which his wife christened the *Macon* on 11 March 1933.

Meanwhile, Hunsaker, as vice president and general manager of International Zeppelin Transport Company, had been lobbying Congress on behalf of the Merchant Airship Bill. It would have authorized the Post Office Department to let contracts for mail be carried by airship, which was a key to the introduction of commercial airship travel. Prospects seemed bright in 1930, and there was talk of erecting another hangar in the Los Angeles area to construct commercial airships so it would not be necessary to wait for the two navy airships to clear the Akron hangar. The collapsing national economy ended that talk, and passage of the bill was delayed by the advent of a new Congress with Democratic instead

February 18, 1915

10¢

Leslie's
Illustrated Weekly N...
Established ...

Winged

The Schweinler Press

At the outbreak of World War I, the press heightened fears in Allied nations that raiding Zeppelin bombers would be invulnerable to attack. The reality proved otherwise, as several German Army Zeppelins fell to defensive anti-aircraft artillery fire in the opening month of the war. Although the United States was officially neutral, its press was often not. The cover of this American news magazine for 18 February 1915 reflected the growing perception among the Allies that Zeppelins were no longer an invincible threat. (Courtesy Charles Jacobs)

Will tomorrow's aircraft carriers FLY?

During World War II, Goodyear Aircraft promoted the concept of a flying aircraft carrier; a 10-million cubic-foot rigid airship equipped with up to ten fighter-bomber airplanes. The design was an updated version of the late 1930s ZRCV airship which was proposed as a replacement for the Akron and Macon. *(Courtesy Eric Brothers)*

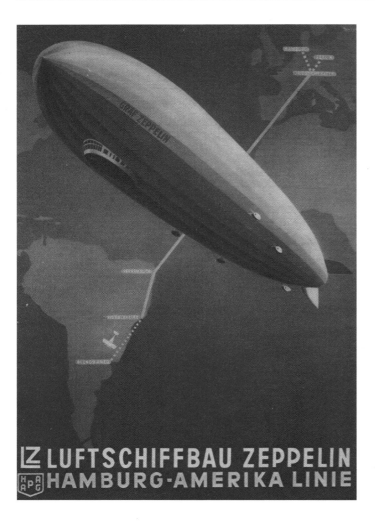

LZ LUFTSCHIFFBAU ZEPPELIN
HAPAG HAMBURG-AMERIKA LINIE

The cover of a brochure promoting the Graf Zeppelin's Europe to South America passenger service in the 1930s. Zeppelins provided the only regularly-scheduled non-stop transatlantic air service until the advent of the "China Clipper" flying boats in 1939. *(The Lighter-Than-Air Society Collection / University of Akron Archives)*

Non-postal stamps like these were printed by collectors to per-
sonalize envelopes they intended to have flown "via air mail" by
Zeppelin. Air mail was expensive and only a small portion of
all mail, with postal items flown by airship an even greater rar-
ity, thus making surviving examples sought-after collectibles.
(Courtesy Charles Jacobs)

Admission to the "reserved guest area" of the Air Dock for the christening ceremony of the USS Akron was by invitation only and
required presentation of this special pass. Afterward, the lucky few
got to keep their passes as souvenirs, which now are prized by collectors of airship ephemera. (The LTA Society Collection / University of Akron
Archives)

In "A Bomber Bombed," aviation artist Charles H. Hubbell portrayed the end of the German Army
Zeppelin LZ 37 on 7 June 1915. Lieutenant R. A. J. Warneford of the British Royal Naval Air Service,
flying a Morane Parasol fighter plane near Ghent, Belgium, overtook the Zeppelin and bombed it, setting the airship on fire. Nine of the ten men aboard perished; they were the first army Zeppelin crew lost
in the war. (Courtesy Western Reserve Historical Society, Cleveland, OH).

This color-tinted postcard shows the south end of the Air Dock open for the ring-laying ceremony of the giant navy airship USS Akron *in November 1929. Two of the airship's ring-shaped frames are under construction on the hangar floor. One of Goodyear's public relations blimps hovers above, tiny in comparison to the massive Goodyear-Zeppelin hangar. (Courtesy Eric Brothers)*

The International Aviation Exhibition of 1909 at Frankkurt am Main was promoted as a major tourist attraction and so was commemorated in colorful postcard souvenirs such as this one, showing one of the featured aircraft, Zeppelin LZ 6. (Courtesy Charles Jacobs)

Graf Zeppelin's Luftschiff über dem Bodensee.

Zeppelins were popular subjects for picture postcards, a new medium introduced in the first decade of the twentieth century. Zeppelin LZ 6 is depicted in vivid color rising above Lake Constance. The old wooden hangar is visible on shore.

(Courtesy Charles Jacobs)

The Goodyear Tire and Rubber Company rarely missed an opportunity to link mundane products such as its automobile tires with the majestic airships being built by the company's Goodyear-Zeppelin division. "150,000,000 Tire Buyers Can't Be Wrong," claimed this advertising card, which was customized for the company's independent tire dealers such as "Michael's Garage" in Pennsylvania. (Courtesy Charles Jacobs)

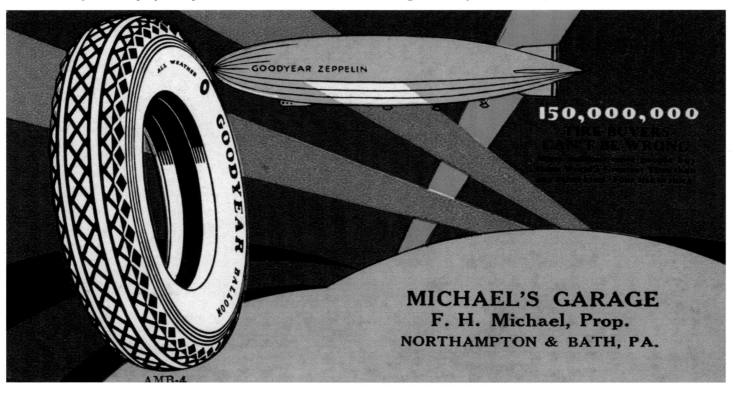

GOODYEAR ZEPPELIN

150,000,000

MICHAEL'S GARAGE
F. H. Michael, Prop.
NORTHAMPTON & BATH, PA.

As the German Zeppelins had been, the U.S. Navy's giant dirigibles were also popular postcard subjects. The silvery airship USS Akron is depicted above the Akron Air Dock backed by a dramatic sunset. (Courtesy Eric Brothers)

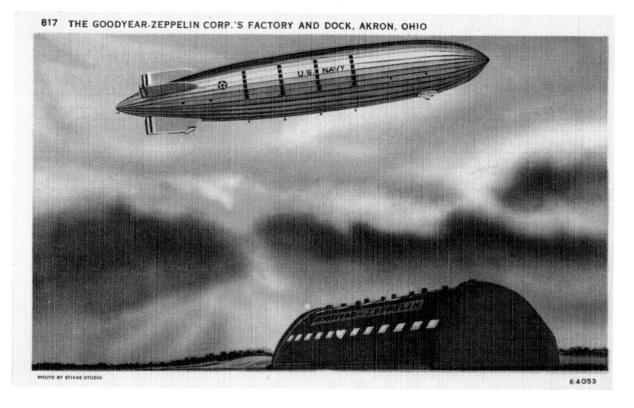

817 THE GOODYEAR-ZEPPELIN CORP.'S FACTORY AND DOCK, AKRON, OHIO

PHOTO BY STIVAS STUDIO

64053

In this postcard, an airship resembling the USS Macon emerges from the big hangar at Moffett Field, California. The former Naval Air Station Sunnyvale was not renamed Naval Air Station Moffett Field (in honor of the admiral and airship advocate who perished aboard the USS Akron) until 1942, so this card was issued long after the navy's rigid airships had passed from the scene. Although similar in shape to the Air Dock in Akron, the steel hangar in California is not as large (1,117 ft. long, 308 ft. wide, 198 ft. high). (Courtesy Charles Jacobs)

GIANT HANGAR, U. S. NAVAL AIR STATION, MOFFETT FIELD, CALIF.

376

3B-H406

One of a series of more than one hundred color-tinted photo postcards from the early 1930s showing steps in the construction of the USS Akron. Part of the giant navy dirigible's dura-lumin skeleton can be seen inside of the Goodyear-Zeppelin Air Dock. The Goodyear public relations blimp Vigilant fits comfortably within the arc of one of the hangar's 600-ton doors, as does a spherical gas balloon used to hold helium during tests. (Courtesy Eric Brothers)

By the 1930s, Zeppelins conveyed an image of power and prestige, and so became popular symbols in advertising. The aerial leviathans continue to fascinate the public, as evidenced by this modern reproduction of a metal sign from the Zeppelin era promoting motor oil.

(Courtesy Charles Jacobs)

of Republican leadership. Pan American Airways intervened to have the bill amended to serve airplanes and flying boats as well as airships, and passage of the bill was further delayed. It passed in the House by a slim margin in July 1932, too late for action by the Senate. After the national elections that fall, the airship bill was scheduled to be voted on by the Senate in lame duck session on 2 March 1933, just two days before Franklin Roosevelt would be inaugurated. Early that morning, however, as bad luck would have it, Senator Walsh of Montana died. The Senate met only to adjourn for the day out of respect for their colleague, and refused to change its calendar, so that business to have been taken up on 2 March was passed over on 3 March. It would be several weeks before the new Congress could consider the Merchant Airship Bill again. By that time, other events would intervene.

A Curtiss F9C-2 "Sparrowhawk" approaches the trapeze on the USS Macon. *Once the airplane's "sky hook" on top of the wing has engaged the trapeze, the biplane can be hauled up into the airship's internal airplane hangar. One of the* Macon's *hull-mounted engine radiators, streamlined propeller struts and the water recovery condensers can also be seen. (The Lighter-Than-Air Society Collection/University of Akron Archives)*

On the night of 3 April 1933, a graduate student studying meteorology at California Institute of Technology, who worked nights loading mail at Western Air Express, was flying from Salt Lake City to Las Vegas. Looking over his weather maps, he noticed what he later described as "a rather intense development on the East Coast." He casually remarked to the radio operator, "I would hate to be flying off New Jersey tonight," and then went to the back of the plane to take a nap. The meteorology student would later become nationally known as Dr. Irving P. Krick, head of his own weather forecasting firm, and weather advisor to General Dwight Eisenhower for the Allied invasion of Normandy and crossing of the Rhine in World War II. He was catapulted into controversy and national prominence as a result of the weather that April night. Krick later recalled that he was asleep in the back of the plane when "about two or three hours later, the radio operator shook my toes and said, 'Do you know that I just received word that the airship *Akron* went down off the New Jersey coast at just the area you were talking about?'"

At six minutes after midnight on 4 April the USS *Akron* fell tail first into the cold, windswept Atlantic. The airship had spent the night flying through a widespread electrical storm and initially it was falsely believed that lightning had set fire to the airship, causing it to plunge into the sea. It would be several hours before the navy would know the full extent of the tragedy.

The following morning in Akron, the newspaper presses rolled out "extra" editions with the preliminary details. At his office, Arnstein "stood tense and grim by a desk heaped with charts and fine drawings," according to one reporter. "I can say nothing now. I must know more," Arnstein told the press. His voice shook as he explained his reticence. There were few details available, since the only survivors of the seventy-six men aboard the *Akron* were Lieutenant Commander Herbert V. Wiley and two crewmen, Moody Erwin and Richard Deal. They were alive only because the German oil tanker *Phoebus* was by chance in the area and miraculously found them in the dark night clinging to pieces of floating wreckage. A fourth man pulled from the cold water, Chief Radio Operator Robert W. Copeland, died of exposure soon afterward. A contributing factor to the great loss of life—the greatest number of casualties in a single aircraft crash up to that time—was that on its last flight, the *Akron* apparently carried no life jackets aboard and only a single rubber raft. The responsibility for such a glaring and tragic omission would have rested with the operators, who, for whatever reasons, chose not to stow that safety equipment on board. Adding to the calamity, the navy blimp J-3 foundered during a search for survivors, claiming two more lives.

By this time, Irving Krick had contacted Kármán, Director of the Guggenheim Aeronautical Laboratory at the California Institute of Technology, who was also director of the Guggenheim Airship Institute at Akron. Krick told him then that it was his opinion that the crash might have been avoided if the weather conditions off the New Jersey coast had been properly evaluated. Kármán immediately sent a message to Arnstein. Krick's analysis of the storm and his public comments were controversial, but they also introduced a new model for predicting weather patterns that launched Krick's meteorological career.

On the day of the crash there was no definitive explanation of what had happened. Arnstein issued a statement to the press which read, "News of the *Akron* disaster comes as a profound shock to me and the entire organization at Goodyear-Zeppelin. From the viewpoint of personnel it is a staggering loss to the nation." Among the dead was Admiral William A. Moffett, the champion of navy airships, who had recently visited Akron for the *Macon* christening. Litchfield, too, expressed his sympathy and offered the services of the company to investigators. President Roosevelt called it a "national disaster" and "grieved with the nation" for the wives and families of the men who were lost.

The people of the city of Akron grieved openly over the loss. In the depths of the Great Depression, the airship had carried the hopes of Akronites that their city would become a center of world air travel. The *Macon* still remained in the Air Dock, ready to fly, but to lose the *Akron* was a painful and demoralizing blow. People wept in the streets. There was grief for the great loss of life, but also for the ship, which had been a source of pride and had become a symbol of Akron the city, and its people. It was like losing a friend, or a member of the family, said some who had worked on the airship.

A naval court of inquiry was held and a congressional investigation was opened; Arnstein was called to testify at the latter. The Joint Committee to Investigate Dirigible Disasters (it did not want to be limited to investigating only the loss of the *Akron*) was organized in April 1933, and on 5 May its members traveled to Akron to tour the Goodyear-Zeppelin facilities. Hearings were held in May and June at which fifty-six witnesses were called, among them the *Akron*'s three survivors.

Airship Investigation, a summary report of the committee's conclusions, was prepared by its counsel, Colonel Henry Breckinridge. His synopsis of the evidence presented to the committee established a chronology of the airship's last flight: "At 7:28 P.M. on April 3, 1933, the USS *Akron* took off from her station at Lakehurst, N.J., on the flight that was to end in her destruction. The ship was proceeding in accordance with an officially authorized mission, for the purpose of training and for calibrating naval radio compass stations in the first naval district at Newport, R.I., and elsewhere. . . ." Lieutenant Commander Herbert V. Wiley, executive officer of the *Akron* and senior survivor of the disaster had telephoned Lieutenant Herbert M. Wescoat, the *Akron*'s aerological officer, at about 11 A.M. that morning "to ask his opinion of the advisability of making the flight." Wescoat told Wiley that he would be able to take the ship out of the hangar at sunset but that he was doubtful that suitable visibility would exist in the vicinity of Newport the following morning.

"When the airship was on the field at about 7 P.M., fog formed rapidly. . . ." In Wiley's opinion, "at the time of departure, from the different weather forecasts, there came no warning as to thunderstorms." It was also his opinion that weather conditions justified the trip and were no cause for apprehension. The officers on the station agreed. However, Charles L. Mitchell, chief forecaster of the Weather Bureau, did not share that assessment. In viewing the disaster in retrospect, he interpreted the weather map at 3 April 1933 as "containing distinct warnings of the possible development of dangerous weather from the Southwest." Mitchell testified that he believed the storm conditions were associated with cold air at high altitudes sinking and overriding rising warmer air at lower altitudes. This motion of air masses set up powerful, spiraling air currents—what Krick and Kármán described as a "vortex effect"—which may have engulfed the airship. But the data, obtained by airplane flights and from weather balloons, was not received in Washington in time to be included in the forecast that would be seen by the *Akron*'s crew.

Another item of testimony that may have been more important than Breckinridge realized was that of Lieutenant Frederick M. Trapnell, one of the pilots of the airplane complement of the *Akron*. He said: "About an hour before the ship was to take off, a rather heavy brown fog came in, which makes it inadvisable to take off in a heavier-than-air plane." Shortly before the *Akron* took off, Trapnell spoke to the airship's captain, Commander Frank McCord, and told him he thought there would be breaks in the fog that would allow him to fly through to make contact with the ship. Trapnell recalled that McCord "told me to wait until he had gone through it himself, and he would radio the ground and tell me whether to come up." Night was falling by the 7:28 P.M. takeoff time. Darkness, even without fog condition, would have made it extra difficult, even hazardous, for Trapnell's plane to hook on to the airship. About ten minutes after the airship left the ground, McCord sent a message instructing Trapnell to remain where he was for the night and to fly the plane to meet the airship in the morning. Trapnell's small N2Y airplane would be needed as a taxi between the airship and the ground at Newport.

There were other considerations for the *Akron* to keep to its scheduled departure. Moffett was waiting, and he was accompanied by an important guest from the Army Reserve, Lieutenant Colonel Alfred F. Masury, vice president of the Mack Truck Company and an officer in the International Zeppelin Transport Company. Moffett's views on the limitations weather imposed on airship operation were well known at Lakehurst in the 1930s. Nearly five years earlier, he had pronounced, "In order for rigid airships to be fully useful . . . they will have to run on practical schedules even in bad weather." Though landing in fog would be a different matter, takeoff would not be dangerous with the *Akron*'s swiveling propellers available for vertical takeoff, and with sufficient fuel aboard for three days or more, a landing would not be necessary until well after the fog was expected to dissipate next morning. McCord must have reasoned that with no storm in the forecast there was no compelling reason not to give Moffett and his guest a ride and the crew more flight experience.

The original plan had been to practice hook-ons, but the airplanes could not safely take off in fog, so that exercise had to be scrapped. "There were other tests they could run," McCord told Wiley, such as fuel consumption tests. When Wiley recounted this, the committee did not pursue it, though one may wonder whether it would have been considered expedient to do such tests in the middle of the night had not Moffett been waiting to take off.

The airship climbed into the fog using the thrust of its propellers swiveled vertically, and proceeded west toward Philadelphia, then southwest along the Delaware River—a direction diametrically opposite to its ultimate destination of Newport. "Between 8:20 and 8:30 P.M.," Wiley said he "observed lightning to the southward at a distance of some 25 miles." About 8:35 P.M., the airship's radio operator received information of a thunderstorm condition at Washington, D.C. Lieutenant Commander Wiley expressed to Commander McCord his judgment that "it was advisable to steer a westerly course," for the reason that a westerly course would take them to a safer area behind the storm. Wiley said, "Commander McCord replied that he had seen lightning likewise to the west," and so ordered the course changed to a southeasterly direction. The *Akron* then made a widely zigzagging course for reasons that remain unclear. The apparently random wandering may have been done to avoid the bad weather, or it could have been an attempt to probe the storm and test the limits of the airship in accordance with the admiral's wishes.

About 11:30 P.M., "A sudden turbulence of air was encountered and the ship made a rapid descent from 1,600 feet to 700 feet as recorded on the altimeter," said Wiley, the only survivor from the airship's control car. After gradually climbing back to its original altitude of 1,600 feet, and maintaining good trim for one to three minutes, the *Akron* made a second rapid descent that that ended only when the airship hit the ocean off Barnegat Inlet, some twenty miles southeast of Lakehurst, whence it had departed five hours earlier.

The *Akron*'s wreckage sat on the seabed in relatively shallow water. If the lower part of the *Akron* had not been flattened and the hull had been intact, the top of the airship would have been above calm water! The navy assigned the submarine rescue ship *Falcon* to the salvage operations, sending divers down during the period 18 to 25 April. They determined that "the wreckage of the *Akron* was of all one piece and no significant parts had been detached from the main wreck except the lower fin . . . and the control car." From the evidence of ruts in the sea bed, "it was assumed that these protuberances were dragged off as the wreck pivoted on the ocean floor." The fin did not break away as the result of the redesigned fin attachment.

In Akron, there was still uncertainty whether the airship had suffered some structural failure which caused the accident, or whether it succumbed to the overpowering elements. For clarification, Arnstein wrote to Wiley on 11 May 1933: "It would help matters materially if you would be kind enough to write to me your personal opinion and conclusion as to whether the ship broke in the air or failed after striking the water. If I am not mistaken you have already made a statement of this character in the course of the Inquiry but this testimony has not yet been made available to us. An expression of your opinion in this matter would help more than anything else in clarifying this problem." Wiley wrote back on 20 May: ". . . it is my personal opinion and conclusion that the *Akron* crash was caused by the ship striking the water on being carried downward by a vertical air current in a thunderstorm.

"My first impression of the event as given in the press on April 4 did not carry this conclusion . . . that the damage to the *Akron* was caused by the ship striking the water and then progressed until the ship entirely rested on the water in a broken condition."

By the date of his reply, the results of the naval court of inquiry had been published, so Wiley quoted from the findings: "The ship was inclined upward by the bow and as the descent continued the lower fin struck the water under the influence of the ship's air speed, the rate of fall of the ship, and probably a quarter wind on the ship's tail of about 40 knots. The immediate effect was to shear the after part of the lower fin carrying with it the lower rudder. This impact probably caused the collapse of the tail portion of the ship and through a combination of bending and shear forces caused breaks in other parts of the ship's structure . . . The tail portion having collapsed in the water the resulting break and the forward movement of the upper structure carried the forward portion into the water causing the final collapse."

Arnstein was reassured that the airship had remained intact until it struck the waves. Some critics had already begun to speculate otherwise, based on the only other eyewitness testimony. But Arnstein countered, based on his conclusion from Wiley's comments, ". . . the structural failures reported by Erwin and Deal, the other two survivors, are clearly associated with the airship's impact with the water, though they are said by some writers to have seen or heard the failures while the airship was in flight." Arnstein reasoned, "It is unlikely that Erwin and Deal, inside the hull on a dark and stormy night, could have been aware of the airship's altitude." He believed the court's conclusion was sound.

Arnstein's own testimony at the hearings did not contribute much to the analysis of the causes of the disaster, in part because of the line of questioning adopted by the committee, but mostly because he did not really know what had happened. The issue of the reduced factor of safety on the tail section indicated by the NACA wind tunnel results did not come up, and frame 17.5 was mentioned only in the light of the accident in which the lower fin had been bashed against the ground at Lakehurst the previous year. Arnstein reassured the committee that the damage that resulted had been adequately and completely repaired.

If Arnstein's testimony as regards the loss of the *Akron* had no great importance, he did make good use of a chance to face down certain slanders dating to the summer of 1924 when certain German nationalists tried to deny that a non-German, Arnstein, was chief designer of the airship *Los Angeles*, the great symbol of German technical supremacy and object of national pride. Frederick S. Hardesty, a consulting engineer from Washington, D.C., who had represented Schütte-Lanz interests in the United States during the 1920s, revived the old falsehoods from the nationalistic German press during the hearings. Citing a 1920 list of high officials of Luftschiffbau-Zeppelin on which Arnstein was credited as head of "Calculations," he denigrated Arnstein as only a mathematician or "calculator," not a designer. Arnstein was present during Hardesty's testimony and was prepared to refute it, once Breckinridge repeated the insult. "This statement is in error," Arnstein replied. "I designed the *Los Angeles*."

After the investigations were complete, Hunsaker summarized the findings of both the naval court of inquiry and the congressional committee of investigation by saying, "Their conclusion is that the loss of the airship was due to an error of judgment, meaning mistaken navigating and operating practice. The ship was found to be well-built and equipped." His assessment may be too harsh on the navy. The crew was experienced, and the ship had logged nearly seventeen hundred flight hours. In the perilous conditions, the airship had dipped very close to the cold Atlantic waves, perhaps closer than her crew realized. Every effort was made to keep the airship steady and on even keel. But no amount of piloting skill could have prevented the airship from reacting to what at the time was a poorly understood phenomenon. The *Akron* likely succumbed to what today would be called a microburst—a sudden, violent, localized downdraft caused by the colliding air masses— that pushed the stern of the airship into the sea.

Breckinridge, analyzing the cause of the accident, commented: "Looking back, it is easy to say that the lives of splendid men and costly Government property would have been saved had the *Akron* remained in her hangar. Officers skilled in the relatively new science of aerology according to the existing standards of competence in the Navy studied the situation and perceived nothing in the available weather data to lead to a decision to cancel the flight." Exactly the opposite opinion was reached by Mitchell, the Weather Bureau's chief forecaster, who testified that the 8 P.M. weather map of 3 April was "loaded with dynamite" in the form of conflicting weather disturbances likely to move northeast. But Mitchell admitted he "had never known of so general a storm area as occurred on the Atlantic seaboard between 3 P.M. on April 3 and 8 A.M. on April 4." Yet the innocuous forecast printed on the map itself—"overcast with occasional rain"—was surely no warning. Krick's forecast that so impressed Kármán and Arnstein was made around 10 P.M. eastern time. By that time the *Akron* was already in the air. Arnstein shared Mitchell's belief that there was enough information available for the flight to have been postponed. He thought the navy aerologists, and perhaps also McCord, had probably allowed their judgment to be swayed by the presence of Moffett with his unspoken but evident desire to fly.

Chapter 16 INTO THE STRATOSPHERE

After the first shock of the loss of the *Akron* had passed, one of the first questions to enter Arnstein's mind was: did the airship fail in midair turbulence because of the known deficiency of the tail attachment structure? If so, then he needed to convince Fulton that the *Macon*'s tail should be reinforced before the airship left Akron, where it could and would be done immediately, with minimum interference to operational needs.

Despite the loss of the *Akron*, and maybe because of it, the Goodyear-Zeppelin workers and the contingent of navy crewmen renewed their focus on getting her sister ship, the *Macon*, ready for a first flight, which took place on 21 April 1933. Arnstein was not successful in persuading Fulton to approve the tail structure reinforcement, and the *Macon* was commissioned in June and flown to Lakehurst commanded by Commander Alger H. Dresel with Rear Admiral Ernest J. King, new chief of the navy's Bureau of Aeronautics, aboard.

Still remaining to be done were the tasks of inspection and liaison engineering, but the engineering staff required for these chores was far smaller than had been needed for the *Akron*. Arnstein had been able to acquire some excellent talent, and since the commercial airship business had not manifested itself, he looked for other suitably challenging work to keep his organization together until it would come. Both he and Litchfield believed it would, despite the *Akron*'s loss. A comparison with the end of airship work at Luftschiffbau in the period after 1919 could not have been lost on Arnstein. With no Zeppelins to build, that company had tried to retain its workforce by manufacturing aluminum boats and cookware. The work stoppage at Goodyear-Zeppelin was not so abrupt, but the Great Depression meant that prospects for new business were slim.

There was some work on modifying the Goodyear blimp fleet, and some work building a new blimp for the army, the TC-13, and refurbishing a navy blimp, the K-1, but nonaeronautical projects were likewise sought. One involved building a duralumin mast for the America's Cup yacht, *Whirlwind*. Another was building the "sky cars" for the Sky Ride at Chicago's Century of Progress Exposition of 1933. The sky cars resembled airship gondolas. Made of steel and aluminum, their streamlined, bus-sized cabins had two passenger decks, one above the other, and large windows. These allowed the passengers a magnificent view of the fairgrounds, the city of Chicago, and the Lake Michigan shoreline from the cars' cableway two hundred feet in the air. Goodyear-Zeppelin built ten of the cars in a corner of the Air Dock not being used for *Macon* construction.

The Century of Progress Exposition spawned another project which led to employment for the Goodyear-Zeppelin engineering department as work on the *Macon* wound down. Swiss balloonist Auguste Piccard had shown the way to the stratosphere in 1931 and again in 1932. Why not have him make another scientific ascent from Chicago as part of the Century of Progress Exposition? At first receptive to the idea, Piccard decided he had other commitments and suggested his twin brother, Jean, who had been employed as a chemical researcher in the United States since 1926. Goodyear agreed to provide the 600,000 cubic foot balloon envelope and suspension at cost, while the Dow Chemical Company offered to furnish at no cost a gondola made of Dowmetal, a lightweight magnesium alloy that it had developed.

In the end, after much politicking, it was not Jean Piccard who took off from Soldier Field in Chicago at 3 A.M. on 5 August 1933, but Lieutenant Settle, who was not only the inspector of naval aircraft during the building of the *Akron* and *Macon* airships at Goodyear-Zeppelin, but an experienced competition balloonist. Settle took off with a malfunctioning gas valve and had to abort after only twenty minutes of flight, landing ingloriously in the Burlington Railroad yards a few miles away. The balloon was saved with only minor damage and a second flight was scheduled. However, a succession of delays due to poor weather, other fair events, and unavailability of science instruments meant the balloon could not launch before the fair's November closing date. Then, in only three days, the gondola, balloon, and gas cylinders were rushed to Akron. On 20 November Settle again climbed into the gondola, accompanied by United States Marine Corps Major Chester L. Fordney, who had helped rescue the balloon's envelope from souvenir hunters in the Chicago railroad yard. The reborn *A Century of Progress* balloon arose outside the Goodyear-Zeppelin hangar from which the *Macon* had departed five months before. As the fifteen-story-tall balloon ascended toward the stratosphere, the crew talked to a nation-wide radio audience and monitored science experiments. Eight hours later, the balloon landed in a southern New Jersey marsh. This flight set an officially recognized world alti-

Tex Settle checks the rigging atop the gondola of the stratosphere balloon A Century of Progress. *The dolly was used to wheel the gondola out of the Air Dock. (Goodyear Tire and Rubber Co. Collection/ University of Akron Archives)*

tude record of 61,237 feet. Of this accomplishment, balloon historian Craig Ryan has written, "It was the most successful stratospheric balloon flight launched from American soil, and Settle and Fordney became the first Americans to take a pressurized cabin beyond the stratosphere." Arnstein was not present to witness the launch. He had left for Germany three weeks earlier aboard the *Graf Zeppelin* after its final stop in Akron following a visit to Chicago.

The *Graf Zeppelin* began commercial air passenger service via airship across the ocean. In the two years after it completed the first airship flight around the world in 1929, the *Graf* had embarked on two notable flights of exploration, one over Siberia and another an international scientific expedition to the Arctic. But these flights were mostly for show. The *Graf* was designed for routine commercial service, to fly six thousand miles nonstop, accommodate twenty passengers in luxurious surroundings and lift twelve tons of freight. Since 1931, the *Graf Zeppelin* had been making scheduled flights across the Atlantic from Germany to Rio de Janeiro, Brazil. At first, there were only three such trips, the next year there were nine. The round trip took ten days. On the last flight of the 1933 schedule, at the request of the promoters of the Chicago Century of Progress Exposition, Eckener brought the *Graf* north via Miami to Akron. Arriving at night, Eckener prudently circled the city until the snow and wind abated toward dawn on 25 October before he landed. Then more than 250 Goodyear-Zeppelin shop people walked the big airship into the cavernous Air Dock. The next day the *Graf*, the left side of its vertical fins now each emblazoned with the swastika of Nazi Germany, flew to Chicago. However, on the right side of the vertical fins, the *Graf Zeppelin* was still painted in the black, red, and white tricolor of the German Republic. Cleverly, Eckener made sure the Zeppelin flew only in a big clockwise circle around the Windy City, keeping the swastika facing away from downtown to avoid offending the Americans. The airship then returned for a brief stopover in Akron. When the *Graf Zeppelin* left the next day, 28 October, Arnstein was on board, bound for Germany. It must have been satisfying for him

as he stepped aboard. This was Arnstein's first experience using a transoceanic airship passenger service, the realization of a dream to which he had devoted nearly a decade of work. And yet he must have been slightly disappointed that the pioneering Zeppelin had not come from Akron, but from Friedrichshafen.

Arnstein was still a consultant for Goodyear-Zeppelin's sister company, Luftschiffbau-Zeppelin, and was going to Friedrichshafen to get his first glimpse of the future of airship travel. Eckener was trying to capitalize on the success of the *Graf Zeppelin*, and Luftschiff-bau had already discarded plans for a new Zeppelin, the LZ 128, in favor of a still larger one, the LZ 129. It would be the largest Zeppelin the world had ever seen, larger even than the *Akron* or *Macon*. A new, larger hangar was required for its construction and a new base at Frankfurt would be built for its passenger operations. Arnstein arrived in Friedrichs–hafen on 2 November after a scheduled stop in Seville, Spain. He then spent the better part of the next three weeks looking at the new Zeppelin under construction, paying par-ticular attention to the passenger accommodations and novel method of installing gas cells around an axial keel within the airship's hull. He met with Eckener, Lehmann, Dürr, pilots Hans Flemming and Anton Witteman, and designer Albert Ehrle. Eckener's amiable son,

Knut, showed him the fabricating shops and wind tunnel, and Arnstein went to Stuttgart to see the new airship's engines, not Maybachs, but Daimler-Benz 16-cylinder, 1,200-horsepower (895 kW) diesels. Of special interest was a visit to the Weather Bureau to get maps and copy data on wind speed and direction over the transatlantic airship routes. After a discussion with Foerster he made notes on the safety factors for main rings "up to 40 to 45 meters diameter."

On 17 November, Arnstein flew from Paris to London via Imperial Airways airplane. On 20 November, Arnstein called on the British Air Ministry. He visited with the designer of the British rigid airship R 100, Barnes Wallis, and later met with a potential customer for Goodyear's aircraft tires. After a visit to the airship sheds at Cardington, Arnstein sailed for home on 23 November.

Back in Akron, the record flight of *A Century of Progress* a few days earlier aroused the interest of army captain Albert W. Stevens, an aerial photography expert at Wright Field in Dayton, Ohio. Stevens wanted Goodyear-Zeppelin to build an even larger balloon to carry him above 80,000 feet. This competition to climb ever higher into the atmosphere was not just a rivalry between navy and army balloonists, but an international contest: the Soviet Union and the United States at this time were each trying to leapfrog each others' altitude records. Stevens first secured the support of his friend, Gilbert Grosvenor, the president of the National Geographic Society, then went to Goodyear with his plan. To reach the altitude Stevens wanted, Arnstein calculated that the new balloon, *Explorer*, would need a capacity of 3,000,000 cubic feet—more gas volume than the airship *Los Angeles*. The balloon would be five times larger than *A Century of Progress* with its envelope covering three times as much area. Goodyear-Zeppelin charged only $25,000 for the balloon and its connecting harness, more than $10,000 below cost. The company considered the loss a contribution to the project's scientific goals, and the project did have some advertising value. The balloon used three weights of rubberized fabric held together by eight miles of seams, and its load-bearing external catenary suspension had 160 bridles terminating in quarter-inch manila lines attached to a new, larger Dowmetal gondola. Even if there were no giant airships to build for now, at least Goodyear-Zeppelin had aeronautic business.

By the early morning hours of 28 July 1934, the *Explorer* was ready to launch. It would ascend from a steep-walled canyon dubbed the "Stratobowl" at Rapid City, South Dakota. In addition to Stevens, army captain Orvil A. Anderson and Major William E. Kepner, both experienced balloonists, were aboard. The balloon rose uneventfully, and its tiny bubble of hydrogen gas began to swell the enormous rubberized fabric bag. About 1 P.M., as the balloon passed 60,000 feet, the giant envelope started to tear. The cause was traced not to the way the balloon envelope had been manufactured, but how it was packed for shipment. The cold air had caused the rubber surface to adhere to itself in the folds of the balloon fabric. As the envelope stretched open, the sticking rubber pulled the fabric apart. Fortunately, the collapsing bag formed a parachute to slow the balloon's descent. Anderson and the others prepared to jump from the gondola to land with their own parachutes once they reached a lower altitude. No sooner had Anderson climbed out of the hatch when the balloon's chafing, rubberized fabric remnants generated a spark (as in early Zeppelin experience) and ignited the remaining mix of hydrogen and air. The bag disintegrated, but all three pilots jumped to safety before the gondola smashed into the ground. The balloon had missed the altitude record by 624 feet—and the last pilot out escaped death by parachuting only 500 feet from the ground.

Undeterred, Stevens wanted to try a return trip to the stratosphere. *Explorer* had been insured, and he was again able to obtain a new endorsement of the army and National Geographic Society. By December 1934 Stevens was in Akron conferring with Arnstein. They soon came up with the design for *Explorer II*, which, because it would use helium for lift, would be even larger than its predecessor. The new balloon would have a volume of 3,700,000 cubic feet—nearly equal to the volume of the airship *Graf Zeppelin*. By early spring 1935, the redesigned balloon envelope was nearly ready. It had heavier cloth in areas likely to rupture and the tacky rubber had been smoothed and dusted with soapstone to keep it from sticking together. The five and two-thirds acres of envelope weighed three tons. A series of mechanical and weather delays pushed the launch of *Explorer*

The stratosphere balloon Explorer *climbs above South Dakota, July 1934.* (The Lighter-Than-Air Society Collection/University of Akron Archives)

II from June into autumn, and it was not until 11 November that the balloon was inflated in well below freezing temperatures. Illuminated by a circle of floodlights, the pale craft looked like a giant jellyfish as it took shape. This time, only Stevens and Anderson were aboard as the thirty-one-story-tall balloon rose above the Stratobowl. The eight hour and thirteen minute flight was a tremendous success. With a lift of nine tons, including one ton of scientific instruments, *Explorer II* ascended to an altitude of 72,395 feet, a new world record. Radio audiences in the United States and Europe listened as the pilots described the curvature of the earth's horizon and the dark but sunlit sky above. The pair took air samples, measured radiation, conducted meteorological experiments, and took lots of photographs. *Explorer II* gently returned to the earth loaded with new scientific information for aeronautic and other research. The crew members were acclaimed by Congress and President Roosevelt. But high-altitude rubberized fabric balloons had reached their limit. *Explorer II*'s envelope was cut into a million bookmarks for National Geographic Society members. Although no one knew it at the time, the *Explorer II* flight proved to be the zenith of balloon exploration for the decade; there were no sequels until well after the Second World War. Then, polyethylene became available to make the envelopes of Sky-hook balloons that could climb above 90 percent of the earth's atmosphere. And not until the space race would there again be such enthusiasm for probing the heavens.

Chapter 17 ALL EYES ON THE "MACON"

During the first half of 1934, the USS *Macon* received a workout with the fleet, participating in a number of exercises in the Pacific and Caribbean. There was pressure on the crew and airship to perform. As Admiral King noted: "This is to be a critical year for airships. We have only one airship. We must not be reckless, but if airships are to justify themselves, the *Macon* has got to show more than she has shown." Frustrating to airship proponents, instead of being put to use as eyes of the fleet, the airship repeatedly was put in congested tactical operations where she was vulnerable to being hypothetically "shot down." It was an uphill battle to convince some of the navy brass of the airship's usefulness. Of more strategic value was the application of a patrol maneuver that allowed the *Macon*'s Curtiss F9C Sparrowhawk airplanes to fly out on a 60-degree track from their "flying carrier," change course 120 degrees and return. By repeating this zigzag course, the faster airplanes could stay parallel with their airship and simultaneously sweep vast areas of ocean looking for the enemy while the airship stayed clear of the surface fleet.

The *Macon* was now stationed at Sunnyvale, California, at the Navy base renamed Moffett Field in honor of the late Bureau of Aeronautics chief. In April the ZRS-5 was expected to participate in a joint exercise with the Atlantic and Pacific fleets in the Caribbean. To get there, the *Macon* would have to traverse the challenging Continental Divide on a passage through Arizona, New Mexico, and Texas. During the seventy-four-hour cross-country flight from California to Opa-Locka, Florida, the *Macon* encountered a severe storm with powerful vertical gusts while flying over the Continental Divide in Texas. The airship was heavy with fuel, its nose pointed slightly up, and in the hot, thin air, her engines were turning at full power to maintain dynamic lift. Meanwhile, the turbulent desert air buffeted the airship. Those were exactly the conditions that could result in excessive loads on the tail surfaces, the potentially serious situation about which Arnstein had warned Fulton. Around noon on 21 April 1934 the *Macon* dived steeply and "a gust of terrific force slammed into her." There was a grinding noise aft, and a repair crew sent to the scene found two diagonal girders broken and another buckled. The damaged parts were structural elements of the main frame supporting the forward part of the left horizontal fin—frame 17.5. The crew made emergency repairs and reinforcements in flight, saving the *Macon* and allowing it to continue its flight to Florida.

Commander Dresel radioed a message to be delivered to Fulton describing the damage, and within an hour Fulton had called Arnstein. The following morning, Arnstein sent Red Coffelt and a mechanic to Florida on Goodyear's private transport plane. By the time the airship arrived at Opa-Locka, Kurt Bauch and two more mechanics were on a train headed south with repair materials. The team replaced the damaged girders while the airship was moored in the open, despite frequent rain squalls and sudden wind shifts, and while distracted by swarms of mosquitoes and the presence of rattlesnakes on the field. The repaired *Macon* was able to join the fleet exercises on 5 May.

The 21 April incident forced Fulton and the Bureau of Aeronautics to accept Arnstein's warning and the NACA test data as the basis for strengthening the tail fins on the *Macon*. Goodyear recommended reinforcements on the airship and readied parts for the installation. But this would have to wait. The navy, Fulton in particular, did not want to take the *Macon* out of operational status to reinforce the fins while the airship was trying to prove its usefulness. Arnstein did not believe the airship should continue to fly, but if he had insisted that the airship be grounded, he would risk Litchfield's ire, because Goodyear could not afford to displease its only customer. In fact, Litchfield wanted Arnstein to okay Fulton's letter saying it was acceptable to fly the airship over the sea if it stayed out of gusts—an impossible requirement, Arnstein felt. Arnstein wrote a reply to Fulton without actually approving the commander's recommended course of action. In deference to Litchfield's admonishing, he marked "personal" on the company letterhead so Goodyear-Zeppelin was never on record as approving or disapproving the urgent need for the reinforcement. Nevertheless, Goodyear made $10,000 worth of reinforcements at company expense and shipped them to Moffett Field.

The navy restricted the airship's operations to the Pacific coast where it was thought conditions similar to those which had damaged the *Macon*'s tail over Texas would not occur, and which was supposed to be free of storms. While believing the airship's structure "amply strong for any operations over the sea," the navy recognized the need for reinforcing the fins and attachment points at ring 17.5. However, the Bureau of Aeronautics expressed the view that, "Because the work is not urgent, it is considered that it can be accomplished from time to time, as opportunity offers, at the discretion of the Command-ing Officer, and, therefore, will not interfere with operating schedules." There was a chance to learn more about the fin pressure concentrations that actually occurred in flight, and the knowledge thus obtained may have settled once and for all the issue about the need to reinforce the fins. In July, Goodyear-Zeppelin and the navy agreed that a simple pressure-measuring instrument in one of the fins would give important information. After accepting the idea for such an instrument, the navy invited a quotation, and one was sub-mitted in September. After that, a Goodyear-Zeppelin memorandum notes, "Nothing more was heard about this project." Meanwhile, the *Macon* saw a change of command, with Commander Herbert V. Wiley, sole surviving officer of the *Akron* disaster, replacing Commander Dresel.

Lieutenant Commander Herbert V. Wiley, U.S.N., last captain of the USS Macon. *(The Lighter-Than-Air Society Collection/University of Akron Archives)*

From July through the end of the year, Wiley worked hard to expand and advance the *Macon*'s capabilities, proving the airship's worth to the fleet. New tools and techniques were tried, including tests of a "spy basket"—a small, wingless aircraft cockpit suspended on a cable below the airship—a device originally developed by Gemmingen and Lehmann in WWI to observe the enemy while the airship remained hidden in the clouds above. Wiley aggressively perfected tactics involving the airship's complement of F9C airplanes, sending them to intercept President Roosevelt at sea aboard the cruiser *Houston*, a stunt that was praised for its initiative but landed Wiley in hot water with his superior officers. There were plans to experiment with radio direction-finding equipment, night operations with its planes, new engines, ballast water recovery, and camouflage. Wiley took his airship flying as much as possible to answer critics within the navy who said the airship had not done enough to demonstrate its performance. But in doing so he came up against the navy's austere budget. Wiley spent his airship's total operating expense for one month just on fuel for a single flight. When he had to curtail operations "on account of meager allot-ments of fuel," Wiley wrote to Admiral King to intercede in getting more aviation fuel. All during this time, Wiley had no knowledge of any urgency to reinforce the fins, nor concern about the proposed schedule of alterations affecting the safety of his airship.

In September, Goodyear-Zeppelin sent the material to Moffett Field to be used in rein-forcing the *Macon*'s fins and frame 17.5. Once the parts arrived, there were further delays in getting the shipment to the officer in charge of assembly and repair. Ben Schnitzer, Arn-stein's representative, kept needling to get the reinforcements made, but since it was past the airship's guarantee period it was no longer the company's responsibility, and Goodyear-Zeppelin could not force the issue. If the airship were in Akron, Goodyear would have completed the repairs with a round-the-clock operation over a long weekend.

Schnitzer reported that navy brass did nothing on weekends except play golf. The navy engineer, Fulton's man, agreed with Schnitzer that the repairs should be made at once, but said, "What can we do?"

This procrastination made Arnstein furious. To him, it seemed the navy "just didn't give a damn!" Arnstein wanted Goodyear to send a crew to install the reinforcements, but Litchfield would not agree. "It's not our airship," he would say, "it is the Navy's responsibility." After a second or third visit from Arnstein on the subject, Litchfield repeated that "in this business, the customer is always right." Arnstein thought this policy was fine for tires, but for an experimental advanced vehicle as complex as a rigid airship, it just wasn't suitable. "And stop insulting Fulton," Litchfield added bluntly.

Burgess also wanted the reinforcements made, and asked Arnstein to pressure Fulton. Arnstein replied he had already done all he could and Litchfield would not let him do more because Goodyear-Zeppelin did not want to risk upsetting its best customer, the navy. While there still remained a calculated risk in flying the *Macon*, that was considered acceptable. As a warning and reassurance, Arnstein outlined the requirements for safe operation of airships in a speech to the Aeronautical Section of the National Safety Council in October 1934. He noted, "The history of airships has shown that when disasters have occurred, there has generally been some combination of . . . coincidences which has magnified a series of minor failures into a major catastrophe." On airship handling he said, "Helmsmen must . . . have the 'feel' of the ship and know how to counteract gusts at their inception." He added, "Engineers and officers must instinctively know when and where to drop ballast or valve gas and when to increase and decrease [engine] power." And he warned, "They should make no move which will tend to augment the severe stresses already imposed on the structure by natural forces." Practically, this meant that an airship should not be flown fast in gusty air, not flown relying too much on dynamic lift (that is, not flown "heavy"), and not be subjected to rapid maneuvers or inputs on the controls. Arnstein could not have known his recommendations for safe airship operation would soon be tested.

The navy set about doing the fin reinforcements on its own schedule. It had assigned a relative order of importance to the work, calling for reinforcements first to frame 17.5 near the horizontal and next the vertical fins, then the horizontal and vertical fins themselves. Between 10 November 1934 and 10 February 1935, reinforcements were put in place around the lower and horizontal fins, since they were the most readily accessible. Reinforcing the upper fin was the last priority, since it would involve deflating two gas cells and opening the hull cover to get access to the structure. This procedure promised to be time-consuming, so it was scheduled for the airship's overhaul in March. On the morning of 11 February 1935 the *Macon* took off for training in strategic scouting.

The exercise went smoothly, with the *Macon* launching and recovering her scout planes that diligently tracked the surface fleet. A little after 5 P.M. on 12 February, the *Macon* was flying parallel to the California coast near Point Sur, running into rain and fog. The airship was just recovering from a shallow dive when suddenly, a sharp gust hit the airship. The 785-foot-long *Macon* lurched toward the shore. According to witnesses who were watching from the Point Sur lighthouse, the airship's upper fin lifted away from the hull at its leading edge, then the whole fin flew to pieces, except the rudder and rudder post. The crewmen on board weren't sure what had happened. The airship's rudder and elevator control wheels had momentarily spun out of the hands of the crewmen holding them, but those in the control car did not immediately know there was a casualty. At the airship's stern, however, helium was rushing into the upper passageway from three ruptured gas cells. The crewmen on the scene sped to the ship's telephones to alert the commander. Orders were quickly given to drop fuel tanks and ballast water gushed from *Macon*'s hull. The action to halt the *Macon*'s descent was too much. Lightened of sixteen tons of gasoline and all ballast aft of midships, the Zeppelin shot skyward. As the airship climbed well above **pressure height**, helium poured from the automatic valves. The starboard engines roared at near standard speed as the ship continued its upward spiral into the clouds. The *Macon*'s fate was sealed. With too much of her lifting gas vented to the sky, she could not remain aloft, and dropped tail first toward the sea. Yet it all happened in slow motion. From the moment of the critical gust to the time the ship touched the ocean thirty-four minutes ticked by. There was plenty of time for *Macon*'s crew to don the life jackets and man the life rafts carried as a consequence of the *Akron* tragedy. All but two of the 83 on board the *Macon* were saved.

The city of Akron was again stunned, but rallied to its Zeppelin builders. At Goodyear-Zeppelin, the mood was downcast. "It is unnecessary to say that the loss of the *Macon* has been a terrible shock to us, and means a very serious set-back," Arnstein wrote at the time. Probably due to the low loss of life, Litchfield remarked, "The popular reaction to the loss of the *Macon* has not been nearly so severe as in the case of the loss of the *Akron*." The reaction from Congress and in the navy was not so charitable. Carl Vinson, House Naval Affairs Committee chairman, said the crash was "possibly 'the death knell' of the navy's experiments in lighter-than-air craft." The navy issued a confidential memorandum saying "The Chief of Naval Operations advises against the building of any additional rigid airships . . ." despite the fact the chief of the Bureau of Aeronautics, Admiral King, "was strongly in favor" of obtaining replacement airships for the *Akron* and *Macon*, or at least a smaller airship for training, to replace the decommissioned *Los Angeles*. While the administration had approved $38 million for naval construction projects, an airship "was not so much as mentioned on the navy's priority list from which the projects were taken." Secretary of the Navy, Claude A. Swanson, said there were other things the navy needed more than airships.

There was another round of investigations, namely, a naval court of inquiry and one conducted by a group from the Science Advisory Board. It was the Special Committee on Airships, the Durand Committee, made up principally of noted researchers and professors of engineering. Among them was Theodor von Kármán. The findings of the Durand Committee were published as a series of five reports from 1936 to 1937. Report Number 3, *Technical Aspects of the Loss of the Macon*, would be a source of pain and aggravation for Arnstein. Before the Durand Committee had even issued this report, one of its members, Dr. Alfred V. de Forest, had leaked to the press that he believed the navy was at fault for not expediting the repairs that Arnstein had suggested. There was an implication that Goodyear-Zeppelin was looking to blame Fulton for the *Macon*'s loss because he had delayed the fin reinforcements. Fulton produced Arnstein's letter marked "personal" as evidence that everyone had agreed the reinforcement did not have to be carried out immediately. Arnstein did not comment publicly, but he believed that his explanation of how easy it would be to install cables "to provide additional reinforcement for the forward part of the fins" should have been enough to alert Fulton to his ongoing concern, especially since he had submitted the idea for Fulton's "personal consideration" and they had discussed the matter repeatedly. Arnstein was disappointed in Kármán, whom he regarded as a friend, for not pointing out during the investigation that there had been some urgency in reinforcing the fins. But no mention of Arnstein's misgivings appeared in the Durand Committee's report. Rather, it stated that the program of reinforcement was "apparently accepted by all concerned." Privately, Kármán explained to Arnstein on two occasions that the Durand Committee "had to protect Fulton" because his navy career was in jeopardy, whereas Kármán believed Arnstein "was in a secure position and would not be hurt by what the committee said." In later years, Arnstein was displeased that Kármán in his autobiography implied that Goodyear-Zeppelin "may have wished to place blame elsewhere to avoid possible criticism of themselves."

On the contrary, it was Goodyear-Zeppelin policy not to comment further on the matter; "the time and energy would be better spent if applied constructively to such things as new commercial projects." Litchfield had taken the attitude that both Goodyear-Zeppelin and the navy had responsibility, "and that neither party would have allowed things to go on as they did, had they realized that so much was at stake." Fulton prepared a twelve-page memorandum expressing his own recollection of events concerning the fin reinforcement, stating that there had been no reason given for grounding the *Macon*, and that none of the airship's officers "felt any concern as to the necessity for the reinforcements to be executed immediately." He noted that the officers who operated the *Macon* continued to believe the airship was structurally sound and safe to fly. Arnstein did not agree with Fulton's memory of their discussions and correspondence, but he wrote to Fulton that "it was company policy to engage in no efforts to assess blame for what had occurred and, in particular, the individual employees were to abstain from any discussion or letter writing on such a subject." He did go so far as to say, "I hope you will not interpret my silence on this subject as denoting agreement, but will realize that it is the company's policy of not further discussing this controversial subject." It was not until a decade later that Litchfield commented on the accident in his book, *Why? Why Has America No Rigid Airships?* "Hindsight would indicate that the ship should have been grounded," he wrote.

The Durand Committee concluded that perhaps the gust was stronger than indicated, and believed that the structure may have been weakened by the Texas incident or in sharp maneuvers subsequently with no outwardly visible sign of damage. In the middle of these conclusions was the opinion "that the methods of analysis employed for determining the stress condition . . . were not . . . capable of taking adequate account of the stress condition in this very complex structure." Clearly, this language pained Arnstein, since it questioned his ability as a stress analyst, and furthermore, its explanation dismissed the later data on fin loading that prompted Arnstein's recommendation for reinforcement. The report said, ". . . it had seemed more reasonable to assume the existence of loads greater than those on which the design had been based, while at the same time admitting the possibility of stress concentrations at certain points of the structure which could hardly be indicated with complete accuracy by purely analytical methods." Had not Arnstein been vindicated by the later series of NACA tests, certainly known to the committee, which had found air pressures on the fins "much larger than had been anticipated"? The report skated over these issues. Arnstein said nothing in his defense, abiding by company policy that prohibited further discussion of the matter. Later, Arnstein admitted that he was probably too sensitive, and remarked with a little smile that he never forgot an insult but easily forgot compliments. Arnstein did recognize that Fulton's actions may have been dictated by navy politics, much as he had to obey Litchfield's instructions not to antagonize the customer, and he believed in accepting the findings of the committee and of all investigation boards, however much he was irritated by those who wanted to hash it all out again.

The naval court of inquiry report was unable to determine whether a gust of wind or a structural failure had caused the casualty leading to the loss of the *Macon*, praised the handling of the airship by Lieutenant Commander Wiley and the "conduct of every officer and man" and concluded that no offenses were committed and no blame incurred on the part of the crew. Despite this finding, several *Macon* crew members believed they knew with certainty what happened, convinced that either a gust, excessive stresses, or undetected metal fatigue caused the structural failure. Arnstein himself believed the navigation officer's report of a gust and agreed with the Durand Committee that it might have amplified the loads put on the fin by maneuvering. He also held out the possibility there could have been hairline cracks from the Texas damage in the upper fin structure, even though Bauch, who had been sent to do the repairs, had been unable to detect any cracks with his naked eye. Arnstein agonized over how he might have taken some further action to prevent the *Macon*'s loss. He thought perhaps that he should have gone through Litchfield to make his case to the secretary of the navy. Of course this was hindsight, and such action risked antagonizing Goodyear's only customer. It was no small risk, either, since Fulton had the whip hand in all dealings with the Bureau of Aeronautics. Goodyear-Zeppelin felt itself protected, having submitted the analysis and the reinforcement parts in ample time. No one knew the precise limits beyond which it was unsafe to fly the *Macon*, but it is ironic that the conditions for successful airship operations that Arnstein had presented to the National Safety Council in October were exceeded on 12 February.

Immediately after the *Macon*'s loss was blamed on failure of its upper fin, there was speculation that a similar failure had caused the *Akron*'s crash. Neither Fulton nor Arnstein believed the two accidents were in any way related. Arnstein was "pained by the suggestion," and Fulton "grumbled that attempts to tie the two together in terms of similar fin failures was 'the stuff of quacks.'" The *Akron* wreckage was examined by divers shortly after the wreck and it was determined that the lower fin had not been dislodged by impact with the water, but only after it had been dragged along the ocean floor. The other fins remained attached to the hull. The hulk of the *Macon* was not rediscovered for many years and not explored until 1990 by remotely operated deep-sea submersible. The largest portion of the *Macon*'s hull lies at a depth of 1,500 feet (457.5 m), but the tail section fell down a sea floor slope beyond the reach of the submersible, so nothing could be concluded about whether the top fin or structure at ring 17.5 failed first.

The entire dream of Goodyear-Zeppelin was in jeopardy. When the *Akron* crashed, there was a sense that it had no business flying into a storm as it had. The loss was overwhelming and inexplicable, since the details of the accident could never be fully ascertained. But the loss of the *Macon* could be examined from many angles, and explanations of the cause would create much rancorous debate. The loss of life was much less, but the future of rigid airships in the United States was uncertain. There would be more delays as the reasons for the failure were scrutinized.

After the loss of the *Akron* and *Macon*, critics accused Arnstein of having forgotten "Dürr's cruciform" tail when he designed the deep-ring structure used in those airships. Arnstein had a patent on the cruciform design, so that was not likely. A cruciform structure is unnecessary. Arnstein knew that a deep ring can be designed to carry any load that a cruciform structure can. The wire-braced deep-ring structure was a valid alternative to the wire-braced frames and cruciform. Arnstein learned of some of the sentiments being expressed privately at Luftschiffbau via Goodyear-Zeppelin's liaison engineers. Other opinions were expressed more openly. Eckener told the press he thought the crash of the *Macon* was due to faulty design. Arnstein could only take offense. Luftschiffbau-Zeppelin had been aware of the design of the ZRS ships from their beginnings via the mutual agreement between the United States and German companies and had offered no criticism of the *Akron-Macon* design drawings. In fact, when Eckener and Dürr came to the United States for the launching of the *Akron* in 1931, they had nothing but praise for it. Arnstein summarized his view of the *Macon*'s loss in a "strictly confidential" memo to his engineers abroad. He wrote, "What was wrong, in our opinion, is that certain girders in the frame were not strong enough to take care of the worst aerodynamic conditions as presented in our analysis of 1934, a copy of which I sent confidentially to Dr. Eckener." Later, Eckener asked Arnstein why, as the designer, he did not ground the airship. "How could I?" Arnstein replied. "It wasn't our airship." This may have taken Eckener a moment to comprehend: it was opposite German practice where the airship builder decided both construction and operational matters.

Suspicion also fell on the cantilevered fins, somehow seen as less able to resist the strain because they lacked cruciform girders. Not so. They had been built to withstand all of the loading conditions known at the time they were designed. Had they been properly reinforced to reflect subsequent load information, doubts about their strength might have been dispelled. Eckener and others alleged that the cruciform design was inherently superior for rigid airships, but the *Los Angeles* suffered upper fin damage from a gust despite having a full cruciform. It, too, had been designed before the later NACA wind tunnel data was known. And consider this: Goodyear's pressure airships have had broad fins similar in shape to the *Macon*'s that are wire-braced externally with no cruciform structure through the airship envelope. No fin failures comparable to the *Macon*'s befell any of the more than two hundred blimps Goodyear later built. The infamous Change Order No. 2 that led to deeper, shorter fins on the ZRS design may not have been as significant in the *Macon*'s fin failure as once assumed. Since the original Project I fin was also designed to load assumptions later shown to be incorrect, it too may have failed in a gust like the one associated with the structural failure in the *Macon*. It should be noted that Arnstein realized the error of the earlier assumptions by the time the *Macon* was in service, and determined that reinforcement was necessary.

There was a fundamental difference in the way the Germans operated their Zeppelins from the approach adopted in the United States. "In America, they want to fly airships the way they drive automobiles—any time, any where," observed Arnstein. "One reason for the success of German airships was that they . . . only flew in good weather." Their operators tried their best to avoid flying into storms, just the opposite of the Americans. Fulton, too, knew there must be some difference in airship operating technique when he wrote, "Therein may lie some part of an explanation why German airships, which were on paper, and actually, much weaker than the *Akron* and *Macon*, were able to operate as they did." A mediocre design can be saved by skill and care in operation. Eckener later explained that the German technique of operation was to fight the gusts "as little as possible." With this care, the *Graf* survived severe weather conditions although the strength of the airship hull was "only about half" of what later airships were expected to have.

The loss of the *Macon* had another kind of stress component: its toll on the health of the Goodyear-Zeppelin engineers. Paul Helma seems to have been particularly affected. He became ill, could not work, and claimed his disability insurance. Helma, who had been with Arnstein from his college days through Züblin, Luftschiffbau, and Goodyear-Zeppelin, voluntarily ended his career. Arnstein did not report to work for several days after the *Macon* went down. When he returned, Litchfield sent him to Friedrichshafen where he visited with Eckener before going on to the Black Forest for some much needed rest. He would need it for the new challenges he was about to face at Goodyear-Zeppelin.

Chapter 18 NEW CHALLENGES, NEW DIRECTIONS

Once the *Macon* was delivered in 1933, the U.S. Navy offered little indication that it would be seeking further rigid airships. Budgets were tight, and the rigid airship's value to the fleet was still a matter of debate. There would be no new orders for dirigibles until the navy had acquired more operational experience with the one rigid airship it still had in commission. With prospects of any rigid airship construction looking remote, Arnstein and his engineers were challenged to find new markets for their talents. They needed to show that their engineering techniques had more applications than just building Zeppelins. One project of which Arnstein was especially proud was instigated by none other than Harry Vissering, the board member of Goodyear-Zeppelin who was the catalyst in getting the rubber company initially involved in rigid airship manufacture. Vissering's other interest was railroads, and he suggested that Goodyear-Zeppelin apply its expertise in building aeronautical structures to surface transport. Other manufacturers, Edward G. Budd in Philadelphia for example, were developing streamlined combinations of locomotives and coaches. These were made of modern materials, notably stainless steel. Vissering thought Goodyear-Zeppelin could compete with its own version of a lightweight, high-speed commuter train. The challenge was to provide the same degree of safety and riding comfort as ordinary trains at speeds in excess of one hundred miles per hour. Goodyear's response was the *Comet*, built for the New York, New Haven and Hartford Railroad to provide fast service between Boston and Providence, with one intermediate stop and a rapid turn around at each end of the line. The train was built at a cost of $250,000 with funds advanced by the Public Works Administration. By early 1934, a design was conceived which would take its final form by midyear. Wind tunnel tests conducted on wooden models at the Daniel Guggenheim Airship Institute determined the shape with the least drag. Aerodynamic efficiency suggested a smooth-surfaced, low-slung configuration of three articulated cars, with the double-ended drive units having rounded, sloping noses. Strength and low weight were prime objectives. The result was a vehicle weighing 40 percent less than a conventional train of the same capacity.

The structural design of the *Comet* was a radical departure from conventional railway car construction. "Many new inventions were embodied in its design," Arnstein observed. He and his engineers designed the entire skin of the roof, side walls, and car bottoms of the *Comet* to carry the load, instead of placing it all on a supporting frame below. The method had been applied successfully in aircraft structures and would later appear in "unibody" autos. Aluminum alloys were used in the rail car frame and body, while cast steel went into the trucks and wheels. "By means of a shorter, more compact wheel-and-shock-absorber arrangement," according to Arnstein, "it was possible to reduce the height of the cars by almost three feet without restricting the passenger space at all." The car bottoms sat a mere ten inches above the rails, and rode on coil springs within hydraulic shock absorbers. "This change not only resulted in a lower center of gravity for safety and stability in high speed turns, but it also resulted in a smaller cross-section or drag area for increased [fuel] economy." The *Comet* was powered by 400 horsepower (298 kW) diesels connected to electric generators driving traction motors. Workers assembled the steel and aluminum cars in the cavernous Air Dock. One visiting engineer who inspected the train as it was being built said it was made "like a Swiss watch." The *Comet* was completed in April 1935, less than two months after the *Macon* went down. In trial runs, its speed topped 110 miles per hour (176 km/h).

Goodyear's "Rail Zeppelin" was a forerunner of much later high-speed trains. Arnstein remarked, "We tried to treat all design features along the lines of airship design and found that such a train could be operated much faster, at very much reduced operating cost and offer a greater riding comfort." The *Comet* went into service that June and had a successful career carrying hundreds of passengers on daily runs until 1951. Unfortunately, only one prototype of the Rail Zeppelin was ever ordered. Permanently coupled "nonstandard" trains like the *Comet* did not find favor with railroad operators because their cars could not be intermixed with other rolling stock. Also, to perform maintenance on one car meant sidelining the whole train.

In spring 1935, with questions about the *Macon* crash still unanswered, there was little work for the Goodyear-Zeppelin engineers to do. Considering the depressed state of the economy, cutbacks were inevitable. In March, Litchfield had already decided to release some of the engineers and most of the other employees. From its peak of over eight hun-

The Goodyear "Rail Zeppelin," a double-ended diesel-electric passenger train set was built for the New York, New Haven and Hartford Railroad. It operated as the Comet beginning in 1935. In addition to its wind tunnel-tested aerodynamic shape, the train featured low-slung unitized construction and extensive use of aluminum to reduce weight. Despite its advanced design, only one example was ordered. *(Lockheed Martin)*

dred employees, the Zeppelin organization was being cut to twenty-two, then finally to ten men. The nucleus of key Zeppelin design personnel was dispersed. Arnstein tried to find jobs for some of his engineers in other Goodyear divisions. Keck had already gone to machine design with the rubber company. Fischer would go there, too, before returning to Germany, as Leonz Rieger did. Arnstein also made discreet inquiries on behalf of his engineers for positions at other aeronautical companies. Klemperer found employment with Douglas Aircraft Company in California. The remaining engineers at Goodyear-Zeppelin would face new and diverse engineering challenges in the second half of the 1930s.

Optimistically, Goodyear-Zeppelin built a full-scale mock-up of the passenger quarters of the rigid airship the company still hoped to build. The passenger dirigibles were visualized as having the same general shape as the ZRS airships, but maybe a million cubic feet larger, with cruising speeds of seventy to eighty miles per hour and possible top speeds of up to one hundred miles per hour. Like an ocean liner, each airship would have staterooms facing inside, outside, and toward a promenade deck. There would be a total of forty-three double staterooms, and an observation car would feature slanted windows. The dining room with its large unobstructed floor would be adaptable "for dancing, ship's concerts or moving pictures." The service personnel would include maids, waiters, porters, and stewards, and a special chef and his staff would cater to the whims of the passengers. "It will be a restless person indeed," Arnstein wrote, "who has time to become bored on an ocean crossing by airship." But there was no new money for rigid airships in 1935. Eckener made a devil's bargain with the Nazi government to continue funding his new airship. In March 1935, the German Air Ministry took control and established a new operating company, the Deutsche Zeppelin Reederei (DZR). Luftschiffbau would build the airships, but Eckener, the grand man of the Zeppelins, would soon be marginalized. The financial backing for a Dutch airship line to the Dutch East Indies—with possible Goodyear-Zeppelin involvement—seemed almost certain before the *Macon*'s loss. Britain's scheme to link its empire by airships also failed. The government-built, hydrogen-inflated R 101 crashed in flames on its first flight to India in October 1930, killing forty-eight of the fifty-four persons on board. The private industry R 100 had flown successfully from England to Canada before the R 101 tragedy, but afterward, it was withdrawn from service and sold as scrap for a mere £100. These failures dimmed the prospects for airship development. The U.S. Special Committee on Airships was making its investigation, but it would not report for another two years. Meanwhile, there would be no money for rigid airships in the United States, either civilian or military. Arnstein lamented, "We now know pretty well how to design a rigid airship, but we did not, before the *Macon*, know enough."

Thwarted in its ambition to obtain another rigid airship, the U.S. Navy seized on the recommendation of the influential General Board, which gave attention not just to rigid airships, but also to pressure airships. The army would soon give up its fleet of blimps, so the role of coastal defender was up for grabs, as far as airships were concerned. The navy had already had its eye on Goodyear's flagship blimp, the *Defender*, the largest blimp in the company's commercial airship fleet. The navy knew *Defender* was more expensive to operate than her sister public relations blimps, so the navy made Litchfield an offer for the airship, but wanted it fitted with a new 183,000-cubic-foot (5,124 cu m) envelope. Litchfield reluctantly agreed to give up the *Defender*, which went to the navy as the G-1. It was the first truly modern pressure airship the navy had purchased in nearly a decade. By 1937, Burgess at the Bureau of Aeronautics issued specifications for a new patrol type and also for a slightly smaller training model, more or less like Goodyear's standard public relations blimp. Goodyear was interested in the contracts, and Arnstein's team submitted a design. The first training blimp was the L-1, with a volume of 123,000 cubic feet (3,444 cu m). It was completed in March 1938 and delivered to Lakehurst to serve as a primary trainer for the expected patrol blimps. The K-2 would become the prototype for the most successful series of pressure airships ever, with 133 more "K-ships" built for service in World War II. The type was to fulfill a role in antisubmarine warfare and as an aerial escort for oceangoing merchant ships.

The K-2, derived from experienced gained with the navy's one-of-a-kind K-1 airship, had an envelope 248.5 feet (75.8 m) long with a volume of 404,000 cubic feet (11,312 cu m), was powered by two 400 horsepower (298 kW) air-cooled radial engines, and could carry a crew of ten on patrol missions lasting up to thirty-nine hours. The K-2 was the first airship to be erected in the mammoth Air Dock since the departure of the *Macon*. The giant orange peel doors rolled open on 6 December 1938 so the K-2 could take its first flight. Ten days later, the K-2 was flown to Lakehurst for delivery to the navy.

While all of this airship activity was centered on a few pressure airships, the goal of building a large rigid airship never completely disappeared. The navy's LTA Design Section continued to refine its ideal rigid airship, giving the scouting airship offensive capability by adding a fleet of nine dive-bombers as hook-on planes. The result was a design for a ten-million-cubic-foot-volume airship nearly 900 feet long, to be known as the ZRCV. This proposal tried to answer all critics by incorporating nearly every suggested improvement and every lesson learned from operating the previous rigid airships. In its details, the ultimate naval airship appeared to be the result of a cross-pollination of ideas from Burgess and Goodyear-Zeppelin. It would have eight engines in four power cars mounted externally, and staggered in height along the hull. Airplanes would be hung externally from the ship's keel.

Following release of the Durand Committee report, there was renewed interest from the navy in securing a rigid training airship, or at least one that could serve as a flying laboratory as the General Board and the Durand Committee had suggested. It seemed that only one nagging problem remained: the Navy Department was unwilling to budget the money for a renewed airship construction program. Airships were inexpensive compared to surface ships, but they were aircraft, and their unit cost appeared staggering compared to the airplanes of the day. There was talk of swapping the decommissioned *Los Angeles* with Goodyear-Zeppelin as partial payment for a new airship, or cutting the ZRS design down in size to meet the more modest goal of a three-million-cubic-foot rigid airship capable of carrying two airplanes. Designs for this airship carried the designation ZRN. Then in 1938 a new restriction emerged: any rigid airship would have to be no more than 325 feet long. It seemed an unreasonable limitation, because in order to maintain the same cubic volume it would have to be impossibly short and bulbous, impractical from an aerodynamic standpoint and severely limited in range and useful load. The restriction appears to have been politically motivated—an attempt by the White House to open up competition for a Metal-clad airship proposal from Ralph Upson's company (the navy had purchased his 202,000-cubic-foot prototype, the ZMC-2, in 1929). Goodyear-Zeppelin tried to comply with the length limit by proposing a conventional, though dwarfish rigid airship that could be lengthened later. Congress authorized the program, but the administration opposed it. "I made it perfectly clear, and have done so for two years," President Roosevelt informed the secretary of the navy in May 1939, "that I do not approve the construction of another large rigid airship for the Navy. . . ." The President was impatient with the Bureau of Aeronautics for its reluctance to accept a smaller airship and so directed that no bids be accepted. "I am not willing . . . to approve the building of the old type of large ship," he wrote, and added, "I deem it unwise to build a smaller ship." Congress did not want to spend money on a small rigid airship intended to be a flying laboratory only and militarily useless. The scouting airships' inability to prove themselves with the fleet came back to haunt them—they had been viewed as land-based aircraft when fleet operations were seen as the desirable role. Since the *Akron* and *Macon* were never integrated within the battle group, they had only a limited constituency to fight for them in the budget battles. On the commercial side, there was now competition from heavier-than-air craft. Large flying boats were in passenger service in the Caribbean in 1935, and an ocean-crossing, four-engine Flying Clipper began transatlantic voyages in 1939.

Although Goodyear-Zeppelin saw no orders for commercial rigid airships, there was more interest in Zeppelin development in Nazi Germany. By 1936 Eckener's new LZ 129 was rapidly nearing completion. The LZ 129 was eventually named the *Hindenburg* in honor of Germany's late president. After the loss of the *Akron* and *Macon*, Arnstein, during a consultation visit to Germany, advised reinforcement of the *Hindenburg* tail. This reinforcement was undertaken, although Luftschiffbau and Arnstein's replacement in stress analysis, Arthur Foerster, denied it during the Nazi era.

The *Hindenburg* was the largest and most advanced airship yet. Its 804-foot (245.2 m) length was dictated by the size of the hangar at Lakehurst, which would be the Zeppelin's American base by special arrangement with the U.S. Navy. From Lakehurst, Zeppelin passengers could continue transcontinental air service by boarding a small by comparison Douglas DC-3 airliner. The new Zeppelin's shape was reminiscent of the *Akron* or *Macon*, but since the *Hindenburg* would be filled with hydrogen, not helium, its four engine cars were arrayed outside the 7.5-million-cubic-foot (210,000 cu m) hull. The *Hindenburg* was designed for transatlantic passenger service, and its spacious lounges and dining room with large windows more than compensated for the small interior staterooms. Up to fifty passengers, if they could afford the $400 fare, could travel across the ocean in half the time of an ocean liner. And they would not be bothered by sea or air sickness. The giant airship cruised along so gently, a fountain pen placed on a table could be stood on end for hours at a time. While cruising in quiet comfort, the passengers would enjoy the last word in luxury. There was a special lightweight aluminum piano at one end of the lounge, gourmet meals, a well-stocked bar, even a smoking room within the airship, pressurized to make absolutely certain no stray molecules of hydrogen could seep in. No matches were allowed—use of the room's sole electric cigarette lighter was carefully supervised by the steward. The airship had an uneventful first season in 1936, making ten round-trip flights from Frankfurt to the United States, carrying 1,021 passengers and 8.6 tons of freight, over half of it the highly sought Zeppelin-postmarked mail (and this does not include figures for several more flights from Germany to South America). The airship was not used exclusively for revenue passenger service, however. As a silver-hued symbol of German superiority in the air, it was a perfect propaganda vehicle, with its vertical tail fins carrying the Nazi Party flag, the large, black swastika set in a white disk against a field of red. The *Hindenburg* participated in a number of propaganda flights, sometimes with the *Graf Zeppelin*, for example, at the Olympic Games held in Berlin in 1936. None of these flights met with the approval of Eckener, who was rapidly losing influence in Germany. His defiant resistance to Nazi schemes to use his airships or hangars prompted Propaganda Minister Joseph Goebbels to have Eckener's name and image banned from all publications.

For its first flight to the United States in May 1937, the *Hindenburg* featured ten extra passenger staterooms on its lower deck. For this flight, former Goodyear-Zeppelin vice president Ernst Lehmann was on board as an observer. Lehmann had become the heir apparent at Luftschiffbau since Eckener had incurred the disfavor of the National Socialist regime. Captain Max Pruss was the Zeppelin's commander, and the crew of sixty-one included trainees plus veteran airship pilots Anton Wittemann, Albert Sammt, and Heinrich Bauer. Eckener did not make the trip. Slowed by head winds, the *Hindenburg* crossed the Atlantic in sixty-seven hours and arrived over a rainy New York City at midday on 6 May. A landing at the Zeppelin's western terminus at Lakehurst, New Jersey, would have to be postponed until later that day, when the weather was expected to improve. Meanwhile, the passengers could enjoy views of the skyscrapers and northern New Jersey pine barrens. During a break in the weather about 7:30 P.M., the airship made its approach for a landing. But as the ship hovered near its pyramid-shaped mooring mast waiting to be taken in hand by more than two hundred ground crew, it burst into flames near the tail. The airship hung in the sky momentarily, as a brilliant fireball rapidly consumed the ship. Tail first, it slumped toward the rain-dampened earth. As the airborne inferno touched down, passengers and crew leapt from the open windows or tried to scramble through the vaporizing outer cover to safety. Within thirty-four seconds, all that was left of the *Hindenburg* was a charred and smoking metal skeleton collapsed in a mangled heap on the sandy soil. Witnesses were stunned. The massive combustion had literally sucked the oxygen from the air, leaving those at the scene breathless. Millions more would relive the experience vicariously. The presence of newsreel cameramen, newspaper photographers, and a radio reporter dramatized in words and images a terrifying accident, seared into the memories of the world. It was not the worst air disaster, however. As bad as the conflagration had seemed, sixty-two of the ninety-seven persons aboard lived. Thirteen of the thirty-six passengers, twenty-two crew members, and one member of the ground crew perished. Among those who would not survive their injuries was captain Ernst Lehmann.

How did the accident occur? What caused the German Zeppelin to catch fire? The German Zeppelin company had been safely operating passenger airships filled with hydrogen since 1910. Investigations were launched on both sides of the Atlantic. The future of Zeppelin transport depended on what could be learned from this accident, and how to prevent its occurrence ever again. The immediate solution seemed to be helium. In fact, the *Hindenburg* was designed from the start to use helium, as a consequence of the disaster that overcame the British airship R 101. Luftschiffbau-Zeppelin knew the United States had a monopoly on helium, but still hoped to use the inert gas, if only in limited amounts, as a nonflammable shield around the airship's hydrogen cells. The special double-chamber gas cells were never installed, so the *Hindenburg* always flew with hydrogen. Besides, Eckener preferred hydrogen because it was cheaper, and thought by using it his company might be able show a profit on its passenger service.

The Hindenburg *burst into flames as it attempted to land at Lakehurst, New Jersey on the evening of 6 May 1937. More than six decades later, the cause of the accident is still debated. Sixty-two of the ninety-seven persons aboard survived the fire. (The Lighter-Than-Air Society Collection/University of Akron Archives)*

Investigators looked deeper into the cause of the tragedy. They examined every moment of the landing, the actions of crew members, the prevailing weather conditions, procedures, the condition of the airship's structure, and functioning status of its various parts. Their findings were published, but they raised more questions than answers. Debate over the causes of the accident and what factors may have contributed to it continues to this day. Arnstein realized the pitfalls of such armchair discussion. As he observed, "Historians can be objective but lack judgment on technical matters requiring interpretation, while those with a background in airships cannot help but be slanted by their own experiences."

From the official record, we know certain facts incontrovertibly. The *Hindenburg* circled the field at Lakehurst twice, according to accepted German practice, after valving for landing. When Captain Max Pruss tried to bring the airship in for landing, the nose would not come down despite the use of all aerodynamic forces available. The airship was tail heavy, unusual after a long flight. Apparently alarmed by this condition, Pruss valved gas forward to bring the nose down and descended immediately without again circling the field. This action may not have allowed sufficient time for the hydrogen to escape through its chimneylike ventilation shaft. When Pruss did get the ship's nose down, the hydrogen would naturally have sought the highest point, which was at the tail where the fire started. If an explosive hydrogen-oxygen mixture was present, anything could have set it off, even the tiniest spark of static electricity.

But there was another explanation for the presence of a hydrogen-oxygen mix. Arnstein speculated that an aft gas valve stuck open. The same thing had occurred at least once before on the *Graf Zeppelin*. If the pressure was low in an aft cell, several crew members would have noticed it. Arnstein thought they should have, but wondered if they did.

Klaus Pruss, son of the captain, noted later that the electrostatic conditions were no worse at Lakehurst that day than had been encountered by the *Graf* and the *Hindenburg* before. Arnstein disagreed, noting that because of electrical storms in the area, all rubber factories in New Jersey were closed down on that day because there was too much atmospheric static electricity for employees to work safely (a static spark could ignite the factories' carbon black and rubber compounds). This was a very uncommon situation.

After the *Hindenburg* fire, Arnstein examined a copy of the German report prepared by Eckener, Dürr, and four others assigned to the investigation, and signed by them at the request of Air Marshal Hermann Goering. Eckener officially may have been a nonperson, but his airship expertise was still valued, and he was useful to the Nazi regime. He and Dürr had difficult positions on this committee. Goering did not want a finding of sabotage since this would make his Nazi police look bad, and the airship crew was "loaded with them." On the other hand, Eckener and Dürr could not afford to make their own company look bad by admitting any errors in design or operation of the airship. Their only way out was to conclude that the accident was an act of God, and that is what the report concluded. Nevertheless, Arnstein drew his own conclusions.

In preparation for landing, hydrogen was valved from all of the gas cells on the *Hindenburg*, then gas was valved three more times from cells near the front. The last valving occurred less than a kilometer from the mooring mast when the airship was traveling about eighteen miles per hour. Arnstein doubted that the vents were designed to be effective in purging valved hydrogen at less than fifty miles per hour. Normal procedure while Arnstein was at Friedrichshafen was to proceed at least once around the field at cruising speed after valving. But Lakehurst's landing field radioed that the *Hindenburg* should land quickly before another storm front arrived so Pruss brought his ship straight in. There was urgency to land so the ship, already delayed, could start its return trip on schedule. Arnstein thought Lehmann was more of a chance taker than Eckener, and believed that had Eckener been aboard, he would not have let Pruss land as he did. Eckener never forgave himself for going to Innsbruck, Austria, to receive an honorary degree instead of being on board the *Hindenburg* for that last flight.

Eckener speculated that the tail heaviness was caused by a bracing wire—snapped during the tight turn the airship made prior to landing—which sliced open a gas cell. Leaking hydrogen poured into the hull at the top of the airship, he believed, and due to the Zeppelin's slow speed was not vented quickly enough. A static electric spark near the vent then ignited the hydrogen-oxygen mix with disastrous consequences. This scenario was least damaging to the company's reputation and it refuted any claim of sabotage, an explanation favored by many, especially those in America. They believed that the Zeppelin's destruction was a protest against the Nazi regime, and they were not convinced the airship or its operation were at fault—only some "infernal machine," as Rosendahl called it, could be responsible. Speculation centered on a crewman or a passenger who may have had motive and opportunity to place an incendiary device in the airship, and no chance to reset its automatic timer to accommodate the airship's delayed landing. But any evidence for sabotage was quickly discounted, although it could not be ruled out entirely by the German and American investigations.

The fiery end of the *Hindenburg* was a devastating blow to passenger airship proponents. Almost forgotten is that this first flight of the 1937 season marked the beginning— and end—of operations with the American Zeppelin Transport Company. Litchfield hoped that a partnership with the successful German airship operator DZR would revive chances to build airships in the United States, at Goodyear-Zeppelin. But the crash of the *Hindenburg*, vividly replayed in theaters and over the radio, shook public confidence in the Zeppelin as a form of transport. The LZ 127 *Graf Zeppelin* was withdrawn from service, and attention was focused on a nearly identical twin of the *Hindenburg*, a new *Graf Zeppelin*, then under construction. This was the LZ 130, and it was decided it would not fly with paying passengers unless helium was used for lift, not hydrogen. Only the United States had helium to sell, but U.S. law forbade its sale to foreign countries. Eckener appealed to his friends in the United States, even going to see President Roosevelt. Eventually, Eckener won a promise to obtain helium, but only if it was used for peaceful, non-military purposes. After the Nazis annexed Austria in March 1938, the United States secretary of the interior, Harold Ickes, refused to allow the shipment of helium. He believed there was too much risk that the helium might be put to military uses, even though nearly everyone by this time had discounted that large airships offered much of a military threat. Ickes's fears were well founded: in August 1939, only weeks before the start of World War II, the LZ 130 made a clandestine flight along the coast of Scotland probing for signals from Britain's new chain of radar stations. Filled only with hydrogen, the new *Graf Zeppelin* never flew paying passengers.

The increasingly warlike stance of Nazi Germany and the anxiety it engendered in much of Europe was having its effect in Akron, too. Europeans saw the United States as a refuge from impending disaster at home, and sought the help of family, friends, old business associates, whomever, with the hope of obtaining their help to emigrate to the United States. Arnstein was not immune from these supplications. He helped many people get out of Czechoslovakia and Austria, beginning with his own brother and sister. (Arnstein's parents were both deceased; his father died in 1922, his mother in 1930.) Arnstein then began to receive numerous letters from persons in his old homeland, people he did not know but who knew about him. Many of the letters begin by inquiring about his health or family, or introducing the writer as a friend of a family member, but their intent soon became clear: could Arnstein help them get a job in the United States so they could relocate legally? The Depression was still a dominant consideration, and for political as well as economic reasons, the U.S. Immigration and Naturalization Service would not allow anyone to immigrate unless that person had a sponsor in the United States. The sponsor had to promise to support the person until he or she could find employment and not be a drain on the American taxpayer. Without fanfare or publicity of any kind, Arnstein signed numerous affidavits for more than a dozen individuals. However, he could not always promise them work at Goodyear-Zeppelin. His engineering staff had reached a low of only ten persons. But he could and did write to his many friends and colleagues, asking for their help. He turned to others within his company, seeking their advice and suggestions. In some extreme instances, and known only to a few, corporate money was made available to influence foreign officials. Some of the people requesting visas were highly trained engineers, others were distinguished professors or doctors, but most were professional people. They found jobs and asylum in the United States, and were able to repay the Arnsteins for their personal loans and kindness. Highly trained or professional people had the best chances of securing a job in the United States, especially if they could be of assistance to a growing defense industry, an industry that would soon earn a reputation as "the arsenal of democracy."

Chapter 19   GOODYEAR–ZEPPELIN BECOMES GOODYEAR AIRCRAFT

By 1939, war in Europe seemed inevitable to many observers. Great Britain and France belatedly responded to Adolf Hitler's aggression and demands for more territory by devoting larger budgets to national defense. For the time being, the United States officially maintained its neutrality. But privately and in public, people were beginning to express their feelings about events in Europe and on whose side the United States should be. Those sentiments became even stronger after 1 September 1939, when Hitler launched his *blitzkrieg* (lightning war) against Poland. Nazi aggression even had its consequences in Akron. "When the remaining disciples conversed among themselves they usually spoke in German," Maynard Flickinger recalled. "But the day that the Nazis drove into Poland Dr. Arnstein ruled that no German should be spoken in Goodyear-Zeppelin."

Now America's Allies of the First World War were hard pressed to counter the Nazi war machine. Great Britain and France turned to the United States to fill orders for war materiel they could not quickly manufacture themselves, or in the quantity they now needed. American industries, slowed by the Great Depression, tooled up to help equip the Allied armies with trucks, aircraft, food, and munitions. At Goodyear-Zeppelin, the dream of building rigid airships was replaced by the practical need to become part of a growing defense industry. To reflect the company's broader goals and aeronautical capabilities, Litchfield created a new company in December 1939 called Goodyear Aircraft Corporation, or simply, GAC. Litchfield would serve as the company's president while Arnstein retained his title of vice president in charge of engineering.

To indicate the new company's interest in work other than airships, Goodyear Aircraft approached the Glenn L. Martin Company and got a contract to build tail surfaces for its

B-26 Marauder bomber. Thirty employees began the work in the Air Dock, in canvas-covered shops on the hangar floor. After Germany invaded Holland and the Low Countries in May 1940, Litchfield grew alarmed that war eventually would draw in the United States, so he made defense production the company's first priority in floor space, personnel, and research. That summer, the company's Aircraft Wheel and Brake Division was started in Plant 3, where the girders for the *Akron* and *Macon* had been produced. By the end of 1940, GAC had obtained contracts to build parts for Grumman Avenger torpedo bombers, Curtiss P-40 Warhawk fighter planes, and Consolidated Coronado flying boats. Much of the engineering for these contracts was only to facilitate manufacturing to other companies' specifications, but the staff was also able to sell its services in design modification. The contracts grew in scope to include sheet metal work and the fabrication of major subassemblies for airplanes: wing panels, control surfaces, fuselage, and tail sections. Demand for these parts necessitated assembly line production methods, and the company was rapidly outgrowing its facilities. It was also moving beyond the need for its sixteen-year relationship with its German business partner.

Goodyear's affiliation with Luftschiffbau-Zeppelin had become awkward. There were no more rigid airships in Germany. In the spring of 1940, Hermann Goering, head of the German Air Force, ordered both *Graf Zeppelins* LZ 127 and LZ 130 dismantled so their aluminum alloy could be used in fighter planes. Goering then had their Frankfurt sheds dynamited because he claimed that they interfered with the operation of his bomber aircraft. The only ties that linked Goodyear with its Zeppelin counterpart now centered on patent litigation of mutual interest. So, in December 1940, the Goodyear-Zeppelin Corporation was dissolved and its rights to Zeppelin patents transferred to a Goodyear holding company, the Wingfoot Corporation. The Zeppelin name passed from the scene in the United States, but not the desire at Goodyear to build rigid airships. The only demand, however, was for Goodyear's blimps. The U.S. Navy saw an increasing role for blimps to serve in maritime patrol and sought to add to its tiny fleet. The U.S. Airship Bill of June 1940 authorized construction of as many as forty-eight of the "useful non-rigid airships." Contracts were placed with Goodyear Aircraft for six airships, two L-type trainers and four patrol K-ships. Within a year, the navy ordered two more K-ships, then asked for an additional twenty-one in the autumn of 1941. During this time, Goodyear also developed a new type of barrage balloon to impede attacks of enemy airplanes. This new balloon was an updated version of the type that had been in use since World War I and was increasingly deployed in Britain. Goodyear's unmanned Strato-Sentinel type could be winched out to altitudes above 15,000 feet (4,575 m).

Goodyear Aircraft had to expand to handle the increased business, but not even the large floor of the Air Dock could contain the new production. Two new buildings, Plant B and Plant C, were erected next to the Air Dock (now called Plant A) to accommodate the overflow. By mid-1941, these buildings added 500,000 square feet of floor space for aircraft part assembly. Another factory was built in Arizona to handle the business Goodyear was receiving from San Diego's Consolidated Aircraft. By June 1941, Goodyear Aircraft had 1,320 employees and was taking on a key role in the United States' ambitious defense program. Litchfield was an easy convert to the doctrine of air power and dedicated GAC to the task of "making America First in the Air." Arnstein was kept busy interviewing and hiring new engineers as well as coordinating their efforts with the production departments.

On 7 December 1941, when Japan attacked Pearl Harbor, the U.S. Navy had only a half dozen blimps capable of patrol duty, including some obsolescent airships given to it by the U.S. Army in 1937. They were all stationed at Lakehurst, New Jersey. Goodyear's four public relations blimps, equivalent to the navy's L-ships, were taken over by the navy and operated on the west coast until larger patrol types could be made available. The navy's sole remaining rigid airship, the *Los Angeles*, had been broken up in the big hangar at Lakehurst and sold for scrap in January 1940.

Arnstein and his five remaining disciples at Goodyear Aircraft, plus the addition of a greatly enlarged engineering staff, suddenly found themselves at the head of a tremendous expansion of military engineering, including airships, airplanes, and aircraft components. Arnstein faced enormous new responsibilities in the rush to full-time war production. Knowing how well organized the Germans were, Arnstein worried that the United States would not be able to prepare its defense in time. He was surprised at how quickly American industry tooled up for war. Goodyear Aircraft grew into a major defense contractor during World War II, a corporation far larger than could have been imagined for Goodyear-Zeppelin just a few years earlier. By the end of 1941, the company employed 3,500. At the end of 1942, the payroll stood at an astounding 31,000 employees. Akron became an aircraft manufacturing center and a magnet for job seekers throughout the United States. Many of the company's young men joined the military during the course of the war. Rosie the Riveter and 12,000 other women took over their jobs.

Germany declared war against the United States on 11 December 1941. One month later, the Battle of the Atlantic came to the shores of the United States when five German submarines attacked Allied shipping virtually unopposed. From 11 January until 6 February when they headed home, this first wave of U-boats sank twenty-five ships, a loss totaling 156,939 tons. For the next several months, U-boat "wolf packs" roamed coastal shipping

A "StratoSentinel" barrage balloon is tested at Goodyear's Wingfoot Lake hangar in 1941. The lobed shape allowed the balloon to expand without bursting as it was winched upward to 15,000 feet. Dozens of these tethered, unmanned balloons flying over a city or military installation forced attacking enemy airplanes to steer clear or risk becoming entangled. (Goodyear Tire and Rubber Co. Collection/University of Akron Archives)

lanes without much fear of discovery, since there were not enough patrol aircraft or ships to protect the sea lanes approaching the eastern coast of North America. U-boats continued to sink freighters and tankers, in several instances only a few miles off shore. By the end of June 1942, U-boats had sent nearly four hundred ships to the bottom, almost all in the Western Atlantic. Merchant ships running along the United States eastern seaboard were on their own until the middle of May when the United States belatedly started to run convoys on the east coast in an attempt to stem the heavy losses. Aircraft of any kind for convoy escort and U-boat chasing were in short supply. Only four patrol blimps were available for the entire eastern sea frontier until May, and even when that number doubled with blimp deliveries in June there were not enough airships to provide adequate coverage. However, these few blimps demonstrated their ability as sub hunters, and in search and rescue operations.

In response to the ship sinkings, Congress increased its previous authorization to allow up to two hundred blimps to be built. Goodyear Aircraft was the prime contractor. The majority of the airships the navy ordered would be improved versions of the K-2 Goodyear built in 1938. By the end of 1942, two dozen blimps had been delivered. By July of the following year, the peak output reached fourteen per month. The one hundredth K-ship was delivered in October 1943.

The K-ship blimps carried radar to track subs running on the surface at night, and these blimps pioneered methods of detecting submarines underwater by their telltale magnetic signature. The presence of air cover for the merchant ship convoys, in which the blimps played a role, led to a dramatic drop in the number of ship sinkings. From August 1942 until May 1943 no ships were sunk along the eastern U.S. coast. The German subs withdrew from coastal waters and moved to attack shipping in the less well-defended Caribbean. Not until the United States instituted convoys in those waters in July 1942 and increased patrols there did shipping losses abate. Those losses declined still further once aircraft were added, and an airship patrol squadron was established in Trinidad, British West Indies, in February 1943. With more vigilant protection came better offensive tactics in hunting U-boats, and the advantage shifted. The Allies were winning the war against the U-boat.

In addition to hunting for enemy submarines, simply having a blimp as an aerial watchdog acted as a deterrent to submarine attacks. The blimps with their day-long endurance were particularly suited to the escort role in coastal shipping lanes, as well as over the congested approaches to North America's sea ports. Even the commander of the German U-boat fleet, Admiral Karl Doenitz, showed respect for the "dwarf dirigibles" in combat-

A U.S. Navy K-ship blimp on patrol with a convoy of merchant ships during World War II. Blimps of this type operated along the east, west, and gulf coasts of the United States, along the eastern shore of South America, and in the Caribbean and the Mediterranean Seas. Armed with depth bombs and machine guns, the blimps served as a deterrent to U-boat attacks on the escorted merchant fleet. Additionally, the airships participated in anti-submarine warfare with navy airplanes and surface ships, performed mine-sweeping, and conducted search-and-rescue missions. (The Lighter-Than-Air Society Collection/University of Akron Archives)

ing his submarines. "It cannot be denied," Doenitz admitted to a German audience in August 1942, "that even the 'blimps' have a certain effectiveness, in defense . . ."

In December 1942 Arnstein noted, "The present war has again shown that the non-rigid airship is one of the most powerful weapons we have against the submarine menace. The modern long-range non-rigid airships do their duty around the clock in convoy and coastal patrol duty. These airships are far superior to the pre-war models and can stay on patrol for protracted periods in all kinds of weather." Personally, Arnstein found it "very gratifying to see that lighter-than-air again [had] its important share" in the war.

The mission of the patrol airships was to seek out enemy submarines, report their positions, hover above, and even destroy them if feasible. A blimp's endurance made it particularly suited to accompany the slow merchant ships. While the presence of any opposing aircraft gave U-boat skippers pause and made them think twice about attacking, the blimp was particularly effective in forestalling submarine attacks. One U-boat captain wrote in his log book, "The amusement at first caused by the appearance of airships has been replaced by a certain amount of respect." Another U-boat log reads: "Alarm, airship! Crash dived while the airship turned towards me." Still another, "Dived on sighting airship." Few U-boat commanders would surface for an attack to risk having an airship drop lethal depth bombs on them. "I did not like the airship which would soon be over me," another U-boat skipper reported, "I turned tail and went to deeper water to lie on the bottom." Blimps, unlike many airplanes, did not have to leave the scene after a short time to return home to refuel. By keeping the U-boats submerged, running on their limited battery power, the airships showed their value as a deterrent.

Better air cover for the convoys forced the U-boats to withdraw to safer waters in midocean where aircraft could not patrol. Merchant ship sinkings there reflected the absence of an effective U-boat deterrent until the air-cover gap was closed in 1943. The navy's patrol airship program was extended to bases along the U.S. Atlantic, Pacific, and Gulf coasts, in the Caribbean, and along the northern and eastern shores of South America. Later in the war, a squadron of K-ships flew across the Atlantic via the Azores to perform antisubmarine duties and minesweeping operations in the Mediterranean. Before the war, few imagined that the blimps built in Akron would be deployed so far away.

The need for still larger and longer range airships led to the development of a new and improved design. The Goodyear Aircraft Corporation built the M-class nonrigid airship of approximately 750,000 cubic foot (21,000 cu m) capacity, which the U.S. Navy put into service over southern waters. The M-ships were approximately the same general volume as the early German rigid airships, the *Bodensee* and the *Nordstern*, which were flown commercially after World War I. The M-ship had a useful load in excess of seven tons, a bomb

Assembly line for K-ship blimp control cars at Goodyear Aircraft's Plant B during World War II. Blimp production peaked in 1943 when eleven K-type patrol airships and three L-ship trainers were delivered during the month of July. (The Lighter-Than-Air Society Collection/University of Akron Archives)

load of 2,400 pounds (1,090 kg), a military range of 2,650 miles (4,240 km), a cruising speed of 50 knots (92 km/h) and a top speed of 67 knots (123 km/h). The long control car spread the loads evenly over the pressurized cotton envelope, which pleased Arnstein from an engineering perspective. Although it was produced in the fewest numbers, Arnstein said "the M-ship was the best airship we ever built at Goodyear."

By 1944 the U.S. Navy had produced the largest airship fleet ever built, including 134 K-type, 22 L-, 8 G-, and 4 M-ships. During the war, up to 2,500 employees worked on blimp production at the Goodyear Aircraft plant's assembly line or at Wingfoot Lake, where the hangar had been doubled in length to 800 feet (244 m).

Few people realize today that the navy blimps of World War II made an important contribution to the war against the U-boats. U.S. Navy Department records show that its fleet of fewer than 150 patrol-type blimps escorted 89,000 vessels without one of the merchant ships ever being lost due to enemy action. The only challenge alleges the loss of one ship to a torpedo in May 1942, when the blimp was more than three miles away. In nearly four years of conflict, the navy's blimps flew 55,900 flights totaling 550,000 hours in the air over both the Atlantic and Pacific frontiers.

Goodyear's reputation grew, not solely based on its blimps, but as a result of its work building components for army and navy aircraft. These assignments included making wing sections for Northrop's Black Widow night fighter and fuselages and tail sections for the Boeing B-29 Superfortress bomber. As the military's needs changed, Goodyear Aircraft quickly altered its assembly line to produce parts for Grumman's Hellcat and Tigercat fighters, and the Lockheed P-38 Lightning. By February 1942, Goodyear was preparing to build not just airplane parts, but complete aircraft. The story of how this came to pass began shortly after the United States declared war. Goodyear's representative in Washington, D.C., was leaving the Bureau of Aeronautics. "If we can do anything for you," he said, "just let us know." Before he had walked too far down the hall, an admiral came to the door and called him back. He asked the Goodyear representative if his company could build fighter airplanes. "I don't know," he said, "but I'll find out."

Goodyear Aircraft responded with an enthusiastic "yes," and sent Arnstein and vice president of sales Thomas A. Knowles to Chance-Vought Aircraft in Connecticut to see the test model of its new navy fighter, the F4U-1 Corsair. After walking around it, looking it over, and talking to a few Vought executives, they decided they could build it. Yet another factory building was needed. Plant D, a sprawling hangarlike structure 1,450 by 450 feet with headroom of 45 feet (442 by 137 by 14 m), was built facing the Air Dock just for Corsair production. Within a year, Goodyear Aircraft rolled out its first FG-1 airplane. The designation stood for "Fighter, Goodyear, Model 1." Outwardly, it was nearly identical to the Vought version, with distinctive inverted gull wings and 2,000 horsepower (1,492 kW) engine. By the summer of 1944, GAC was at peak production of 200 planes per month.

Because of their success, GAC was given a contract to design an advanced version of the Corsair, which received the designation F2G. It was designed to counter the threat of Japanese kamikaze airplanes attacking navy ships. The idea was to put a 28-cylinder, 4,360-cubic-inch (71.4 l) radial engine in an airframe strong enough to handle its 3,000 horsepower (2,238 kW). Although only a few were built toward the end of war, this aircraft became the fastest piston engine fighter of its day, flying at speeds in excess of 450 miles per hour (720 km/h). Arnstein once asked his test pilot what the powerful airplane was like to fly. "It's a homesick angel," the pilot replied. Altogether, Goodyear's "Aircrafters" produced over 4,000 Corsairs in Akron during the war. Most of these ended up in U.S. Navy markings, though some went to Britain's Royal Navy Flying Corps.

Goodyear's company policy was always to take any contract that would provide work for its engineers. Not all of the projects were on a grand scale. The workers in one plant produced self-sealing fuel tanks for fighter planes. If hit in combat, the self-sealing tanks helped to protect the plane from fire and explosion. Other workers built rubber life rafts to save airmen downed at sea. There was also production of thousands of aircraft tires, brake assemblies, and lightweight magnesium aircraft wheels. Goodyear Aircraft repeatedly added or expanded buildings around the huge, black Air Dock. Its four principal Akron production facilities—Plants A, B, C, and D—now offered as much floor space as Henry Ford's Willow Run factory at Detroit, and employed more people than any other Akron company. Production went on twenty-four hours a day in three shifts. Management personnel worked extra hours during the week with Saturday overtime. Wartime brought increased demands on Karl's time and the expectation of all-out effort. Nearing age fifty-five, Arnstein admitted that at times it "was pretty hard to keep up," but thought he did well considering the work pressure. At home there was some respite. The Arnsteins' four children had grown up. Renée, the eldest, was married on Thanksgiving Day 1942 before enrolling in graduate school. Suzy was at university in Michigan and the boys, Frank and Gerry, were in prep and grammar school. They faced an unexpected problem. When World War II started, the Arnsteins' boys were subjected to considerable teasing from their classmates at school because their name sounded too German. In the mid-1920s when the Arnsteins first came to the United States, they were asked by immigration officials if they wanted to anglicize their family name. Arnstein said no; he had a professional reputation and was well known by his current name. There was a solution, and it came from around the dinner table. One of the daughters suggested the boys change their names. It would not be an issue for the girls, she argued, because when they married they

Arnstein family photo, May 1935.
Top row: Renée, Bertl, Karl, Suzy.
Bottom row: Frank, Gerry. (Karl Arnstein Collection/University of Akron Archives)

would have the last name of their husband. Mrs. Arnstein agreed. She felt that for the boys, anglicizing their name to Austen would put an end to the taunting and be more suitable in the future as well.

When he was at work, Arnstein could look out of his glass-walled office at what seemed like "acres of desks" where his engineers kept busy. The engineering department had never been so busy, and work areas were hastily created for the additional engineers as needed. He took a keen, personal interest in his engineers, and every day he visited the engineering department, stopping by a drawing board or desk for a moment to chat about the work each engineer was doing, discussing progress or any problems or new ideas. Even on the hottest days, one of those engineers remembered, Arnstein still wore his trademark double-breasted wool suits and never seemed the least bit uncomfortable.

As Goodyear Aircraft grew, Arnstein found a new role as an executive. His days supervising a few engineers in a small, close-knit shop were behind him. Now he oversaw a staff of 2,500 engineers, and had the responsibility of keeping them satisfied in regard to their status, contracts, and benefits. He was a member of the operating committee where the plans, limitations, and contract requirements of the company were discussed. With many departments in the Engineering Division working on a multitude of projects, it was important to Arnstein that their needs were represented in company decisions. In spite of long hours, there arose among the defense workers a special spirit of comradeship and patriotism and national pride which lifted their spirits above the daily grind. As diverse as the workforce was, with many of its workers entering or leaving military service, Goodyear Aircraft never experienced a strike during World War II, although there were two against the rubber company, one lasting for five days, the other for eighteen days.

Planning for future industrial manufacturing at Goodyear Aircraft became increasingly important as military contracts were completed or cut back. Since it often took more than a year to progress from contract to actual production, it was necessary to secure new business so the factory and workers would not be idle. But what type of production? Much depended on Allied success in the war. The Allies were determined to win; they believed it was only a matter of time until their superior production capabilities overwhelmed the Axis on all fronts. Litchfield looked forward with enthusiasm to the postwar era. Despite all of the advances in heavier-than-air technology during the war, his dream of the commercial passenger-carrying rigid airship had not died. On 6 June 1944, a day remembered as the beginning of the Allied landings in Normandy, Arnstein and Litchfield were in Washington, D.C., talking to the navy's General Board, promoting the idea of a ten-million-cubic-foot airship. They discussed plans for a cargo-carrying version, a troop transport, and a hospital ship. After the war, they argued, these giant aircraft could be converted to passenger service to give the United States the edge in a global air transport market that even then was being envisioned. The navy, however, had no specific need for a rigid airship and no funds to construct one. Besides, the board argued, the Air Dock was already in use and its workforce largely committed to the contracts on hand. But the accelerated pace of production did not last. Wartime orders slowed as the Allies won victory in Europe, then in Japan.

After the war ended in August 1945, Goodyear Aircraft received a well-deserved army-navy "E" for excellence. Originally a navy gunnery award, it had been broadened in World War II "to recognize exceptional performance on the production front." Only 5 percent of the nation's war plants won the award. With the coming of peace, the company would have to find new markets for its products, but the advances in materials and construction techniques achieved during the war promised a bright future.

Chapter 20 POSTWAR INTO COLD WAR

Akron was exhausted by war work, and when the war was over, the city seemed to pause to catch its breath. The pace of life slowed while industry changed over from war production to peacetime manufacturing. Companies downsized while technologies developed during the war—synthetic rubber, plastics, advanced electronics—were being adapted to civilian applications. There were lean years for GAC, too, as war production wound down. Aircraft manufacturer Glenn L. Martin continued contracts with Goodyear to produce parts for its Martin 202 and 303 transport aircraft, but these type of contracts were becoming rare. Goodyear Aircraft found itself taking odd jobs to keep its employees busy, as had Goodyear-Zeppelin. Among the products it manufactured were aluminum storm windows, metal furniture, Wilson and York refrigerators, Seeburg jukeboxes—and metal coffins.

During the war, with its eye on the postwar private aviation market, GAC had developed a small amphibious airplane, the GA-2 Duck. Later, the company built a larger version, the GA-22 Drake. However, the postwar market for new aircraft did not boom as expected. Several other manufacturers already offered competing products, so Goodyear did not put these planes into production.

Nor were there any buyers for airships. The navy returned its borrowed blimps to Goodyear Tire and Rubber. Nearly all of the wartime patrol blimps were deflated and stored. Others were sold to private contractors, including Howard Hughes, to be used for advertising purposes. Arnstein focused on refining the technology and science of airship flight. To pursue this line of research, he initiated a project measuring the swimming characteristics of goldfish. Fish had a streamlined form and were able to move through a fluid medium with minimum effort. How could an airship, also streamlined, be made to travel through the medium of air with similarly low expenditure of energy? That was the knowledge his engineers hoped to discover. Their apparatus, a water tunnel, was similar to wind tunnels in that the subject was held stationary while the fluid rushed past.

As Goodyear's workforce settled into a postwar routine, there was time to re-establish personal ties that had been disrupted by World War II. Many people had expressed considerable concern for the welfare of Arnstein's former colleague, Hugo Eckener. His outspokenness had not endeared him to the Nazi regime, and he had lost his home to Allied bombing. Friedrichshafen was a prime target, because the resources of Luftschiffbau-Zeppelin and Maybach were used in war production, and much of the Zeppelin factory was destroyed. After the war, Friedrichshafen fell within the French zone of occupation, and living conditions were harsh for the seventy-seven-year-old Eckener. In order to make life a little easier for the elder statesman of airships, Litchfield tried to arrange for Eckener to visit the United States. Shortages of food and other essentials made the visit appealing. But red tape involving Eckener's connection to wartime industry required bringing him in to the country under the auspices of Project Paper Clip, the same government operation that expedited the arrival of German rocket scientists to the United States. In the spring of 1947, Eckener came to Akron and stayed at the Portage Country Club, not far from the homes of Litchfield and Arnstein. In early May, Eckener was the center of a discussion at the Arnstein home on the commercial rigid airship. Four of the original disciples were in attendance, as were other Goodyear engineers and a navy representative. Eckener still saw advantages for the airship, despite the competition from airliners, especially believing in its practicality for long over-water flights in the South Pacific.

Still later, another German employee of the old Luftschiffbau, Arthur Foerster, came to the United States. After working for the navy at Lakehurst, he came to Goodyear Aircraft. He now admitted that the *Hindenburg*'s tail section had been reinforced according to Arnstein's recommendation, despite the airship company's earlier denials. He also accepted Arnstein's mathematical analysis of the reasons behind the fin failures of the *Macon*. It was a satisfying admission for Arnstein, who felt some vindication after enduring the slights directed at him from overseas during most of the 1930s.

The navy had retired or stored most of its fleet of K-ship blimps at the end of the war, but in the late 1940s, there was renewed interest in building an even larger airship with a much greater range and endurance for antisubmarine missions. When the navy decided it wanted this new type of blimp, Goodyear Aircraft was ready with a design. Its team of airship builders proposed an N-class airship with a long car, similar to that used on the M-ship, which Arnstein believed was his best blimp design. Besides distributing the weight load along more of the airship's envelope (which reduced wrinkles in the envelope), the articulated car permitted isolating the engines to reduce noise.

"We did propose a long car for the N-airship," Arnstein explained: "But the American system of procurement is one of compromise. You not only have to please yourself and the procurement officer, but not displease any of his four or five superior officers."

"One Navy officer insisted on a short—'modern' he called it—control car." The navy officer was Commander Willard Hanger, chief of the Airship Desk at the Bureau of Aeronautics. He had seen a proposal for an airship with a short car from Douglas Aircraft Corporation, which was also competing for the navy airship contract. The navy had wanted some competition for the contract, and had persuaded Douglas to submit a proposal in addition to those coming from GAC. Arnstein believed it was Klemperer, his former disciple who had been at Douglas Aircraft Corporation since 1936, who developed the competing airship proposal.

Hanger and others in the bureau thought the short car was the optimal choice, thinking that it should be compact like an airplane cockpit, with everything within reach. Structurally, however, the short car was undesirable because it required a higher envelope pressure to prevent wrinkles, and this made the airship more dependent on precise pressure maintenance. Arnstein met with Hanger, who informed him that other than to order a blimp envelope from GAC, he was going to give the contract to Douglas. "You are not either," Arnstein protested, "because if you do we are going to raise hell. Here Goodyear spends a lot of its own money on development of airships, and when a contract comes along you are going to give it to someone else?" Hanger thought it over, and said, "Well, all right, give us a short car and you can have the contract."

Arnstein shaved a little off the length of the car but it was not enough. He kept trimming until the car was about what Douglas had proposed. Only then did Hanger accept it. Arnstein did not want to do this, but Litchfield told him to give the customer what he wanted. As built by GAC, the N-ship was similar to what Douglas Aircraft had proposed. The new blimp was distinctive for other reasons: it had a double-deck crew quarters, complete with bunks and galley, and engines mounted inside the car driving the propellers by transmission shafts. These were the first internally mounted airship engines since the *Akron* and *Macon*. Another design departure involved canting the tail fins forty-five degrees, so the familiar vertical and horizontal cross now resembled an "X."

Using the short car created various pressure and suspension system troubles on the N-ship and subsequent models. The car was barely long enough for the N-ship, and when a larger radar was added to the cars of later N-ships, Arnstein believed that the car should have been lengthened by an internal keel. GAC made this request, but was turned down by the navy mostly due to lack of funds for a new control car design.

The late 1940s saw another attempt to revitalize interest in the rigid airship as a passenger vehicle. Litchfield wrote a book on the subject, *Why? Why Has America No Rigid Airships?*, which examined the issue in economic terms. Congress also became involved, approving funding for an airship, but the legislation did not survive a pocket veto by President Harry Truman.

International tensions heightened in the late 1940s, with the United States and its western allies frequently opposing the actions of the Soviet Union and its communist partners. The Iron Curtain, the blockade of Berlin and the Berlin Airlift, the Soviet Union's development of an atomic bomb, the communist revolution in China, the Korean War, and numerous other confrontations around the world became hallmarks of the Cold War. The perpetually simmering conflict prompted the U.S. Congress to increase defense spending, and the military's budget continued to grow during the next four decades. GAC would once again become a major defense contractor.

Another postwar adjustment made at Goodyear Aircraft was the hiring of women to fill jobs once the exclusive domain of men. Many women worked at GAC during the war, but afterward, most of them returned to their former roles as wives, mothers, and homemakers. There were some exceptions, and besides clerical workers, a few women were hired at GAC to work at engineering tasks such as drafting and calculating. At first, there were only seven, and while they were not warmly welcomed, they were tolerated. These women were pioneers of the modern feminist movement.

The idea that women should be able to have some career away from the home also took root at the Arnstein household, where education and academic achievement were highly valued. It is not surprising that the scholarly but practical pursuits that had shaped Arnstein's early life were encouraged at home. Arnstein's ambition to teach was in part realized by his wife. Bertl had graduated from the University of Akron's Buchtel College of Liberal Arts with a bachelor of arts degree in 1935. After WWII she taught German and French in the university's Department of Modern Languages. Arnstein saw to it that all four of his children went to good universities and on to graduate school at a time when that was not so common as it is today. Arnstein's eldest daughter, Renée, had obtained a master's degree in personnel management from Radcliffe College, and she and her husband had started a family. Daughter Suzy had married after the war and had received her master's degree in occupational therapy from the University of Southern California. In high school, both sons had attained the rank of Eagle Scout. Now they were away at college. Encouraged by their mother, they were studying to be doctors—not of engineering, but medicine.

Renée and her family lived not too far west of Akron, so there was opportunity for the Arnsteins to see their grandchildren regularly. It promised to be a happy situation. But that joy was shattered exactly one week before Christmas 1949. The Arnsteins were awakened from their sleep to news that no parent should have to receive: Renée had been killed in an auto accident. It took a moment for the dreadful news to sink in. Their beautiful Renée was gone—dead at the age of twenty-nine. The car her husband was driving had slammed into the back of a slow-moving truck on Tallmadge Parkway hill in northeast Akron. The emotional impact on the Arnsteins was devastating. Their son-in-law would survive, but now three young children had no mother. Bertl, who had suffered the loss of both of her parents as a youngster, helped to raise the two boys and a girl. There was a long period of grief.

Dr. and Mrs. Arnstein's three surviving children have been successful in their personal and professional lives. Suzy became an accomplished sculptress. The two sons each went on to have their own distinguished careers. Frank became a professor of medicine at Harvard Medical School and was chairman of rheumatology and immunology at Boston's Brigham and Women's Hospital for twenty-five years. Gerald, a hydraulic engineer turned physician, a cardiac specialist, became a professor of surgery at Harvard Medical School and was surgeon in chief at the Massachusetts General Hospital for twenty-nine years. The Arnsteins had sixteen grandchildren and many great-grandchildren.

At a time when Arnstein could have retired, he continued to work. Progress on the N-ship continued. In the 1950s, Arnstein would see Goodyear Aircraft build more of the large pressure airships to serve in antisubmarine warfare for the U.S. Navy. Some of these blimps, nearly a million cubic feet (28,000 cu m) in volume, were given a new mission: to provide early warning against a surprise air attack by Cold War foes. No longer were airships to be just "eyes for the fleet." They were now "eyes in the sky" for the nation, capable of flying for two or more days at a time without refueling. Four of these blimps were 1,500,000 cubic feet (42,000 cu m) in volume and over 400 feet (122 m) long—the largest nonrigid airships yet built. They carried powerful radars forty-feet (12 m) in diameter inside their envelopes. Several of the large blimps set new flight records for duration and distance. One navy blimp flew a triangular route nonstop across the Atlantic ocean, from the northern United States to above the African coast, and returned to Florida. The blimp stayed aloft eleven days, besting the endurance of the *Graf Zeppelin*.

The Cold War created an atmosphere of unease and distrust, and as a defense contractor, GAC was required to maintain its vigilance against possible espionage. In that era of heightened security, even doodle pad notes were subject to being burned in front of guards. One infraction of the strict security rules by a junior engineer prompted Arnstein to accept personal responsibility for the young man's errors. As he had done in the past,

A U.S. Navy ZPG-2W type Airborne Early Warning blimp flies over the even larger ZPG-3W class in the late 1950s. The bumps atop their envelopes housed height-tracking radars. The large horizon-scanning search radar to warn of attacking enemy aircraft at long range was carried in a dome on the bottom of the 2W-type control car and inside the envelope of the 3W type. (The Lighter-Than-Air Society Collection/University of Akron Archives)

Arnstein again showed his loyalty to his engineers. The offending engineer had left some documents in his desk, under only one lock, instead of in the double-locked safe where they should have been returned. The navy's security officer made an issue of the security violation. The young man feared for his job. He went home early to return the first thing the following morning to face Arnstein, and possibly receive the pink slip terminating his employment. Instead, Arnstein advised him not to make the same mistake again: "Sometimes the rules are lousy, but in the future, go by the rules." There were no recriminations, the man was not fired, nor demoted, nor reprimanded. Arnstein, in defending his man, had taken the heat of the navy's legitimate complaint upon himself. He trusted his engineers, and rewarded their trust in kind. But he would not tolerate disobedience. Arnstein's heir apparent in engineering at GAC, Elgin L. Shaw, showed signs of insubordination when he did not report to the office for several days after a business trip to California. Arnstein told Shaw that he would have to change his ways or resign, and gave him two weeks to make up his mind. Shaw had been Arnstein's chief assistant, and it was a difficult ultimatum to give. Shaw decided to quit, and formed a competing company that made envelopes for navy airships. Arnstein felt Shaw had betrayed his commitment to Goodyear, and when Shaw came to Goodyear asking for business, Arnstein "did not think he could give it to a disloyal employee who had done harm to GAC."

Defense contracts multiplied as a result of the Korean War, and Arnstein and his engineers soon had over three hundred projects to keep them busy. They were designing and building aircraft canopies, crosswind aircraft landing wheels, guided missile and satellite systems, analog computers, helicopter components, radar, radar housings, and airplane fuel tanks. They also promoted uses for new products, such as the company's lightweight *Bondolite* honeycomb material and laminated plastics. And they were developing new types of manned aircraft. One of Arnstein's favorite projects of this period was a lightweight one-person helicopter, the Gizmo. Another novel project was a rubber inflatable aircraft, the Inflatoplane, to be used by fighter pilots to escape from behind enemy lines. GAC also developed rocket booster casings and guidance systems for the Matador and Mace guided missiles, as well as other defense products in the 1950s.

Arnstein was also interested in getting GAC involved in human space exploration. The topic was still in the realm of science fiction in the mid- to late 1950s, and Litchfield was unconvinced that this was a wise investment of research and development money. Arnstein dug into his own pocket to send one of his engineers to a conference in Europe about space flight. When the engineer returned, he reported that practically every nation was getting involved in space flight, but that one nation was far ahead—the Soviet Union. With

Even before the Soviet satellite Sputnik *opened the eyes of the world to space travel, Goodyear Aircraft Corporation developed an ambitious proposal for a reusable, manned space vehicle. This artist's concept depicts the nearly 200-foot (60 m) high Air Dock filled with Goodyear "Meteor, Jr." rockets undergoing assembly and a large rigid airship occupying the remainder of the hangar.*

(Lockheed Martin)

Karl Arnstein in his office shortly before retirement. Behind him is a model of a U.S. Navy ZPG-2 blimp. On the table at right are models of airplanes designed and built at Goodyear Aircraft, the F2G-2 Super Corsair and the GA-22 Drake amphibian. (A. D. Topping Collection/ University of Akron Archives)

that report in front of him, Litchfield gave Arnstein no more argument about a budget for astronautics research and development. Goodyear Aircraft imaginatively developed a number of projects, and even proposed a rocket for travel to the moon. It was among the first corporations to do so, even before the Soviet Union launched its *Sputnik* satellite, and well before the United States contemplated its "put a man on the moon" Apollo Project. Appropriate to its gas-filled fabrics heritage, Goodyear Aircraft later envisioned an orbiting space station made out of inflatable structures. The Goodyear Aircraft Corporation had come a long way from its Zeppelin-building roots, but without the knowledge gained from its earlier endeavors, it would not have been ready for the space age.

As his career came to a close, Arnstein was honored by the U.S. Navy with its Distinguished Public Service Award for his many contributions to its airship program. He received the Wingfoot Lighter-Than-Air Society's Achievement Award and he was recognized by the American Bar Association with the Naturalized American Award. Arnstein retired in January 1957, shortly before reaching age seventy. Maybe it was a coincidence, but that same year the U.S. Navy began the cutbacks that would eliminate its naval airship program by 1961. The naval airship cause was hurt still further by a tragic accident in July 1960 that destroyed a navy Airborne Early Warning blimp and claimed the lives of eighteen of its twenty-one crew members. Arnstein once again was called in to investigate an airship disaster. The facts were quickly ascertained. Unknown to the pilot, an automatic pressure control device unintentionally had been disabled. As a result, the ZPG-3W airship lost pressure and its envelope buckled. The pilot's reaction sent the ship nose first into the sea off New Jersey, the impact with the water burst the envelope, and the ship sank. A lawsuit alleged that the bag failed before it struck the water, but that was never proven. Suspicions lingered among some Navy personnel, who also believed the bag was at fault. The court case continued for several years. Goodyear Aircraft was exonerated, but it did not matter—the navy had deflated its remaining blimps on schedule. It was not the end of airships, however. Commercial blimps continued to flourish as public relations vehicles.

Although Arnstein continued to keep his hand in airship work as a consultant after retirement, he and Mrs. Arnstein had time to pursue other interests. One of these was art. Bertl became a longtime member of the board of directors of the Akron Art Institute. She was credited with initiating its annual masked ball fund-raiser, which raised hundreds of thousands of dollars over the years, and in guiding acquisition of the art museum's collections. Dr. Arnstein could give attention to his fine art prints and stamp collection, and pursue his hobby of graphology, the study of handwriting. Moreover, he could devote more time to his rose garden, a passion for twenty years. At one time he had four hundred rose bushes under cultivation. He watched each one with careful expectation, noting the soil conditions, light, and location in the garden to track the progress of their growth.

Arnstein continued to receive accolades, including an honorary doctorate degree from the University of Akron in 1967. Goodyear Aerospace (the designation of Goodyear Aircraft from 1963 until 1987) named an annual employee award for technical achievement after Arnstein, giving a grant for $5,000 to the college or university of the winner's choice. Later, Arnstein was enshrined in the Western Reserve Aviation Hall of Fame in Cleveland. He continued to live in Akron at the same residence he had occupied for more than forty years. Karl Arnstein died on 12 December 1974, aged eighty-seven. His widow, Bertl, survived him by another twenty-five years. She passed away at the age of 101 on 29 November 1999.

When he retired Arnstein summarized his feelings about his profession, about being an engineer: "The tougher the problems, the greater the satisfaction," he said. "If we succeed—and if we do *not* succeed—we still highly treasure the value of the experience." Arnstein believed "there is no such thing as 'Life without worries.'" He told his engineers, "If we do not have serious problems to worry about we will eventually acquire the habit to worry about trifles."

Arnstein also had time to reflect on his career. "Naturally there were disappointments," he said later. "One of the most glaring in my business life was to find our original high hopes for the prospects of airships not fully obtainable. Fortunately, as it frequently has happened in the history of human endeavor, some good has come from most of our past work and studies, and so with the joint efforts of so many of our associates and friends, the much broader form of aviation industry emerged in Akron."

Even toward the end of his life, Arnstein believed that while the airship would never return as a competitor in commercial air travel, for special applications it still had a place, specifically sight-seeing and luxury cruises. Such a future may again come to pass. At

Friedrichshafen, the small German town on Lake Constance where the Zeppelins began, their story continues. A small prototype called the *New Technology* airship was built in the late 1990s, created by a company with its roots in the business empire Count Zeppelin began nearly a century before. Although it is in many ways more reminiscent of a blimp, if it is successful, it could allow the building of larger airships for scenic cruises. The ring then would be complete, as the technology of the twentieth century is reborn and adapted for the twenty-first century. Karl Arnstein's legacy is providing a link to this future. His accomplishments in aeronautical engineering, and the understanding of airship technology he pioneered, have formed a basis for pursuit of these adventures in lighter than air.

Chapter 21 THE LEGACY: UP SHIP!

Karl Arnstein's life was defined by the wars that shattered Europe not once, but twice during the first half of the twentieth century. Were it not for the consequences of such belligerence, his life's work would likely have been far different, and even less likely would they have involved the construction of airships.

He could have been a philosopher or mathematician, but a desire to be practical attracted Arnstein to civil engineering. His teacher was a pioneer in the design of reinforced concrete structures, and Karl had the fortune of having him as a mentor while pursuing his doctoral degree. This led to employment with a firm renowned for its construction in reinforced concrete. In this company he likely would have stayed, known for his work in stabilizing the Strasbourg Cathedral tower. In such a position Arnstein likely would have continued to refine the techniques of structural analysis realized so successfully in building the railroad bridge at Langwies. But the upheaval of World War I caused whatever plans he made for his career to be pushed aside, and ultimately altered the course of his life's work. Arnstein's knowledge of civil engineering spared him from the horrors of trench warfare, and a favorable impression he made on airship pioneer Count Zeppelin unexpectedly took him from the front to an aircraft factory in Friedrichshafen, Germany. Here Arnstein adapted his analysis of utilitarian structures fixed firmly to the ground to examination of flying structures, the Zeppelins. In this endeavor Arnstein excelled, and he was among the first to apply stress analysis to aircraft design. His innovative solutions to structural problems were not only patentable, but of such usefulness that most were immediately adopted. Arnstein codified the intuitive, guesswork approach to Zeppelin design then existing and replaced it with scientific understanding of the physical forces acting on a Zeppelin's structure. Zeppelins could be built larger and lighter with confidence that they were strong enough to survive the rigors of flight, if not always the misfortunes of war. Arnstein's technical contributions helped to refine the Zeppelin as a flying machine, an engineering accomplishment evidenced in more than eighty Zeppelin airships produced with Arnstein's design expertise, or more than two-thirds of all the airships built by Luftschiffbau-Zeppelin.

Following the First World War, the Zeppelin technology that Arnstein had improved was on the verge of being banned outright by the victors where it was not being seized by them. The old empires that determined and maintained Europe's social order disintegrated in the 1914–18 war. Arnstein's Bohemian homeland was subdivided. Following one last hurrah in the form of the Zeppelin *Los Angeles* built for the U.S. Navy, German airship expertise looked to be lost forever. Arnstein then might have become a professor of civil engineering in his hometown of Prague, but by another twist of fate he was chosen to bring his Zeppelin knowledge—and a small group of airship experts—to America. That he did, and he applied his knowledge to further the Zeppelin dreams of his new sponsor, rubber industrialist Paul W. Litchfield. Arnstein's decision to transplant himself to the United States and become one of its citizens altered the course of his life yet again, for his benefit as well as that of his family, and ultimately to the benefit of his adopted nation.

Litchfield wanted to fill the skies with Zeppelin airliners, but the only orders came from the U.S. Navy, which asked for Zeppelins to carry airplanes and serve as "eyes in the sky" for the fleet. Arnstein complied with a design for what was at the time the world's largest airship, one that could carry airplanes inside its hull. Arnstein oversaw the design and construction of two of these giant dirigibles, the *Akron* and *Macon*, as well as the creation of the enormous hangar in which they were built. This hangar, the Air Dock in Akron, Ohio, was for decades the largest building in the world without interior columns, and Arnstein was proud that it was built in accordance with aerodynamic principles. The building was worthy of a patent, as were more than thirty of Arnstein's engineering ideas. The most important of these showed how to make a simple metal box girder lighter and stronger by giving it holes with formed edges. This girder type found widespread use in many aircraft structures.

As the result of unexpected tragic events and a pervasive, dreadful economy, the dream of building and operating passenger Zeppelins from North America to South America, Europe, and Asia was never fulfilled. It was, however, transformed and supplanted by the times, and knowledge of airship building was of value later, technologically and organizationally. While waiting to build the passenger Zeppelin fleet, Arnstein and his team developed the enduring pressure airships, the Goodyear blimps. They also built the research balloons *A Century of Progress* and *Explorer II* that carried men to record altitudes in the stratosphere. Closer to earth, Arnstein and his engineers developed a high-speed passenger train, the *Comet,* utilizing aircraft construction methods. Its aerodynamic shape, diesel-electric power plant, use of aluminum, low-slung suspension, and other design features were precursors of the Japanese and French high speed trains built after WWII.

Arnstein's role in Germany's rigid airships of the 1930s has been overlooked, yet he served as a consultant and an advisor to Luftschiffbau-Zeppelin, and his advice to reinforce the fins on the *Hindenburg* was followed although not credited until years later. When Nazi Germany swallowed up Arnstein's Bohemian homeland in the late 1930s, Arnstein did not shun his moral responsibility to offer help to friends and family who wished to escape the growing tyranny.

After the outbreak of another war in Europe in 1939, Arnstein's engineering insight helped to build a company, known primarily for tires and rubber goods, into a substantial aircraft contractor for defense work. As a result, when the United States and her Allies desperately needed every bit of efficient production that could be mustered, Goodyear Aircraft was able to become a silent partner with a dozen airplane manufacturers, helping to produce tens of thousands of airplanes. Goodyear Aircraft Corporation made its own mark as airplane manufacturer by building over four thousand of Corsair navy fighters.

The Second World War added another dimension to Arnstein's airship-building career. Unlike in the First World War, the need was not for giant rigid Zeppelins, but smaller pressure airships. Arnstein helped to perfect the blimp, and saw it into serial production. Goodyear built for the U.S. Navy over one hundred and thirty K-ship patrol blimps—more airships than had ever been made of a single class, either rigid or non-rigid. These blimps proved valuable in coastal defense, serving as submarine chasers, as convoy escorts, and in rescue operations.

World War II propelled the phenomenal growth of Goodyear Aircraft Corporation from fewer than a dozen to more than 30,000 employees, making the company the largest single employer in Akron. Although military contracts decreased after the war ended in 1945 and many workers returned to peacetime pursuits, the company had benefited from its diversification. The engineering base Arnstein helped to establish gave GAC the confidence to branch into other areas of national defense in the next decade, including the building of missiles, computers, flight simulators, parachutes, and radar equipment. New techniques and products gave the company entry into plastics fabrication, development of lightweight composite materials, high-performance fabrics, aerospace electronics, and nuclear energy. During these years approaching retirement, Arnstein worked as a team leader, preparing the company to pursue business it otherwise would never have been able to undertake. And GAC still built blimps, such as the giant radar-carrying platforms constructed for the navy in the 1950s. Some of these pressure airships, the ZPG-3Ws, were larger in volume than any one of seventy-six Zeppelins made by Luftschiffbau. When Arnstein retired in 1957, he had the satisfaction of having nurtured a generation of engineers who were competent to perform in a world that had made the transition from the zeppelin era to the space age.

Karl Arnstein's life, while rich in professional accomplishments and contributions to Akron's and aviation history, is also a study in frustration. Some of this frustration was born of economic conditions; some was due to politics and cultural traditions. But the greatest frustration Arnstein experienced was not realizing the dream of a commercial rigid airship business in the United States. The ideal moment technologically for such an endeavor—what might have become the rigid airship's golden decade—was one overshadowed by the Great Depression. Arnstein was the instrument chosen to make Litchfield's airship dream a reality, and in this he was only partially successful. Arnstein, a designer of over a dozen distinct classes of rigid airships for Luftschiffbau-Zeppelin, built only two rigid airships in the United States. These, the *Akron* and *Macon*, were experimental prototypes. Their design did not have the luxury of serial production to perfect them, resulting in no commercial application—a disappointment to both Arnstein and Litchfield. We are left wondering about the what-ifs. Commercial airship transport, which saw only limited development in England and Germany, proved too expensive to be viable principally because of the steep price of acquiring and operating airships. The competition, heavier-than-air planes, with their lower unit cost, replaced airships as the fastest transportation across the oceans. Would the rigid airship industry have thrived with subsidies, such as airmail contracts, that helped other segments of air commerce? Possibly. Was Goodyear-Zeppelin's exclusivity as United States patent holder of Zeppelin technology ultimately a hindrance to broader acceptance of commercial airships, since there were no multiple producers of rigid airships in America? Probably. Did the cumulative failures of commercial airship programs in other countries influence public opinion against rigid airships? Undoubtedly. The *Hindenburg*'s fiery crash was captured dramatically in sound and pictures as no other air disaster had been, to be revisited endlessly by the news media. What if the press had not been witness? With no "as it happened" recordings, would such an indelible negative impression of Zeppelins have been made on the public? Arguably, no. The *Hindenburg* crash and loss of the navy's dirigibles halted development work on rigid airships in a way no comparable single crash—or even numerous crashes—of airplanes could affect heavier-than-air craft progress. Airships could not sustain the losses. There were too few Zeppelins, and they were not easily replaced. Airplanes could be built in a matter of weeks, but it took years to produce an airship.

Investigations of the airship crashes added further delays that could not be made up. By the time the official committees reached conclusions about what caused each airship wreck, too much valuable time had been lost. In the interim, economic and political conditions worsened while airplanes continued to progress. Built in far greater numbers and greater diversity, airplanes continuously evolved, and they gradually achieved acceptance as a form of transport. The same was not true for the Zeppelin.

The loss of both the *Akron* and the *Macon* and members of their crews deeply affected Arnstein. Later in life, he said poignantly, "Talking about them is like talking about one's own dead children." These airships should have been the crowning achievement in Arnstein's airship design career. Instead, some lingering doubt has remained about the structural integrity of these airships and the ability of their designer. The facts indicate the navy airship *Akron* was lost to an unexpectedly severe storm, not due to any design flaw. The *Macon*'s loss may have been prevented had the dirigible's only known weak point been reinforced earlier or if the damage that occurred in the flight off Point Sur had been handled differently. Arnstein had recognized the potential problem with the fin, and made the remedy available to the navy. It might be argued that Arnstein could have been more insistent that the fin structure reinforcements be made before the *Macon* was allowed to continue to operate. However, it was not his style to challenge the authority of his corporate leader, or that of the airships' military operators. Arnstein's Old World view of the manufacturer having the last word on matters of design clashed with New World ideas of how an airship should be built and operated. The differences in procedure contributed to the frustration Arnstein later felt, especially in instances where his original airship designs were altered to suit the customer. Arnstein believed that compromise could never produce excellence. But he accepted the rules and endured the consequences, never complaining publicly. As a result, his side of the story has rarely, if ever, been told.

Arnstein was a quiet, self-effacing man who generally shunned publicity, and with justifiable reason. On several occasions when he was thrust into its spotlight, he was misrepresented. In Germany, not only his words but his deeds were contrived by journalists eager to embellish a story, often for nationalistic purposes. Once Arnstein came to the United States, the reporters were less strident, but often more patronizing in tone. Frequently, they were no more accurate in reporting the facts than their continental counterparts. As detail-oriented as Arnstein was, it is little wonder that he disliked such journalists.

To give a correct account of Arnstein's life and career and to recognize his achievements has been the goal of this book. Arnstein's engineering legacy can be found in bridges and a cathedral foundation, and in the scale of Akron's Air Dock. It includes the design of a high speed train and one of the fastest piston-engine fighter planes of World War II. An equally important legacy was the knowledge Arnstein patiently shared with engineers on two continents and the inspiration he gave them. One of the young engineers working on his engineering staff in Akron looked up from his drawing board one day and remarked to a coworker, "Arnstein knows everything there is to know about Zeppelins." The neighboring engineer replied, "I think he knows everything there is to know about engineering."

Arnstein will be remembered best for his work with the majestic Zeppelins—the Zeppelins that pioneered aeronautical technology, the Zeppelins that were the focus of his career. Arnstein recognized their importance in a speech shortly after his retirement: "It was the airship and my association with its supporters that gave me a strong and enduring stimulation in my professional life for over forty years. The airship experience allowed me also to expand from this fascinating though specialized field of aviation to other aeronautical developments."

And it is not just for his contributions to Zeppelin design that Arnstein should be remembered. The skills he and his twelve disciples brought to the United States ensured in no small way that three-quarters of a century after its commercial debut, the Goodyear blimp remains the tire company's corporate icon. Indeed, the blimp has become symbolic to the citizens of Akron, serving as a familiar mascot that recalls the city's large airship heritage. Arnstein and his team produced a blimp design that is still current today, nearly identical in basic form and operation from its mid-1920s antecedents, although modern in its materials and equipment.

Counting both Zeppelins and blimps, Arnstein participated in the design and development of more airships than anyone else—more than eighty rigid airships and over 230 pressure airships. He was the designer of three of the U.S. Navy's five rigid airships, the *Los Angeles, Akron,* and *Macon.* The other two naval airships, the *Shenandoah* and ZR-2, were copies of his designs.

At the beginning of the twenty-first century, the promise of the airship beckons again. Large rigid airships have been proposed as luxury sight-seeing cruise liners and as cargo haulers to fulfill a niche between fast but costly airplanes and inexpensive but slow surface ships. Airships are being contemplated as communications relay platforms to replace satellites for transmitting cellular voice and data signals. Other applications for airships include monitoring pollution or natural resources such as forests and fisheries. Large, long-endurance airships could serve in surveillance roles in peacekeeping missions, to monitor the flow of refugees, border crossings, or the movements of troops or materiel. Arnstein's design legacy may yet live on in a new generation of rigid airships. For them, the traditional airship launching command serves as fitting encouragement: "Up Ship!" The same words should serve to remind us of Dr. Karl Arnstein, whose life was so inextricably linked with airships, and to the airships to which he contributed so much.

REFERENCE MATERIAL

APPENDIX A: KARL ARNSTEIN'S PATENTS

U.S. Patent No.	Title	Date	Assigned to	Co-inventor
1,449,721	Light Weight Girder	27 March 1923	Luftschiffbau-Zeppelin	—
1,456,497 (Reissue 15,855)	Skeleton Frame Construction for Airship Fins and the Like	29 July 1924	—	—
1,486,623	Anchoring Means for Airships	11 March 1924	Luftschiffbau-Zeppelin	—
1,502,227	Panelwork for Light Structures	22 July 1924	Luftschiffbau-Zeppelin	—
1,502,417	Wire and Rope Clamp	22 July 1924	Luftschiffbau-Zeppelin	—
1,502,418	Wire and Rope Clamping Device	22 July 1924	Luftschiffbau-Zeppelin	—
1,503,293	Skeleton Framework Construction for Airships and the Like	29 July 1924	Luftschiffbau-Zeppelin	—
1,505,689	Rigid Frame for Airships	19 August 1924	Luftschiffbau-Zeppelin	—
1,517,885	Stern Construction of Rigid Airships	2 December 1924	Luftschiffbau-Zeppelin	—
1,521,590	Joint for Frames for Airships	6 January 1925	Luftschiffbau-Zeppelin	—
1,526,198	Aircraft Structure	10 February 1925	Luftschiffbau-Zeppelin	—
1,527,728	Hollow Bar in Two Pieces	24 February 1925	Luftschiffbau-Zeppelin	—
1,553,061	Airship	8 September 1925	Luftschiffbau-Zeppelin	—
1,553,586	Landing and Starting Carriage for Airships	15 September 1925	Luftschiffbau-Zeppelin	—
1,614,519	Airship with Structural Compensating Surfaces	18 January 1927	Luftschiffbau-Zeppelin	—
1,620,507	Hull Construction of Rigid Airships	8 March 1927	Luftschiffbau-Zeppelin	—
1,623,951	Airship Frame	5 April 1927	Luftschiffbau-Zeppelin	—
1,623,952	Stabilizing Apparatus for Rigid Airships	5 April 1927	Luftschiffbau-Zeppelin	—
1,631,908	Rigid Airship	7 June 1927	Luftschiffbau-Zeppelin	—
1,642,005	Aircraft	13 September 1927	Luftschiffbau-Zeppelin	—
1,656,810	Hollow Girder for Light Structures	17 January 1928	Luftschiffbau-Zeppelin	—
1,658,876	Gas Cell for Airships	14 February 1928	Luftschiffbau-Zeppelin	Ernst A. Lehmann
1,662,021	Hull Structure for Rigid Airships	6 March 1928	Goodyear-Zeppelin	—
1,665,872	Assemblage Point Device	10 April 1928	Luftschiffbau-Zeppelin	—
1,669,592	Rigid Airship	15 May 1928	Luftschiffbau-Zeppelin	—
1,673,481	Airship Hull	12 June 1928	Luftschiffbau-Zeppelin	—
1,779,387	Main Ring for Rigid Airships	21 October 1930	Goodyear-Zeppelin	—
1,797,186	Fastening Means for Airship Envelopes	17 March 1931	Goodyear-Zeppelin	Paul Helma, Kurt Bauch
1,818,952	Bulkhead for Rigid Airships	11 August 1931	Goodyear-Zeppelin	Paul Helma
1,841,321	Aircraft Hangar and Method of Building It	12 January 1932	Goodyear-Zeppelin	Paul Helma Wilbur J. Watson
1,883,455	Method and Apparatus for Building Airship Bulkheads	18 October 1932	Goodyear-Zeppelin	Paul Helma
1,913,325	Airship Bulkhead	6 June 1932	Goodyear-Zeppelin	Paul Helma
2,349,584	Flying Boat Hull	23 May 1944	Wingfoot Corp.	Benjamin J. Schnitzer

"Influence Lines of Continuous Beams Supported by Three or Four Elastic Supports."* Vienna: R. V. Waldheim and Co., 1910.

"Theory of Multiple Strut Framed Bridges."* Prague: J. G. Calve, 1910.

Influence Lines of Indeterminate Structures on Elastic Supports. * Berlin: W. Ernst and Son, 1912.

"Theory of a Series of Continuous Silos."* *Armierter Beton,* 1913.

"Influence Lines of Indeterminate Bridge Structures."* *Beton and Eisen*, 1913.

"Theory of Circular Foundation Plates."* *Beton and Eisen*, 1913.

"Group of Continuous Silos."* *Betonbau*, 1914.

"Cylindrical Containers with Flat Bottom."* *Architektur and Ingenieurwesen,* 1916.

"Axially Compressed Column under Bending Through Series of Side Loads."* *Eisenbau*, 1919.

"Stresses in Columns under Combined Axial and Side Loads." National Advisory Committee for Aeronautics, July 1922.

"Theory of Large Bridges of Reinforced Concrete Arch Construction."* *Melan Anniversary Volume* Leipzig: F. Deuticke, 1923.

"The Development of Large Commercial Rigid Airships." American Society of Mechanical Engineers *Transactions* 1928, Paper No. AER-50-4.

"Developments in Lighter-Than-Air Craft." *Society of Automotive Engineers Journal* (May 1929).

"What We Need Now is Less Invention and More Application of Basic Principles." *U.S. Air Services Magazine* (April 1930).

"Why Airships?" *U.S. Air Services Magazine* (December 1932).

"Logical Development of Airships for Fast Ocean Transportation." *Metal Progress* (December 1932).

"Some Airship Problems." *Zeitschrift für Flugtechnik* (Berlin) (January 1933).

"Some Design Aspects of the Rigid Airship." American Society of Mechanical Engineers Paper No. AER-56-10, 1934.

"The Comet—High-Speed Train." *Mechanical Engineering* (August 1935).

"Transoceanic Airships." *Aviation* (June 1936).

"Aerodynamic Theory." Vol. 6, Ch. 4 in *Performance of Airships.* Berlin: Julius Springer, 1936.

"Wind Pressures on the Akron Airship Dock." *Journal of the Aeronautical Sciences* (January 1936).

"The Field of the Large Commercial Airship." *Journal of the Aeronautical Sciences* (August 1936).

"On Methods of Calculating Stresses in the Hulls of Rigid Airships." Proceedings of the Fifth International Congress of Applied Mechanics, 1938.

"Notes on Recent Structural Research of the Goodyear-Zeppelin Corporation." *Journal of the Aeronautical Sciences* (1939).

"Fatigue Problems in the Aircraft Industry." *Metals and Alloys* (July 1939).

"The Engineering Treatment of Ring or Wheel Problems, Applied Mechanics." *Kármán Anniversary Volume*, 1941.

"Recent Developments in Airships." *Aeronautical Engineering Review* (June 1942).

"Design Aspects of the Goodyear Model M Airship." *Industrial Aviation* (January 1946).

"Fatigue Failures in Aircraft." *Proceedings* of the Society for Experimental Stress Analysis 3, no. 2 (1946).

"On American Aeronautics." *L'Air* (Paris) (April 1946).

"Rigid Airship Competes for Long Range Hauling." *Society of Automotive Engineers Journal* (August 1946).

"An Effective Air-Power Team." *Technical Data Digest* (1 May 1949).

"Discussion of the Fifteenth Wright Brothers Lecture 'Experimental Approach to Aircraft Structural Research' by Dr. P. B. Walker." *Journal of the Aeronautical Sciences* (March 1952).

* These are Arnstein's translations of the titles. The originals are in German.

APPENDIX C: LUFTSCHIFFBAU-ZEPPELIN AIRSHIPS

Builder's Number	Designation	Operator*	Gas Volume (cubic feet)	Length x Max. Diameter (feet)	No. of Motors (Total HP)	First Flight	Remarks
LZ 1		LZ	399,000	420 x 38.5	2 (28)	2 July 1900	Dismantled early 1901
LZ 2		LZ	366,000	414 x 38.5	2 (170)	30 Nov 1905	Forced landing Jan 1906; dismantled
LZ 3		LZ	404,000	414 x 38.5	2 (170)	9 Oct 1906	Lengthened 1908; dismantled 1913
	Z I	Army	431,000	440 x 38.5	2 (210)	21 Oct 1908	
LZ 4		LZ	530,000	446 x 42.5	2 (210)	20 June 1908	Burned on the ground at Echterdingen 5 Aug 1908
LZ 5	Z II	Army	530,000	446 x 42.5	2 (210)	26 May 1909	Wrecked on the ground at Weilburg April 1910
LZ 6		LZ	530,000	446 x 42.5	3 (375)	25 Aug 1909	Lengthened early 1910; burned in hangar 14 Sept 1910
		DELAG	565,000	474 x 42.5			
LZ 7	Deutschland	DELAG	683,000	486 x 46	3 (360)	19 June 1910	Stranded in storm 28 June 1910
LZ 8	Deutschland (replacement)	DELAG	683,000	486 x 46	3 (360)	30 March 1911	Damaged against hangar at Düsseldorf, 16 May 1911
LZ 9	Z II (replacement)	Army	584,000	430 x 46	3 (435)	2 Oct 1911	Lengthened; dismantled Aug 1914
			628,000	460 x 46			
LZ 10	Schwaben	DELAG	628,000	460 x 46	3 (435)	26 June 1911	Burned on the ground at Düsseldorf 28 June 1912
LZ 11	Viktoria Luise	DELAG	660,000	486 x 46	3 (510)	14 Feb 1912	Wrecked upon landing Oct 1915
LZ 12	Z III	Army	628,000	460 x 46	3 (435)	25 April 1912	Dismantled at Metz Summer 1914
LZ 13	Hansa	DELAG	660,000	486 x 46	3 (510)	30 July 1912	Dismantled Summer 1916
LZ 14	L 1	Navy	793,000	518 x 48.5	3 (495)	7 Oct 1912	Lost in storm off Heligoland; 14 dead
LZ 15	Z I (replacement)	Army	690,000	466 x 48.5	3 (510)	16 Jan 1913	Forced landing, wrecked by storm, Karlsruhe 19 March 1913
LZ 16	Z IV	Army	690,000	466 x 48.5	3 (510)	14 March 1913	Dismantled Autumn 1916
LZ 17	Sachsen	DELAG	690,000	466 x 48.5	3 (510)	3 May 1913	Dismantled Sept 1916
		Navy	736,000	486 x 48.5	3 (540)		
LZ 18	L 2	Navy	953,000	518 x 54.5	4 (660)	6 Sept 1913	Burned in air 17 Oct 1913; 28 dead
LZ 19	Z I (replacement 2)	Army	690,000	466 x 48.5	3 (495)	7 June 1913	Wrecked upon landing at Diedenhofen 13 June 1914
LZ 20	Z V	Army	690,000	466 x 48.5	3 (495)	8 July 1913	Shot down by artillery in Poland, 27 Aug 1914
			736,000	486 x 48.5	3 (540)		
LZ 21	Z VI	Army	736,000	486 x 48.5	3 (540)	10 Nov 1913	Damaged by gunfire at Liege, stranded near Cologne 6 Aug 1914
LZ 22	Z VII	Army	782,000	510 x 48.5	3 (540)	8 Jan 1914	Shot down by artillery, Lorraine 22 Aug 1914
LZ 23	Z VIII	Army	782,000	510 x 48.5	3 (540)	21 Feb 1914	Shot down by artillery near Luneville 22 Aug 1914

(continued)

Builder's Number	Designation	Operator*	Gas Volume (cubic feet)	Length x Max. Diameter (feet)	No. of Motors (Total HP)	First Flight	Remarks
LZ 24	L 3	Navy	794,000	518 x 48.5	3 (630)	11 May 1914	Forced landing, Fanö Island, Denmark 17 Feb 1915
LZ 25	Z IX	Army	794,000	518 x 48.5	3 (630)	13 July 1914	Bombed in hangar by British airplane, 8 Oct 1914
LZ 26	Z XII	Army	882,000	528.5 x 52.5	3 (630)	14 Dec 1914	Built in Frankfurt, dismantled in Jüterbog Aug 1917
LZ 27	L 4	Navy	794,000	518 x 48.5	3 (630)	30 Aug 1914	Forced landing in Denmark 17 Feb 1915
LZ 28	L 5	Navy	794,000	518 x 48.5	3 (630)	22 Sept 1914	Hit by artillery fire near Riga; forced landing May 1915
LZ 29	Z X	Army	794,000	518 x 48.5	3 (630)	13 Oct 1914	Hit by artillery; forced landing, St. Quentin, France 21 March 1915
LZ 30	Z XI	Army	794,000	518 x 48.5	3 (630)	11 Nov 1914	Blew away from hangar and burned, May 1915
LZ 31	L 6	Navy	794,000	518 x 48.5	3 (630)	3 Nov 1914	Accidentally burned in hangar Sept 1916
LZ 32	L 7	Navy	794,000	518 x 48.5	3 (630)	20 Nov 1914	Shot down by British ships 4 May 1915; 11 dead, 7 POWs
LZ 33	L 8	Navy	794,000	518 x 48.5	3 (630)	17 Dec 1914	Hit by artillery fire and stranded in Belgium 5 March 1915
LZ 34	LZ 34	Army	794,000	518 x 48.5	3 (630)	6 Jan 1915	Hit by artillery fire, stranded and burned in E. Prussia, May 1915
LZ 35	LZ 35	Army	794,000	518 x 48.5	3 (630)	11 Jan 1915	Hit by artillery fire, stranded in Belgium 14 April 1915
LZ 36	L 9	Navy	879,000	529 x 52.5	3 (630)	8 March 1915	Accidentally burned in hangar Sept 1916
LZ 37	LZ 37	Army	794,000	518 x 48.5	3 (630)	28 Feb 1915	Shot down by British airplane over Ghent 7 June 1915; 9 dead, 1 survivor
LZ 38	LZ 38	Army	1,126,000	536.5 x 61.3	4 (840)	3 April 1915	First airship for which Arnstein performs stress analysis; bombed in hangar by British plane, 7 June 1915
LZ 39	LZ 39	Army	879,000	529 x 52.5	3 (630)	24 April 1915	Hit by artillery fire, forced landing in Russia, 18 Dec 1915
LZ 40	L 10	Navy	1,126,000	536.5 x 61.3	4 (840)	13 May 1915	Struck by lightning, burned in air, Neuwerk Island 3 Sept 1915; 19 dead
LZ 41	L 11	Navy	1,126,000	536.5 x 61.3	4 (840)	7 June 1915	Dismantled at Hage early 1917
LZ 42	LZ 72	Army	1,126,000	536.5 x 61.3	4 (840)	15 June 1915	Dismantled in Jüterbog, Feb 1917
LZ 43	L 12	Navy	1,126,000	536.5 x 61.3	4 (840)	21 June 1915	Hit by artillery fire, stranded and burned at Ostend, 10 Aug 1915
LZ 44	LZ 74	Army	1,126,000	536.5 x 61.3	4 (840)	8 July 1915	Stranded on a hill in fog, 8 Oct 1915
LZ 45	L 13	Navy	1,126,000	536.5 x 61.3	4 (840)	23 July 1915	Dismantled at Hage early 1917
LZ 46	L 14	Navy	1,126,000	536.5 x 61.3	4 (840)	9 Aug 1915	Wrecked by crew, Nordholz June 1919
LZ 47	LZ 77	Army	1,126,000	536.5 x 61.3	4 (840)	24 Aug 1915	Shot down by artillery, France 21 Feb 1916; 11 dead

Builder's Number	Designation	Operator*	Gas Volume (cubic feet)	Length x Max. Diameter (feet)	No. of Motors (Total HP)	First Flight	Remarks
LZ 48	L 15	Navy	1,126,000	536.5 x 61.3	4 (960)	9 Sept 1915	Brought down by artillery in Thames River, 1 April 1916; 1 dead, 17 POWs
LZ 49	LZ 79	Army	1,126,000	536.5 x 61.3	4 (840)	2 Aug 1915	Hit by artillery, stranded in Ath, Belgium, Jan 1916
LZ 50	L 16	Navy	1,126,000	536.5 x 61.3	4 (960)	23 Sept 1915	Wrecked in training, 19 Oct 1917
LZ 51	LZ 81	Army	1,126,000 1,264,000	536.5 x 61.3 585.5 x 61.3	4 (960) 4 (960)	7 Oct 1915 lengthened Sept 1916	Hit by artillery, stranded Bulgaria 27 Sept 1916
LZ 52	L 18	Navy	1,126,000	536.5 x 61.3	4 (960)	3 Nov1915	Accidentally burned in hangar 15 Nov 1915
LZ 53	L 17	Navy	1,126,000	536.5 x 61.3	4 (960)	20 Oct 1915	Accidentally burned in Tondern hangar 28 Dec 1916
LZ 54	L 19	Navy	1,126,000	536.5 x 61.3	4 (960)	19 Nov 1915	Brought down at sea 2 Feb 1916; 16 dead
LZ 55	LZ 85	Army	1,126,000	536.5 x 61.3	4 (840)	12 Sept 1915	Brought down by artillery Salonika 5 May 1916
LZ 56	LZ 86	Army	1,126,000 1,264,000	536.5 x 61.3 585.5 x 61.3	4 (840) 4 (840)	10 Oct 1915 lengthened Summer 1916	Wrecked in landing 6 Sept 1916; 9 dead
LZ 57	LZ 87	Army	1,126,000 1,264,000	536.5 x 61.3 585.5 x 61.3	4 (960) 4 (960)	6 Dec 1915 lengthened Aug 1916	Dismantled at Jüterbog, July 1917
LZ 58	LZ 88 L 25	Army Navy	1,126,000 1,264,000	536.5 x 61.3 585.5 x 61.3	4 (840) 4 (960)	14 Nov 1915 lengthened Sept 1916	Dismantled at Potsdam 15 Sept 1917
LZ 59	L 20	Navy	1,126,000	536.5 x 61.3	4 (960)	21 Dec 1915	Wrecked in Norway 3 May 1916
LZ 60	LZ 90	Army	1,126,000 1,264,000	536.5 x 61.3 585.5 x 61.3	4 (960)	1 Jan 1916 lengthened Summer 1916	Blew away in storm unmanned 7 Nov 1916
LZ 61	L 21	Navy	1,126,000	536.5 x 61.3	4 (960)	10 Jan 1916	Shot down off England 28 Nov 1916; 17 dead
LZ 62	L 30	Navy	1,949,600	649.5 x 78.5	6 (1440)	28 May 1916	First airship for which Arnstein was fully responsible for structural design; awarded to Belgium, dismantled 1920
LZ 63	LZ 93	Army	1,126,000 1,264,000	536.5 x 61.3 585.5 x 61.3	4 (840) 4 (840)	23 Feb 1916 lengthened Summer 1916	Dismantled Summer 1917
LZ 64	L 22	Navy	1,264,000	585.5 x 61.3	4 (960)	2 March 1916	Shot down at sea by British aircraft 14 May 1917; 21 dead
LZ 65	LZ 95	Army	1,264,000	585.5 x 61.3	4 (960)	31 Jan 1916	Hit by artillery, stranded 22 Feb 1916 near base
LZ 66	L 23	Navy	1,264,000	585.5 x 61.3	4 (960)	8 April 1916	Shot down at sea by British 21 Aug 1917; 18 dead
LZ 67	LZ 97	Army	1,264,000	585.5 x 61.3	4 (960)	4 April 1916	Dismantled July 1917, Jüterbog
LZ 68	LZ 98	Army	1,264,000	585.5 x 61.3	4 (960)	28 April 1916	Dismantled Aug 1917
LZ 69	L 24	Navy	1,264,000	585.5 x 61.3	4 (960)	20 May 1916	Accidentally burned in Tondern hangar 28 Dec 1916
LZ 70							Not built
LZ 71	LZ 101	Army	1,264,000	585.5 x 61.3	4 (960)	29 June 1916	Dismantled Sept 1917, Jüterbog

(continued)

Builder's Number	Designation	Operator*	Gas Volume (cubic feet)	Length x Max. Diameter (feet)	No. of Motors (Total HP)	First Flight	Remarks
LZ 72	L 31	Navy	1,949,600	649.5 x 78.5	6 (1440)	12 July 1916	Shot down over London by British aircraft 2 Oct 1916; 19 dead
LZ 73	LZ 103	Army	1,264,000	585.5 x 61.3	4 (960)	8 Aug 1916	Dismantled Aug 1917
LZ 74	L 32	Navy	1,949,600	649.5 x 78.5	6 (1440)	4 Aug 1916	Shot down over London by British aircraft 24 Sept 1916; 22 dead
LZ 75	L 37	Navy	1,949,600	644.7 x 78.5	6 (1440)	9 Nov 1916	Awarded to Japan, dismantled 1920
LZ 76	L 33	Navy	1,949,600	644.7 x 78.5	6 (1440)	30 Aug 1916	Forced down by artillery near London 24 Sept 1916, 22 POWs
LZ 77	LZ 107	Army	1,264,000	585.5 x 61.3	4 (960)	16 Oct 1916	Dismantled July 1917
LZ 78	L 34	Navy	1,949,600	644.7 x 78.5	6 (1440)	22 Sept 1916	Shot down by British aircraft, coastal England 28 Nov 1916; 20 dead
LZ 79	L 41	Navy	1,949,600	644.7 x 78.5	6 (1440) 5 (1200)	15 Jan 1917 modified Spring 1917	Wrecked by crew at Nordholz 23 June 1919
LZ 80	L 35	Navy	1,949,600	644.7 x 78.5	6 (1440) 5 (1200)	12 Oct 1916 modified Spring 1917	Broken up at Jüterbog, 15 Nov 1918
LZ 81	LZ 111	Army	1,264,000	585.5 X 61.3	4 (960)	20 Dec 1916	Dismantled Aug 1917, Dresden
LZ 82	L 36	Navy	1,949,600	644.7 x 78.5	6 (1440) 5 (1200)	1 Nov 1916 engine removed 1 Feb 1917	Forced landing in France 7 Feb 1917
LZ 83	LZ 113	Army	1,949,600	644.7 x 78.5	6 (1440)	22 Feb 1917	Given to Navy; awarded to France, dismantled Oct 1920
LZ 84	L 38	Navy	1,949,600	644.7 x 78.5	6 (1440)	22 Nov 1916	Forced landing in Russia 29 Dec 1916
LZ 85	L 45	Navy	1,949,600	644.7 x 78.5	5 (1200)	2 April 1917 modified Aug-Sept 1917	Forced landing in France 20 Oct 1917
LZ 86	L 39	Navy	1,949,600	644.7 x 78.5	6 (1440) 5 (1200)	11 Dec 1916 engine removed 1 Feb 1917	Shot down by artillery, France 17 March 1917
LZ 87	L 47	Navy	1,949,600	644.7 x 78.5	5 (1200)	1 May 1917 modified Sept-Oct 1917	Accidentally burned in hangar, Ahlhorn 5 Jan 1918
LZ 88	L 40	Navy	1,949,600	644.7 x 78.5	6 (1440) 5 (1200)	3 Jan 1917 engine removed 1 Feb 1917	Wrecked in landing, Neuenwald June 1917
LZ 89	L 50	Navy	1,949,600	644.7 x 78.5	5 (1200)	9 June 1917	Wrecked in France 20 Oct 1917; 4 dead, 16 POWs
LZ 90	LZ 120 *Ausonia*	Army Italian Army	1,949,600	644.7 x 78.5	6 (1440)	30 Jan 1917	Awarded to Italy 1920; dismantled June 1921
LZ 91	L 42	Navy	1,960,000	644.7 x 78.5	5 (1200)	21 Feb 1917 modified June–July 1917	Wrecked by crew at Nordholz 23 June 1919
LZ 92	L 43	Navy	1,960,000	644.7 x 78.5	5 (1200)	6 March 1917	Shot down by British aircraft, North Sea 14 June 1917; 24 dead
LZ 93	L 44	Navy	1,970,000	644.7 x 78.5	5 (1200)	1 April 1917	Shot down by artillery, France 20 Oct 1917; 18 dead
LZ 94	L 46	Navy	1,970,000	644.7 x 78.5	5 (1200)	24 April 1917	Accidentally burned in hangar, Ahlhorn 5 Jan 1918

Builder's Number	Designation	Operator*	Gas Volume (cubic feet)	Length x Max. Diameter (feet)	No. of Motors (Total HP)	First Flight	Remarks
LZ 95	L 48	Navy	1,970,000	644.7 x 78.5	5 (1200)	22 May 1917	Shot down by British aircraft over England 17 June 1917; 14 dead, 3 POWs
LZ 96	L 49	Navy	1,970,000	644.7 x 78.5	5 (1200)	13 June 1917	Forced landing in France 20 Oct 1917; 19 POWs
LZ 97	L 51	Navy	1,970,000	644.7 x 78.5	5 (1200)	6 July 1917	Accidentally burned in hangar, Ahlhorn 5 Jan 1918
LZ 98	L 52	Navy	1,970,000	644.7 x 78.5	5 (1200) 5 (1225)	4 July 1917 new motors May 1918	Wrecked by crew, Wittmund 23 June 1919
LZ 99	L 54	Navy	1,970,000	644.7 x 78.5	5 (1200) 5 (1225)	13 Aug 1917 new motors March 1918	Bombed in Tondern hangar by British plane 19 July 1918
LZ 100	L 53	Navy	1,977,000	644.7 x 78.5	5 (1200) 5 (1225)	8 August 1917 new motors April 1918	First with 15m (not 10m) frame spacing; shot down in North Sea by British planes 11 Aug 1918; 19 dead
LZ 101	L 55	Navy	1,977,000	644.7 x 78.5	5 (1200)	1 Sept 1917	Stranded in Thuringen 20 Oct 1917
LZ 102	L 57	Navy	2,420,000	743 x 78.5	5 (1200)	26 Sept 1917	Burned landing at Jüterbog 8 Oct 1917
LZ 103	L 56	Navy	1,977,000	644.7 x 78.5	5 (1200) 5 (1225)	24 Sept 1917 new motors July 1918	Wrecked by crew, Wittmund 23 June 1919
LZ 104	L 59	Navy	2,420,000	743 x 78.5	5 (1200)	10 Oct 1917 Rebuilt early 1918	Africa Flight 21-25 Nov 1917, 4200 mi; burned in air near Italian coast 7 April 1918; 23 dead
LZ 105	L 58	Navy	1,977,000	644.7 x 78.5	5 (1225)	29 Oct 1917	Accidentally burned in hangar, Ahlhorn 5 Jan 1918
LZ 106	L 61 *Italia*	Navy Italian Army	1,977,000	644.7 x 78.5	5 (1225)	12 Dec 1917	Awarded to Italy; wrecked Jan 1921
LZ 107	L 62	Navy	1,977,000	644.7 x 78.5	5 (1225)	19 Jan 1918	Accidentally burned in air near Heligoland 10 May 1918
LZ 108	L 60	Navy	1,977,000	644.7 x 78.5	5 (1225)	18 Dec 1917	Bombed in Tondern hangar by British plane 19 July 1917
LZ 109	L 64	Navy	1,977,000	644.7 x 78.5	5 (1225)	11 March 1918	Awarded to England 1920; dismantled 1921
LZ 110	L 63	Navy	1,977,000	644.7 x 78.5	5 (1225)	4 March 1918	Wrecked by crew, Nordholz 23 June 1919
LZ 111	L 65	Navy	1,977,000	644.7 x 78.5	5 (1225)	17 April 1918	Wrecked by crew, Nordholz 23 June 1919
LZ 112	L 70	Navy	2,195,000	694 x 78.5	7 (1715)	1 July 1918	Shot down near English coast by British aircraft 5 Aug 1918; 22 dead
LZ 113	L 71	Navy	2,195,000 2,420,000	694 x 78.5 743 x 78.5	7 (1715) 6 (1470)	29 July 1918 lengthened Oct 1918	Awarded to England July 1920; dismantled at Pulham 1923
LZ 114	L 72 *Dixmude*	Navy French Navy	2,420,000	743 x 78.5	6 (1470)	8 July 1920	Awarded to France; burned in air off Sicily 21 Dec 1923; 50 dead
LZ 115	L 100		2,650,000	743 x 82.5	6 (1470)		Cancelled
LZ 116	L 73						Project, not built
LZ 117	L 74						Project, not built
LZ 118	L 75						Project, not built

(continued)

Builder's Number	Designation	Operator*	Gas Volume (cubic feet)	Length x Max. Diameter (feet)	No. of Motors (Total HP)	First Flight	Remarks
LZ 119	L 100		3,810,000	781 x 96.5	10 (2450)		Project, not built
LZ 120	*Bodensee* *Esperia*	DELAG Italian Army	706,000 795,000	393.3 x 61.3 426 x 61.3	4 (980)	20 July 1919	Passenger service July–Dec 1919; awarded to Italy 1921; dismantled 1928
LZ 121	*Nordstern* *Méditeranée*	DELAG French Army, Navy	795,000	426 x 61.3	4 (980)	Dec 1919	Awarded to France 1921; dismantled Sept 1926
LZ 122-125							Projects, not built
LZ 126	ZR-3 *Los Angeles*	USN	2,762,000	658.3 x 90.7	5 (2000)	27 Aug 1924	Built for US Navy, flown to US 15 Oct 1924; dismantled 1939
LZ 127	*Graf Zeppelin*	LZ DZR	3,995,000	775 x 100	5 (2650)	18 Sept 1928	Round-the-World flight Aug 1929; S. Atlantic passenger service 1931–37; dismantled Spring 1940
LZ 128			5,288,000	776.4 x 127.8	8?		Project, not built
LZ 129	*Hindenburg*	DZR	7,062,000	804 x 135	4 (4200)	4 April 1936	Passenger service, Germany to North and South America; burned while landing, Lakehurst 6 May 1937; 36 dead (22 flight crew, 1 ground crew, 13 passengers), 61 survivors
LZ 130	*Graf Zeppelin 2*	DZR	7,062,000	804 x 135	4 (4200)	14 Sept 1938	No passenger service, but made 30 flights, including "spy flights" off English coast July–Aug 1939; dismantled Spring 1940
LZ 131-132			7,995,000	863 x 135			Projects, 1937–1938; not built, although some parts were fabricated for LZ 131

*LZ = Luftschiffbau-Zeppelin; DELAG = Deutsche Luftschiff A.G.; Army = German Army; Navy = German Navy; USN = U.S. Navy; DZR = Deutsche Zeppelin Reederei. Sixteen airships were built at Potsdam, twelve at Staaken, one at Frankfurt, and the remainder built in or near the town of Friedrichshafen (including the first six at Manzell and twenty-one wartime Zeppelins at Löwenthal)

U.S. NAVY RIGID AIRSHIPS

Builder	Designation	Name	Gas Volume (cubic feet)	Length x Max. Diameter (feet)	No. of Motors (Total HP)	First Flight	Remarks
Naval Aircraft Factory, Phila. (Assembled at NAS Lakehurst, NJ)	ZR-1	Shenandoah	2,115,000	680 x 78.8	6 (1800) 5 (1500)	4 September 1923 one engine removed 1924	Rebuilt 1924; broke up in air over Ava, Ohio 3 Sept 1923; 14 dead, 29 survivors
Royal Airship Works, Cardington (UK)	(R 38) ZR-2		2,724,000	699 x 85.5	6 (2100)	23 June 1921	Broke up in air over Hull, England 24 Aug 1921; 44 dead, 4 survivors
Luftschiffbau-Zeppelin, Friedrichshafen	(LZ 126) ZR-3	Los Angeles	2,600,000	658.3 x 90.7	5 (2000)	27 August 1924	Delivered to US 15 Oct 1924; decommissioned 30 June 1932; dismantled Dec 1939
Goodyear-Zeppelin, Akron	ZRS-4	Akron	6,850,000	785 x 133	8 (4480)	23 September 1931	Crashed at sea off Barnegat, NJ 3–4 April 1933; 73 dead, 3 survivors
Goodyear-Zeppelin, Akron	ZRS-5	Macon	6,850,000	785 x 133	8 (4480)	21 April 1933	Crashed at sea off Point Sur, Calif. 12 Feb. 1935; 2 dead, 81 survivors
Aircraft Development Corp., Detroit	ZMC-2		202,000	149.5 x 52.8	2 (440)	19 August 1929	A "pressure-rigid" Metalclad airship; dismantled 1941

SOURCES

The primary source of information for this book was a series of conversations the author had with Dr. Karl Arnstein in Akron, Ohio, from 1958 to 1969. Additional information came from correspondence and conversations with Mrs. Arnstein, especially during the period 1981 to 1993, and from conversations and correspondence with persons who knew or worked with Dr. Arnstein. Supplemental material also came from scholars and other parties familiar with the history of the period in question, and from a variety of secondary sources. Unless otherwise noted, the original research is in the A. D. Topping Collection of the University of Akron Archives in Akron, Ohio.

Another extremely valuable resource was the collection of Dr. Karl Arnstein's papers at the University of Akron Archives, which includes personal and professional correspondence, drawings, speech notes, photographs, and published articles. An inventory of the collection is available online at: **http://www.akron.edu/archival/arnstein/arnstein.htm**.

The Goodyear Tire and Rubber Company Corporate Collection at the University of Akron Archives, particularly the aviation category, contains a wealth of information on the aeronautical activities of this company. The Lighter-Than-Air Society Collection, also housed at the University of Akron Archives, has documents and photographs pertaining to airship history not found elsewhere. Some archival records of the former Goodyear-Zeppelin Corporation and Goodyear Aircraft Corporation are to be found in the Lockheed Martin Collection at the University of Akron Archives.

The National Archives in Washington, D.C., houses records of the U.S. Navy's involvement with rigid airships, with Record Group 72, the Bureau of Aeronautics, General Correspondence Files 1925–1942, being the most relevant.

Works frequently cited in the source notes are identified with the following abbreviations:

ADT: A. Dale Topping Collection, University of Akron Archives
ABJ: Akron Beacon Journal
ATP: Akron Times-Press
BA: Bertha (Bertl) Arnstein, wife of Karl
CPD: Cleveland Plain Dealer
GTR: Goodyear Tire and Rubber Company Collection, University of Akron Archives
KA: Karl Arnstein
KAC: Karl Arnstein Collection, University of Akron Archives
LMC: Lockheed Martin Collection, University of Akron Archives
LTAS: The Lighter-Than-Air Society Collection, University of Akron Archives
NARA: National Archives and Records Administration, Washington, D.C.
WFC: The Wingfoot Clan, house organ of the Goodyear Company, issued in various editions by several of the company's factories. A bound set is to be found in the University of Akron Archives. The Aircraft Edition is of particular research value.
WLTAS: Wingfoot Lighter-Than-Air Society. Its publication, the WLTAS

Bulletin, was the predecessor of The Lighter-Than-Air Society and its publication, *Buoyant Flight*. The name change occurred in 1971, effective with volume 18, no. 2, of the Bulletin.

N.B.: Sources cited for each chapter are listed by their first appearance in the text.

INTRODUCTION

Peter Fritzsche, *A Nation of Fliers* (Cambridge: Harvard University Press, 1992); The Curtis Publishing Co., *The Aviation Industry* (Philadelphia: The Curtis Publishing Co., 1930); Paul W. Litchfield, *Industrial Voyage: My Life as an Industrial Lieutenant* (Garden City, N. Y.: Doubleday and Co., 1954).

CHAPTER ONE

Karl Arnstein (KA), untitled speech notes, c. 1935, KAC; Bertl Arnstein (BA), letters to author, October 1981–October 1984; BA, conversation with author, 23 October 1984; Zbynek Zeman, *The Masaryks: The Making of Czechoslovakia* (London: Weidenfeld and Nicholson, 1976); Leslie C. Tihany, *A History of Middle Europe from the Earliest Times to the Age of the World Wars* (New Brunswick, N.J.: Rutgers University Press, 1976); Wilfred van de Walle, conversation with author, 12 March 1975; BA, conversations with author, 23 October 1982; BA, conversation with editor, 7 August 1998; "Arnstein in der Nikolanderrealschule," *Prager Tagblatt*, 21 September 1924 (unless noted, all translations are by the author); Karl Arnstein, "Curriculum Vitae," c. 1923, KAC; KA, conversations with author, 24 June 1965 and 17 June 1962; *Encyclopedia Americana* (1980), s.v. "Charles University"; Ctibor Rybár, *Prag: Reiseführer—Informationen—Fakten* (Prague: Olympia Verlag, 1983); Charles Elmer Rowe, *Engineering Descriptive Geometry* (New York: D. Van Nostrand Co., 1939); KA, untitled speech notes, c. 1935, KAC; David B. Steinman and Sara Ruth Watson, *Bridges and Their Builders* (New York: G. P. Putnam's Sons, 1941); August Nowak, "Joseph Melan," in *Joseph Melan zum Siebzigsten Geburtstage* (Leipzig: Franz Deuticke, 1923); Richard Sheldon Kirby, et al., *Engineering in History* (New York: McGraw-Hill, 1956); Stephen P. Timoshenko, *History of Strength of Materials* (New York: McGraw-Hill, 1953); Joint Committee to Investigate Dirigible Disasters, 73rd Cong., 1st sess., *Hearings*, 1933; *Le Nouveau Journal de Strasbourg*, 1 November 1924, newspaper clipping in KA's scrapbook, KAC; M. Foerster, "Eduard Züblin," *Armierter Beton* (January 1917): 1–3; Hale Sutherland and Raymond C. Reese, *Introduction to Reinforced Concrete Design*, 2nd ed. (New York: John Wiley and Sons, 1943); Bruno Frei, "Der Erbauer des 'ZRIII,'" *Der Abend* (Vienna), 29 September 1924; Lillian and Phillip Van Doren, *Beyond Paris* (New York: W. W. Norton Co., 1967); Goodyear Aircraft Corp., *A Tribute to Dr. Karl Arnstein* (Akron: Goodyear Aircraft Corp., 1957); Leopold Singer, "Der Statiker," *Prager Tagblatt*, 19 October 1924; KA, conversation, 27 February 1965; A. D. Topping, "Karl Paul Helma" [obituary], WLTAS *Bulletin* 12, no. 6 (April 1965): 6; Paul Caminada, *Der Bau der Rhätischen Bahn* (Zürich: Orell Füssli Verlag, 1982); *Le Nouveau Journal de Strasbourg*, clipping in scrapbook, KAC; KA, "Engineering Experiences," speech notes, c.

1942, KAC; Gustav Bener, *Ehrentafel Bündner Ingenieure* (Chur, 1927), quoted in Paul Caminada, *Der Bau der Rhätischen Bahn* (Zürich: Orell Füssli Verlag, 1982).

CHAPTER TWO

KA, conversation with author, 13 January 1962; H. S. Ede, "Zeppelin Over Nuremberg," in *Savage Messiah* (New York: Literary Guild, 1931) [The airship KA saw over Strasbourg was probably the *Schwaben* (LZ 10), which in 1911 was based at Baden-Oos, about twenty-five miles away.]; A. D. Topping, "Count Zeppelin's American Balloon Ascent," WLTAS *Bulletin* 12, no. 10 (September 1965): 3–7; F. Stansbury Haydon, *Aeronautics in the Union and Confederate Armies*, vol. 1 (Baltimore: Johns Hopkins Press, 1941); A. D. Topping, "Letter from Hans von Schiller," WLTAS *Bulletin* 13, no. 5 (March 1966): 9; Rhoda R. Gilman, "Zeppelin in Minnesota: A Study in Fact and Fable," *Minnesota History* 39, no. 7 (fall 1965): 278–285; Maria Bach Dunn, trans., "Zeppelin in Minnesota: The Count's Own Story," *Minnesota History* 40, no. 6 (summer 1967): 265–78; A. D. Topping, "Count Zeppelin's American Balloon Ascent," part 3, WLTAS *Bulletin* 13, no. 3 (January 1966): 2–4; Hugo Eckener, *Count Zeppelin*, trans. Leigh Farrell (London: Massie Publishing Co., 1938); Rolf Italiaander, *Ferdinand Graf von Zeppelin* (Konstanz: Verlag Friedrich Stadler, 1980); Douglas H. Robinson, *Giants in the Sky* (Seattle: University of Washington Press, 1973); T. E. Guttery, *Zeppelin: An Illustrated Life of Count Ferdinand von Zeppelin 1838–1917* (Aylesbury, United Kingdom: Shire Publications, 1973); Otto Skall, "Die weitestgespannten Eisenbeton-Bogen-brücken der Welt," *Technische Rundshau: Wochenschrift des Berliner Tageblatts* 27, no. 16 (13 July 1921): 15; Caminada, *Rhätischen Bahn;* Hans Knäusel, *LZ 1: Das erste Luftschiff des Grafen Zeppelin—Eine Dokumentation* (Friedrichshafen: Zeppelin-Luftschiffbau GmbH and Zeppelin-Metallwerke, 1975); Hans Knäusel, *LZ 1: Der erste Zeppelin: Geschichte einer Idee 1874–1908* (Bonn: Kirschbaum Verlag, 1985); Arthur F. Foerster, review of *David Schwarz, Carl Berg and Graf Zeppelin*, by Carl Berg Jr., WLTAS *Bulletin* 8, no. 8 (June 1961): 6; Ernst A. Lehmann with Leonhard Adelt, *Zeppelin: The Story of Lighter-Than-Air Craft*, trans. Jay Dratler (London: Longmans, Green and Co., 1937); Alfred Colsman, *Luftschiff Voraus!* (Stuttgart: Deutsche Verlags-Anstalt, 1933); Thor Nielsen, *The Zeppelin Story: The Life of Hugo Eckener* (London: Allan Wingate, 1955); Ingeborg Colsman, quoted in Italiaander, *Ferdinand Graf von Zeppelin;* Henry Cord Meyer, "Eckener's Struggle to Save the Airship for Germany, 1919–1929," *Buoyant Flight* 29, no. 2 (January–February 1982): 2–9; Rolf Italiaander, *Ein Deutscher namens Eckener* (Konstanz: Verlag Friedrich Stadler, 1981); KA, conversation with author, 20 February 1958; Hugo Eckener, *My Zeppelins*, trans. Douglas Robinson (London: Putnam, 1958); Oliver E. Allen, *The Airline Builders* (Alexandria, Va.: Time-Life Books, 1981); Len Deighton, *Blood, Tears and Folly: An Objective Look at World War II* (New York: Harper Collins Publishers, 1993).

CHAPTER THREE

Goodyear Aircraft Corp., *A Tribute to Dr. Karl Arnstein;* KA, conversation with author, 2 June 1967; BA, conversation with author, 23 October 1982; *Webster's Collegiate Dictionary*, 5th ed., s.v. "sapper"; KA, conversations with author, 17 April 1961, 13 January 1962, 30 May 1966 ,and 17 May 1969; BA, letter to author, 31 July 1985; Committee to Investigate Dirigible Disasters, *Hearings;* Colsman, *Luftschiff Voraus!;* Eckener, *Count Zeppelin;* Robinson, *Giants;* Italiaander, *Ferdinand Graf von Zeppelin;* KA, conversation with author, 5 July 1963; Peter W. Brooks, *Historic Airships* (Greenwich, Conn.: New York Graphic Society, 1973); Hans von Schiller, *Zeppelin: Wegbereiter des Weltluftverkehrs* (Bad Godesberg, Germany: Kirschbaum Verlag [1967]); KA, conversation with author, 6 November 1959; KA, "Factors of Safety," unpublished speech notes, n.d., KAC; Ludwig Dürr, *Fünfundzwanzig Jahre Zeppelin-Luftschiffbau* (Berlin: V.D.I.-Verlag, 1924); Douglas H. Robinson and Charles L. Keller, *Up Ship! A History of the U.S. Navy's Rigid Airships 1919–1935* (Annapolis, Md.: U.S. Naval Institute Press, 1982); Douglas H. Robinson, *The Zeppelin in Combat*, 1st ed. (London: G. T. Foulis and Co., 1962); Karl Arnstein, "Rigid Airships" (speech presented to the American Society of Automotive Engineers, Akron, 15 March 1946); Karl Arnstein, "Engineering Treatment of Ring or Wheel Problems," in *Kármán Anniversary Volume* (1941); Theodor von Kármán, "Some Remarks on Mathematics from the Engineer's Viewpoint," *Mechanical Engineering* (April 1940); Karl Arnstein and E. L. Shaw, "On Methods of Calculating Stresses in the Hulls of Rigid Airships," *Proceedings*, Fifth International Congress of Applied Mechanics (1938); Otto Kägi, "Ein Leben im Dienste der Technik," *Heimatspiegel*, in *Zürcher Oberländer* 3 (March 1969), 2, 19–21; KA, conversation with author, 20 January 1968; Nevil Shute, *Slide Rule* (New York: William Morrow and Co., 1954); Dürr, *Fünfundzwanzig Jahre;* C. C. Carr, *Alcoa: An American Enterprise* (New York: Rinehart, 1952); *The Lincoln Library of Essential Information*, 39th ed., s.v. "duraluminum"; Ovid W. Eshbach, ed., *Handbook of Engineering Fundamentals*, 2nd ed. (New York: John Wiley and Sons, 1952); KA, conversations with the author, 2 August 1963, and 11 May 1968; Douglas H. Robinson, letter to the author, 30 May 1985; KA, "Bericht über die Beobachtungen wahrend der ersten Werkstattenfahrt von L 30 am 28 Mai 1916" (notebook), LTAS; KA, "Reise nach Ahlhorn zwecks Untersuchung der Schaden am L 41, 17.2.1917" (travel report), LTAS; A. D. Topping, "The Death of Count Zeppelin," *Buoyant Flight* 29, no. 6 (September–October 1982): 2–8; KA, untitled speech notes, KAC; KA, conversation with the author, 19 June 1969; Hermann Moedebeck, "Berict über den ersten Fahr-Versuch mit dem Luftschiff des Grafen von Zeppelin," *Illustrierte Aëronautische Mitteilungen* (August 1990), reprinted in Knäusel, *LZ 1: Der erste Zeppelin;* Lehmann, *Zeppelin;* Ernst Lehmann and Howard Mingos, *The Zeppelins* (London: G. P. Putnam's Sons, [1927]); William F. Kerka, letter to the author, 3 December 1991; KA, conversation with the author, 27 February 1965; A. D. Topping, "Dr. Karl Arnstein" [obituary], *Buoyant Flight* 22, no. 3 (March–April 1975): 2–6; KA, "Arnstein über Reise nach Hage–Ahlhorn vom 12 April bis 19 April 17" (travel report), LTAS; [KA?] "Extract aus den techn. Berichten LZ 85 (L 45) am 2 April 1917," LTAS; Nielsen, *The Zeppelin Story;* Robinson, *Giants;* Douglas Robinson, letter to author, 30 May 1985 [Robinson interviewed Arnstein in 1955 and Dose in 1957. The quoted passage is from the original manuscript for *The Zeppelin in Combat*, and does not appear in the published version.]; KA, U.S. Patent 1,665,872, "Assemblage Point Device," 10 April 1928 [the German patent was applied for in 1917, but the U.S. patent was not granted until 1928. Similar late dates apply to U.S. patents on all of KA's patents originally applied for in Germany.]; KA, U.S. Patent 1,527,728, "Hollow Bar in Two Pieces," 24 February 1925; KA, U.S.

Patent 1,502,227, "Panelwork for Light Structures," 22 July 1924; KA, U.S. Patent 1,449,721, "Light Weight Girder," 27 March 1923; Wilhelm's Cross honors, unidentified clipping (8 August 1917) in KA scrapbook and unidentified clipping (22 July 1917) via Isa von Brandenstein.

CHAPTER FOUR

BA, letters to the author, 17 December 1980, 23 October 1985, 19 February 1987, 6 March 1987, and 20 April 1987; BA, conversations with the author, 23 October 1982, 15 November 1982, and 7 October 1985; KA, conversations with the author, 13 January 1962 and 20 January 1968; Josephine Van de Grift, clipping, *ABJ*, 2 May 1925, in KA's scrapbook, KAC; Jay M. Winter, *The Experience of World War I* (London: Macmillan, 1988); Anne Millbrooke, *Aviation History* (Englewood, Colo.: Jeppesen Sanderson, 1999); Elmer L. Kuhn, "Industrialisierung in Oberschwaben und am Bodensee," *Geschichte am See* 24, part 1 (1984), 403–21; Colsman, *Luftschiff Voraus!;* Peter Fritzsche, *Germans into Nazis* (Cambridge: Harvard University Press, 1998).

CHAPTER FIVE

Robinson, *Giants;* Lehmann and Mingos, *The Zeppelins;* Nielsen, *The Zeppelin Story* [The Treaty of Versailles, Section III, Air Clauses, Article 198, paragraph 4, states that in Germany "No dirigible shall be kept."]; Rick Archbold, *Hindenburg: An Illustrated History* (New York: Warner/Madison Press, 1994); BA, conversations with author, 7 October 1985 and 9 October 1987; BA, letters to the author, 15 November 1982, 29 May 1984, and 19 February 1987; KA and BA, conversation with the author, November 1964; Patrick Abbott, *Airship* (New York: Charles Scribner's Sons, 1973); Peter Allen, *The 91 Before Lindbergh* (Eagan, Minn.: Flying Books, 1985); Robinson and Keller, *Up Ship!;* Charles L. Keller, "The Hensley Incident," WLTAS *Bulletin,* 9, no. 9 (July–August 1962): 2–5; Robinson, *Zeppelin in Combat;* Hans Knäusel, *Zeppelin and the United States of America,* 2nd ed., trans. M. O. McClellan (Friedrichshafen: Luftschiffbau-Zeppelin GmbH and Zeppelin-Metallwerke, 1981); Harry Vissering, *Zeppelin: The Story of a Great Achievement* (Chicago: Wells and Co., 1922); Charles E. Rosendahl, *Up Ship!* (New York: Dodd, Mead and Co., 1931); Lester D. Gardner, *Who's Who in American Aeronautics,* 3rd ed. (New York: Aviation Publishing Corp., 1928); Richard K. Smith, letter to the author, 31 July 1987 [notes from Smith's interview with Weyerbacher, Boonville, Indiana, 8 July 1960]; KA, conversation with the author, 13 January 1962; BA, letter to the author, 9 August 1987; Volker R. Berghahn, *Modern Germany: Society, Economy and Politics in the Twentieth Century,* 2nd ed. (Cambridge: Cambridge University Press, 1987); Winter, *The Experience of World War I;* Norman Beasley, *Men Working: A Story of the Goodyear Tire and Rubber Company* (New York: Harper and Brothers, 1931); Litchfield, *Industrial Voyage;* Meyer, "Eckener's Struggle"; Henry Cord Meyer, *Airshipmen, Businessmen and Politics, 1890–1940* (Washington: Smithsonian Institution Press, 1991); Richard K. Smith, "The Airship in America, 1904–1976," in *Two Hundred Years of Flight in America: A Bicentennial Survey,* Eugene M. Emme, ed. (San Diego: American Astronautical Society, 1977): 76; KA, conversations with the author, 20 February 1958, 13 and 16 January 1962, 2 August 1963, 30 May 1966, 2 June 1967, and 11 May 1968; C. P. Burgess, *Airship Design* (New York: Ronald Press, 1927); William H. Longyard, *Who's Who in Aviation History: 500 Biographies* (Novato, Calif.: Presidio Press, 1994); Hugh Allen, *The House of Goodyear,* 3rd ed. (Cleveland:

Corday and Gross, 1949); A. D. Topping, "A Conversation with Arnstein," *Buoyant Flight* 35, no. 2 (January–February 1988), 5–6; Frank R. Gross, "Matters of Language," *Buoyant Flight* 33, no. 4 (May–June, 1986), 11–12 [re: chefkonstrukteur]; BA, letter to the author, 9 August 1987; KA, U.S. Patent 1,526,198, "Aircraft Structure," 10 February 1925; KA, U.S. Patent 1,502,417, "Wire and Rope Clamp," 22 July 1924; KA, U.S. Patent 1,502,418, "Wire and Rope Clamping Device," 22 July 1924; Dürr, *Fünfundzwanzig Jahre;* KA, U.S. Patent 1,505,689, "Rigid Frame for Airships," 19 August 1924; KA, U.S. Patent 1,521,590, "Joint for Frames for Airships," 6 January 1925; KA, U.S. Patent 1,503,293, "Skeleton Framework Construction for Airships and the Like," 29 July 1924; KA, U.S. Patent 1,553,586, "Landing and Starting Carriage for Airships," 15 September 1925; KA, U.S. Patent 1,553,061, "Airship," 8 September 1925; KA, U.S. Patent 1,614,519, "Airship with Structural Compensating Surfaces," 18 January 1927; KA, U.S. Patent 1,673,481," Airship Hull," 12 June 1928; KA, U.S. Patent 1,623,951, "Airship Frame," 5 April 1927; KA, U.S. Patent 1,658,876, "Gas Cell for Airships," 14 February 1928; KA, U.S. Patent 1,656,810, "Hollow Girder for Light Structures," 17 January 1928; KA, U.S. Patent 1,623,952, "Stabilizing Apparatus for Rigid Airships," 5 April 1927; KA, U.S. Patent 1,517,885, "Stern Construction of Rigid Airships," 2 December 1924; *Zeppelin: Ein bedeutendes Kapitel aus der Geschichte der Luftfahrt,* 5th ed. (Friedrichshafen: Zeppelin-Luftschiffbau GmbH and Zeppelin-Metallwerke, 1983); KA, U.S. Patent 1,620,507, "Hull Construction of Rigid Airships," 8 March 1927; KA, U.S. Patent 1,631,908, "Rigid Airship," 7 June 1927; KA, U.S. Patent 1,669,592, "Rigid Airship," 15 May 1928; KA, U.S. Patent 1,642,005, "Aircraft," 13 September 1927.

CHAPTER SIX

Special Committee on Airships [Durand Committee], *Report* No. 2 (Washington, D.C.: National Academy of Sciences, Stanford University Press, 1937); Burgess, *Airship Design;* Dürr, *Fünfundzwanzig Jahre;* Robinson and Keller, *Up Ship!;* Hugh Allen, *The Story of the Airship,* 8th ed. (Akron, Ohio: The Goodyear Tire and Rubber Co., 1932); Italiaander, *Ferdinand Graf von Zeppelin;* KA, conversation with author, 20 February 1958; Richard K. Smith, letter to author, 31 July 1987; KA, conversation with author, 15 May 1966 [It is not unusual to have material written by subordinates appear under the signature of a busy high-ranking company officer. The author wrote short reviews of technical articles that appeared over Arnstein's byline in *Applied Mechanics Review.*]; BA, letter to author, 19 October 1981; Anton Wittemann, *Die Amerikafahrt des Z.R. III* (Wiesbaden: Amsel Verlag, 1925); "Q" [pseud.], "A Tale of The Clan," *WFC,* Akron edition (1 October 1924): 3 [Reprint of letter, J. M. Yolton to V. M. Braden, manager of Goodyear Aeronautics Dept., 7 September 1924]; clippings from the *Prager Tagblatt,* 31 August 1924; *Prager Abendblatt,* 1 September 1924; *Prager Presse,* 17 September 1924, rotogravure section; *Bohemia,* 17 September 1924; *Seeblatt* [Friedrichshafen], 6 September 1924; Bruno Frei, "Der Erbauer des ZRIII," *Der Abend* [Vienna], 29 September 1924; *Prager Tagblatt,* 15 October 1924, KA scrapbook, KAC; BA, letter to author, 4 December 1988; Fritzsche, *A Nation of Fliers;* Robert S. Ross, letter to editor, 14 January 2000; BA, letters to author, 10 April 1985 and 23 November 1991; Berghahn, *Modern Germany;* Lindley Fraser, *Germany Between Two Wars* (London: Oxford University Press, 1944).

CHAPTER SEVEN

Gordon A. Craig, *Germany 1866–1945* (New York: Oxford University Press, 1978); Gordon A. Craig, *The Germans* (New York: Putnam, 1982; reprint, Penguin Books, 1991); Berghahn, *Modern Germany;* BA, conversation with author, 9 October 1987; BA, letter to author, 7 March 1988; Erich Ludendorff, *The General Staff and Its Problems: The History of the Relations Between the High Command and the German Imperial Government as Revealed by Official Documents,* Vol. 1, trans. F. A. Holt (New York: E. P. Dutton, 1920); Winter, *The Experience of World War I;* Armin Treibel, "Variations in Patterns of Consumption in Germany in the Period of the First World War" in *The Upheaval of War: Family, Work and Welfare in Europe, 1914–1918,* Richard Wall and Jay Winter, eds., (Cambridge: Cambridge University Press, 1988): 159–96; BA, letter to author, 9 August 1987; Karl Arnstein, "Weitgespannte Eisenbetonbogenbrücken" in *Joseph Melan zum Siebzigsten Geburtstage* (Leipzig: Franz Deuticke, 1923), 1–26; BA, letter to author, 25 January 1989; Kägi, "Ein Leben im Dienste der Technik"; Knäusel, *Zeppelin and the United States of America;* Lehmann and Mingos, *The Zeppelins;* Litchfield, *Industrial Voyage;* U.S. Naval Institute, *Naval Aviation 1943* (Annapolis, Maryland: U.S. Naval Institute, 1943); Allen, *House of Goodyear;* Maurice O'Reilly, *The Goodyear Story* (Elmsford, N. Y.: The Benjamin Co., 1983); Henry Cord Meyer, letter to author, 27 January 1988; BA, conversation with author, 23 October 1982; KA, conversation with author, 30 May 1966; KA, unpublished speech, 30 years' reminiscences [1954], KAC; KA, unpublished notes for a speech to manufacturing supervisors, c. 1950s, KAC; James M. Diehl, *Paramilitary Politics in Weimar Germany* (Bloomington, Ind.: Indiana University Press, 1977); Dürr, *Fünfundzwanzig Jahre;* KA, conversation with the author, 17 January 1962; Ralph Block, "Herman T. Kraft" [obituary], WLTAS *Bulletin* 7, no. 6 (April 1960): 4; Ralph Upson, letter [H. T. Kraft eulogy], WLTAS *Bulletin* 7, no. 7 (May 1960): 6; H. T. Kraft, letter to P. W. Litchfield, 23 June 1924, GTR; W. C. Young, letter to P. W. Litchfield, 24 June 1924, GTR; KA, untitled speech notes, KAC; KA, conversation with author, 24 June 1965; Hugh Allen, letters to author, 15 August, 1962 and 11 March 1969 [Eckener's doctorate was in psychology, but it is true that he was working on an economic treatise.].

CHAPTER EIGHT

Robinson and Keller, *Up Ship!;* Hugo Eckener, "Die Amerikaflug des Z.R. III," in *Graf Zeppelin—Sein Leben—Sein Werk,* Ludwig Fischer, ed. (Munich: R. Oldenbourg Buchdruckerei, 1929), 238, 242–44; J. Gordon Vaeth, *Graf Zeppelin: The Adventures of an Aerial Globetrotter* (New York: Harper and Bros., 1958); Eckener, *My Zeppelins; Seeblatt,* 15 October 1924, KA scrapbook, KAC; Wittemann, *Amerikafahrt; Neues Wiener Journal* and *Seeblatt,* 16 October 1924, KA scrapbook, KAC; Nielsen, *The Zeppelin Story;* Clifford W. Seibel, *Helium: Child of the Sun* (Lawrence, Kans.: University Press of Kansas, 1968); Bradley Jones, *Elements of Practical Aerodynamics,* 2nd ed. (New York: John Wiley and Sons, 1939); Special Committee on Airships, *Report No. 2;* KA, conversation with author, 17 April 1961; Dürr, *Fünfundzwanzig Jahre;* Robinson, *Giants;* Kajetan, "Arnstein," *Die Stunde* [Vienna], 17 October 1924, and other clippings, KA scrapbook, KAC; Antonia Vallentin, *The Drama of Albert Einstein,* trans. Moura Budberg (Garden City, N. Y.: Doubleday and Co., 1954); KA, conversation with author, 11 May

1968; BA, letters to author, 4 December 1988, and 25 January 1989; KA, conversation with author, 13 November 1963; Kurt Bauch, interview with author, Akron, Ohio, 20 October 1982; BA, conversation with author, 16 October 1984; Theodor Troller, letter to author, 12 May 1988; clipping, *Stuttgarter Neues Tagblatt,* 11 November 1924, KA scrapbook, KAC; BA, letter to author, 5 March 1989.

CHAPTER NINE

Kurt Bauch, interview with author, Akron, Ohio, 20 October 1982; BA, letter to author, 5 November 1984; M. L. Flickinger, letter to author, 6 May 1983; A. D. Topping, "Kurt F. Bauch" [obituary], *Buoyant Flight* 33, no. 3 (March–April 1986): 6–7; A. D. Topping, "Benjamin J. Schnitzer" [obituary], The WLTAS *Bulletin* 10, no. 8 (June 1963): 2–4; A. D. Topping, "H. R. Liebert" [obituary], WLTAS *Bulletin* 17, no. 8 (July–August 1970): 4; A. D. Topping, "Eugen Brunner," [obituary], WLTAS *Bulletin* 6, no. 9 (July–August 1959): 13; Mary Schmid [Brunner relative], conversation with author, Pittsburgh, c. 1960; "Lucky 13," *CPD,* 4 October 1931; A. D. Topping, "Walter Gustav Emil Mosebach" [obituary], *Buoyant Flight* 21, no. 3 (March–April 1974): 6–7; "Wolfgang Klemperer" [obituary], WLTAS *Bulletin* 12, no. 7 (May 1965): 8 [The Versailles treaty banned the manufacture or import of aircraft in Germany for a time; thereafter, strict limits on aircraft engine horsepower severely limited aircraft development until the ban was lifted in the late 1920s.]; Gardner, *Who's Who;* M. L. Flickinger, interview with author, Akron, Ohio, 19 October 1982; M. L. Flickinger, letter to author, 12 October 1989; BA, letters to author, 14 May 1989 and 5 June 1989; Steve Love and David Giffels, *Wheels of Fortune: The Story of Rubber in Akron* (Akron, Ohio: University of Akron Press, 1999); KA, conversations with author, 13 January 1962 and 2 August 1963; Hugh Allen, *Rubber's Home Town: The Real Story of Akron* (New York: Stratford House, 1949); KA, speech, American Bar Association Naturalized American Awards Banquet, Akron, Ohio, 17 September 1959, KAC; clippings, *Kansas City Star,* 15 November 1924, *San Francisco Call,* 15 November 1924, KA scrapbook, KAC; clippings from the *CPD,* 25 and 26 November 1924; P. W. Litchfield, "Super-Zeppelin Airships," *Aero Digest* (January 1925): 11–13; Richard K. Smith, *The Airships Akron and Macon: Flying Carriers of the United States Navy* (Annapolis, Md.: Naval Institute Press, 1965); KA and BA, conversation with author, 24 June 1965; "Christmas as Observed in Many Christian Countries," *WFC,* 24 December 1924; Goodyear Aircraft Corp., *A Tribute to Dr. Karl Arnstein;* Goodyear-Zeppelin, "Prospectus for a 3 million cu ft airship," c. 1924, GTR; Zenon Hansen, *The Goodyear Airships* (Bloomington, Illinois: Airship International Press, 1977); John S. Mitchell, *The Army Airship Roma* (Hampton, Va.: Syms-Eaton Museum, 1973); R. K. Smith, "Design No. 60," WLTAS *Bulletin* 10, no. 10 (September 1963), 4–6; Rosendahl, *Up Ship!;* Robinson and Keller, *Up Ship!;* KA, conversations with author, 6 November 1959, 17 April 1961, and 16 January 1962; Thom Hook, *Shenandoah Saga* (Annapolis, Md.: Air Show Publishers, 1973); M. L. Flickinger, "Training Airship with Hangar—Wingfoot Lake," G-Z Project YF-16, Drawing YL-46 (28 November 1925), ADT. Robinson, *Giants.*

CHAPTER TEN

U.S. House of Representatives, Committee on Naval Affairs, *Hearings,* 122 (13–26 January 1926); Frederick S. Hardesty, ed., *Key to the Development of the Super-Airship; Luftfahrzeugbau Schuette-Lanz, Mannheim-Rheinau, Germany, 1909–1930* (New York, 1930); U.S. House of Representatives, Committee on the Public Lands, 67th Congress, 4th sess. *Hearings on H.R. 11549 "Helium Gas"* 113 (5–14 December 1922); Meyer, *Airshipmen;* Garland Fulton, letter to author, 12 August 1963; "Coming: Overnight Airships, New York to Chicago," *Literary Digest* (24 March 1923): 58–61; Frederick S. Hardesty, et al., "Commercial Airways," (August 1925) [a memorandum prepared for the Airways Corporation of America, Boston, Massachusetts]; KA, U.S. Patent 1,662,021, "Hull Structure for Rigid Airships," 6 March 1928; KA and Paul Helma, U.S. Patent 1,818,952, "Bulkhead for Rigid Airships," 11 August 1931; KA, U.S. Patent 1,779,387, "Main Ring for Rigid Airships," 21 October 1930; KA and Paul Helma, U.S. Patent 1,913,325, "Airship Bulkhead," 6 June 1933; KA and Paul Helma, U.S. Patent 1,883,455, "Method and Apparatus for Building Airship Bulkheads," 18 October 1932; KA, Paul Helma, and Kurt Bauch, U.S. Patent 1,797,186, "Fastening Means for Airship Envelopes," 17 March 1931; Allen, *House of Goodyear;* Hansen, *The Goodyear Airships.*

CHAPTER ELEVEN

Meyer, *Airshipmen;* Sailendra Nath Dhar, *International Relations and World Politics Since 1919,* 2nd ed. (New York: Asia Publishing House, 1967); Umberto Nobile, *My Polar Flights,* trans. Frances Fleetwood (London: Frederick Muller, 1961); Special Committee on Airships, *Report No. 2;* Robinson, *Giants;* KA, conversations with author, 17 April 1961 and 20 January 1968; Committee to Investigate Dirigible Disasters, *Hearings;* KA, letter to Alfred Colsman, 23 December 1926; Colsman, letter to KA, 9 January 1927; KA, letter to Colsman, 28 January 1927; Claudius Dornier, letter to KA, 17 March 1927; Colsman, letter to KA, 18 April 1927; KA, letter to Colsman, 24 June 1927; KA, letter to Dornier, 24 June 1927; Dornier, letter to KA, 12 July 1927; Gardner, *Who's Who;* KA, letter to Colsman, 13 August 1927 [Copies of letters quoted in this chapter were graciously provided to the author courtesy of the Luftschiffbau-Zeppelin Archive, Zeppelin-Metallwerke, Friedrichshafen, Germany.]; Goodyear Aircraft Corp., *A Tribute to Karl Arnstein;* KA, "Resume," KAC; "50 Years Ago," *Aeronautics and Astronautics* (April 1976): 48; KA, letter to Colsman, 23 March 1927; Smith, *Airships Akron and Macon;* KA, conversation with author, 12 December 1966; Ralph Block, "Bill Young: Lighter-Than-Air Sales Problems," WLTAS *Bulletin* 5, no. 8 (June 1958): 1; William F. Trimble, *Admiral William A. Moffett: Architect of Naval Aviation* (Washington, D.C.: Smithsonian Institution Press, 1994); Robinson, *Giants;* Burgess, *Airship Design.*

CHAPTER TWELVE

Ralph Block, "B. E. 'Shorty' Fulton: Akron's Part in Aviation," WLTAS *Bulletin* 7, no. 2 (December 1959): 1; clippings about the search for a hangar site, *ABJ,* 6 January 1928; *Los Angeles Times,* 25 January 1928, KA scrapbook, KAC; James H. Farmer, *Celluloid Wings* (Blue Ridge Summit, Pa.: TAB Books, 1984); James H. Farmer, "Howard and Hell's Angels," *Air Classics* (December 1990): 73–76; Howard Hughes, telegrams to KA, 5 and 10 March 1928, KAC; *Hell's Angels* (n.p. [1930]); *The Akronian* 1, nos. 10–11 (October–November 1928): 2–3 [Akron Chamber of Commerce publication]; Allen, *House of Goodyear;* Akron officials, letter to P. W. Litchfield, 22 October 1928 [copy in LTAS]; P. W. Litchfield, letter to Akron officials, 27 October 1928 [copy in LTAS]; KA, conversations with author, 6 November 1959 and

13 January 1962; KA, "The Development of Large Commercial Rigid Airships," American Society of Mechanical Engineers *Transactions* (January–April 1928) [preprint]; Allen, *House of Goodyear;* Wilbur Watson, "Building the World's Largest Airship Factory and Dock," [pamphlet, 1930]; Allen, *Story of the Airship;* Christopher Dean, et al., *Housing the Airship* (London: Architectural Association, 1989); James R. Shock, *American Airship Bases and Facilities* (Edgewater, Fla.: Atlantis Productions, 1996); "Goodyear-Zeppelin to Construct Mammoth Hangar," *ABJ,* 29 October 1928; KA et al., U.S. Patent 1,841,321, "Aircraft Hangar and Method of Building It," 12 January 1932 [filed 28 March 1929]; "Airdock construction completed," *ABJ,* 18 February 1930; Steve Love and David Giffels, *Wheels of Fortune;* KA, letter to Nesbitt H. Bang, associate ed., *Bulletin of the American Meteorological Society,* 7 March 1930, KAC.

CHAPTER THIRTEEN

Burgess, *Airship Design;* Smith, *Airships Akron and Macon;* KA, "Development of Large Commercial Airships"; Allen, *House of Goodyear;* A. D. Topping, "D. W. Brown Remembers," *Buoyant Flight* 34, no. 5 (July–August 1987): 4–6; Theodor von Kármán, *The Wind and Beyond* (Boston: Little, Brown and Co., 1967); Michael H. Gorn, *The Universal Man: Theodore von Kármán's Life in Aeronautics* (Washington, D.C.: Smithsonian Institution Press, 1992); Vaeth, *Graf Zeppelin;* Eckener, *My Zeppelins;* Rosendahl, *Up Ship!;* M. L. Flickinger, interview with author, 19 October 1982; M. L. Flickinger, letter to author, 6 May 1983; A. D. Topping, "M. L. Flickinger" [obituary], *Buoyant Flight,* 38, no. 3 (March–April 1991): 7–8 [Arnstein recalled that it was Rosendahl who insisted on being able to see the fin control station. The *Graf Zeppelin* also had an auxiliary control station in the lower fin, but the view forward was limited.]; Harold G. Dick and Douglas H. Robinson, *The Golden Age of the Great Passenger Airships Graf Zeppelin and Hindenburg* (Washington, D.C.: Smithsonian Institution Press, 1985); Harold G. Dick, letter to author, 6 April 1990; C. P. Burgess, "Design Memorandum No. 91, A Discussion of Methods for Providing a View of the Bottom Fin and Rudder from the Control Car of the ZRS-4," U.S. Navy Bureau of Aeronautics (November 1929).

CHAPTER FOURTEEN

KA, speech, 25 September 1956, KAC; Smith, *Airships Akron and Macon;* Allen, *Story of the Airship;* BA, letter to author, 15 November 1982; A. J. MacDonald, conversation with author, April 1959 [This is not the MacDonald of the MacDonald-Underwood affair mentioned later in this chapter.]; KA, letter to W. H. Collins, 30 June 1930, KAC; "Zepp builder becomes U.S. Citizen" *ABJ,* 26 June 1930; Congressional Hearings, clippings, KAC; Lt. Col. E. C. MacDonald, "Why Did the *Akron* Crash?" *Real America* (October, 1933), KAC; Charles M. Kelley, "The Truth About Flying Coffins," *Machinists Monthly Journal* (April 1935): 198–99, 249–50, KAC; KA, memorandum [defending hiring foreign workers], 10 November 1932, KAC; W. F. Gonder, "Experiences of an Airship Worker," audiotape of talk to The Lighter-Than-Air Society, Akron, Ohio, 13 January 1972, ADT; Trimble, *William A. Moffett;* Robinson, *Giants; ATP,* 8 August 1931, and *ABJ,* 8 August 1931 [USS *Akron* christening editions]; Robert Hedin, ed., *The Zeppelin Reader* (Iowa City: University of Iowa Press, 1998) [reproduces *ATP* cartoon by Paton Edwards]; "Mrs. Hoover Christens Airship USS *Akron,*" *Goodyear Triangle* 13, no. 32 (11

August 1931): 1–2; KA, speech, 25 September 1956, KAC; Paton Edwards cartoon, *ATP*, 24 September 1931; Thom Hook, *Sky Ship: The Akron Era* (Annapolis, Md.: Air Show Publishers, 1976); A. D. Topping, "An Evening of Recollections with 'Flick,'" *Buoyant Flight* 29, no. 5 (July–August 1982): 2–4; M. L. Flickinger, "*Akron* Control Surface Balances," *Buoyant Flight* 29, no. 6 (September–October 1982): 8; "*Akron* arrives at Lakehurst," *ABJ*, 22 October 1931; Allen, *Story of the Airship*, 7th ed.; A. D. Topping, "D. W. Brown Remembers," *Buoyant Flight* 34, no. 5 (July–August 1987): 4–6.

CHAPTER FIFTEEN

Smith, *Airships Akron and Macon;* Keith W. Bose, "FDR and the Schütte Airship Patents," *Buoyant Flight* 37, no. 5 (July–August 1990): 2–6; The Daniel Guggenheim Airship Institute, *Publication No. 1* (Akron, Ohio: Daniel Guggenheim Airship Institute, 1933); Dr. Theodor H. Troller, letter to author, 12 January 1988; H. B. Freeman, "Pressure Distribution on the Hull and Fins of a 1/40-Scale Model of the U.S. Airship 'Akron,'" NACA Technical Report No. 443" (Washington, D.C.: NACA, 1932); KA, conversations with author, 17 January 1962 and 2 August 1963; Special Committee on Airships [Durand Committee], Report No. 3, *Technical Aspects of the Loss of the Macon* (Stanford, Calif.: Stanford University Press, 1937); KA, conversations with author, 13 January 1962 and 6 November 1967; Robinson and Keller, *Up Ship!;* R. K. Smith, letter to author, 2 April 1986; Kármán, *The Wind and Beyond;* Irving P. Krick, "Meteorology in the Space Age," a lecture before the Cleveland Engineering Society, 25 May 1959, quoted in "Meteorology and the Loss of the *Akron*," WLTAS *Bulletin* 13, no. 5 (March 1966): 6–8; "*Akron* Plunges Into Sea," *ABJ*, 4 April 1933; KA, Statement to the Press, 4 April 1933, KAC; Trimble, *William A. Moffett;* A. D. Topping, "Experiences of an Airship Worker," *Buoyant Flight* 19, no. 3 (March–April 1972): 9–10; Joint Committee to Investigate Dirigible Disasters, 73rd Cong., 1st sess., *Airship Investigation: Report of Col. Henry Breckinridge*, 1933; Committee to Investigate Dirigible Disasters, *Hearings;* "Zepps Carry Mail Must Weather Storms," *ABJ*, 13 October 1928 [Moffett quote]; James R. Shock, *U.S. Navy Pressure Airships 1915–1962* (Edgewater, Fla.: Atlantis Productions, 1993); KA, letter to H. V. Wiley, 11 May 1933, KAC; H. V. Wiley, letter to KA, 20 May 1933, KAC; KA, American vs. German Development [of Airships], notes and correspondence, 1935–1936, KAC; J. C. Hunsaker, "Airships for Commercial Purposes," speech notes for the International Automotive Engineering Congress of the Society of Automotive Engineers, 28 July–4 September, 1933, KAC; Joint Committee to Investigate Dirigible Disasters, *Report of Col. Henry Breckinridge;* "*Akron* Plunges Into Sea," *ABJ*, 4 April 1933; Committee to Investigate Dirigible Disasters, *Hearings;* Joint Committee to Investigate Dirigible Disasters, *Report of Col. Henry Breckinridge;* Superintendent of Documents, "Washington, D.C., Monday, April 3, 1933—8 A.M. (E.S.T.), Forecasts until 8 P.M. Tuesday: Marine forecasts," (Washington, D.C.: Superintendent of Documents, 1933) [weather map].

CHAPTER SIXTEEN

Smith, *Airships Akron and Macon;* Robinson and Keller, *Up Ship!;* ADT, notes on comments by William Leib, n.d., ADT; KA, notes on yacht mast, April and June 1930, KAC; Hansen, *The Goodyear Airships;* Craig Ryan, *The Pre-Astronauts: Manned Ballooning on the Threshold of Space* (Annapolis, Md.: Naval Institute Press, 1995); David H. DeVorkin, *Race to the Stratos-phere: Manned Scientific Ballooning in America* (New York: Springer-Verlag, 1989); Clippings on *Graf Zeppelin* flight, *ABJ*, 25 and 28 October 1933, KA scrapbook, KAC; KA travel notes [photocopies], November 1933, ADT; Karl Arnstein, "The Design of the Stratosphere Balloon 'Explorer,'" in *The National Geographic Society–U.S. Army Air Corps Stratosphere Flight of 1934 in the Balloon "Explorer"* (Washington, D.C.: National Geographic Society, 1935): 90–105; Karl Arnstein and F. D. Swann, "The Design of the Stratosphere Balloon 'Explorer II,'" in *The National Geographic Society–U.S. Army Air Corps Stratosphere Flight of 1935 in the Balloon "Explorer II"* (Washington, D.C.: National Geographic Society, 1936): 240–44.

CHAPTER SEVENTEEN

Admiral E. J. King, quoted in Smith, *Airships Akron and Macon;* KA, conversations with author, 20 January and 14 February 1968; KA, "personal" letter to Garland Fulton, 8 July 1933, KAC; Garland Fulton, letter to KA, 10 July 1933; KA, "History of Tail Surface Load Assumptions," 21 March 1935 [draft], KAC; Lehmann and Mingos, *The Zeppelins;* H. V. Wiley, letter to E. J. King, 22 July 1934, and E. J. King, letter to Aircraft Battle Force, "Subject: USS *Macon*—Operational Expenses," 20 August 1934, ZR5/A4 files in General Correspondence, Records of the U.S. Navy Bureau of Aeronautics, 1925–1942, Record Group 72, National Archives Building, National Archives and Records Administration, Washington, D.C. [hereafter, "Gen. Corresp., RG 72, NARA"]; H. V. Wiley, "Court of Inquiry, Record of: Compilation of Testimony by Subject," 23 August 1935, ZR5/A17 files in Gen. Corresp., RG 72, NARA; KA, conversations with author, 17 January 1962, 24 June 1965, 12 December 1966, and 10 November 1967; KA, speech, "Safety Problems of Airships," presented to the Aeronautical Section, National Safety Council, Inc., Cleveland, Ohio, 3 October 1934; Robinson and Keller, *Up Ship!;* Special Committee on Airships, *Report No. 3;* USS *Macon* Log Book, 1 January 1934 to 12 Feb 1935, RG 72, NARA; "Dirigible *Macon* Sinks at Sea," *CPD*, 13 February 1935; KA, letter to H. G. Dick and George Lewis, 2 March 1935 [Dick and Lewis were Goodyear-Zeppelin's liaison engineers assigned to Luftschiffbau-Zeppelin in Friedrichshafen.], KAC; P. W. Litchfield, letter to H. G. Dick and George Lewis, 26 March 1935, KAC; Claude Swanson, memorandum to LTA Operations, 18 February 1935, Gen. Corresp., RG 72, NARA; Kármán, *The Wind and Beyond;* Thomas A. Knowles, letter to KA, 23 September 1935, KAC; KA, letter to Garland Fulton, 6 November 1935, KAC; P. W. Litchfield, *Why? Why Has America No Rigid Airships?* (Cleveland: Corday and Gross, 1945); James G. McHugh, "Confidential Memorandum Report for Bureau of Aeronautics Navy Department, Pressure Distribution Measurements on Fins of Different Aspect Ratio on a 1/40th Scale Model of the U.S. Navy Rigid Airships ZRS-4 and -5," (Washington, D.C., NACA, 28 December 1935); KA, conversation with author, 11 May 1968; "Macon Report Praises Wiley," *Associated Press*, 22 May 1935; Calvin Bolster, memorandum to Garland Fulton, "USS *Macon*," 26 March 1935; Donald M. Mackey, "What Really Happened to the *Macon*," memorandum [1966?]; KA, conversation with author, 2 August 1963; R. K. Smith, "Books and LTA," *Buoyant Flight* 24, no. 5 (July–August 1977): 5–8; R. K. Smith, "The *Akron* Wreckage," *Buoyant Flight* 25, no. 5 (July–August 1978): 13; A. D. Topping, "Newslog," *Buoyant Flight* 37, no. 6 (September–October 1990): 10; Eric Brothers, "The NAA [Naval Airship Association] Reunion," *Buoyant Flight* 39, no. 1 (November–December 1991): 12–14; Jeffrey Cook, *An Engineering History of the ZRS-*

4/5 Fin Design (n.p., 1997); A. D. Topping, letter to the editor of USNI *Proceedings*, 29 February 1968, ADT; Harold G. Dick, with Douglas H. Robinson, *The Golden Age of the Great Passenger Airships Graf Zeppelin and Hindenburg* (Washington, D.C.: Smithsonian Institution Press, 1985); KA, conversations with the author, 16 November 1959 and 13 January 1962; Charles Rosendahl, memorandum, 17 January 1937, Gen. Corresp., RG 72, NARA; Garland Fulton, "Memorandum," 6 August 1935, 12, KAC; A. D. Topping, letter to the editor, USNI *Proceedings*, 29 February 1968; KA, "Memorandum for File, Discussion of Commercial Rigid Airship," 8 May 1947 [summary of Hugo Eckener's remarks in Akron], KAC; Thomas A. Knowles, conversation with author, 16 July, 1992; KA, conversation with the author, 27 February 1965.

CHAPTER EIGHTEEN

KA, "'The Comet'—High Speed Train," *Mechanical Engineering* (August and September 1935): 479–82, 553–60; Hansen, *The Goodyear Airships;* "Comet races at 100 m.p.h.," *ABJ* (26 April 1935); "Streamliner Hits 110-Mile Top Speed," *New York Times* (30 April 1935); Meyer, *Airshipmen;* KA, "The Airship's Contributions to Modern Aviation," 15 April 1953 [speech notes]; KA, untitled speech notes, n.d., KAC; P. W. Litchfield, letter to H. G. Dick and George Lewis, 26 March 1935, KAC; A. D. Topping "Here's What Happened to Original LTA Group," WLTAS *Bulletin* 13, no. 5 (March 1966): 8; "Last 'Disciple' Mosebach retires," *WFC* (17 February 1966): 1–2; KA, speech notes for Manufacturing Supervision, c. 1955, KAC; KA, quoted in "Roomy Deck for Airship," *New York Times* [undated clipping, c. 1934], KAC; Vaeth, *Graf Zeppelin;* H. G. Dick and George Lewis, letter to KA, 25 February 1935, KAC; Robinson, *Giants;* KA, conversation with author, 16 January 1962; General Board, *Hearings*, 1936; General Board No. 449, Record Group 72, Confidential Correspondence, U.S. Navy Bureau of Aeronautics, National Archives Building, National Archives and Records Administration, Washington, D.C. [hereafter, "General Board 449 files, NARA"]; Dow W. Harter, "Design and Construction of Airships," (27 January 1936) *Congressional Record*, 74th Cong., 2nd sess., 1936; ZN files, RG 72, NARA; A. D. Topping, "Walter Gustav Emil Mosebach" [obituary], *Buoyant Flight* 21, no. 3 (March–April 1974): 6–7; LTA Design Bureau, Bureau of Aeronautics, "Specifications for a Non-Rigid Airship . . ." [three specifications for L-, G-, K-2 blimps], (15 April 1937), ZN files, RG 72, NARA; Shock, *U.S. Navy Pressure Airships;* C. P. Burgess, "Design Memorandum No. 193, Requirement for Proposed Airship K-2," (March 1935); Smith, *Airships Akron and Macon;* Lewis Compton, "Memorandum for the Aide to the President," 27 April 1939, ZRN-6/L4-2, ZRN files, Gen. Corresp., RG 72, NARA; Franklin Roosevelt, memo for the secretary of the navy, 3 May 1939, ZRN-6 files, Gen. Corresp., RG 72, NARA; Thomas A. Knowles, conversation with author, 20 November 1983; KA, conversations with the author, 6 November 1959 and 17 April 1961; "Summary of LZ 129 1936 Westward and Eastward Crossings, North Atlantic Service," LMC; Vaeth, *Graf Zeppelin;* "Eckener Dishonor: Name Eradicated from Berlin Streets," (22 April 1936), newspaper clipping, GTR; Dick, *Golden Age;* Rick Archbold, *Hindenburg: An Illustrated History* (New York: Warner/Madison Press, 1994); Lutz Tittel, *LZ 129 "Hindenburg"* (Friedrichshafen, Germany: Zeppelin-Museum Friedrichshafen, 1987); KA, conversations with author, 13 January 1962, 2 August 1963, and 13 November 1963; A. D. Topping, letter to Douglas Robinson, 12 February 1961, ADT; Robinson, *Giants;*

R. W. Knight, Report No. 11, *The Hindenburg Accident: A Comparative Digest of the Investigations and Findings, With the American and Translated German Reports Included* (Washington, D.C.: U.S. Dept. of Commerce, 1938); Richard van Treuren and Addison Bain, "The *Hindenburg* Fire at Sixty," *Buoyant Flight* 44, no. 3 (March–April 1997): 2–7 [claims inherent flammability of the outer cover as origin of *Hindenburg* fire]; Harold G. Dick, letter to KA, 19 May 1937, KAC; [Books by A. A. Hoehling (*Who Destroyed the Hindenburg?*, Boston: Little, Brown and Co., 1962), Michael Mooney (*The Hindenburg*, New York: Dodd, Mead and Co., 1972), and the motion picture *The Hindenburg* (directed by Robert Wise, Universal Studios, 1975) explored *Hindenburg* sabotage theories]; Manfred Bauer and John Duggan, *LZ 130 "Graf Zeppelin" and the End of Commercial Airship Travel* (Friedrichshafen, Germany: Zeppelin-Museum Friedrichshafen, 1996); Hepburn Walker Jr., review of *The Zeppelin Dream*, by James F. Danner, *Buoyant Flight*, 28, no. 1 (November–December 1980): 10–11; KA, personal correspondence [re affidavit requests], 1938–1940, KAC; T. A. Knowles, letter to KA, 17 October 1939, GTR.

CHAPTER NINETEEN

M. L. Flickinger, letter to the author, 6 May 1983; Hugh Allen, *Goodyear Aircraft* (Cleveland: Corday and Gross, 1947); Thomas A. Knowles, conversation with author, 20 November 1983; O'Reilly, *Goodyear Story;* Robinson, *Giants;* Bauer and Duggan, *LZ 130;* E. J. Thomas, "Assignment," 27 December 1940 [assignment of rights, patents, etc., of Goodyear-Zeppelin Corp. to the Wingfoot Corp.], GTR; Shock, *U.S. Navy Pressure Airships;* James R. Shock, *The U.S. Army Barrage Balloon Program* (Bennington, Vt.: World War II Historical Society, 1996); Hugh Allen, *The Story of the Airship (Non-Rigid)* (Chicago: Lakeside Press, 1943); Goodyear Aircraft Corp., "Goodyear Aircraft Capabilities," (publicity booklet, c. 1958); BA, letter to the author, 16 October 1984; J. Gordon Vaeth, *Blimps and U-Boats: U.S. Navy Airships in the Battle of the Atlantic* (Annapolis, Md.: Naval Institute Press, 1992); Marc Milner, *The U-Boat Hunters of the Royal Canadian Navy and the Offensive Against Germany's Submarines* (Annapolis, Md.: Naval Institute Press, 1994); A. Timothy Warnock, *Air Power versus U-Boats* (n.p.: Air Force History and Museums Program, 1999); A. Timothy Warnock, *The Battle Against the U-Boat in the American Theater* (n.p.: Center for Air Force History, [1992?]); William F. Althoff, *Sky Ships: A History of the Airship in the U.S. Navy* (New York: Crown Publishers, Orion Books, 1990); Roy A. Grosnick, ed., *Kite Balloons to Airships . . . The Navy's Lighter-Than-Air Experience* (Washington, D.C.: Government Printing Office, 1987); Charles E. Rosendahl, *How Soon We Forget: A History of Navy Airships in World War II* (Unpublished manuscript, 1977), LTAS; T. G. W. Settle, memorandum to P. W. Litchfield, 10 November 1942; Karl Doenitz, "Some Questions on Submarine Warfare, Answered by the Commander of Submarines Admiral Karl Doenitz," interview by Gerhart Weise, *Voelkischer Beobachter*, 4 August 1942 [transcript of radio program, translated by the U.S. Navy], KA, "Contributions of Lighter-Than-Air Aeronautics," speech given to the Akron Branch of the Institute of Aeronautical Sciences, 16 December 1942; KA, conversation with author, 4 November 1959; Roy D. Schickedanz, "The M-ship," *Buoyant Flight* 23, no. 5 (July–August 1976): 2–4; Naval Airship Training and Experimental Command, *"They Were Dependable": Airship Operations in World War II* (U.S. Naval Air Station, Lakehurst, N. J.: Naval Airship Training and Experimental

Command, 1946); Thomas A. Knowles, conversation with author, 20 November 1983; Thomas A. Knowles, letter to author, 26 February 1984; O'Reilly, *Goodyear Story;* Nicholas A.Veronico with John M. and Donna Campbell, *F4U Corsair* (Osceola, Wis.: Motorbooks International, 1994); Donald Armstrong, *I Flew Them First: A Test Pilot's Story* (Mesa, Ariz.: Champlin Fighter Museum Press, 1994); Shafto Dene, *Trailblazing in the Skies* (Akron, Ohio: The Goodyear Tire and Rubber Co., 1943); Carl Pennig, conversation with editor, 9 January 2000; KA, letters to Harry Vissering, 13 February 1942 and 4 February 1943, KAC; BA, letter to author, 23 October 1982; BA, interview with editor, 7 August 1998; "Rigid Airships for Naval Transport Purposes," 6 June 1944, General Board 449 files, NARA; Suzanne Gravette, "Valiant Service Describes Ohio's WWII 'E' Companies," Ohio Historical Society *Echoes* 39, no. 2 (April–May 2000): 1–2.

CHAPTER TWENTY

Love and Giffels, *Wheels of Fortune;* KA, speech notes, c. 1953, KAC; Harry Vissering, letters to KA, 10 February 1944, 3 March 1945; KA, speech notes, n.d., Herman Van Dyk, "Zeppelin and the A-4 Rocket," *Buoyant Flight* 46, no. 4 (May–June 1999): 6–10; KA, conversations with author, 4–5 November 1959, 17 April 1961, 13 January 1962, 13 November 1963, and 24 June 1965; Robert E. Hunter, conversation with editor, 4 October 1999. KA, conversation with author, 16 January 1962; Ralph M. Holmes, "In the Editor's Mail," *Buoyant Flight*, 42, no. 1 (November–December 1994): 7–8; Lillian Sokol, interview with editor, 31 January 1998; Allen, *Goodyear Aircraft;* O'Reilly, *Goodyear Story;* Althoff, *Sky Ships,* Shock, *U.S. Navy Pressure Airships;* KA, letter to Harry Vissering, 4 February 1943; "Daughter of Dr. Arnstein Killed as Car Hits Truck," *ABJ,* 19 December 1949; Jack Waldman, conversation with author, 9 October 1985; KA, conversation with author, 17 January 1962; KA, speech notes to Manufacturing Supervision, c. 1955, KAC; Grosnick, *Kite Balloons to Airships;* "Meteor Jr.," and "Space Station," Aviation files, GTR; Ralph Block, "Darrell Romick Speaks," WLTAS *Bulletin,* 6, no. 5 (March 1959): 2; A. D. Topping, "Investigation of the ZPG-3W Accident," WLTAS *Bulletin* 16, no 3 (January 1969): 2–5; KA, "Personal" [speech on ZPG-3W loss], 9 August 1960, KAC; KA, speech notes, 1957; "U.S. Leads in Airship Design Progress, Says Dr. Karl Arnstein," *WFC,* 15 October 1958; Ralph S. Block, "6th Annual Banquet," WLTAS *Bulletin* 6, no. 1 (November 1958): 2–8; "Dr. Karl Arnstein To Be Enshrined in Hall of Fame," and "GAC's Highest Technical Honor: Nominations Sought for Arnstein Award," *WFC,* 3 September 1981; W. G. Austen, letter to editor, 13 October 1998; Ken Nichols, "Around Town," *ABJ,* 7 August 1972; David Giffels, "Akron Art Influence Arnstein, 101, Dies," *ABJ,* 30 November 1999; William Garvey, "Return of the Zeppelin," *Popular Mechanics,* July 1994.

CHAPTER TWENTY-ONE

R. K. Smith, letter to author, 9 March 1992; KA, speech, Naturalized American Awards Banquet, 17 September 1959; Nick Costakos, conversation with Anne Topping, 1994; Chris Lyford, "Rigid Airships: U.N. Peacekeepers," U.S. Naval Institute *Proceedings,* October 1992.

GLOSSARY

airship: a dirigible or powered lighter-than-air vehicle. Formerly used to describe both lighter-than-air and heavier-than-air craft but now understood to mean only the former.

ballast: a movable, usually expendable counterweight to a lighter-than-air craft's lifting gas. Sand or metal shot is commonly used by gas balloons; water has been the preferred agent in rigid airships. Small sand-filled bags weighing twenty-five to thirty-five pounds are commonly used to "weigh off" (or balance by static equilibrium) most pressure airships. In an emergency, ballast is anything with weight that can be separated from the vehicle. Ballast may be dropped by an airship to compensate for lost lifting gas, to counter adverse aerodynamic loads or to ascend more quickly than by use of propulsion or aerodynamic pressure on the hull or fins.

blimp: a term coined in 1915 as a friendly synonym for a pressure airship. The word is said to have mimicked the sound made when a man snapped his thumb on the airship's gas-filled envelope. It is *not* derived from the description of an apocryphal type of World War I British airship, the "Balloon, Type B, limp." There was never a "Type B" nor a designation "limp" applied to a British airship before, during, or after WWI. The term most likely originated with Lieutenant (later Air Commodore) A. D. Cunningham of the Royal Naval Air Service, commanding officer of the British airship station at Capel, France, in December 1915. During a weekly inspection, Lieutenant Cunningham visited an aircraft hangar to examine a "Submarine Scout" pressure airship, His Majesty's Airship SS-12. Cunningham broke the solemnity of the occasion by playfully flipping his thumb at the gasbag and was rewarded with an odd noise that echoed off the taut fabric. Cunningham imitated this sound by uttering: "Blimp!" A young midshipman, who later became known as Air Marshal Sir Victor Goddard, repeated the tale of this humorous inspection to his fellow officers in the mess before lunch the same day. The author of this book believes it is by this route that the word "blimp" came to the world.

catenary curtain: a fabric curtain hung inside the envelope of a pressure or semirigid airship, to which an external gondola or control car is attached by cables. Ideally, it spreads the load of the car across a sufficiently large part of the envelope so as to minimize distortions and stretching. Its shape is not a true catenary in the mathematical sense, but its similarity in shape to an inverted rope suspended by its ends was close enough for the name to stick.

cruciform: a cross-shaped arrangement of girders that extends through the hull of an airship and is used to connect and reinforce the tail fins.

DELAG: Deutsche Luftschiffahrts Aktien-Gessellschaft (German Aerial Transportation Company), the pre-WWI German passenger Zeppelin service. Between 1909 and 1914, the hydrogen-inflated vehicles of this airline flew a total of 107,180 miles carrying 34,288 persons without so much as a scratch.

dirigible: a term used to describe any steerable or directable airship, including blimps (pressure airships), semirigid airships, and Zeppelins (rigid airships). In American usage, it has been improperly employed to describe only the latter type.

duralumin: originally the trade name of a lightweight but strong alloy of aluminum mixed with smaller amounts of copper, magnesium, manganese, iron, and silicon. Its high strength with little weight has made it a preferred choice for building the structure of rigid airships. It was patented in 1909 by Alfred Wilm, who granted an exclusive license for its manufacture to the company, Dürener Metallwerke. The "duralumin" name was derived from *Düren*er Metallwerke, and *alumin*um.

dynamic lift: the vertical movement of an airship created by aerodynamic forces acting on the shape of the vehicle, as opposed to static lift, which is generated by the buoyancy of a lighter-than-air lifting gas.

envelope: the gasbag of a pressure or semi-rigid airship. Unlike a rigid airship gas cell, an envelope forms an external barrier to the elements, and when pressurized, serves an integral role in maintaining the airship's shape. It also has fittings for attaching the fins, control car, and other structural components. The envelope is usually made of a high-strength fabric combined with a sufficiently impermeable barrier coating or film to minimize loss of the buoyant gas it contains. Formerly made of rubberized cotton, envelopes are now mainly constructed of synthetic materials with their seams cemented, glued, or sealed.

factor of safety: Arnstein defined this as the ratio between the *best estimate* of the strength of a structure and the *best estimate* of the worst loads to which it will be subjected. As used in airship design, a factor of two is the accepted value of predicted excess strength, although a larger ratio will sometimes be figured for some nominal loading condition much less severe than the worst to which a structure will be subjected. "The *real* safety of a structure," Arnstein noted, "depends on how the engineer's 'best estimates' are made—that is, on his knowledge and care, his experience with or ability to foretell the possible unfavorable conditions which may occur and his optimism or pessimism regarding factors which are uncertain—as much as it depends on the value of the 'factor of safety' used."

fineness ratio: the ratio of an airship's length to its diameter; the higher the number, the longer and more slender the ship.

finite element analysis: a method of engineering investigation that assumes that a structure with a complex shape may be analyzed by obtaining experimental data from a number of fixed points along its surface. The measurements may be subjected to computer analysis and used to model complex phenomena like stress on materials or aerodynamic loads.

gas cell: on a rigid airship, the gas-impervious, balloon-like container of lifting gas housed within the rigid framework. These cells were built as light and gas-tight as possible, using a variety of fabrics and gas barrier materials. They were held in place by wire and cord netting, and their volume could vary with atmospheric pressure, since the shape of a rigid airship was maintained by its framework and outer cover.

gold beaters' skin: when airship pioneers discovered that using rubber to make gas cells nonporous posed a risk of fire due to sparks from static electricity, they lined the cells with a product that would not generate static—the outer membrane of cow intestines. This delicate tissue was used by jewelers as a barrier when hammering down gold into thin sheets. Its gas-impervious quality and light weight were prized by airship constructors. Since each skin, one from each bovine cecum, measures on average only six by thirty-nine inches, huge numbers of them were needed, up to 50,000 skins per gas cell. They required careful handling from the slaughterhouses until they were assembled into gas cells by skilled handwork, and so were extremely expensive. The skins were washed and glued to the lightweight cell fabric one at a time. This disagreeable work was often relegated to women.

gondola: a term used to describe the variously shaped external pods on an airship that house engines or control stations. The term was coined to describe the open top, boat-shaped structures on the earliest Zeppelins. In U.S. practice, the preferred term is "car," as in "control car" or "engine car."

loads: in stress analysis or aerodynamics, the forces or pressures exerted on an object. If they are too great for the material or structure to handle, the latter will fail (buckle, fracture, or break).

lighter-than-air (LTA): that branch of aeronautics, actually aerostatics, that includes flight vehicles that depend upon the displacement of air for their lift. Such vehicles include balloons and dirigibles of all types, piloted or unpiloted. LTA does not include kites, except when the word encompasses the use of tethered balloons, often called kite balloons or aerostats. In practice, airships are rarely flown lighter-than-air; such vehicles would simply float away were it not for their engine power. However, an airship that weighs only slightly more than the air supporting it is more easily controllable during the critical phase of takeoff and landing and still derives nearly all the benefits of a craft which weighs the same as the air it displaces. A vehicle in such perfect equilibrium then requires motive power solely to travel through the air, not dependent at all upon power to move enough air over an airfoil to generate lift. Its opposite is HTA, for heavier-than-air, which is flight by vehicles such as airplanes or helicopters that depend solely on the action of aerody-

namic forces to provide lift. The distinction has been blurred by some hybrid vehicles that rely on a combination of lighter-than-air (a gas cell or envelope) and heavier-than-air (wings, stationary or rotary) to achieve flight.

pressure airship: a term used to describe those airships whose shape is dependent on having a higher pressure inside the gas envelope than is found in the atmosphere outside. With no gas in its envelope, a pressure airship is only an empty bag on the ground; the only rigid structures are the control car, fins, and fittings. Also called a non-rigid airship.

pressure height: the maximum altitude at which an airship can no longer contain its lifting gas due to its greater pressure compared to the surrounding atmosphere. At this altitude, the airship's spring-loaded automatic valves open to relieve the pressure or else the gas cell or envelope will burst.

rigid airship: an airship whose shape is maintained by an internal framework and whose lifting gas is contained by a separate gas cell or cells within that structure. The external fabric covering on a rigid airship is not completely gas-tight and is used for streamlining and to protect the more delicate gas cells and other interior components from wind and weather. Rigid airships include Zeppelins and similar aircraft built by other companies. The term "rigid" is a bit of a misnomer, since even the metal skeleton of a rigid airship must flex a little under loads or else it would break.

ring: the circular frame element perpendicular to the long axis of a rigid airship used to support the longitudinal (lengthwise) girders. To be more precise, the ring is actually a polygonal approximation of a circle made of many smaller straight members. Main rings help carry an airship's primary structural load, while intermediate rings carry less but help to smooth the faceted circumference. In naval architecture and naval usage, the ring is properly called a frame, but since the German name for the structure used the word "ring" that has carried over as a popular term.

Schütte-Lanz: the rigid airship manufacturing company founded in Mannheim-Rheinau, Germany, by Johann Schütte and Karl Lanz. From 1909 until shortly after WWI, it was a competitor to the Zeppelin Company and introduced many innovative refinements to rigid airship design. These improvements appeared in Zeppelins due to a wartime patent-sharing agreement. Although Schütte-Lanz airships generally were more streamlined and advanced the state of airship science, most examples were flawed by their use of plywood instead of duralumin girders. The wooden girders could not be made to resist moisture completely and in service often weakened to the point where structural integrity was jeopardized.

semi-rigid airship: an airship with a rigid keel but whose envelope is maintained by gas pressure. The keel at the bottom of the envelope is used as a support for control car, engines, ballast, and sometimes tail surfaces. Critics have complained that a semi-rigid has none of the advantages of either a rigid or a purely pressure airship, and incorporates the disadvantages of both.

However, a semi-rigid airship, the *Norge*, is now believed to have been the first aircraft to fly over the North Pole in 1926. (Admiral Richard E. Byrd's claim to have done so in a trimotor airplane has now been discounted.)

shear deflection: the physical displacement of a piece of structure placed under a load and measured parallel to its surface. (Bending forces and deflection are measured perpendicularly.)

shearing force: the force or pressure applied to a structure parallel to its surface.

static lift: the vertical force exerted on an airship created solely by the buoyancy of its lighter-than-air lifting gas, unlike dynamic lift, which is generated by aerodynamic forces acting on the shape of the vehicle.

streamlining: the application of aerodynamic theory to achieve a shape with the least wind resistance, hence allowing it to be moved through air with less effort and more speed. The elongated teardrop form of most airships is the result of this study.

Zeppelin: The often generic term for any rigid airship, derived from the name of its inventor and tireless promoter, Ferdinand Graf von Zeppelin (1838-1917). The first aircraft of this type flew in 1900 near Friedrichshafen, Germany. After many trials and tribulations, Zeppelin was able to form a company, Luftschiffbau-Zeppelin, to manufacture this type of airship. Luftschiffbau-Zeppelin produced a total of 117 rigid airships—more than any other manufacturer. The word is properly capitalized when referring to airships produced by the Zeppelin Company, but may be used lowercase to describe any similar, cigar-shaped rigid airship.

SELECTED BIBLIOGRAPHY

Abbott, Patrick. *Airship: The Story of R.34 and the First East-West Crossing of the Atlantic by Air.* New York: Charles Scribner's Sons, 1973.

Allen, Hugh. *Goodyear Aircraft: A Story of Man and Industry.* Cleveland, Ohio: Corday and Gross Co., 1947.

———. *The House of Goodyear,* 3rd ed. Cleveland, Ohio: Corday and Gross Co., 1949.

———. *The Story of the Airship,* 8th ed. Akron, Ohio: The Goodyear Tire and Rubber Co., 1932.

———. *The Story of the Airship (Non-Rigid): A Study of One of America's Lesser Known Defense Weapons.* Chicago: The Lakeside Press, R. R. Donnelley and Sons Co., 1943.

Allen, Oliver E. *The Airline Builders.* Alexandria, Va.: Time-Life Books, 1981.

Allen, Peter. *The 91 Before Lindbergh.* Eagan, Minn.: Flying Books, 1985.

Althoff, William F. *Sky Ships: A History of the Airship in the United States Navy.* New York: Crown Publishers, Orion Books, 1990.

Archbold, Rick. *Hindenburg: An Illustrated History.* New York: Warner/Madison Press, 1994.

Armstrong, Donald. *I Flew Them First: A Test Pilot's Story.* Mesa, Ariz.: Champlin Fighter Museum Press, 1994.

Bauer, Manfred, and John Duggan. *LZ 130 "Graf Zeppelin" and the End of Commercial Airship Travel.* Friedrichshafen, Germany: Zeppelin-Museum Friedrichshafen, 1996.

Beasley, Norman. *Men Working: A Story of the Goodyear Tire and Rubber Co.* New York: Harper and Brothers, 1931.

Berghahn, Volker R. *Modern Germany: Society, Economy and Politics in the Twentieth Century.* 2nd ed. Cambridge: Cambridge University Press, 1987.

Brooks, Peter W. *Historic Airships.* Greenwich, Conn.: New York Graphic Society, 1973.

Burgess, Charles P. *Airship Design.* New York: Ronald Press, 1927.

Caminada, Paul. *Der Bau der Rhätischen Bahn.* Zürich: Orell Füssli Verlag, 1982.

Colsman, Alfred. *Luftschiff Voraus!* Stuttgart: Deutsche Verlags-Anstalt, 1933.

Craig, Gordon A. *The Germans.* New York: Putnam, 1982; reprint, New York: Penguin Books, 1991.

———. *Germany 1866–1945.* New York: Oxford University Press, 1978.

Curtis Publishing Co. *The Aviation Industry: A Study of Underlying Trends.* Philadelphia: The Curtis Publishing Co., 1930.

Deighton, Len. *Blood, Tears and Folly: An Objective Look at World War II.* New York: Harper Collins Publishers, 1993.

Dene, Shafto. *Trailblazing in the Skies.* Akron, Ohio: The Goodyear Tire and Rubber Co., 1943.

DeVorkin, David H. *Race to the Stratosphere: Manned Scientific Ballooning in America.* New York: Springer-Verlag, 1989.

Dick, Harold G., with Douglas H. Robinson. *The Golden Age of the Great Passenger Airships Graf Zeppelin and Hindenburg.* Washington, D.C.: Smithsonian Institution Press, 1985.

Diehl, James M. *Paramilitary Politics in Weimar Germany.* Bloomington, Ind.: Indiana University Press, 1977.

Dürr, Ludwig. *Fünfundzwanzig Jahre Zeppelin-Luftschiffbau.* Berlin: V.D.I.-Verlag, 1924.

Eckener, Hugo. *Count Zeppelin: The Man and His Work.* Translated by Leigh Farrell. London: Massie Publishing Co., 1938.

———. "Die Amerikaflug des Z.R. III." In *Graf Zeppelin—Sein Leben—Sein Werk,* ed. Ludwig Fischer. Munich: R. Oldenbourg Buchdruckerei, 1929.

———. *My Zeppelins.* Translated by Douglas Robinson. London: Putnam, 1958.

Fraser, Lindley. *Germany Between Two Wars: A Study of Propaganda and War-Guilt.* London: Oxford University Press, 1944.

Fritzsche, Peter. *Germans Into Nazis.* Cambridge: Harvard University Press, 1998.

———. *A Nation of Fliers: German Aviation and the Popular Imagination.* Cambridge: Harvard University Press, 1992.

Gardner, Lester D. *Who's Who in American Aeronautics,* 3rd ed. New York: Aviation Publishing Corp., 1928.

Goodyear Aircraft Corporation. *A Tribute to Dr. Karl Arnstein.* Akron, Ohio: Goodyear Aircraft Corp., 1957.

Gorn, Michael H. *The Universal Man: Theodore von Kármán's Life in Aeronautics.* Washington, D.C.: Smithsonian Institution Press, 1992.

Grosnick, Roy A., ed. *Kite Balloons to Airships . . . The Navy's Lighter-Than-Air Experience.* Washington, D.C.: Government Printing Office, 1987.

Guttery, T. E. *Zeppelin: An Illustrated Life of Count Ferdinand Von Zeppelin 1838–1917.* Aylesbury, United Kingdom: Shire Publications, 1973.

Hansen, Zenon. *The Goodyear Airships.* Bloomington, Ill.: Airship International Press, 1977.

Hedin, Robert, ed. *The Zeppelin Reader: Stories, Poems and Songs from the Age of Airships.* Iowa City: University of Iowa Press, 1998.

Hell's Angels. N.p., [1930?]. Motion picture publicity booklet.

Hook, Thom. *Shenandoah Saga.* Annapolis, Md.: Air Show Publishers, 1973.

———. *Sky Ship: The Akron Era.* Annapolis, Md.: Air Show Publishers, 1976.

Italiaander, Rolf. *Ein Deutscher namens Eckener.* Konstanz, Germany: Verlag Friedrich Stadler, 1981.

———. *Ferdinand Graf von Zeppelin: Reitergeneral, Diplomat, Luftschiffpionier.* Konstanz, Germany: Verlag Friedrich Stadler, 1980.

Kármán, Theodore von, with Lee Edson. *The Wind and Beyond: Pioneer in Aviation and Pathfinder in Space Theodore von Kármán.* Boston: Little, Brown and Co., 1967.

Knäusel, Hans Georg. *LZ 1: Das erste Luftschiff des Grafen Zeppelin: Eine Dokumentation.* Friedrichshafen: Zeppelin-Luftschiffbau GmbH and Zeppelin Metallwerke, 1975.

——. LZ 1: *Der erste Zeppelin: Geschichte einer Idee 1874–1908*. Bonn: Kirschbaum Verlag, 1985.

——. *Zeppelin and the United States of America*, 2nd ed. Translated by M. O. McClellan. Friedrichshafen: Luftschiffbau-Zeppelin GmbH and Zeppelin-Metallwerke, 1981.

Knight, R. W. Report No. 11 *The Hindenburg Accident: A Comparative Digest of the Investigations and Findings, With the American and Translated German Reports Included*. Washington, D.C.: U.S. Dept. of Commerce, 1938.

Lehmann, Ernst A., with Leonhard Adelt. *Zeppelin: The Story of Lighter-Than-Air Craft*. Translated by Jay Dratler. London: Longmans, Green and Co., 1937.

Lehmann, Ernst, and Howard Mingos. *The Zeppelins*. London: G. P. Putnam's Sons, [1927].

Litchfield, Paul W. *Industrial Voyage: My Life as a an Industrial Lieutenant*. Garden City, New York: Doubleday and Co., 1954.

Litchfield, Paul W., and Hugh Allen. *Why? Why Has America No Rigid Airships?* Cleveland, Ohio: Corday and Gross Co., 1945.

Longyard, William H. *Who's Who in Aviation History: 500 Biographies*. Novato, Calif.: Presidio Press, 1994.

Love, Steve, and David Giffels. *Wheels of Fortune: The Story of Rubber in Akron*. Akron, Ohio: University of Akron Press, 1999.

Ludendorff, Erich. *The General Staff and its Problems: The History of the Relations Between the High Command and the German Imperial Government as Revealed by Official Documents*. Volume 1. Translated by F. A. Holt. New York: E. P. Dutton, 1920.

Meyer, Henry Cord. *Airshipmen, Businessmen and Politics, 1890–1940*. Washington, D.C.: Smithsonian Institution Press, 1991.

Millbrooke, Anne. *Aviation History*. Englewood, Color.: Jeppesen Sanderson, 1999.

Milner, Marc. *The U-Boat Hunters of the Royal Canadian Navy and the Offensive Against Germany's Submarines*. Annapolis, Md.: Naval Institute Press, 1994.

Naval Airship Training and Experimental Command. *"They Were Dependable": Airship Operations in World War II*. U.S. Naval Air Station, Lakehurst, N.J.: Naval Airship Training and Experimental Command, 1946.

Nielsen, Thor. *The Zeppelin Story*. London: Allan Wingate, 1955.

Nobile, Umberto. *My Polar Flights*. Translated by Frances Fleetwood. London: Frederick Muller, 1961.

O'Reilly, Maurice. *The Goodyear Story*. Elmsford, N. Y.: The Benjamin Co., 1983.

Robinson, Douglas H. *Giants in the Sky: A History of the Rigid Airship*. Seattle: University of Washington Press, 1973.

——. *The Zeppelin in Combat: A History of the German Naval Airship Division, 1912–1918*. London: G. T. Foulis and Co., 1962. (An enlarged, well illustrated edition of this title was printed by Schiffer Publishing, Atglen, Pennsylvania, in 1994.)

Robinson, Douglas H., and Charles L. Keller. *"Up Ship!" U.S. Navy Rigid Airships 1919–1935*. Annapolis, Md.: Naval Institute Press, 1982.

Rosendahl, Charles E. *Up Ship!* New York: Dodd, Mead and Co., 1931.

Ryan, Craig. *The Pre-Astronauts: Manned Ballooning on the Threshold of Space*. Annapolis, Md.: Naval Institute Press, 1995.

Rybár, Ctibor, *Prag: Reiseführer—Informationen—Fakten*. Prague: Olympia Verlag, 1983.

Schiller, Hans von. *Zeppelin: Wegbereiter des Weltluftverkehrs*. Bad Godesberg, Germany: Kirschbaum Verlag, [1967].

Shock, James R. *American Airship Bases and Facilities*. Edgewater, Fla.: Atlantis Productions, 1996.

——. *The U.S. Army Barrage Balloon Program*. Bennington, Vt.: World War II Historical Society, 1996.

——. *U.S. Navy Pressure Airships 1916–1962*. Edgewater, Fla.: Atlantis Productions, 1993.

Shute, Nevil. *Slide Rule*. New York: William Morrow and Co., 1954.

Smith, Richard K. *The Airships Akron and Macon: Flying Aircraft Carriers of the United States Navy*. Annapolis, Md.: Naval Institute Press, 1965.

Tihany, Leslie C. *A History of Middle Europe from the Earliest Times to the Age of the World Wars*. New Brunswick, N.J.: Rutgers University Press, 1976.

Timoshenko, Stephen P. *History of Strength of Materials*. New York: McGraw-Hill, 1953.

Tittel, Lutz. *LZ 129 "Hindenburg."* Friedrichshafen, Germany: Zeppelin-Museum Friedrichshafen, 1987.

Treibel, Armin. "Variations in Patterns of Consumption in Germany in the Period of the First World War," in *The Upheaval of War: Family, Work and Welfare in Europe, 1914–1918*, Richard Wall and Jay Winter, eds. Cambridge: Cambridge University Press, 1988.

Trimble, *William F. Admiral William A. Moffett: Architect of Naval Aviation*. Washington, D.C.: Smithsonian Institution Press, 1994.

U.S.Congress, Joint Committee to Investigate Dirigible Disasters. 73rd Cong., 1st sess., *Hearings*, 1933.

Vaeth, J. Gordon. *Blimps and U-Boats: U.S. Navy Airships in the Battle of the Atlantic*. Annapolis, Md.: Naval Institute Press, 1992.

——. *Graf Zeppelin: The Adventures of an Aerial Globetrotter*. New York: Harper and Bros., 1958.

Veronico, Nicholas A., with John M. and Donna Campbell. *F4U Corsair*. Osceola, Wis.: Motorbooks International, 1994.

Vissering, Harry. *Zeppelin: The Story of A Great Achievement*. Chicago: Wells and Co., 1922.

Warnock, A. Timothy. *Air Power versus U-Boats*. N.p.: Air Force History and Museums Program, 1999.

——. *The Battle Against the U-Boat in the American Theater*. N.p.: Center for Air Force History, [1992?].

Winter, Jay M. *The Experience of World War I*. London: Macmillan, 1988.

Wittemann, Anton. *Die Amerikafahrt des Z.R. III*. Wiesbaden: Amsel Verlag, 1925.

Zeman, Zbynek. *The Masaryks: The Making of Czechoslovakia*. London: Weidenfeld and Nicholson, 1976.

Zeppelin Metallwerke. *Zeppelin: Ein bedeutendes Kapitel aus der Geschichte der Luftfahrt*, 5th ed. Friedrichshafen: Zeppelin-Luftschiffbau GmbH and Zeppelin-Metallwerke, 1983.

INDEX

Series on Ohio History and Culture

ABOUT THE AUTHOR AND EDITOR

Dale Topping (1917–1993) held a Ph.D. from the University of Illinois in theoretical and applied mechanics. During his career he worked for Goodyear Aerospace Corporation and Bell Aerospace-Textron.

Eric Brothers is a native of Akron and a freelance journalist. He succeeded Dale Topping as editor of *Buoyant Flight*, the bulletin of The Lighter-Than-Air Society.

ABOUT THE BOOK

When Giants Roamed The Sky: Karl Arnstein And The Rise Of Airships From Zepplin To Goodyear was designed and typeset on a MacIntosh in QuarkXPress in 11/16 Bulmer MT with Techno display type by Kachergis Book Design of Pittsboro, North Carolina.

When Giants Roamed The Sky: Karl Arnstein And The Rise Of Airships From Zepplin To Goodyear was printed on eighty-pound Sterling Litho and bound by Sheridan Books, Ann Arbor, Michigan.